BY YOUR COMMAND

The Unofficial and Unauthorised Guide to *Battlestar Galactica*
Volume I • The Original Series and *Galactica 1980*

TO TRACY
LOVE
From Ron

Tracy
Love
from Alan St...

BY YOUR COMMAND

The Unofficial and Unauthorised Guide to *Battlestar Galactica*
Volume I • The Original Series and *Galactica 1980*

Alan Stevens and Fiona Moore

First published in the UK in 2012 by
Telos Publishing Ltd
17 Pendre Avenue, Prestatyn, Denbighshire LL19 9SH
www.telos.co.uk

Telos Publishing Ltd values feedback. Please e-mail us with any comments you
may have about this book to: feedback@telos.co.uk

ISBN: 978-1-84583-060-1 (paperback)

Internal design, typesetting and layout by Arnold T Blumberg
www.atbpublishing.com

Printed in England by Good News Digital Printing

British Library Cataloguing in Publication Data.
A catalogue record for this book is available from the British Library.

To Ayesha and Zhukov
'Orwell's Rats'

CONTENTS

THE BOOK OF THE WORD: AUTHORS' INTRODUCTION

Before we begin the book, we would like to briefly outline our approach to *Battlestar Galactica*. As people who have become fans of both the original and the reimagined series (and willing to acknowledge that *Galactica 1980* at least has some merit), we intend to celebrate *Battlestar Galactica* in all its diverse televisual incarnations, and to show the connections, homages, and interplay between the various interpretations of the story of a space-borne exodus in search of Earth.

Writing books which cover the 1978, 1980 and 2003-onwards series has thrown up a unique set of challenges. For the first volume, our main concern was to track down behind-the-scenes information which contextualises the series for the modern reader, given that over thirty years had passed since the making of the programmes. In the second book, however, there exists so much information about the reimagined series available via blogs, websites, news services and recorded interviews with cast and crew that the challenge has instead been to figure out what should be included, and what left for our readers to discover through other sources. This has made for a corresponding shift in emphasis in the content of the two volumes, with the first leaning more heavily on production details than the second; however, in both we have aimed to focus on the series' main strength, its development of strong continuing narratives and character arcs.

For reasons of space we have chosen to focus on the televised series, covering the comic-book, game and novel spinoffs in overview essays.

As with our earlier Telos books, *Liberation: The Unofficial and Unauthorised Guide to Blake's 7* and *Fall Out: The Unofficial and Unauthorised Guide to The Prisoner*, we do not here propose to have the 'last word' on a series as dynamic and long-lived as *Battlestar Galactica*. We do hope to be able to contribute a guide which will be interesting, analytical and thought-provoking – and occasionally, given our 'unofficial and unauthorised' designation, challenging received wisdom – as we trace the evolution of the series from its 1970s origins to the present day.

We would like to acknowledge the help of, in no particular order: Paul Winter, Nick Lewis, Ilana Rain, Shawn O'Donnell, Richard Hatch, Andy Swinden and Ben Keywood from Galaxy 4 in Sheffield, Mark Oliver, Jane and Robert Moore, Bronwen Moore and David Clark, David Howe and Stephen James Walker at Telos, and all the many people who work tirelessly to make draft scripts, production information, concept art and so forth available to fans, particularly on the websites named below, all of which we would encourage our readers to visit. Special thanks are due to Marcel Damen for allowing us to see advance copies of interviews for his website www.galactica.tv, and for providing us with rare copies of draft and unfilmed scripts and out-of-print interviews.

The main books consulted for this volume are: *An Analytical Guide to Television's Battlestar Galactica* (2005, McFarland and Co) by John Kenneth Muir, *Frak You!: The Ultimate Unauthorized Guide to Battlestar Galactica* (2007, ECW Press) by Jo Storm, *Finding Battlestar Galactica* by Lynnette Porter, David Lavery and Hillary Robson (2008, Sourcebooks Inc) and *Somewhere Beyond The Heavens: The Battlestar Galactica Unofficial Companion* (2006, Imprint) by David Criswell and Richie F Levine.

Although we have consulted far too many websites and forums to be able to acknowledge them all, our key sources have been: www.battlestarwiki.org and its affiliate sites, www.kobol.com, www.battlestargalactica.com, galactica.tv, www.colonialfleets.com, www.byyourcommand.net, www.battlestarfanclub. com, Colonial Defence Forces (www.cdfcommand.com), Galactica Sitrep (www.galacticasitrep.blogspot.com), www.tombsofkobol.com, Susan J Paxton's *Battlestar Galactica* website (geocities.com/sjpaxton/, sadly unavailable at the time of writing, though it can be accessed through archive.org), www.cylon. org (also now unavailable outside of archive.org), www.annelockhart.com, www.richardhatch.com, *Sheba's Galaxy* (galactica1981.tripod.com/), and the satirical website WikiFrakr (wiki.frakr.com).

Finally, a brief word on the title of these books. The most obvious reason for choosing 'By Your Command' is that it is the only phrase which appears in all three series of *Battlestar Galactica* and its spinoffs. However, the phrase also evokes themes common to all of televised *Battlestar Galactica*: the nature of totalitarianism, the legitimacy of command, the question of when to submit to authority and when to resist it, and the way in which the characters of all series ultimately find themselves following the plans of divine beings.

BATTLESTAR FOREWORD 2012

BY RICHARD HATCH

It is hard to believe that 35 years have gone by since the debut of the original *Battlestar Galactica* movie and series on ABC television back in 1978. Considered to be the biggest and most expensive TV series in history up to that date, *Battlestar Galactica* survived only one season yet made a lasting and indelible impact on the public, and has spawned four additional programmes: *Galactica 1980*; *Caprica*; *Blood and Chrome* and the critically acclaimed reimagined version, which ran from 2003 to 2009 on the Sci-Fi Channel. In an era when every network seems to have lost interest in producing shows that originate in space, *Battlestar Galactica* has continued to expand its audience and has produced a loyal following demanding more *Galactica* programming.

Thinking back on my journey playing Apollo in the original series I have to say that that period of my career was life-changing. This epic story of survival and courage not only inspired me, but introduced me to some of the most talented and famous actors in the business – like Ray Milland, Fred Astaire, Patrick Macnee – and forged meaningful friendships that have lasted until this day. It introduced me to a world that ignited my imagination and inspired me to create in for over three decades writing many *Battlestar Galactica* novels, and unless you've gone through the baptismal fires of being cast in a new series you have no idea of the powerful bonding process that takes place bringing together creative artists from every background, culture and philosophy in such a synergistic and collaborative way that is unparalleled in my experience. To have been a significant part of that and to have experienced and watched first hand the process of highly gifted artists creating and bringing to fruition an epic concept like *Battlestar Galactica* changed my life forever and gave me the hunger to be part of something that powerful and transformative again and again in my career.

We all lived like a family on the back lot of Universal where we filmed on many a cold night until the sun came up trying to keep up with our impossible production schedule. We even filmed on Saturdays and Sundays trying to keep ahead of the curve, but ultimately time, money and ratings, while good, still in the top 20, didn't justify the biggest budget in TV history.

But, as this new book on the series shows, what stood the test of time was the iconic story of mankind surviving a holocaust, overcoming fear, and finding the courage to face and conquer the impossible. Fans of all ages and from all walks of life related to this powerful story and have passed the series down to their children from generation to generation. And now, the future of *Battlestar Galactica* lies before us.

So hold your hats, buckle your seat belts and fire your thrusters! *Battlestar Galactica* is too powerful and viable a concept to disappear. It will continue to come back time and time again to thrill and inspire generations of passionate fans throughout the world. By your command!

Richard Hatch
April 2012

BATTLESTAR GALACTICA

Created by:
Glen A Larson

Executive Producer:
Glen A Larson

Supervising Producers:
Leslie Stevens (1), Donald P Bellasario (4 – 17)

Associate Producers:
Winrich Kolbe (1), David G Phinney (2, 5 – 17), Gary B Winter (3 – 4, 6 – 17),

Produced by:
John Dykstra (1, 5), Donald Bellisario (2, 3), David J O'Connell (2, 4, 6 – 17)

Co-Producer:
David J O'Connell (2, 3)

Art Directors:
John E Chilberg II (1), Richard D James (2, 4, 5, 7, 9), Mary Weaver Dodson (3, 6, 8), Paul Peters (10 – 12, 14 – 17), Bill Camden (10, 12 – 14, 16), James J Murakami/Muraikami[1] (11, 13, 15, 17)

Story Editors:
Jim Carlson (9 –17), Terrence McDonnell (9 – 17)

Theme by:
Glen A Larson & Stu Phillips

Music by:
Stu Phillips conducting the Los Angeles Philharmonic Orchestra

Directors of Photography:
Ben Colman (1, 10 – 17), H John Penner (2 – 4, 6, 7, 9), Enzo A Martinelli ASC (5), Frank Thackery (8)

---

1 Given as 'James J Muraicami' in 'Greetings from Earth'.

Set Decorations:
Mickey S Michaels (1), Lowell Chambers (1 – 9), Sam Gross (1, 10 – 17)

Casting by:
Mark Malis (1, 2, 4, 5), Patti Hayes (3, 6 – 17)

Film Editors:
Robert L Kimble, ACE (1), Larry Strong (1), Leon Ortiz-Gil (1, 2, 6 – 10), John F Schreyer (3 – 4), David Howe (5, 8, 10, 12, 16), John Dumas (5), George R Potter (2, 6, 8, 10, 13, 14), Michael Berman (2, 7, 9, 11, 13, 14, 17), Frederic L Knudtson (15)

Assistant Film Editors:
Bill Young (1), Tom Benko (1), Walton Dornisch (1)

Set Decorators:
Mickey S Michaels (1), Lowell Chambers (1, 2)

Sound:
Jim Alexander (1, 5), Earl N Crain, Jr (2 – 4, 6, 7, 9 – 13, 15), John Kean (8), John Dignan (8), Mike Frankovich, Jr (9), Clyde Sorensen (14), Charles L King III (16, 17)

Sound Re-recording:
Robert L Hoyt (1)

Unit Production Managers:
Harker Wade (1– 4, 6 – 8, 10 – 17), Rowe Wallerstein (5)

1st Assistant Directors:
Phil Cook (1, 2, 4, 6, 9, 11, 13, 15), Bill Holbrook (2 – 3, 5, 7, 10, 11, 12, 14, 16), Britt Lomond (8), Walt Gilmore (17)

2nd Assistant Directors:
Nick Marck (1), Charles Watson Sanford (2 – 4, 6, 7, 9 – 15), Kate/Katy Emde (5), Bruce Hanson (8), Chuck Lowry (8), Herb Adelman (16, 17)

Costume Designer:
Jean-Pierre Dorleac

Costume Supervisor:
Mark Peterson (5 – 17)

Makeup:
Scott Eddo (1), Tommy Thompson (1)

Hair Stylists:
Joy Zapata (1), Paul Griffin (1)

Sound Effects Editors:
Peter Berkos MPSE (1 – 6), Dick Wahrman (7 – 17)

Dialogue Editor:
Cliff Bell Jr MPSE (1)

Music Editors:
James D Young (1 – 4), Herbert D Woods (1, 5 – 17)

Title Design:
Wayne Fitzgerald (1)

Titles & Optical Effects:
Universal Title

Special Electronic Effects:
John Peyser, Jr (1)

Camera:
David Augsburger (1), Don Dow (1), David Robman (1), Jonathan Seay (1), Douglas Smith (1), Jody Westheimer (1)

Key Grip:
Mark Cane (1)

2nd Unit Directors:
Gene Montanino (1), Guy Magar (2), Winrich Kolbe (15)

2nd Unit Director of Photography:
Mario Dileo (1)

2nd Unit Cameramen:
George Voellmer (2), Don Dow (2)

Chief Model-maker:
Grant McCune (1)

Model Builders:
Deborah Armstrong (1), David Beasley (1), John Erland (1), Steve Gawley (1), Richard Gilligan (1), Lane Liska (1), Lorne Peterson (1), Tom Rudduck (1), David Scott (1), David Sosalla (1), Kenneth Swenson (1)

Effects Illustration and Design:
Dan Goozee (1), Joseph Johnston (1), Ralph McQuarrie (1)

Additional Artwork:
Martin Kline (1), Andrew Probert (1)

Special Mechanical Equipment:
Richard Alexander (1), William Shourt (1), Don Trumbull (1)

Special Electronics:
Alvah J Miller (1)

Animation and Rotoscope Design:
Harry Moreau (1)

Animators:
Angela Diamos (1), Sherry Epperson (1), Peter Kuran (1), Maxwell Morgan (1)

Optical Photography:
David Berry (1), William Brier (1), James N Catania (1), Frederick Langenbach (1), Errol D McCue (1), Bruce Nicholson (1), Masaaki Norihiro (1), Eldon Rickman (1), James Rickman (1)

Miniature and Effects Unit Supervised by:
John Dykstra and Apogee, Inc (1)

Production Supervisor:
Robert Shepherd (1)

Production Assistants:
Patricia Rose Duignan (1), Cass McCune (1), Steven McCarthy (1), John Shourt (1), Michael Sweeney (1)

Editorial Assistants:
Mary Lind (1), David Miller (1), Conrad Buff (1), Leslie Dennis (1), Jeff Freeman (1), Dennis Kelly (1), Cory McCrum (1)

Test and Display Equipment by:
Tektronix

The Landram Vehicle was Furnished by:
Thiokol

Special Effects:
Joe Goss (1), Karl Miller (1)

Production and Special Effects Consultants
David M Garber (4 – 17), Wayne Smith (4 – 17)

Special Effects Photography:
Richard Edlund (1), Dennis Muren (1)

A Glen A Larson Production/
Produced in Association with Glen A Larson Productions

REGULAR CAST
Captain Apollo – Richard Hatch
Lieutenant Starbuck – Dirk Benedict
Commander Adama – Lorne Greene
Lieutenant Boomer – Herbert Jefferson, Jr
Lieutenant Athena – Maren Jensen (1, 2, 4, 5, 8 – 10, 12, 13)
Flight Sergeant/Lieutenant Jolly – Tony Swartz (1 – 3, 6, 8, 10, 11, 13)
Boxey – Noah Hathaway (1 – 10, 13)
Colonel Tigh – Terry Carter
Count Baltar – John Colicos (1, 2, 4, 5, 7, 8, 10, 12, 14, 17)

Cassiopea[2] – Laurette Spang (1 – 4, 7 – 13, 16, 17)
Lieutenant Sheba – Anne Lockhart (8 – 14, 16, 17)
Flight Corporal/Sergeant Rigel – Sarah Rush[3] (1, 2, 4, 5, 6, 14)
Flight Officer/Sergeant Omega – David Greenan[4] (1, 2, 4 – 6, 8 – 11, 13 – 17)
Doctor Salik – George Murdock (2, 9, 10, 13)
Doctor Wilker – John Dullagham (1, 10, 12 – 14)
Ensign Greenbean – Ed Begley, Jr (1, 2, 6, 10)
Giles – Larry Manetti (2, 3, 5)
Corporal Komma – Jeff MacKay (5, 9, 12)
Imperious Leader – Dick Durock (1, 2, 8)
Imperious Leader (voice) – Patrick Macnee (1, 2, 8)
Lucifer – Felix Silla (1, 2, 4, 5, 7, 8, 10)
Lucifer (voice) – Jonathan Harris (2, 4, 5, 7, 8, 10)
Muffit II – Evie (1, 2, 3 – 9)

2 Most sources spell the character's name 'Cassiopeia', which is the proper Greek spelling. However, as her name never appears in the credits, and all draft scripts bar 'The Long Patrol' and the deleted final scene of 'The Young Lords' (in both of which the name is misspelled as 'Casseopia') spell her name 'Cassiopea', we will be using the 'Cassiopea' spelling throughout.
3 Parts one and two of 'The Gun on Ice Planet Zero' credit Rigel's rank as 'Flight Corporal'; however, the computer readout seen onscreen in 'The Long Patrol' gives her rank as 'Sergeant'. 'Saga of a Star World' credits Sarah Rush as 'Woman on Duty'. The 2 October 1978 terminology document, a compilation of notes on the characters and language of the series, does not cite Rigel's rank at all, which no doubt contributed to the confusion.
4 Part two of 'The Gun of Ice Planet Zero' credits Omega's rank as 'Flight Officer', but the readout seen in 'The Long Patrol' gives his rank as 'Sergeant'.

THE ORIGINAL SERIES: BACKGROUND AND PRODUCTION

The original *Battlestar Galactica* series premièred on US television in September 1978, but less than a year later was off the air. Nonetheless, its brief run was marked by a number of dramatic events, giving it a history and genesis unique among telefantasy series.

COME BACK MRS NOAH: ADAM'S ARK AND THE GENESIS OF BATTLESTAR GALACTICA

Series creator Glen Larson (whose early career included, among other things, a stint with a band of moderate success called The Four Preps) has often said that the origins of *Battlestar Galactica* date back to his first attempt to write for television, a failed 1967 pitch to Universal Studios for a series to be called *Adam's Ark*. Larson has given two outlines of what this series would have involved, initially saying that it 'was sort of about the origins of mankind in the universe, taking some of the Biblical stories and moving them off into space as if by the time we get to Earth they're really not about things that happened here but things that might have happened someplace else in space', and, elsewhere, that the series involved a Howard Hughes-type billionaire who gathers together a group of elite scientists, athletes, artists and so forth to flee Earth (which is facing destruction) on a spacecraft. The discrepancy between the two synopses has led some to suggest that, in fact, *Adam's Ark* was not the precursor of *Battlestar Galactica*, and director Alan Levi has suggested in an interview that *Galactica*'s origins lie instead in an idea developed by *The Outer Limits* creator Leslie Stevens, who, he said, had mentioned to him a *Battlestar Galactica*-like idea that Stevens was planning to discuss with Larson. However Stevens has never made any claims of idea theft (in a 1981 interview with *Fangoria* [issue 10], he attributes the concept, story, and the script for 'Saga of a Star World' entirely to Larson), and indeed not only worked on an early version of the *Battlestar Galactica* story which later became 'The Gun on Ice Planet Zero' (and contributed the unmade script 'The Beta Pirates'), but also worked closely with Larson to develop *Buck Rogers in the 25th Century* for television. It is perhaps more likely that Larson, in the wake of assertions that *Battlestar Galactica* plagiarised *Star Wars*, has been emphasising the similarities between *Adam's Ark* and *Battlestar Galactica* in order to cement his claim that the concept was his original idea.

In the late 1970s, Larson, who had gone on to write for, create, and executive-produce a number of television series in the intervening ten years, pitched the *Battlestar Galactica* concept to Universal in the wake of the success of *Star Wars*. At the time it was common for TV studios to pick up popular movie ideas to turn into TV series, and, although Larson was far from the only writer involved in this practice, he had developed a reputation for being good at it (his creations *Alias Smith and Jones*, *McCloud* and *BJ And the Bear*, for instance, bearing strong resemblances to the films *Butch Cassidy and the Sundance Kid* [1969], *Coogan's Bluff* [1968] and *Every Which Way But Loose* [1978] respectively), such that writer Harlan Ellison nicknamed him 'Glen Larceny'. By positioning the *Adam's Ark* concept as a saga of humans from doomed alien planets fleeing to Earth, Larson was able to pitch the series as another movie tie-in along these lines.

The premise of the series was also crafted so as to include Western and World War II film ideas as well, which Larson said in a contemporary interview with *Time* was an attempt to 'make space comfortable for the Midwest', that is, to encourage people not normally inclined to watch science fiction to tune in. The idea ultimately developed was that, somewhere in space, twelve colonies of humans, with names strikingly similar to those of the signs of the Zodiac (picking up on the contemporary mania for astrology) have been at war with a race of robots, called Cylons, for centuries. Following the destruction of the colonies in a Pearl Harbour-style surprise attack, a group of survivors, led by Commander Adama on the battlestar *Galactica*, a warship, flee into space looking for a fabled thirteenth colony, known as Earth, and the series would follow their adventures as they search for Earth with the Cylons in pursuit (the chase being led by a human traitor, Count Baltar), resulting in a sort of cross between *Wagon Train* and *The Cruel Sea* (1953) in space. Indeed, although *Star Trek* was originally pitched as '*Wagon Train* to the stars', it has been noted by many, including Larson, that the description fits *Battlestar Galactica* rather better. As it developed, the series also began to evidence serial elements, in the form of a sort of prototypical story arc, of a kind rare in American telefantasy of the time (though frequently seen in 1970s British telefantasy, for instance *Doctor Who*, *Survivors* and *Blake's 7*).

BUILDING THE SHIP: PRODUCTION ON THE SERIES

Battlestar Galactica was originally greenlighted as a seven-hour miniseries (comprising a three-hour pilot and two subsequent two-hour stories) to air in autumn 1978. John Dykstra, who had worked on the special effects of *Star Wars*, was recruited as special effects supervisor, and the effects were thus initially done at George Lucas' company Industrial Light and Magic; while Lucas was at first happy for this to happen, he then became nervous about the similarities between *Battlestar Galactica* and *Star Wars* and, in a meeting with Glen Larson, *Star Wars* producer Gary Kurtz gave him a list of things which he wanted changed to make a greater distinction between the two (this apparently included the use of laser beams firing from pistols, which seems odd as these have been a staple of space opera since the 1930s, but it must be said that the use of beamless guns in *Battlestar Galactica,* based, according to a contemporary interview with John Dykstra, on an electronic strobe effect, does give it a more realistic feel). Ralph McQuarrie, who had worked on the pre-production art for *Star Wars* and *Close Encounters of the Third Kind* (1977), did the pre-production art for *Battlestar Galactica,* and the costumes were designed by Jean-Pierre Dorelac, with Joe Johnson and Andrew Probert being the primary designers of the Cylon Centurians. An October 1978 article in *Future* magazine stated that Carlo Rambaldi (later to create ET for Spielberg's film of the same name) was hired to design the Imperious Leader, though Rambaldi himself denies all knowledge of this (a 16 August 1977 letter indicates that Rambaldi was indeed hired to design creature masks for the series, but does not specify the creature). The series' supervising producer was Don Bellisario, an ex-Marine (which may have inspired some of the series' military focus) best known today for creating *Magnum PI* (with Larson), *Quantum Leap,* and, more recently, *NCIS.* The theme tune was composed by Stu Phillips and, recalling his musical past, Glen Larson.

The series is frequently said to have had the highest budget in TV history at the time, reportedly $1 million per episode (though, since some episodes are clearly more expensive than others, this is likely to have been an average amount over the whole series), and various sources claiming that 'Saga of a Star World' alone cost between $7 and $14 million. The Tektronix corporation, which had made computers for actual NASA spacecraft, put real, functioning computers on the bridge set, which they estimate cost $850,000, with $23,000 of that going on TV monitors, and the landram vehicle was designed by Thiokol, an American industrial designer and manufacturer which at the time possessed a division focused on producing vehicles for ski resorts. The *Galactica* miniature was 72 inches long, weighing over 60 pounds, and the space sequences involved lots of matte shots and back projection, the latter of which, since the film strips used were often only a few seconds long, required careful timing and precision on the part of the actors, as well as interminable numbers of takes if the actor was even a tiny bit out of sync with the film.

Network executives, impressed with the quality of production, took the decision late in the day to develop the programme into a full weekly series, and, while Larson had, according to Richard Hatch on the documentary *Remembering Battlestar Galactica,* hoped to have a year to prepare the show, they insisted that this be done straight away. This led to an increasingly frenetic pace of production, with actors and crew frequently working seventeen-hour days, and actors being handed their scripts literally minutes before shooting (Anne Lockhart remembers being given rewrites of one scene *after* it had been filmed, on one occasion, and writer Terence McDonnell recalls the episode 'Murder on the *Rising Star*' being commissioned on a Wednesday with the deadline for the final draft being that coming Friday). Bellisario said in a contemporary interview that filming often finished barely ten days before the airdate, and that editing could carry on as late as the day before transmission. John Dykstra left early on, reportedly expressing an unhappiness with the rapid pace of production and the quality of the show, and also with the decision to show a recut version of the pilot episode in Canada as a theatrical film in July 1978, in order to recoup some of their costs for the studio and provide a test audience for the network (saying that his effects had been designed specifically for television and thus film did not show them at their best). After his departure, Universal's Hartland facilities took over the effects. Despite the chaos, most performers and production crew have good memories of the series, and Larson has said that in hindsight it was one of the most fun projects he has ever been involved with.

One well-remembered concept of the series was Muffit, the robot pet of Apollo's young stepson Boxey, an attempt to cash in on the cute robot craze of the late 1970s while also appealing to the perennial fondness of children for dogs, resulting in a sort of cross between the two 1970s children's icons Benji and K9. Cleverly, the robot was played by a young female chimpanzee called Evie (short for 'Evolution'), directed by her trainer Boone Narr, giving the creature a simultaneously organic yet inhuman movement.[5] However, chimps are not known for taking direction, and, as the shooting hours got longer, Evie frequently made it known when she did not feel up to performing, and the sheer number of outtakes involving Evie doing something inappropriate, while funny to subsequent viewers, make it plain how frustrating and time-consuming working with her must have been, and go some way towards explaining why the character was written out in later episodes. Like other such robot characters, Muffit seems to have a been a love-it-or-hate-it figure for most commentators: the authors of this book wish to come clean and say that we actually quite like the character, finding it rather cute without being too saccharine.

Finally, the Cylons, the series' key villains, are also distinctive, looking like

---

5 According to actor Tony Swartz, a second chimp, a male named 'Doc', played Muffit for part of 'Saga of a Star World', but was replaced after he refused to go back into the daggit suit following an incident in which the suit overheated, causing the chimp to become sick.

a cross between medieval knights, Roman soldiers, the Cyclops, and Samurai warriors (although designer Andrew Probert has said that his original design was inspired by ancient Greek armour). To keep the camera crew from reflecting in their polished bodies, they were usually shot in darkness or in blue or red coloured light, and/or using starburst filters, which had the added benefit of making them sinister and atmospheric. The costumes were difficult to get into and out of, resulting in many humorous anecdotes about Cylon actors having to avoid trips to the bathroom as much as possible; visibility was also limited to a small number of holes above the red 'scanning eye', leading to a number of tripping and falling incidents (attentive viewers will note that Cylons tend to run very, very carefully). They were played by stuntmen, due to the pyrotechnic and physical demands of the role (except for the IL-class Cylon Lucifer, portrayed by dwarf actor Felix Silla, who had played Cousin Itt on *The Addams Family*, was also Noah Hathaway's stunt double on *Battlestar Galactica* and would go on to play the robot Twiki on *Buck Rogers*). The Cylons also incurred their share of production costs: the original costume and headpiece for the Imperious Leader reportedly cost $50,000, but then remained in the shadows when Larson objected to the final result (cut footage suggests an attractively eerie, lizardlike look to the costume), and many of the Cylon Centurian suits were rendered unusable by pyrotechnics or falls, and, when the production team ran out of money to make new costumes, they cobbled together replacement suits using parts of damaged ones.

SHIP'S ROSTER: CASTING THE SERIES

Battlestar Galactica also had a distinctive cast. Lorne Greene, a distinguished Canadian actor and announcer (whose stint reading the news on CBC Radio during WWII earned him the nickname 'The Voice of Canada'), was cast as Commander Adama, being then best known for playing the widowed patriarch of the Cartwright family on the Western series *Bonanza*, a part which, ironically, he had been offered after an appearance as a widower with small children on *Wagon Train*. Greene is often said by cast members to have been a popular presence on the set, getting on well with everyone and being a font of off-colour jokes.

Supporting Greene were Richard Hatch as Captain Apollo, and Dirk Benedict as Lieutenant Starbuck. Hatch was cast at the network's recommendation, having appeared in the soap *All My Children* and the police drama *The Streets of San Francisco,* as well as having initially auditioned for the part of Luke Skywalker, and being seen as having the necessary sex appeal for a programme like *Battlestar Galactica*. Hatch himself was more reluctant (in the documentary *Looking Back at the Future*, he says that at the time he was searching for a project which would challenge him as an actor, and didn't think that *Battlestar Galactica* was it), but Larson eventually wore him down. Benedict (whose credits at the time were less impressive, his main ones being the Aaron Spelling drama *Chopper One* and a snake-based 1973 movie called *Ssssss*) proved more controversial: Larson, who had met the actor in New York, wanted him to play the role of Starbuck from the outset, but the network objected, while Larson in turn objected to their choice of actor (saying later that he was too short). A number of other actors went up for the role, including Don Johnson, later of *Miami Vice* fame, whom Larson auditioned three times before turning him down eventually on the grounds of not liking his accent (which Larson later described as 'redneck'). Although Larson eventually got his way over Benedict, this is said to have been the source of some of the bad blood between the studio and the network over *Battlestar Galactica*.

Further controversy emerged over Starbuck's cigar (or 'fumarello', as it is called in the series) habit. Starbuck is described as a cigar smoker from early drafts of 'Saga of a Star World' onwards, and Benedict, reportedly a smoker since the age of ten, employed the cigars to iconic effect in his performance. ABC, however, objected, saying that women found cigars a turnoff and insisted that the cigar be dropped. The network relented when hundreds of female fans sent in cigars for Benedict, but Benedict, as well as the character he played, continued to be a source of controversy for the series.

Also cast were Maren Jensen as Athena, Herb Jefferson Jr as Boomer, Laurette Spang as Cassiopea and Terry Carter as Tigh. Jensen, a model with no acting experience bar a guest spot on Larson's *The Hardy Boys* series, proved to have little acting ability and was rapidly sidelined, with Laurette Spang, who had rather more acting experience prior to *Battlestar Galactica*, having appeared in, among others, *Happy Days*, *Charlie's Angels* and *The Gemini Man*, rapidly replacing her as the main female character and regular love interest for Starbuck. Anne Lockhart, daughter of June Lockhart of *Lost in Space* fame, was introduced halfway through the series to add to the number of strong female characters (after Jane Seymour, whose character Serina had proved successful in the pilot series, insisted on returning only for the second two-part story). Herb Jefferson Jr, a graduate of the American Academy of Dramatic Arts, had built up a reputation as a character actor on series like *Columbo* and *McCloud*, while Terry Carter was another *McCloud* veteran who had also done three years as one of Sergeant Bilko's sidekicks, Private Sugarman, and had been the first black newscaster in New England. Carter had impressed Larson with his flair for deadpan comedy; initially he was cast as Boomer, but was recast as

Tigh when he broke his ankle roller-skating (although this is not visible, he wore a cast throughout the whole of 'Saga of a Star World').

John Colicos was cast as the main human villain, Count Baltar. Colicos was another Canadian, who had previously appeared with Lorne Greene in a production of *Hamlet,* and whose past credits included a memorable stint as a Klingon, Kor, on the *Star Trek* episode 'Errand of Mercy' (a role he would later reprise in *Star Trek: Deep Space Nine*). A press document clearly intended to accompany the Canadian film release of 'Saga of a Star World' has Colicos remarking that, while he does not generally regret being typecast as villains, such characters do tend to get killed off at the end of the episode, costing him a steady paycheck, suggesting that he was pleased by the decision to keep Baltar as a recurring figure in the series. He was described by colleagues as 'larger than life'. Colicos was supported by Jonathan Harris, best known for playing Doctor Smith in *Lost in Space,* as the voice of Lucifer, and Patrick Macnee, the well-known British actor of *The Avengers* and *James Bond* fame, as the voice of the Cylon Imperious Leader (also, for reasons which add to the intrigue of the series, providing the introductory voiceover on many episodes).

FAITH OF OUR FATHERS: RELIGION AND POLITICS IN BATTLESTAR GALACTICA

Battlestar Galactica is noteworthy among telefantasy series for the way in which it deals with politics and religion. Although there are a number of American telefantasy shows which, tacitly or explicitly, embrace a right-wing philosophy, it is rare to find one which, as *Battlestar Galactica* does, actually explores the social and philosophical implications of conservatism. In particular, *Battlestar Galactica* appears to embrace an early form of neoconservatism: as defined by John Gray in his book *Black Mass,* David Harvey in his book *The New Imperialism,* and Adam Curtis in his documentary *The Trap,* neoconservatism is an, initially American, political movement which takes the Utopian stance that democracy is the natural state of all political systems, which will emerge if the impediments to it are removed, and as such advocates active intervention in other states in order to encourage them to democratic ideals, as well as advocating the striving towards these ideals at home. Significantly, this did not feature long-term involvement abroad, aside from brief sojourns to topple dictators and demonstrate democratic principles.

Battlestar Galactica itself developed in the context of the late Carter Administration, under which America, wounded by its recent forays in Vietnam, pursued a policy of non-intervention and détente: it's worth noting, in light of the series' seeming obsession with disarmament, that in the late 1970s Carter was involved in the controversial SALT II armament reduction treaty, and that the Russian newspaper *Izvestia* accused *Battlestar Galactica* of pumping up anti-Soviet hysteria through using the peace negotiations sequence in 'Saga of a Star World' as an allegory of the SALT talks. With rising prosperity, however, and Vietnam becoming a more distant memory, many were questioning the rightness of Carter's policies and articulating neoconservative ideas. While the development of political philosophy in *Battlestar Galactica* will be covered in depth during the episode reviews, it should be noted that it was very much in line with the neoconservative movement of the day (please note that, although neoconservatism has recently accrued negative associations, this is stated not to detract from *Battlestar Galactica*, but to point out how it was influenced by its political context). It had a strongly Utopian premise – fleeing disaster to seek a better world – and the idea of 'higher' civilisations interfering with others to improve them is continually portrayed as a good thing, with the consequences of failing to do so shown as severe. Significantly, also, the *Galactica* tends not to linger after having put matters to rights. Although this philosophy is given a fairly sophisticated exploration in early episodes, the ideas became cruder as the series wore on and the production schedule became tighter, approaching self-parody in 'Experiment in Terra'.

The series also shows clear religious influences. While again these will be discussed in detail in individual episode reviews, Larson, a former Mormon, incorporated aspects of Mormon belief into the series (earning himself accusations of blasphemy from Mormons, and proselytising from non-Mormons), as well as bringing in aspects of the Moses legend, in which a visionary, patriarchal figure leads a desperate tribe towards a promised land (with additional echoes of President of The Church of Jesus Christ of Latter-day Saints, Brigham Young, and his followers' journey to Utah). Early drafts of 'Saga of a Star World' have the subtitle 'Exodus' appearing, either when Adama announces the formation of the rag-tag fleet or as an episode title for the second hour. There are also influences from Erich von Däniken's book *Chariots of the Gods* (1968), which argued that aliens have visited Earth in the past and influenced human development; this idea was popular in the 1970s, when the public were keen on the idea that myths and paranormal phenomena could be explained through science, and Larson says, in the documentary *The Creation of Battlestar Galactica*, that he likes to think that humans are 'robots of a higher god', created through alien intervention. Despite occasional misunderstandings by critics led astray by the names of such characters as Apollo and Athena, and by the fact that the novelisation of 'Saga of a Star World' speculates that Earth may be the origin world of the Colonial societies (and that Larson himself occasionally contradicts the premise of the series in interviews), it is made clear through the series' opening narrative, and fully articulated in episodes such as 'The Hand of God', that the *Galactica* crew are not, in fact, the ancestors of humans on Earth, but rather that Earth's mythologies and ancient cultures come from the same common source as those of the Colonials, all of them having been originally settled from Kobol.

BATTLESHIP SHIPPERS: THE CRITICAL AND POPULAR REACTION

Battlestar Galactica was released to much publicity in the prestigious Sunday 8 pm time-slot, and was an immediate ratings success: although CBS and NBC had, respectively, scheduled the Emmy Awards and a screening of the 1976 remake of *King Kong* against it, the series premièred in the top ten of the Nielsen ratings (although the pilot episode is said frequently to have peaked at 65 million viewers by, among others, Larson, Hatch and the *Sciography* documentary, this, admittedly astonishing, figure has been called into question; however, all industry sources, including many with no stake in promoting the programme, acknowledge that it certainly made a strong showing. For the record, the book *Battlestar Galactica: Somewhere Beyond the Heavens* cites the figure of 44.6% audience share and 33.230 million households for the première, which they extrapolate to an audience of 66 million). Although ratings did drop later on, the series continued to perform well, averaging 20.4 million households (most successful new shows in the late 1970s averaged about 18 million), strongly beating out *Mary*, Mary Tyler Moore's comeback show, which was then replaced with firm ratings favourite *All in the Family*, against which *Battlestar Galactica* continued to hold its own. The annual Nielsen's Sweepstakes placed it as #24, which was the best showing for a network science fiction programme until *The X-Files*. It is worth noting that, after *Battlestar Galactica* was cancelled, its replacement, *Mork and Mindy*, bombed spectacularly when up against the same competition, making *Battlestar Galactica*'s achievement even more notable.

Viewer reaction was generally positive, with Benedict and Hatch finding themselves mobbed by female fans, and the series being nominated for a NAACP Image Award for its portrayal of positive African-American figures in Terry Carter and Herbert Jefferson Jr in the episode 'Fire in Space'. According to *Frak You!* and *Finding Battlestar Galactica*, the series also won the People's Choice Award for Best New TV Drama Series and Emmy awards for its costumes and visual effects, as well as being nominated for a number of high-profile awards, including the Golden Globes, the Saturn Award and the Grammy Award for Stu Phillips' score, and Noah Hathaway was nominated for a Young Artists Award (more recently, the DVD release of the series was nominated for a Saturn Award for Best Television DVD Release in 2003). In a rather appropriate tribute, US Air Force pilots reportedly nicknamed the then-new F-16 multirole jet fighter aircraft 'the Viper' after the Colonial fighter craft. Critical reaction was more mixed, although a lot of the negative press, significantly, seems to have ended once the *Star Wars* copyright infringement lawsuit was resolved, suggesting that much of it may have been inspired by critics attempting to take sides with Lucas against the newcomer. It is worth noting that writer Isaac Asimov, who initially criticised the series harshly, was later said to have agreed to act as an advisor on *Battlestar Galactica*'s abortive second season.

The most famous reaction, however, was the series of lawsuits exchanged between Universal and Fox over perceived similarities between *Star Wars* and *Battlestar Galactica*. This is often erroneously reported as George Lucas having sued Universal; however, although the lawsuit was apparently taken out at Lucas' instigation, and although he has repeatedly gone on record as saying that he was unhappy with the similarities between the two, it is also worth noting that it was not unknown at the time for studios to launch such lawsuits over alleged copyright infringement with the understanding that this would simply lead to an out-of-court settlement (see, for instance, John Kenneth Muir's detailed reporting of the Universal versus Dino de Laurentiis lawsuit over the rights to *King Kong* in *An Analytical Guide to Television's Battlestar Galactica*). Fox may also have been concerned about the fact that the *Battlestar Galactica* multi-part episodes were intended for subsequent cinematic re-release, making it not only a television programme, but a possible rival film series for the *Star Wars* movies.

The initial lawsuit was launched in June 1978 by Fox, well before the series had aired (its first release, the Canadian theatrical première, was in July 1978), for copyright infringement, citing 34 counts of similarity between the film and the series. Universal promptly countersued for copyright infringement on the 1972 film *Silent Running* (on which John Dykstra had worked), specifically saying that R2-D2 imitated the robots Huey, Dewey and Louie, and, reportedly, filed a second lawsuit for copyright infringement of the 1939 *Buck Rogers* serial. Fox further countersued, forbidding the sale of *Battlestar Galactica* merchandise (tie-in merchandise was a relatively new concept, but already recognised as profitable), and Universal countersued in turn, citing violation of the California business and professional code. By 22 August 1980, all lawsuits were resolved, with *Galactica* being ruled to have not infringed *Star Wars*' copyright (one of the points of similarity, for instance, was said to be the close male friendships between a charming rogue and a strait-laced hero at the centre of both, which, as expert witness Jerry Pournelle indicated, is one of the staples of mythology), but *Star Wars*, equally, as having not infringed the copyright of *Silent Running*. Ironically, when a further lawsuit emerged following an incident in December 1978 in which a child choked on a projectile from a Colonial Viper toy, the judge singled out *Star Wars* toys in his ruling against the toy company Mattel, and Kenner was also forced, as a result of the ruling, to undertake a hasty redesign in its Boba Fett *Star Wars* toys. However, the problem for *Battlestar Galactica* has been that the lawsuit, firstly, produced a persistent myth that Lucas was behind the series' cancellation, and, secondly, means that people are still inclined to perceive *Battlestar Galactica* as a kind of inferior televised *Star Wars*, and failing to take the series on its own merits.

RIDING IN THE HAND OF GOD: THE SERIES' CANCELLATION AND SUBSEQUENT FALLOUT

Despite the series' ratings success, ABC was not pleased with its showing. They had, according to most accounts, predicted top ratings for it, and, according to their official statements on the subject, simply doing quite well did not justify the continued expense. William J Adams, author of a sociological study on the impact of scheduling on ratings success, elaborates on this statement in a 1982 article in *Fantastic Films* magazine, noting that the expense of making the series would have been largely borne by the studio (ABC itself paid only $750,000 for the rights to broadcast each episode twice), which would have recouped its costs; however, the cost-to-profit ratio on science fiction programmes is generally low compared to that on cheaper-to-produce series such as sitcoms and dramas, and, he argues, this ratio prompted ABC to tacitly try to engineer the series' cancellation by overhyping it (thus ensuring a media backlash when it fails to live up to expectations, a move which apparently did not succeed in *Battlestar Galactica*'s case) and by subjecting it to last-minute postponements and reschedulings. It is certainly true that episodes of the series were subject to postponement by up to three weeks during its initial run, although that might be equally down to the fact that the production on the series was documentably running further and further behind schedule as it wore on, which might have led to the studio being unable to release some episodes on time. When the series was made, also, most American networks still operated on the principle that the best television was the 'Least Objectionable Programming', or LOP, and, even though the controversies which affected *Battlestar Galactica* did little, if any, harm to the ratings, they may have made the executives nervous. Whatever the truth behind the move (and whether it deliberately tried to engineer the series' collapse as Adams claims, or simply damaged it through their insistence on a tight production schedule, ABC must ultimately take the blame for the final product's shortcomings), ABC took the decision to cancel *Battlestar Galactica* abruptly after only a single season.

The suddenness of the cancellation led to a certain amount of fallout, with not all the actors hearing about it directly: Laurette Spang claims that she found out about its cancellation on television while on a family visit to Michigan, and Anne Lockhart from reading newspapers while on holiday in Hawaii. A number of scripts were left unfilmed and plans under way for a second season had to be shelved (to be discussed later in detail). The series had also, no doubt to Universal's dismay, not recorded enough episodes to go into syndication and recoup more of the studio's costs, and the cancellation also inspired a suicide by Eddie Seidel, a fifteen-year-old fan of the series, prompting the threat of yet another lawsuit from the youngster's parents. While rival networks CBS and NBC considered picking up *Battlestar Galactica* as a mid-season replacement show in 1979, negotiations failed for unknown reasons (possibly the cost-to-profit ratio mentioned by Adams).

Despite this, the series did not fade away. In 1979 Universal included a *Battlestar Galactica* section into their studio tour, which proved popular throughout the 1980s. Dirk Benedict went on to play other wisecracking womanisers (most famously on *The A-Team*) through his association with the role of Starbuck, and Richard Hatch maintained a close connection with the series over the years. *Battlestar Galactica* also experienced a new lease on life in the 1980s in film and telemovie form. Following the success of Universal's release of the *Buck Rogers* pilot as a theatrical film, 'Saga of a Star World' was released to US audiences (under the title *Battlestar Galactica*), grossing $10 million and inspiring Universal to subsequently rerelease the rest of the *Battlestar Galactica* episodes, cut into feature-length films, domestically and internationally, as theatrical films and telemovies. While most of the series fit neatly into feature-length slots ('Saga of a Star World', 'Lost Planet of the Gods', 'The Gun on Ice Planet Zero', 'Greetings from Earth', 'War of the Gods' and, with the addition of material from 'Fire in Space', 'The Living Legend', retitled as *Mission Galactica: The Cylon Attack*), others involved cutting together sometimes disparate episodes, such as *The Phantom in Space* (compiling 'The Lost Warrior' and 'The Hand of God'), *Space Prison* ('The Man with Nine Lives' and 'Baltar's Escape'), *Space Casanova* ('Take the *Celestra*' and 'The Long Patrol'), *Curse of the Cylons* ('The Magnificent Warriors' and 'Fire in Space') and *Murder in Space* ('Murder on the *Rising Star*' and 'The Young Lords'). The 'Experiment in Terra' telemovie is unusual in having had new footage added, in the form of a prologue which will be discussed in the episode review, as well as some cut-down material from the *Galactica 1980* episode 'The Return of Starbuck'.

Finally, mention needs to be made of *Buck Rogers in the 25th Century*, a kind of intellectual stablemate and successor to *Battlestar Galactica*, being another project which Larson was associated with around the same time, and which overlapped it in production; also, according to an interview with Leslie Stevens in *Starlog* 21 (1979), after John Dykstra resigned from the *Battlestar Galactica* project, he and Larson recruited replacement special effects personnel off *Buck Rogers*. Consequently, various models, props and costumes from *Battlestar Galactica* were reused in *Buck Rogers*, which will be noted as relevant throughout the episode reviews (our comments are also not to be taken as comprehensive, as we will only be noting the more blatant or amusing reuses); *Galactica* hangar crew uniforms appear throughout the series on people performing the analogous function, and Colonial Warrior uniforms were even recycled as guard uniforms in the episode 'Cosmic Whiz Kid'. In the pilot episode of *Buck Rogers*, 'Awakening', Viper joysticks were reused as the joysticks of Earth Defence Directorate fighters (though by the time the series was commissioned, a distinctive set of joysticks were made for the EDD).

The fact that production on the two series overlapped meant that this also occasionally worked in reverse, as Buck's shuttle from 'Awakening' was redressed to be used in the *Battlestar Galactica* episode 'Greetings from Earth'. Many actors also appeared in both series, including Anne Lockhart in 'A Dream of Jennifer', Ana Alicia (from 'Take the *Celestra*' and *Galactica 1980*'s 'Space Croppers') and Richard Lynch (from 'The Gun on Ice Planet Zero' and *Galactica 1980*'s '*Galactica* Discovers Earth') in 'Vegas in Space', John Quade (from *Galactica 1980*'s 'The Super Scouts') in 'The Plot to Kill a City', and, finally, Wilfred Hyde-White (from 'Saga of a Star World') had a regular role in Season Two of *Buck Rogers* as Doctor Goodfellow. The series do also have some conceptual similarities, having a strong female lead and a male lead who is something of an amalgam of Apollo and Starbuck (a slightly wistful and introspective type who is also a ladies' man and hedonist; early drafts of *Battlestar Galactica* scripts suggest that Starbuck originally shared Buck's penchant for rescuing lost or wayward women), as well as a certain exploitation of male sexuality (with Buck, like Apollo and Starbuck, frequently displaying a good deal of flesh). Twiki, a cute android who looks like a little boy with a bowl haircut, resembles an amalgam of Boxey and Muffit, and the second series, in an inversion of *Battlestar Galactica*'s premise, featured a quest to locate lost colonies of Earth. Overall, *Buck Rogers* appears to have had more time and thought put into its production than *Battlestar Galactica*, coming across as slicker and less chaotic; however, the finished product, in our opinion, is correspondingly blander, failing to hit the narrative heights of *Battlestar Galactica*, despite being somewhat redeemed by the suggestion, hinted at in the pilot and in the title theme lyrics ('What kind of world am I going to find/will it be real or just all in my mind?') that the whole thing is a self-aggrandisement/softcore pornographic fantasy in the mind of a dying astronaut, with Twiki as a kind of ambulatory phallic symbol.

Battlestar Galactica thus has had an impact on the public out of proportion to the brevity of its initial run, and strongly captures the zeitgeist of the 1970s.

I ● SAGA OF A STAR WORLD (PARTS ONE, TWO AND THREE)

US TRANSMISSION DATE: Sunday 17 September 1978
WRITER: Glen A Larson
DIRECTORS: Richard Colla (Uncredited: Alan J Levi)
CREDITED CAST: Lew Ayres (President Adar); Wilfrid Hyde-White (Sire Anton); John Fink (Doctor Payne); Jane Seymour (Serina); Ray Milland (Sire Uri); Rock Springfield (Lieutenant Zac); Randi Oakes (Young Woman); Norman Stuart (Statesman); David Matthews (Operative); Chip Johnson (1st Warrior); Geoffrey Binney (2nd Warrior); Paul Coufos (Pilot); Bruce Wright (Deck Hand)
KNOWN UNCREDITED CAST: Carol Baxter (Woman in Elevator); Myrna Matthews (Little Supreme/Tucana Singer); Patti Brooks (Big Supreme/ Tucana Singer); Sandy Gimpel (Seetol); Diane L Burgdorf (Lotay); Jim Peck (Commentator on Caprica); Peanuts (Muffit); Doc (Muffit II)

SYNOPSIS: The people of the Twelve Colonies are preparing to sign an armistice with the Cylon Alliance, putting to an end a thousand yahren-long war, but Commander Adama of the battlestar *Galactica* has doubts. Adama's sons, pilots Apollo and Zac, discover that the Cylons are in fact preparing an ambush, and rush to warn the Colonies, though Zac is killed in the process. The Cylons launch a devastating attack, through the treachery of the human Count Baltar. Adama gathers the survivors in a 'rag-tag fleet' of diverse vessels, and announces that their destination will be the long-lost Thirteenth Colony: Earth. Aboard the Fleet, the situation rapidly degenerates, with many people lacking in food and supplies, and others, like Council member Sire Uri, living in luxury, while Apollo and his friends Boomer and Starbuck attempt to ensure fair distribution of resources. Apollo befriends a woman, Serina, whose son, Boxey, is despondent over the death of his pet daggit Muffit in the attack, and he arranges for Boxey to have the care of an experimental robot daggit, 'Muffit II', as a replacement. Starbuck forms a friendship with a socialator, Cassiopea, which places a strain on his extant relationship with Apollo's sister Athena.

As the Council debate the best planet to go to for the restocking of resources, Apollo suggests that he can get them quickly to the planet Carillon through clearing a minefield at the Nova of Madagon, which they approve, and which is successful. On Carillon, the fugitives unexpectedly discover a resort with a casino. The travellers avail themselves of the facilities, while Adama suspects a Cylon trap. The Council, led by Uri, resolve to disarm completely, and plan to get around Adama's opposition to this move by putting it to the people at a ceremony to honour Starbuck, Boomer and Apollo for their deeds at the Nova of Madagon; Adama, however, devises a plan to secretly keep enough warriors back among the Fleet to fight off an attack by sending non-combatants dressed in warrior uniform to the ceremony. Apollo and Starbuck, suspicious of the bogus warriors, investigate, and discover, first, that the Ovions, who run the facility, are kidnapping their 'guests' (including Cassiopea) to feed to their offspring and that the Cylons are allied with the Ovions. Rescuing Cassiopea (and Boxey and Muffit, who have wandered into the Ovions' tunnels), Apollo and Starbuck return to sound the alarm. A pitched battle ensues between the Cylons and the humans, in which the Cylons' Imperious Leader is killed. His successor reprieves Baltar, who has been under threat of execution, and tells him to go and propose a truce with the human fleet.

ANALYSIS: 'Saga of a Star World', the opening three-hour pilot serial (although, as this figure includes over 40 minutes of adverts, the actual length of the story is closer to two and a quarter hours), quickly establishes the series' premise, central characters and some of its continuing themes, proving, on the whole and despite a few shortcomings, a strong start for *Battlestar Galactica*.

STARTING THE SAGA: THE NARRATIVE FROM SCRIPT TO SCREEN

The story is structured in three parts, such that it can be viewed as three separate (albeit linked or 'arced') episodes, or as a single story. The first section (from the betrayal of the armistice through to the start of the exodus of the fleet from the Colonies) is the best developed in narrative and character terms; the second (covering the food-hoarding incident, the creation of Muffit II and the clearing of the minefield at Nova of Madagon) is less strong, but still has good characterisation. The final section is the weakest, and provides no sense of resolution; even if the story is the setup for an ongoing series, there should be some form of internal closure to the episode itself.

'Saga of a Star World' underwent a series of changes over its development, which make for interesting comparisons with the final version. The earliest draft we could locate, dated 3 November 1977 (the third section of which includes a number of mistakes, like mixing up which character is in which scene and inconsistencies over the words for currency and measurement, which suggests that the writer was still trying out different concepts), has the same tripartite structure mentioned above (and, while the first section is very close to how it appears on screen, the second two are much sketchier and narratively weaker). The second third of the early draft is also less dramatic than what was finally shown on screen, with the food-hoarding and starving population mentioned rather than actually depicted, and the section focusing around the mine clearing, the discovery of Carillon, and the development of Muffit. The final third is much more vague, without the plotline of Sire Uri planning to disarm, and with a rather melodramatic ending involving Baltar kidnapping Adama, Athena and Boxey, and Starbuck engaging in a daring rescue. Baltar's relationship with the Cylons is more openly duplicitous; at the climax of the story, with the Cylons on the verge of attacking the remaining humans, he offers Adama a deal, whereby Baltar would continue to supply the Cylons with tylium from Carillon in exchange for the lives of the humans, whom Baltar would then govern (and, should the Cylons fail to comply, threatening to blow up the planet instead), foreshadowing the way in which Baltar in the finished series vacillates between the Cylons and the humans, but continually looks out for his own interests under all circumstances.

Cassiopea is conspicuous by her absence; later drafts of the script, after she is introduced, have her being killed by the Ovions. Cassiopea's reprieve came mainly because of doubts concerning the ability of Maren Jensen to carry off the role of main romantic interest for Starbuck. Baltar, in the early draft, begs for his life and is given a chance to redeem himself by the Imperious Leader, before being shot by Starbuck, where later drafts, and the film, have him executed by the Cylons, then the final version as screened gives him a reprieve in a tacked-on epilogue. Adama uses the phrase 'an infamy' to describe the Cylon attacks in early drafts, where later he will change it to 'a holocaust' in the broadcast episode.

Some of the characters also underwent changes. Athena loses a lot of dialogue over successive drafts (possibly due to problems with Maren Jensen's performance); in the earlier drafts, she is described as a 'trainee', and comes across as something of a fusspot, continually making accusatory and short-sighted complaints about her father and brother's actions. Apollo, then known as Skyler, initially appears as a cold man who finds it difficult to express his emotions, an idea which does survive up to a filmed but cut scene in which Athena accuses Apollo, in an unusually clumsy sequence, of having 'the simple mind of a mechanical drone programmed only to fight' (Adama, equally awkwardly, replies 'Athena, please, let's not turn what's left of our family into a vortex of invective'), but which is quite different to Richard Hatch's portrayal of Apollo as a sensitive man in touch with his emotions who is not afraid to cry in public. Zac undergoes a number of changes, from an experienced fighter to an inexperienced fighter to the situation finally aired, in which Starbuck gives up his place on patrol to Zac so that Zac can have his first patrol before peace is formally declared.

Serina, initially known as 'Lyra' and being no relation to Boxey (he is an orphan she takes under her wing) was intended to be a continuing character (as attested by her presence in the draft script 'The Nari of Sentinel 27'), who would subsequently become a Quorum of Twelve member, but later drafts have her dying of pluton poisoning; the scripts seem to imply that this is incurred through being burned by a Cylon laser during the attack on Caprica, which may explain why Boxey is not also suffering from the complaint. Scenes of her learning of this and urging Apollo to take care of Boxey after her death were filmed (the death itself was planned to take place offscreen), but the idea was dropped after test audiences who were shown rough cuts of the episode found it too depressing, and Jane Seymour was persuaded to stay on for another two episodes; however, including it would have provided the final third with a more satisfactory, if downbeat, ending. In a 1980 interview with *Starlog*, Seymour says that she hadn't planned on doing the series and hadn't been keen on continuing when the production team asked her to (saying that she had gone down best with test audiences of all the female characters), that she was angry that the scenes of her illness were cut, and that she felt the character had been changed completely in 'Lost Planet of the Gods'.

A couple of scenes deleted late in the day flesh out Starbuck and his relationships more thoroughly. Starbuck originally had a couple of scenes in which he plays cards against Gemon officers and loses not only his, but also Boomer, Jolly and Greenbean's, gambling money in the process, explaining more fully his comment to Cassiopea about the religious scruples of the Otori sect on Gemini against sex making them good card players. He also had a little more banter with Cassiopea in the shuttle about her choice of profession (in which he tells her he has been experiencing terrible headaches and needs to release some tension, and she replies, 'make an appointment'), explaining his apology to her later. Starbuck and Cassiopea's love scene was originally more explicit, with Starbuck said in draft scripts to be naked, and in the first filmed version he is shirtless, but the network censors' fears that it was too racy for prime time on Sunday nights led to it being reshot in a toned-down, fully-clothed version. Another deleted scene features the crew singing a crypto-Christian hymn, beginning 'Hail to thee, o Lord of manna, bounteous be thy hand ...' and getting steadily worse, throwing in references to freedom, liberty and Zion. Although it is tempting to believe it was axed on grounds of taste, it was actually probably only removed because this scene features Serina telling Apollo to look after Boxey once she is dead.

A few changes seem to have been made to avoid too close a comparison with *Star Wars*. The name 'Saga of a Star World' (which never actually appears onscreen) is formed from a number of early alternate titles for the series (which include *Star World*, *Starworld*, *Galactica: Star Worlds*, and *The Saga of the Battlestar Galactica*), some of which do seem a little too close to the title of the Lucas epic. Richard Hatch has suggested that the change of the young male lead's name from 'Skyler' to 'Apollo' was one of these, and early drafts refer to Muffit as a 'droid' rather than, as in the finished version, a 'drone'[6] and an apparently humanoid droid named 'Zeus', a bit of a C-3PO type with an 'effete' voice, appears in the 1977 draft. More focus is placed upon alien races in early drafts as well (with a feline, four-breasted waitress, with the ability to pick up glasses with her tail, appearing in the casino), and the abandonment of these, no doubt for cost and time reasons, also can be seen as a way of distinguishing *Battlestar Galactica*, with its largely isolated human population, from the multispecies universe of *Star Wars*.

The 1977 draft script also shows some interesting points of continuity. Boomer's ethnic origin is specified explicitly from the outset (though not Tigh's); the wrist-clasping handshake is mentioned, as are early versions of some familiar Colonial swearwords, including 'Feljurcreb' as an early version of 'Felgercarb' (the word 'aresford' as a substitute for 'ass' also appears). The idea of distinctive Colonial terms for units of time, distance and currency appears, although not yet in its final form ('millitons' alternates with 'microns' as a Colonial equivalent for 'seconds', the term 'years' is used instead of the televised series' more alien 'yahrens', and 'centon' seems to be a unit of currency as well as of time, whereas later Colonial currency will be established as based on 'cubits'). The double-mouthed Tucana singing trio are mentioned as far back as the 1977 draft, and described as looking like the Supremes (on Carillon, they sing a song with the prescient lyrics, written by John Tartaglia, Sue Collins and Glen Larson, 'No matter where you go, it won't matter what you do/cause something's always after you ...'); the one with whom Starbuck negotiates is described as 'Big Supreme' from the 27 February 1978 draft onwards, and they are also referred to as the 'Android Sisters' in the drafts from 1978[7] (Starbuck's conversation scene in the 27 February 1978 draft has him speaking with all three; at one point 'two sisters begin to bawl from all four mouths and rise to scurry out'). They were originally to have been seen in the hymn-singing sequence which closed the serial. The 1978 drafts contain a rather hideous line for Adama when he describes the ships of the fleet as being

---

6 This change was made so late in the day that the word 'drone' had to be audibly dubbed in to Doctor Wilker's dialogue.

7 Which is clearly a joking reference to the American swing-era trio the Andrews Sisters, rather than implying that the singers are robots.

'as forgotten and abandoned as a womb after childbirth'.

The story has also produced a few behind-the-scenes anecdotes. The visual effects for the Cylon attack sequence had been done before the footage of the humans reacting to it was shot, so the director had to work out the choreography and pyrotechnics with the effects people around the existing visual effects footage. The director, Richard Colla, reportedly fell out with Glen Larson during the shooting and was replaced by an uncredited Alan J Levi. The sequence of Starbuck, Apollo, Cassiopea, Muffit and Boxey fleeing across a narrow walkway was shot on the *Phantom of the Opera* soundstage at Universal, on a walkway which was forty feet in the air; Noah Hathaway was too frightened to go on it and so was doubled by Felix Silla, while Evie, who was also initially reluctant to cross at speed, was then scared by the pyrotechnics, shot across the walkway and climbed into the rafters, needing to be coaxed down by the production team. In the sequence right after Serina's news broadcast is cut off by the sound of the approaching Cylon fighters, as the fighters soar over the city in darkness one can quite clearly see the words 'FUCK OFF' spelled out in the city's lights to the immediate right of the third fighter as it approaches the centre of the screen (this effect is even clearer in the photonovel of the pilot).

THE MASK OF APOLLO: CHARACTERISATION AND WORLDBUILDING

From its first episode, the series' central characters are well drawn. Adama is a strong and believable creation, suspicious to the point of paranoia (a cut line from the 1977 draft script has Tigh saying, 'I once read a book on tactical survival in an alien world. It said a little paranoia was good for you', and Adama replying, 'I'm familiar with that book. I wrote it.'), but also fiercely loyal (originally backing Sire Uri because he knew and liked him from earlier associations) and a good tactician who understands the power of faith, encouraging people to believe in Earth even though most think it is a myth. He is also shown as capable of being wrong, and letting his personal feelings get in the way of his professional work, opposing Apollo's plan for him to guide the ships through the minefield, even though it is a sensible one, out of fear that his son might be killed. Lorne Greene gives a powerful performance, even apparently shedding genuine tears in the scene where Adama learns of the death of his wife.

Apollo, Starbuck and Boomer are well characterised for an initial outing, though still possessing scope for development at this stage. Starbuck probably gets the most development of the three; his later anxiety about the safety of his fellow-officers can be seen to have its origins in his feelings of responsibility for the death of Zac, and the fact that, although Starbuck and Apollo seem close initially, Starbuck gravitates more towards Boomer as the story progresses, then back to Apollo at the end, suggesting a subtext in which Starbuck and Apollo tacitly work through their feelings about Zac's death. Starbuck is seen early on to favour Cassiopea over Athena, as Athena offers commitment, which he doesn't want (and also, going out with Athena provides any number of potential opportunities for offending her father Adama), whereas Cassiopea recognises and accepts him as a philanderer, much as he accepts her profession as a socialator, essentially a legitimised prostitute (the 2 October 1978 terminology document, tongue firmly in cheek, defines a socialator as 'a great date'). When Athena says to Starbuck that she can't commit to him because of her feelings over Zac's death, Starbuck promptly uses the same excuse to explain his philandering behaviour to her in the casino, which might make him initially seem callous and manipulative, but it is explained over the course of the series that Starbuck's family background does give him genuine commitment issues.

Boxey and Muffit, or 'Muffy', are far less cutesy than some of their detractors claim, with Boxey being capable of sulking, fretting and getting into trouble, as well as a credible talent for manipulation (disingenuously suggesting to his mother that Apollo would make a good stepfather). Muffit is said here to be a prototype for a line of cybernetic guard dogs, and certainly has jaws powerful enough to bite into a Cylon's leg. Sire Uri is also well-characterised to the point where one rather regrets that he didn't continue in the series (an actor of Ray Milland's status presumably being too expensive to have as a regular). However, not only does the character feature heavily in the uncanonical Marvel spinoff comic, but a 'Sire Geller' turns up in 'Greetings from Earth', suggesting ongoing homages to a particular Israeli spoon-bender. The character is clearly motivated throughout the latter two-thirds of the story by Apollo and Boomer's raid on his nest-egg; he backs Apollo's minefield-clearing plan and also the allowing of civilian visits to Carillon as revenge against Adama for the earlier action.

The story is also impressive in the way it makes the audience care about even minor characters. We only meet Zac briefly, and yet the timing and manner of his demise (burning to death in a decidedly graphic fireball), and the way the other characters react to it, make us feel for him. Similarly, the destruction of the battlestar *Atlantia* is genuinely shocking due to its scale and the characters' reactions. The sequence in which Tigh steals the warriors' uniforms for Adama's masquerade deception establishes the character's quick thinking abilities (as well as Terry Carter's flair for comedy), and the scene in which a Viper pilot complains 'hey, Starbuck, it's dangerous around here', followed by Starbuck's double take as his wingman explodes, establishes, through graveyard humour, the genuine peril of their situation. We also see a few points which will become significant later on; the security guards, here seen as private ships' security, will evolve into a *de facto* police force over the series, and the term of abuse 'Boray', heard briefly in this story, will be revealed in 'The Magnificent Warriors' to refer to a race of porcine primitives. The single collar insignia which Apollo gives Boxey will be worn by the child throughout the rest of the series.

The initial political situation of the episode (which was screened at the time of the Yom Kippur war, and was interrupted by a news bulletin on the Camp David summit between Egypt and Israel) has also been given a lot of thought. The Colonials' sense of betrayal is credible in that everyone does genuinely believe that the armistice is going to happen, even hardened warriors like Apollo, and, although Adama is suspicious, he himself acknowledges that he believes his feelings to be baseless, and only fully accepts that the Cylons have broken the armistice when he receives hard evidence in the form of the attack on Zac and Apollo. Baltar himself, although the audience can see the villainy in the characterisation, has clearly manufactured the persona of a trustworthy man, and, since no one in their right mind is going to set themselves up to be killed, the idea of a human betraying his own race to a genocidal enemy is counterintuitive. It is later explained that he struck a deal with the Cylons to spare his own planet so that he could continue to rule over it, but the rest of the humans don't know about this. Furthermore, Baltar's people had investigated Carillon as a mining prospect and reported that it had too little tylium to be financially worthwhile, suggesting that Baltar in fact set up a mining operation on the planet in secret, which further implies that he has been clandestinely fuelling the Cylon fleet (an idea which appears in explicit form in the 1977 draft), and thus that he's actually been in touch with the Cylons for longer than any of the Colonials suspect (which might also explain why he betrays humanity to the Cylons, as he would thus have had some idea of the scale of the Cylon forces and might have decided to support the stronger group, an idea supported by the 2 October 1978 terminology document, which states that Baltar defected to the Cylons 'as soon as he discovered his side was losing'). In this story, a total of five Colonial battlestars are seen, and four named in the background radio transmissions heard on the *Galactica* (these being the *Atlantia*, *Pacifica*, *Acropolis*, and *Triton*).

The subsequent portrayal of life in the Fleet is also believable. There are said to be 220 ships (including one designated 'Gemini Freight' and another

'Colonial Movers', presumably a spaceborne moving van; the *Rising Star*, on which Sire Uri is based and which will feature repeatedly throughout the series, appears here for the first time), but it is not stated whether or not this includes the *Galactica* (the matter is resolved in 'The Living Legend', in which it is implied that it does not). The Quorum of Twelve (in some instances, referred to as the Council of the Twelve, or the Council of Twelve) govern, along with the President, making a ruling council of thirteen (as Larson has stated, bringing in Biblical imagery of the Last Supper and Jesus' betrayal by Judas). Baltar was also a member of the Quorum, but it is never stated which planet he represents. The subsequent Quorum established after the exodus begins was elected by a few, frightened people under fairly distressing conditions, explaining how a profiteer like Sire Uri could creep into power, as it is indicated in dialogue that his wife was well-respected, and seems to have been a restraining influence on him back on the Colonies, suggesting that he used his wife's good name to get himself elected in the absence of a rigorous political process. This also indicates what will become a theme throughout the series, of people becoming overcautious after a traumatic event; when Apollo accuses Adama of failing to act against Uri for this reason. In light of subsequent events, it is worth noting that the Fleet at this stage is not under martial law, as the Quorum can, and do, overrule Adama, and he defers to them.

The Ovions' characterisation is explicitly based on insects, primarily ants. Their leader, Lotay, is called a 'Queen' in the 1977 and the 27 February 1978 drafts; this and later drafts describe the Ovions as having female voices, which survives in the final in that the translation device uses a feminine tone to render Lotay's speech. The 1977 draft implies that male Ovions are killed after they have served their reproductive purpose, and states that the species is known to the Colonials previously as migrant workers, and in the final, it is observed that they are not native to Carillon as there is no indigenous food source (which also implies that they are feeding their guests on the remains of other guests).

We also get some limited backstory on the war between the humans and the Cylons. Early drafts, and the 2 October 1978 terminology document, refer to the Cylons as being part of a multispecies Alliance,[8] and that warring factions of humans had to band together to fight off this common enemy, which survives into the episode in Boomer's line 'every creature in

---

8 Tigh refers to them as the 'Cylon Empire', a term which is frequently used to describe the Cylon forces throughout the series, suggesting that, whatever the initial nature of the Alliance, the Cylons are currently the dominant power within it.

the universe is out to exterminate us' and in the Imperious Leader's reference to the Alliance before ordering Baltar's execution. There is also a filmed but cut scene in which Baltar, proposing a toast to the assembled Quorum, notes in his speech that humans have recently joined together, following which negotiations with the Alliance were initiated, and it is worth noting that the alien species encountered thus far are all either tacitly or explicitly helping the Cylons (although the Hasari, whom Adama alludes to the humans having helped when they were attacked by Cylons, are never specified as being human or alien; the 2003 *Battlestar Galactica* video game depicts them as whale-like creatures, picking up on the idea that the Hasari might well be nonhumans. The 1977 draft mentions two other races as having been saved from the Cylons by the humans, the Galics and the Tucana, the latter of which are known to be aliens). In Baltar's execution scene, the Imperious Leader, after saying that he can't trust someone who would betray his own people, asserts that Baltar has 'missed the point of the war' and that all humans must be destroyed. The idea was played down in later drafts, no doubt because of the moral questions it raises over the humans' position in the universe (what did they do to get every species' hand against them?). The idea of warring factions of humans uniting, however, explains why no one questions the Cylons' abrupt decision to sue for peace, as the unification of the human groups would have made them a credible enemy for the Cylons, and thus it is plausible that they would seek a non-military settlement.

Although the series would go on to be noted for its right-wing sympathies, these do not really emerge in explicit form (aside from the fact that Adar, an ageing President involved in a disarmament treaty, played by an American actor,[9] bears certain resemblances to Jimmy Carter; Carter is also famous for having explicitly linked his religious beliefs with his politics, reflected in the mingling of faith and governance in the *Battlestar Galactica* universe) until the final third of the story, when Sire Uri's radical disarmament plan is shown as a foolish move, and Adama makes a spoken defence of interventionist politics. Although Adama defends the move, it is stated that the humans' intervention on behalf of the Hasari was what started the war with the Cylons. While a deleted scene from Apollo's discussion on the ethics of war with Boxey has Apollo telling the child that the opposite of war isn't necessarily peace, and that it's OK to fight back if you're attacked first, he also acknowledges that the issue is complex and there are no cut-and-dried answers. It is, furthermore, strongly indicated that Adama is a reluctant leader (with cut footage showing

---

9 Lew Ayres, the actor in question had, ironically, been a conscientious objector during WWII.

him attempting to resign from the Quorum of Twelve; the 1978 drafts make it plain that he resigns and Anton takes over as its leader), introducing the series' theme that people who desire power are evil and/or foolish, but those who have it thrust upon them are trustworthy. It might be worth noting, however, that it is a common allegorical trope in American SF cinema and, later, television, to represent Communists as insects or robots, so the presence of villainous robots allied with insects (whose lifestyle is a caricature of American beliefs about Communism, presenting a bounteous society in which all work in harmony and the rich share with the needy, but which is really fatally exploitative) is likely to have an unconscious resonance with the intended audience.

RED EYES IN THE SUNSET: THE INTRODUCTION OF THE CYLONS

The Cylons are also introduced here. While there is little in the way of characterisation at first, some of the celebrated Cylon Centurian[10] sarcasm appears in the final section (Imperious Leader: 'How? We took them by surprise.' Centurian: 'Apparently it was not as big a surprise as we had hoped for.') A Cylon Centurian identifies himself as Flight Leader Serpentine, in the first indication that Cylons have names. It is shown in the epilogue that Cylon politics changes; the new Imperious Leader, having been, or so he claims, programmed at a less warlike time than his predecessor, is more inclined to negotiate, suggesting a degree of individual differentiation and political responsiveness among Cylons. We also learn that there are different types of Cylons, with the introduction not only of the Imperious Leader but, at the end of the story, of IL-class Cylon Lucifer, who looks like the offspring of *Doctor Who*'s Cyberman Controller from the 1967 story 'The Tomb of the Cybermen' and *Buck Rogers*' Twiki (and is played by the man who would go on to operate the latter robot), and whose costume changes over the course of the series, suggesting that he has a wardrobe hidden away somewhere. The idea that there are physically different types of Cylons occurs even in early drafts, in which the Cylons are lizards rather than robots.

It is in this adventure, also, that one of the few fragments of Cylon backstory which the original series provides appears. We learn from Apollo, talking to Boxey, that the Cylons are 'machines created by living creatures a long time ago. In some ways they're smarter than us, and programmed to think a lot faster, but they're not as individual ... they were made by a race of reptiles called Cylons.

---

10 The spelling of the name varies, with some scripts and outside sources giving it as 'Centurian' and others giving it as 'Centurion'. For the sake of clarity, we will be using the former spelling when referring to the original series and *Galactica 1980* , but using the latter when referring to the reimagined series, in which the spelling appears to have been standardised as 'Centurion'.

After a while the Cylons learned that humans were the most practical form of life through the system, so they copied our bodies … there are no more real Cylons, they died off thousands of yahrens ago, leaving behind a race that's purely machine, but we still call them Cylons'. The lizard concept survives in early drafts, in which the Centurians are said to be armour-clad beings rather than robots (though the familiar postage-slot style scanning eye seems to have been a feature of this armour from the outset; the change to robots came at the instigation of the network, which viewed the destruction of machines as less morally objectionable than the shooting of living beings in armour). Even in the 6 April 1978 draft, in which Muffit's biting the Cylon's leg causes it to spark and short, implying a robot being, Apollo still insults a Cylon by calling it a 'creepy, crawly creature'. The final design of the Imperious Leader, furthermore, appears reptilian (he also has a cute little lizard pet with stuck-on dragon wings which perches on his arm like Blofeld's cat, and which is still visible on his left arm in the high-angle shots from behind). The 2 October 1978 terminology document cites the Imperious Leader as being 'the last surviving member of an intelligent reptilian race'. Early drafts, including one as late as 6 April 1978 say that the Imperious Leader should have multiple eyes, an idea not followed up in the design. The fact that the Imperious Leader is shot in shadow gives it a further sinister cast, recalling the scenes of Marlon Brando receiving clients in semi-darkness in *The Godfather* (1972). Although the fact that Patrick Macnee provides not only the voice of the Imperious Leader but also the opening voiceover (and, later, portrays Count Iblis) causes much speculation (which will be discussed in more detail in 'War of the Gods'), this was not always the case: the 1977 draft indicates that Adama was initially to have done a somewhat differently phrased opening voiceover (as he does in later drafts up to 6 April 1978), and cut footage indicates that an alternate, slightly mechanical-sounding, voice was tried for the Imperious Leader.

While it is not explicitly stated in the episodes, there is a tacit explanation as to why, if the Cylons have been in a war with humans for a thousand yahrens without either side gaining a definite advantage, they can return now to smash the humans with overwhelming force. The answer comes when Adama alludes to the Cylons attacking other groups than just the Twelve Colonies, which suggests that the Cylons may have been fighting a multi-front war (presumably against other species), meaning that they could have cleared up the other fronts without the humans knowing and were using the armistice as a cover for the attack, an idea which fits in with the fact that much of this story is based on the Battle of the Bulge (in which Hitler stripped his forces on the Eastern Front to launch an armoured strike on the West, which the Allies, supposing him to be still committed in the East, did not anticipate). It also recalls the situation towards the end of World War I, when the surrender of Russia meant that a million German soldiers were promptly released to fight in the West, overwhelming the Allies for a time. This is supported by the line where Apollo notes with surprise that the concealed Cylon force has enough firepower to destroy the Fleet; generally, military forces that are capable of overwhelming their opponents don't enter into peace negotiations, meaning that the humans were not expecting the Cylon force to be as large as it is.

THE OWL OF ATHENA: THE MYTHOLOGICAL ORIGINS OF THE STORY

'Saga of a Star World' draws strongly not only on Biblical and Greek mythology, but also on American myths of origin. In terms of its Old Testament connections, leaving aside the earlier concept's imagery of humans driven from Paradise through the actions of reptiles, there are strong parallels with the Exodus of the Israelites, with the Twelve Colonies, like the Twelve Tribes of Israel, seeking a promised land; the clearing of the minefield standing in for the parting of the Red Sea, the discovery of Carillon for the provision of manna from heaven, and the casino scenes paralleling the story of the Golden Calf (particularly the Cecil B De Mille film *The Ten Commandments'* [1956] depiction of the incident). Moses, significantly, is said to have been born and died in the month of Adar. While others have written extensively on the Mormon parallels of the story, the focus on lost tribes links in with the Mormon belief that Native Americans stem from a lost tribe of Israel, and the Quorum of Twelve take their name directly from the Mormon religious leaders, the Quorum of the Twelve Apostles.

There are also connections with Greek and Roman mythology, not only with the story of Aeneas (a man leading his family and followers out of a ruined city to find a new land), but also the Odyssey, with the Carillon sequence resembling the stories of the Lotus Eaters, in which some of Odysseus' sailors are induced to abandon their quest for home and embrace instead a life of idle pleasure, and of Circe, who offered the sailors hospitality but repaid them by turning them into animals (a parallel to the way the Ovions' seeming generosity is a cover for their use of the Colonials as food for their grubs). While the names in the series are frequently mythological, these vary between those with clear symbolic connotations (such as Adama, named for a Biblical patriarch who was the first human), and others which seem to have been picked simply for their classical sound (for instance Cassiopea, whose mythological namesake is a proud and vain queen, who thus bears no resemblance to the modest woman of that name in the series). The concept of socialators appears to have been drawn from the sacred prostitutes of Ishtar, while elements of the series' design also evoke ancient mythologies, such as the Egyptianate look of the Viper pilots' helmets and the *Galactica*'s resemblance to an ancient Mesoamerican crocodile.

Another sort of mythology that will also pervade the series is modern American mythology: the Western and the WWII story. The Western, as noted, is evoked in the series' 'wagon train' setup (and reinforced in the presence of Lorne Greene's *Bonanza* connections). Early drafts of the script (including that which provided the material for the novelisation), include, like Westerns, livestock as well, on a 'livery ship' (which, perhaps recalling the idea of Noah's Ark, are in breeding pairs, including a pair of unicorns, a whimsical idea which will return to unfortunate effect in 'The Young Lords'). Although Starbuck does not really resemble his namesake from *Moby-Dick*, this name also, through Melville's story, evokes America's cultural and literary past; interestingly, the American alternative comic, *Star*Reach* (1974-79) featured the adventures of a space rogue named Cody Starbuck. Baltar bears some resemblances to Benedict Arnold, the American revolutionary who defected to the British side, and to Vidkun Quisling, the Norwegian politician who gave away military secrets to the Nazis with the aim of being made their leader in Norway once they had taken it over; significantly, given Baltar's involvement in supplying the Cylons with tylium, the Nazis were largely interested in obtaining the natural resources which Norway could supply.

The story is also extensively based on American activities in World War II, or at any rate the subsequent Hollywood depiction of these, being one part Pearl Harbour to one part Battle of the Bulge, with a liberal salting of elements from the Battle of Midway. Pearl Harbour, of course, involved a nation which had pursued a policy of disarmament following an exhaustive involvement in a war, which then finds itself attacked unexpectedly by a powerful imperialist force (note that the name 'the Cylon Alliance' suggests an Axis-style collaboration, and it is evident from Adama's speech in the third section that the Cylons have been attacking more than just the Twelve Colonies). The film *The Battle of the Bulge* (1965) sees Adama and Apollo's roles merge in the Henry Fonda character, Lt Col Kiley, who suspects the Germans of being up to something when no one else in the American forces will do so; later, after the Germans' plans have been revealed, a scene occurs where Kiley, on a reconnaissance flight to find the Germans in the fog-bound Ardennes forest, spots first a fuel depot, and then, beyond that, hundreds of tanks (paralleling the empty Cylon tanker and the hundreds of Cylon ships seen by Apollo and Zac). After warning the Americans, the plane he is flying in crashes, killing the pilot and wounding him. There are also elements of the film *Midway* (1976) in this sequence, which has a scene of American pilots flying through cloud cover to discover the Japanese fleet. The final climactic battle, in which the Cylons, while attacking the *Galactica,* are taken by surprise by unexpected squadrons of Vipers rising from the surface of Carillon, recalls an incident in the Battle of Midway itself, where the Japanese carrier fleet launched an attack on the island of Midway, but were then taken by surprise by American bombers, who had already taken off before the strike began.

The *Galactica* itself also recalls an American aircraft carrier (and it is explicitly likened to one in the 2 October 1978 terminology document), being long and flat, defending itself and surrounding ships not only with its own guns, but with squadrons of Vipers (the early draft also refers to the *Galactica* as having a 'catapult deck', a signalling tower and ground crewmen). The Vipers' flexible, individualistic tactics, breaking formation frequently to pursue dogfights, are very like the American pilots' tactics in WWII (which allowed them to make quicker and more effective use of information obtained in battle than the tactics of the disciplined, strategy-focused Japanese pilots). We also see some Cylon fighters using *kamikaze* manoeuvres against the *Galactica*, reinforcing the Japanese connection. The fact that the Cylons have an Alliance, while the humans don't, despite not seeming particularly prejudiced towards other groups, recalls the fact that, although Americans do form alliances, they are generally short-lived, operating only for the duration of the relevant military or economic operation, rather than lasting confederacies. The story thus reinforces American self-perceptions.

FELGERCARB HAPPENS: PROBLEMS WITH 'SAGA OF A STAR WORLD'

Although most of them are in the third, and weakest, section, there are unfortunately a few problems with the story. If tylium is so volatile that Starbuck and Apollo shooting at the ceiling would cause a chain reaction which would blow up the whole planet, one wonders why there haven't been some serious accidents before this, as any Ovion sneaking a crafty cigarette behind the egg maturation chambers is going to be at risk of destroying the entire civilisation. It's also stretching credibility that no one on the Colonies appears to have noticed their holiday-making friends going missing (although the early draft suggests that letters are sent back to the Colonies to reassure friends and relatives and encourage them to come, much, one assumes, like the letters sent by the Nazis to reassure Jews that their relatives, actually in death camps, were all right, sooner or later someone is likely to notice that they don't come back). Although Maren Jensen's acting seems fine in the extant footage, a number of outtakes lend credibility to the reports that her role was reduced due to problems with her performance. Serina's broadcast refers to the peace negotiations taking place on the 'star Kobol', where 'Lost Planet of the Gods' has Kobol being the origin world of humans which is rediscovered by the fleet.

There are also a few problems with the political setup at the end of the story. Although it is believable that Sire Uri would play to the gallery by allowing a tired and starving people on to Carillon, it is less believable that the only person offering any opposition to this is Adama, particularly since the Carillon setup practically screams 'it's a trap': Baltar's connection to the planet is made obvious early on, and a casino where people win all the time ought to arouse anyone's suspicions (while the novelisation claims that the Ovions had managed to doctor their food with a drug that made the Councillors more suggestive, and had encouraged them thus to support universal disarmament, none of this is even hinted at onscreen). Also, even the most disarmament-keen real-life politicians never suggest destroying their arms completely. While the series remains largely within the realms of credibility on the political front here, the gullible-politicians-versus-clever-Adama scenario will return again in the series, to bad effect. There also appears to be a minor continuity error in that Boomer says that he and Starbuck are to receive the Fleet's highest military honour, the 'Gold Cluster', and then later Apollo says that he is to receive the 'Star Cluster' at the same ceremony; this is due to the omission of a line from the 27 February and 28 March 1978 drafts which makes it plain that the two honours are synonymous.

Despite these occasional problems, 'Saga of a Star World' is a genuinely splendid blockbuster as well as displaying a flair for drama and characterisation, and it is easy to see why the series succeeded as well as it did at the box office and on television.

2 • LOST PLANET OF THE GODS (PARTS ONE AND TWO)

US TRANSMISSION DATES: 24 September 1978 and 1 October 1978
WRITERS: Glen A Larson & Donald Bellisario
DIRECTOR: Christian I Nyby II
CREDITED CAST: Sheila DeWindt (Deitra); Janet Louise Johnson (Brie); Jane Seymour (Serina); Bruce Wright (1st Lt Guard); Paul Coufos (2nd Guard); Janet Lynn Curtis (Sorell); Jennifer Joseph, Leann Hunley, Gay Thomas, Millicent Crisp (Female Warriors)

SYNOPSIS: The Fleet heads into a magnetic void, which Adama, consulting the religious text the *Book of the Word*, believes may lead the way to Kobol, origin world of the Twelve Colonies. After most of the Viper pilots fall ill with a plague which Boomer and Jolly unwittingly brought to the *Galactica* through failing to follow proper decontamination procedures, the decision is taken to draft in the all-female shuttle pilots as replacement warriors, including Serina, who has become a trainee shuttle pilot. Although Starbuck and Apollo are sceptical, the women pilots successfully protect a mission to the asteroid's surface to find a cure for the plague. Meanwhile Baltar, commanding a Cylon base ship[11], has tracked down the *Galactica* and kidnaps Starbuck. Apollo and Serina hold their wedding ceremony, at the climax of which a star appears, which turns out to be the system of the planet Kobol. Adama, Serina and Apollo search the ruins on Kobol for a clue to the location of Earth; Baltar follows them and attempts to broker a deal with Adama, whereby the *Galactica* would pretend to surrender to the Cylons, be guided to their homeworld, and then destroy it. He releases Starbuck as a purported sign of his good intentions. Lucifer, on Baltar's base ship, having heard nothing from his leader and mindful of his own personal ambitions, attacks Kobol. The hieroglyphics that Adama is seeking are destroyed, and Baltar is trapped in the ruins, while the Colonial forces engage the Cylons in battle, with the now-recovered male warriors providing much-needed reinforcements. Serina is fatally wounded during the encounter, and Apollo promises to look after Boxey.

ANALYSIS: 'Lost Planet of the Gods', the second story in the series, is a strong follow-up to 'Saga of a Star World', building on the themes and ideas established in the pilot, and developing the story and characterisation of *Battlestar Galactica*'s protagonists and villains.

---

11 The terms 'base star' and 'base ship' are used interchangeably for the Cylon craft throughout the series.

KEEPING THE WAGONS ROLLING: ARC DEVELOPMENT

It is with 'Lost Planet of the Gods' that *Battlestar Galactica* shows the development of an arc, as well as the exploration of the fictional universe set out in 'Saga of a Star World'. Cassiopea is now working as a medtech, a move which, although it was originally sparked by the fact that the network was nervous about having a regular character who works as a prostitute, fits in with the idea that the Fleet is now geared for survival: a scene in which Cassiopea explains her career change to Apollo, saying that one good thing which came out of the destruction of the Colonies was the chance for people to start anew, was cut, although the same function is fulfilled by the scene in which Serina tells Apollo that everyone is being trained in some useful function. From a narrative point of view, having Cassiopea working as a medtech puts her in the thick of the action, whereas the writers might have more trouble finding reasons for a socialator to get involved with the various adventures in which the character finds herself.[12]

Boxey also gets more development in the story. It seems his father was killed, or disappeared, at some point prior to the attack, as he appears fairly well-adjusted to a fatherless state, and actively encourages his mother to remarry. He is also very cheeky, accusing Apollo of being a bit slow to catch on in the dinner-party scene, and, as Apollo and Serina square off over Serina's decision to become a shuttle pilot, wandering out with the observation, 'come on, Muffy, they're going to have an argument' (this is followed by Serina retorting 'we are *not* going to have an argument!', Boxey remarking, as the door closes, 'yes, they are', and Apollo turning to Serina to say 'Yes, we are!'). He wears what appears to be a child-sized bridge officer's uniform in the wedding sequence. Tigh also gets in another bit of deadpan humour, as, after driving the security officers (referred to in the first-draft script as 'Colonial sentries') away from the pilots' party, he informs the pilots that the only thing worse than stealing drink from the officers' mess is getting caught stealing drink from the officers' mess (although the irony is that, had the security officers succeeded in breaking up the party, the entire squadron might not have been laid low by the infection).

We also get some more development of the Colonial culture. The word 'fumarello' for cigar is used here for the first time (when Apollo rescues Starbuck from the magnetic void, Starbuck tells his friend that he owes him a fumarello), and, when Adama remarks 'if I were a hundred yahrens younger ...' there is

---

12 The 2 October 1978 terminology document contains the rather wonderful observation that, after Cassiopea has given up prostitution for medicine, 'the men still look at her lithe sensuous blondeness longingly'.

also an indication that Colonials might live for longer, and stay younger, than Earth humans (or, possibly, that a yahren might last for less time than an Earth year[13], although the amount of time specified suggests that Colonials still have longer lifespans than Earth humans; in 'War of the Gods', we will learn that Colonials can expect to live for about 200 yahrens). Lucifer states that the Fleet is travelling at less than light speed, meaning that they would take years just to get out of the solar system (a fact conveniently ignored by all involved in the scriptwriting process). A few more ships are named, these being the freighters *Yarborough* and *Astrodon*, and a ship of unknown type called the *Edana*. The mummified corpse Baltar tries to pull the sceptre from is the Ninth Lord of Kobol, who, according to the fifth-draft script, was the last to rule before the planet was abandoned.

Starbuck's attempt to replace Serina on the mission is also not simply down to his feelings about female pilots, but clearly relate to his guilt over Zac's death after he took the patrol originally assigned to Starbuck. Here, he attempts to replace Serina so that she won't have to take a potentially fatal risk. Apollo, also, says 'he's trying to protect Serina – or me'; however, in protecting Serina he is also protecting Apollo, from experiencing the loss of another loved one, and, in that Starbuck takes the deep probe position, he is the one who is caught by the Cylons, thus saving both of them. Ironically, however, the Cylons who kill Serina later are undoubtedly the ones who escorted Starbuck to the surface, making him indirectly responsible for her death.

This is also the story in which the collectivist attitude which characterises *Battlestar Galactica* is made plain. While most American telefantasy series, like *Star Trek*, tend to be characterised by an ethos which places the rights of the individual above all else, and feature whole starship crews being put in jeopardy in order to save a single lost crewman, the opposite is true of *Battlestar Galactica*. Although Adama loves Serina as his future daughter-in-law, and knows the risks of putting her on the front line, he does it, as otherwise everyone else's life would be in danger. Although Adama offers Apollo the chance to hold Serina back, saying that he can leave out any pilot who he doesn't consider qualified enough to fly the mission, Apollo also refuses to play favourites, and in a cut line, Tigh says to Adama afterwards 'you knew he wouldn't hold her back'.

THE WOMEN WARRIORS: IS 'LOST PLANET OF THE GODS' SEXIST?

One of the most common accusations levelled at 'Lost Planet of the Gods' is that

---

13 The 1978 terminology document defines a yahren as 'a year', but does not specify which planet it is a year of.

it is sexist. However, it would seem that the opposite is the case, as the women are shown as acquitting themselves well as pilots, and the only two characters who doubt their abilities, Apollo and Starbuck, get their comeuppance.

At the start of the story, there does seem to be a gender division in the Fleet's military. Although women do become pilots and warriors (as Serina points out to Apollo), they serve as shuttle pilots and bridge officers, and are only considered as Viper pilots due to the sudden virus outbreak. Apollo says that 'the Viper is the most advanced flying machine ever designed by man. You don't just turn one over to a ... shuttle pilot' with the clear implication that Apollo is actually hesitating over the word 'woman'. However, while the women-pilots plotline initially looks rather dodgy, with Serina undermining Apollo's classroom authority by audibly saying 'I love you' to him in front of the other trainees, and with a sequence of Starbuck flirting with women in form-fitting pressure suits, the later sequences show them as competent warriors. Deitra, particularly, seems to be a ruthless fighter, Apollo is forced to acknowledge that Serina's a good pilot and even the slightly flaky Brie overcomes her nervousness on her first outing to fly the rest of the mission competently (a cut scene from the first draft had her screwing up badly during training, adding an extra level of nuance to her nerves on her first flight). Starbuck, finally, says 'we lost a lot of good pilots up there', at the end of the story, acknowledging that the women did a better job than he expected.

The original scenes as defined in the first-draft script, while still containing the sense of the finished version, are also much more explicit. When Apollo and Starbuck first meet the women, they are said to be all young and 'quite beautiful', and wearing different sorts of outfits; Starbuck is described as 'admiring each backside as the girls jump through the hatch'. The women then go to the quartermasters' and receive G-suits and put them on, suggesting there might have been a lot of flesh on display. Starbuck also enjoys a sensual moment with Brie, when he offers to help her put on her flightsuit properly (Athena dampens his efforts to demonstrate proper military dress to Brie with a 'withering glare'; the draft script heavily implies that Starbuck is attracted to Brie, and even in the televised version she is the first person he approaches when he returns to the Colonials). However, the women's experience is also highlighted in early versions; Deitra's rank and background are given (she is said to be 'Lieutenant Deitra, formerly of the *Atlantia*', who was on a run when it was destroyed by the Cylons), where Brie is stated to be a flight sergeant.

It is firmly established in the script that the only problems the women face are their own inexperience and the prejudice of others (particularly Starbuck, whose belittling of Brie's reports means that the squadron could have been surprised by the approaching Cylon fighter, and, as it is, his reluctance to check the situation probably lost them valuable time), but that is all; there is no talk of them returning to shuttle pilot duty afterwards. The scene in which the women talk in the officers' mess underlines this: although their discussion is in a feminine, girls-night-out style, they are clearly competent and aware warriors, and the only nasty note is struck by Starbuck and Apollo's unkind mimicry. However, this again reflects more on the prejudices of the warriors rather than the women's abilities, in that, while the women are holding an intense technical discussion, the men are frivolously and campily going on about curtain fabric. Ironically, also, the women's inexperience may have saved them in their initial mission, as the Cylons were unprepared for their erratic tactics.

The wedding subplot also ties in with the women-pilots storyline. Starbuck becomes visibly jealous of Serina after she and Apollo become engaged, and treats Apollo as if marriage is the equivalent of death (a hilarious cut sequence also has Starbuck likening it to castration: in a conversation beginning with Starbuck comparing marriage to flying into a Cylon base ship with all guns blazing, and Apollo countering by comparing it to a gentle long-term reconnaissance mission, Starbuck retorts 'yeah, with your cannon sawed off', before desperately trying to retract the statement by saying 'what I mean is, you don't need weapons on a reconnaissance mission'). This is also probably one of the motivating factors behind his treatment of the women pilots, as Serina is one of them, and it is not insignificant that Starbuck mentions Apollo's wedding when he pokes fun of the women pilots in the officers' mess.

Another common myth is that women pilots, bar Sheba later in the series, only appear in this story. In fact, Brie returns as one of the pilots captured by the Ship of Lights in 'War of the Gods', and the reuse of some of the launching sequence footage from this story means that she is also seen launching in 'The Living Legend', and Deitra is seen preparing for launch in 'The Hand of God'. A deleted tag scene which appears in the draft of 'The Young Lords' refers to Deitra and Athena flying a recon patrol. We also hear numerous references to female pilots, and see women in pilot uniforms in crowd sequences, elsewhere in the series. It is true that there is no further character development on the part of the female pilots seen in this story, which is a shame as it could have made for some interesting ongoing storylines, but presumably issues of cost and actor availability made this less achievable. It also has to be said that the series almost completely avoids the common late-seventies convention of having women as the continual targets of stalking and kidnap, with the only such cases appearing in the unused script 'The Beta Pirates' and briefly in

'The Magnificent Warriors' (in which the woman in question, the assertive hexagenarian Siress Belloby, is far from the traditional helpless victim).

SMILE AND SMILE AND BE A VILLAIN: THE BALTAR STORY

By far the most interesting piece of development in this story comes in Baltar's personal arc. In the epilogue of 'Saga of a Star World', which is given a recap in reedited form with additional material near the start of 'Lost Planet of the Gods' (although it's absent from the first-draft script of part one), the Imperious Leader tells Baltar that he wishes to extend the hand of truce to the humans. The Imperious Leader's motives in saying this are unclear; on the one hand, it is true that the Cylons have different personalities and attitudes, and that they regard humans well enough to copy their design, so it could be taken at face value, but, on the other hand, he could be manipulating Baltar into trying to negotiate with the *Galactica*.

Baltar's reaction is to the general effect that he believes the offer to be true, but, it is revealed later, he also clearly considers the possibility that it is a trap, and the Imperious Leader is lying to him. If this is the case, then, as he notes in a cut line in draft five of the second part of the script, 'I am obviously of no further value to the Cylons once I have delivered [the Fleet]', and he will himself be killed by the Cylons. Consequently, what he does is to capture a pilot, land on Kobol, meet Adama and release the pilot as a gesture of goodwill, and tell Adama that he believes the Imperious Leader to be trying to deceive them under the guise of peacemaking, and proposes that instead they pretend to surrender, return 'to Cylon' (their home planet) and launch a devastating counterattack against the heart of the Cylon Alliance, while, as he asserts, the Cylons are 'scattered throughout the star system', searching for the human fleet (which they evidently are, as Adama, despite his paranoia and scepticism, clearly believes him, and Lucifer, as discussed below, has anticipated Baltar's plan). He refers to the Cylons as 'demons', which is a significant foreshadowing of later revelations about their relationship with Count Iblis. This can be seen as Baltar trying to play two sides off against each other; on the one hand he is acting as if he believes the Imperious Leader and is attempting a ruse to bring the *Galactica* into Cylon space, but he is doing this in such a way as to aim the *Galactica* directly at the Cylons' area of greatest vulnerability, thus, potentially, redeeming himself in the eyes of the humans. Either way, Baltar is seen to have a keen sense of his own survival, even if he is somewhat overconfident and less sceptical than he would like to appear. Although he is fairly sacrilegious at first, when the bombs fall on the tomb, he immediately assumes that its collapse is an act of God, indicating both that he is so sure his plan would work that he was not expecting the attack, and that his cynicism is underlain with the same faith as the rest of the humans.

Lucifer clearly figures out Baltar's scheme. In a conversation with a Centurian, he says 'I'm afraid Baltar's plan has failed, whatever that plan truly was', then, when the uncomprehending Centurian restates the original idea of escorting the *Galactica* back to Cylon, 'yes, the thought that always intrigued me was, just who was to be whose prisoners?' And then, when the Centurian says it believed the humans were to be the prisoners of the Cylons, says, 'you Centurians are so limited in your appreciation of the human mind', indicating that Lucifer understands that Baltar would rather be a prisoner of the *Galactica* than believe the Imperious Leader's assurances, and thus that Lucifer is far shrewder than Baltar gives him credit for.

However, Baltar is nonetheless in a strong position. His plan to use the *Galactica* to take out Cylon and decapitate the Cylon Empire is sound, and he is also indicated to be a brilliant demagogue, when Apollo remarks 'you should have seen the effect he has on our new warriors. They're all ready to follow him right into another trap. We don't dare expose him to the Council' (note also the implication, once again, that new warriors and Council members are gullible, but that old warriors are too sharp to be taken in). Baltar's fatal flaw was that he thought he could talk his way around anyone, even the Cylons, but didn't realise that the Imperious Leader, with whom he was dealing, was bent on genocide. By showing up with a base ship, also, Baltar is loading the dice in his favour, as it sends the obvious message that, if the humans choose not to follow his plan, the Cylon force accompanying him could easily take them on in a fight. Baltar's position is actually even stronger than he realises, due to the epidemic on the *Galactica*.

Adama, however, shows clear signs of letting obsession overcome his good judgment. When Baltar appears, Adama must surely know that there must be some sort of Cylon presence in the area; however, even when Starbuck confirms that there is indeed a base ship nearby, Adama refuses to leave. While one can understand the need to find out the location for Earth, the sensible thing to have done would be to flee the situation. As it is, even though they do remain, they are still prevented from learning the location of Earth by the Cylon attack. The strategic situation is only saved by the fact that the recovered pilots are able to come into the fight at the last minute and take the Cylons by surprise, and the reason the Cylons don't attack the Fleet itself is because it's hidden by the magnetic void's instrument-scrambling properties (they only know the humans are on Kobol in any case because of Baltar's inside knowledge; both parties appear to be close enough to Kobol to detect it – hence the *Galactica* discovering that the Cylons are in the vicinity through observing their attack on the planet – but not close enough to each other's positions to pick each other up through the void, in another iteration of the Battle of Midway).

At the end of the story, Baltar appears to be in a serious condition, with blood around his mouth; when Baltar is trapped under the pillar, Adama says 'your friends have sealed your fate and ours', and, after Adama, Serina and Apollo leave, the fifth-draft script also says Baltar 'examines his surroundings, seeing them suddenly as his final resting place'. The audience are thus clearly supposed to be left with the impression that it could be the end of Baltar.

WE HAVE BEEN HERE BEFORE: BACKGROUND AND EXTERNAL REFERENCES

This particular story clearly shows the influence of popular writer Erik von Däniken on the series, in that religion is presented not just as collections of symbols and expressions of faith, but as having a practical or factual basis. The Colonials do not simply sing hymns about, worship, and swear by the Lords of Kobol, they also know them to be real, historic people, and Adama's ritual medallion opens the doors on Kobol (which would be a bit like learning that the Pope's crucifix can be used as a key on an alien planet). The *Book of the Word*, the Colonial equivalent to the *Bible*, tells the Colonials how to get to Kobol, rather than simply providing moral advice and allegorical narratives. In a discussion in part two, Tigh and Adama argue over this, with Tigh taking the atheist's, and Adama, the believer's, position; however, a line in which Tigh argues that their ancestors misinterpreted scientific phenomena as acts of God was cut from the final version.

The story was partly filmed in Egypt, although, according to director Christian Nyby II, none of the regulars were present for the Egyptian filming, and they were doubled by local people. Due to Egyptian scruples against women wearing trousers, Jane Seymour was doubled by a twelve-year-old boy. Egypt was, of course, undergoing a surge in popularity at the time, fuelled by the world tour of the Tutankhamun artifacts between 1972 and 1979 (which ran in the USA between November 1976 and April 1979). Cut dialogue between Serina and Apollo also indicates that Kobol was destroyed by pollution, and that, when the people of Kobol established their colonies, they eliminated all their old technology (presumably to stop the destruction happening again, but also neatly explaining why Earth has no indications of space-faring early civilisations), in reference to the 1970s concerns about environmentalism and fears of technology.

There are also references to Mormonism in the story. Apollo and Serina's wedding is apparently based on a Mormon wedding ceremony, and 'Kobol' (which is ancient Persian for 'heaven') is an anagram of 'Kolob', the planet or star which Mormons believe to be nearest to the throne of God (one of the oldest computer languages is also called COBOL). There are Biblical references in that the largest city on Kobol is called 'Eden', and they are guided to Kobol, like the Magi to Jesus, by a star (in the original script, the star appears prior to the wedding ceremony, in a scene on the bridge, but the finished version highlights the connection between the star's appearance and religious belief). Starbuck, however, swears 'for Sagan's sake', at one point, a deliberate in-joke about astronomer Carl Sagan's famous scepticism regarding spiritual matters.

SOMEWHERE OUT THERE: DEVELOPMENT AND PRODUCTION

While the basic story has remained intact from early scripts to the final treatment, there are some significant changes along the way aside from those already alluded to. The story was called 'Tombs of Kobol', at least up to the fifth-draft script (a name which suits it rather better, since at no point are the inhabitants of Kobol explicitly identified as gods in this story, and their divine status is left ambiguous in the rest of the series, although there is a line in 'War of the Gods' part one in which Adama speculates that the Lords of Kobol may have come from a species who had evolved to a more advanced level than their own, making them godlike). Several scenes are in different order, as well as a few being altered or cut; the first-episode cliffhanger originally ends with Apollo announcing to the pilots that the Cylons are attacking, where the final version ends with the destruction of the base being reported to Baltar, a scene which appears in part two of the original version.

Some of the scenes with the women had their sexual overtones scaled back, as noted above, and the scene where Apollo and Starbuck undergo decontamination originally had decidedly homoerotic overtones, with the two men getting into the same decon chamber and stripping off together, and later being seen wearing rather groovy-sounding 'decon clothing', loose-fitting white jumpsuits. Also cut is a sequence where Apollo and Starbuck reminisce over a flight academy incident involving two Gemon girls, presumably, from the context, not members of the sect which insists that sexual contact happen every seven years mentioned in 'Saga of a Star World' (although if they are, that casts an interesting light over the sect and its members, suggesting as it does that they can be quite free with their favours if approached in the right year). More prosaically, the training scenes are heavily cut back (although one, cut at a late date, appears in both the teaser for part one and the recap for part two), presumably for time reasons, and some of the technical discussion among the women is also cut, presumably both for time reasons and because it makes them look like they have gone from novice to expert Viper pilots in a relatively short space of time.

There are also some differences in terminology between the original and final versions. In the first-draft script, the word 'sealed' appears throughout as a synonym for 'married' (the 2 October 1978 terminology document states that the terms should appear interchangeably), and, in the fifth-draft version of part two, the word 'sealed' appears a couple of times, with the words 'marriage' and 'wedding' also appearing, whereas in the televised version, the word 'sealed' appears only during the wedding ceremony (when Adama says 'I declare you sealed'). A drink called 'vinyon' appears in the first-draft script, in a cut scene with Boomer and Jolly, but is apparently abandoned somewhere along the way, and instead 'ale' and 'ambrosa' are mentioned in the onscreen version.

On a more technical front, the opening prologue has changed slightly from the pilot, with references to Lemuria and Atlantis being dropped, and the monologue shortened. Christian Nyby II is the son of Christian Nyby, who directed the 1951 horror classic *The Thing from Another World*. The sequences of the women pilots training against a simulator with back-projection is an inside joke, as the Viper sequences were actually filmed in a similar way, with a Viper being physically moved about by production crewmembers against a filmed back-projection. On the casting front, Maren Jensen has complained in an interview about the women pilots being all very conventionally beautiful, but one has to say that the nature of television makes it unlikely that it would have been otherwise. Doctor Salik makes his first appearance in this story, played by George Murdock, who is also known for playing 'God' in the movie *Star Trek V: The Final Frontier* (1989). Finally, the attack on the tents and pyramids on Kobol is spectacular, standing up well over thirty years later.

'Lost Planet of the Gods' is an interesting story, with a number of ironic twists and implied motivations as well as a sharp message against gender prejudice, establishing the precariousness of the Fleet's situation and the deviousness of the series' central antagonists, which ends on a very downbeat note, with the tragic and futile death of Serina.

3 ● THE LOST WARRIOR

US TRANSMISSION DATE: Sunday 8 October 1978
TELEPLAY: Donald Bellisario
STORY: Herman Groves
DIRECTOR: Rod Holcomb
CREDITED CAST: Kathy Cannon (Vella); Lance LeGault (Bootes); Claude Earl Jones (Lacerta); Red West (Marco); Johnny Timko (Puppis); Jason Donahue (Jason); Carol Baxter (Macy); Mary Kay Mars (Vi)
KNOWN UNCREDITED CAST: Rex Cutter (Red-Eye)

SYNOPSIS: While decoying a group of Cylon fighters away from the Fleet, Apollo runs out of fuel and crash-lands on the planet Equellus. Meeting up with a local young boy, Puppis, his mother, Vella, and uncle, Bootes, Apollo learns that he is in an agricultural settlement which is dominated by a local gangster named Lacerta, backed up by his henchman, Red-Eye, who turns out to be a Cylon. Although Bootes and Puppis urge Apollo to take on the Cylon, Apollo refuses, as he is unsure of the Cylon's motives, causing Bootes to brand him a coward. Vella, however, whose ex-Colonial warrior husband was killed by Red-Eye, approves of his action. Puppis sneaks out of the settlement to stalk a local predator called a lupus; at his mother's request, Apollo follows him, and winds up bonding with the child. Apollo hatches a plan to find Red-Eye's ship and comrades, and steal fuel from them to allow him to return to the Fleet. Bootes, inspired by drink, attacks Red-Eye and loses. Learning that Red-Eye was found, damaged and alone, in the wreckage of a ship, Apollo challenges him to a duel and wins. Vella reveals the location of her husband's crashed Viper, providing Apollo with the fuel he needs to return to the Fleet.

ANALYSIS: 'The Lost Warrior' is quite clearly not part of the original seven hours of the series. It feels like a filler episode, with a rushed script and clumsy insertion into the ongoing narrative. After the five hours of top-notch space-opera which were 'Saga of a Star World' and 'Lost Planet of the Gods', this episode shows a marked drop in quality on the script and production front.

LOST IN SPACE: PRODUCTION AND WRITING

The production of the story detracts strongly from it; it looks cheap, and most of the effects, such as they are, are problematic. While the 'ovines', essentially orange-dyed sheep, just about get away with it through being seen mostly in long shot, the growling horses painted with tiger stripes are rubbish. A draft script, dated 25 August 1978, describes the growling horses, and unfortunately adds a rooster which hoots 'like an owl' to the menagerie (Bootes also refers to Lacerta as a 'pig', which, along with references to these animals in 'The Beta Pirates' and the original draft of 'Fire in Space', suggests that some familiar Earth creatures can be found in the Colonies). Even in pre-CGI days, a creative and resourceful designer might have done something less ambitious but more alienesque with the idea (as, for instance, would later be achieved in 'The Magnificent Warriors'). Johnny Timko may not be the worst child actor to appear in the series, but his performance is wooden and stilted, aside from the rather good reaction when Apollo pulls a gun on him. While having Red-Eye mounted on a horse in medieval tilting armour (the draft script simply has it in leather harness, though states that the horse should have tusks) is effective, reinforcing the medieval-knight resemblance of the Cylons, the studio's gag reel shows an undignified outtake of the actor falling off the horse while attempting a dismount, suggesting that the idea had some problems in the execution.

This story is another in which the names are extensively drawn from Greek mythology, and specifically that enshrined in constellations. Bootes is one such; however, despite a possible tenuous connection between the mythological Bootes, a hunter, and the gun-wielding *Battlestar Galactica* character, it might have been better to have chosen a classical Greek figure whose name was not so easily mispronounced as 'booties' by speakers of American English. Jason is, of course, another mythological name, while Puppis is a constellation which forms part of a larger constellation, Argo Navis, named after Jason's boat, the *Argo* (significantly, another part of the Argo Navis constellation, the sail, is named 'Vela'; *Argo Navis* would also be the name of one of the ships in the reimagined series). Literally, 'puppis' means 'the poop deck', and, as if that weren't bad enough, it sounds too much like 'puppy' to allow one to take the character remotely seriously. There is also a constellation called 'Equuleus', meaning 'the foal' or 'the little horse', which again has a tenuous connection with the story, in its use of horselike creatures and Western pastiche motifs. Director Rod Holcomb would go on to win an Emmy for his work on *ER*, and also directed episodes of *Lost*.

GHOST RIDERS IN THE SKY: 'THE LOST WARRIOR' AS WESTERN

While many telefantasy series find themselves branded as 'space Westerns', 'The Lost Warrior' takes this literally, down to swinging saloon doors and silver cowboy hats. There is nothing inherently wrong in the idea of a space series drawing on Western motifs: *Battlestar Galactica* generally draws on the 'Wagon

Train' metaphor to good effect, and the Tattooine-based portions of *Star Wars: A New Hope* (1977) are all the more effective for being heavily influenced by Westerns in much the same way as 'The Lost Warrior' (featuring as they both do, isolated farms, small corrupt towns run by grotesque fat crime-lords, and desperadoes shooting each other in drinking establishments). However, 'The Lost Warrior' fails in this regard through sheer heavy-handedness. The Equellus sequences flag up their roots far too much, with men in cowboy hats, women in bustiers, and a fat Boss Hogg-style villain with a (scripted) white suit and Colonel Sanders string tie. Puppis' obsession with killing a 'lupus' (which is beyond contrived as a name for a wolf-like animal) is heavily drawn from the whole boys-coming-of-age subgenre of Westerns.

The draft script indicates that something more creative was intended with the idea. An early stage description says 'the location should be dressed to look as unusual as possible. Although it is basically a western setup, it should not look like Little House on the Prairie', and later says that the saloon should resemble an old ship's boiler room, suggesting that the writer's idea was to have the village looking like it was built out of reused colony ships (the saloon set as realised looks like a Western saloon with some spaceship parts added). Lacerta's henchmen are said to be dressed in black outfits with silver vests, chaps and possibly a helmet, to the general effect that they are attempting to emulate Red-Eye, but, although Marco and another of Lacerta's men do wear spangly white and silver cowboy suits in the final version, the imitating-Red-Eye effect doesn't actually read.

In the story's favour, 'The Lost Warrior' is an interesting riff on the Western trope of the stranger who rides into town, kills the heavy and sorts out the corrupt boss, then rides out again. On the face of it, this is exactly what Apollo does, but, unlike the abovementioned stranger, he is concerned about the repercussions of engaging Red-Eye, out of fear that if he kills him, he will betray his presence on the planet to the other Cylons, and they will come after him, perhaps even wiping out the colony. Unfortunately, the heavy-handed invoking of the Western genre makes it difficult to appreciate any innovation in the story's treatment of this idea.

Although comparisons to *Shane* (1953) are normally made in reviews of this story, what is less often noted are its resemblances to another classic Western, *Destry Rides Again* (1939), which starred Jimmy Stewart as the eponymous deputy sheriff who refused to carry a gun, to the initial derision of the townsfolk, but he rapidly earned their respect through other means. Like Apollo in 'The Lost Warrior', Destry had a strategic purpose in refusing to carry a gun, rather than acting out of pacifism or idealism, and, like Apollo,

Destry eventually wielded a gun to good effect when he deemed the situation demanded it. However, *Destry Rides Again* was actually a rather subversive movie, in that Destry, during his period of going weaponless, solved his problems with lateral thinking instead, demonstrating to the townsfolk that wielding a gun can be a sign of cowardice, lack of imagination and stupidity as much as of courage and manliness, where 'The Lost Warrior' is more straightforward on the issue, and does not cause the viewer to question or challenge the idea of solving problems through gunfights.

While the message of 'The Lost Warrior' (which contains a literal Chekhovian gun on the wall, in Puppis' numo-rifle) is not particularly anti-gun, it does have to be said that it is strongly in favour of caution and using one's intelligence. The conclusion is not to go in with all guns blazing, but to learn what the situation is and how one can turn it to best advantage, before deciding whether or not to go for the gun. Bootes and Vella's late husband Martin, who choose fighting as a way to solve their problems, are hardly shown to be great role models, and the townsfolk generally, looking primarily to a violent solution against Red-Eye rather than seeking to defeat him through their powers of observation and reasoning (the number of dents in the Cylon's bodywork suggesting a repeated pattern of opponents simply trying to have a pot at him and getting blown away for their troubles), continue to be oppressed by those stronger than they are.

HOLD IT, STRANGER: CHARACTER DEVELOPMENT

The story does have some strengths in its portrayal of the central characters. Vella sees in Apollo a possible substitute for Martin, a Colonial warrior who was killed in a fight with Red-Eye; taking Apollo's reluctance to carry a gun for pacifism rather than strategising, she evidently hopes that she has found a similar warrior who is less inclined to throw his life away, continuing the theme of characters who react to a traumatic event by becoming overcautious. When she learns that Apollo has a child at home and that he is planning to go for the Cylon fuel dump he believes to be on the planet, she starts to tell him something reluctantly, but is interrupted by the report of Bootes going on an alcohol-fuelled tear in town; after that issue has been resolved, she tells him about Martin's ship and its fuel reserves, suggesting that this was what she was going to tell him earlier. She seems surprised to learn that Apollo has a son, suggesting that family does not fit into her idea of a Colonial warrior's lifestyle, and, no doubt, raises the question in her mind that Martin, who never spoke about his life as a Colonial warrior, also had connections he never told her about.

Red-Eye provides other examples of the weird capacity Cylons have for intuition and humour. He recognises from Apollo's body language that he wants to kill him, suggesting that he understands human behaviour on an intuitive as well as a logical level, and he gets the entertaining line 'humans deceive, not sound waves'. His well-timed 'uh oh', when he sees that Apollo has a Colonial sidearm and is thus in a position to kill him, is another example of a Cylon giving a momentary emotional display. Right before Red-Eye fires his gun, his scanning eye stops dead in the centre, which gives Apollo a distinct advantage in terms of knowing when he will fire (although, despite this, Red-Eye draws first; Apollo succeeds by being quicker on the trigger). The idea that a Cylon with a dent in its head might start following a portly and domineering human in a white suit oddly foreshadows the implication, in 'War of the Gods', that Count Iblis had something to do with the development of the Cylons, as Lacerta resembles Patrick Macnee in a white robe rather more than he resembles a Centurian, an IL-series Cylon or the Imperious Leader. Apollo initially doesn't carry a gun because he assumes from what he has seen of Cylons formerly, that, where there is one, there will be many; he does not know why this Cylon is seemingly living in harmony with humans, and he suspects it of something. The answer to the machine's peculiar behaviour is actually rather pathetic – it's damaged, such that it follows Lacerta without really knowing what it's doing or why. The draft script also provides an explanation for why Red-Eye acquires an extra dent in his helmet between his fight with Bootes and his confrontation with Apollo; as scripted, Bootes draws first and shoots Red-Eye in the forehead, whereas the filmed version has edited this out.

On board the *Galactica,* there is a rather sweet interlude in which Starbuck and Boomer try to keep Boxey from worrying about his father by inviting him to sleep over in the bachelor officers' quarters. Boxey reacts with glee, launching himself at Boomer, and proceeds to thoroughly enjoy his evening of 'adult privileges', staying up late and playing cards for sweets (and reproaching Starbuck for eating his own bet), until Cassiopea steps in to play mother and restore order. In an interesting development, Boxey is referred to by Apollo as his son, not his stepson, and Adama is referred to by Starbuck as Boxey's grandfather.

CORNERS OF THE UNIVERSE: DEVELOPING ARCS AND WORLDBUILDING

The story adds somewhat to our knowledge of the *Battlestar Galactica* universe. For the first time, it is revealed that there may be other forgotten settlements of humans than simply the fabled Lost Colony; the Equellus settlement appears to be of Colonial origin, but the Fleet didn't know it was there (suggesting that it had been largely forgotten about). Although they appear to be technologically backward compared to the Fleet, this makes sense in the light of their being an outpost: Colonial America was fairly primitive compared to European countries of the time, and, in a subsistence-agriculture situation, the colonists are not in a position to make massive technological advances. The fact that Equellus is on the fringes of the Colonial space means that the audience gets a glimpse of the war, not from the perspective of the participants, but of the people on the sidelines, who have no idea what it's about or who the enemy are, but who are affected by it anyway (although the setup on Equellus does invite comparison with the wider political situation in the series, as Lacerta's brutal reign over the town draws parallels with Sire Uri's attempt to maintain power through a security force, and the Cylons' assertion of superiority over the humans; Apollo draws a connection between Lacerta, the Cylons and the fuel dump he believes to be on the planet, recalling the details of Baltar's secret provision of fuel for the Cylons as revealed in the final part of 'Saga of a Star World'). Curiously, the Colonials don't attempt to recruit the Equellus colonists into the Fleet, or even to warn them about the encroaching Cylons.

The philosophy of putting the collective ahead of the individual also returns. Apollo acts as a decoy to save the Fleet from Cylon attack and, after he crashes on Equellus, he doesn't expect rescue, but tries to figure out a way off the planet himself. Although Starbuck and Boomer do go after him, it's made plain that this is not considered a normal way of proceeding, and that they are running a risk (annoyingly, a scientific error which continually dogs this series also appears, in that, when Starbuck and Boomer cut their engines and drift to conserve fuel, they imply that they will have to restart the ships to keep moving, and the script has their ships slowing 'practically to a stop', overlooking the fact that, since there's no drag factor in space, there's no reason for the ships to slow down; this can arguably be excused by virtue of the fact that the series continually employs the metaphor of planes and boats for its vehicles). The neoconservative doctrine alluded to in the series background essay also appears, in that Apollo sorts out the situation on Equellus, then leaves, with the assumption that, having been put on the right path, they can now figure things out for themselves.

While there are more interesting things in 'The Lost Warrior' than it may first appear, the story is unfortunately not really clever enough to warrant prolonged consideration, and visibly is in need of further development.

4 • THE LONG PATROL

US TRANSMISSION DATE: 15 October 1978
WRITER: Donald Bellisario
DIRECTOR: Christian I Nyby II
CREDITED CAST: James Whitmore Jr (Robber); Ted Gehring (Croad); Sean McClory (Assault); Tasha Martel (Adulteress); Ian Ambercrombie (Forger); Robert Hathaway (Enforcer); Nancy DeCarl (Slayer)
KNOWN UNCREDITED CAST: Cathy Paine (Voice of CORA); John Holland (Maitre d')

SYNOPSIS: As the Fleet heads into an unknown galaxy, Starbuck volunteers to test Recon Viper One, an unarmed reconnaissance vessel. Finding a small shuttlecraft pursued by an armed ship, he helps the shuttle to escape and lands to meet its pilot, who, after Starbuck learns that he is smuggling ambrosa, promptly knocks Starbuck out, steals the Recon Viper and flees, emitting a transmission in an unknown code which is picked up by the Cylons; in the Fleet, Apollo and Boomer are sent out to investigate. Starbuck is accused of stealing the shuttle by the pilot of the armed vessel, and taken to the prison asteroid of Proteus, whose inhabitants are the descendants of the guards (the Enforcers) and the original prisoners (the Prisoners), serving out the sentences of their ancestors; they have been out of touch with the Colonies for centuries, and do not know the outcome of the war. Starbuck incites the Prisoners to rebellion against the Enforcers. Apollo and Boomer find the Recon Viper and the thief, Robber, who has fled Proteus with his family, and, learning of the situation, arrive on Proteus in time to help Starbuck fight off a Cylon attack. The surviving Proteans join the Fleet.

ANALYSIS: 'The Long Patrol' is, like 'The Lost Warrior', an obvious 'filler' episode, this time focusing on Starbuck instead of Apollo; while it isn't atrocious, and does have a few things to like, it's also far from outstanding and strikes a few sour notes on the characterisation front.

KEEP ON PATROLLING: EPISODE PRODUCTION

'The Long Patrol' was probably the fifth story filmed, according to prolific fan writer, researcher and interviewer Susan J Paxton (who has some evidence that 'The Gun on Ice Planet Zero' was second in the order of filming, making 'Lost Planet of the Gods', 'The Lost Warrior' and 'The Long Patrol' third, fourth and fifth). Some have suggested that, since this episode focuses on Starbuck while the previous one focused on Apollo, both 'The Lost Warrior' and 'The Long Patrol' were filmed more or less simultaneously; this would make sense, given the near-complete absence of Athena and Cassiopea from one of the two episodes, and given that the studio were under pressure to produce the series quickly, but reports of this are unsubstantiated at present. The title of the episode is something of a misnomer, as the patrol is not actually long, but, rather, lost; however, having had the word 'lost' in the previous two story titles, the scriptwriting team presumably didn't want to go there again.

The exterior of Robber's shuttle is the same prop which serves as the exterior of the Colonial shuttles in 'The Gun on Ice Planet Zero, part one' and 'Baltar's Escape'. The Universal backlot's standing Western set, on which 'The Long Patrol' was filmed, also appeared in 'The Lost Warrior' and would be seen later in 'The Magnificent Warriors'. Robert Hathaway, father of Noah, has a small role as an Enforcer; in a recent interview, Noah Hathaway revealed that he was indirectly responsible for this, as, since labour regulations required one of his parents to be on the set at all times, and, as Robert was an actor himself who was continually hanging around with the cast and crew while providing parental supervision, he was recruited to play the role. Arlene Martel (credited here as Tasha Martel), who plays Adulteress 58, is best known for playing Spock's bride-to-be in the *Star Trek* episode 'Amok Time'. There are also a couple of nice touches to the production design, such as the Enforcers flying what is visibly an older version of a Viper (whose guns fire in a similar way to the Vipers in the reimagined series), and the fact that, when one of Apollo's gunshots hits the fountain, a cloud of steam goes up.

PROTEUS MANIFESTO: NARRATIVE AND WORLDBUILDING

From a narrative point of view, it's worth noting that, where the characters had driven the events in the previous two stories, here a lot more happens in the way of coincidence. Cassiopea just happens to be on the bridge at the right moment to see the coded transmission, and just happens to recognise Arian merchant code by virtue of being the daughter of an Arian (it's also straining credibility to suggest that Arian merchant code has stayed more or less the same for centuries), and the whole French-farce sequence where Starbuck has dinner with both Athena and Cassiopea in separate dining rooms without either knowing, until they run into each other in the corridor, also hinges on coincidence and timing, and is contrived (and, again, it's straining credibility to suggest that, in a close-knit community like the *Galactica*, the fact that Starbuck had taken Cassiopea to dinner, and, indeed, was dating both her and Athena at the same time, wouldn't be common knowledge by this point). The

Cylons, who have featured strongly up to this episode, are here very much a peripheral menace: there is a brief scene with Lucifer and Baltar which gives no indication of what they've recently been through and the mutual suspicion which is undoubtedly brewing between them (as will be seen in the next story); a draft script from 12 July 1978 indicates that the scene was originally to feature the Imperious Leader and a Centurian, which explains this discontinuity.

The episode does add a few things to the development of the series' universe and its arcs. Although hydronic mushies (called simply 'mushies' in the series itself) were seen in the dinner party sequence of 'Lost Planet of the Gods', they are actually named here for the first time; these are apparently a popular snack or *hors d'oeuvre*, described in the 1978 writers' guide for the series as 'a very tasty health food', but which actually look like dyed tofu. The Cylons are again referred to as 'the Alliance', this time by the Prisoners, although, aside from working together with the Ovions for the last third of 'Saga of a Star World', the Cylons have thus far been seen mainly to operate on their own. Perhaps the Cylons have come to dominate what was formerly a more equitable alliance, or have wiped out or subjugated their former allies. The Enforcers, characterised as the villains, wear white uniforms (which are scripted), in another example of white being used as an identifying marker for antagonists. The scene where Boxey can't sleep and Adama tells him a bedtime story is a complement to the scene later in 'The Young Lords', in which Adama is ill in bed and Boxey tells him a story to cheer him up. We also learn that the Fleet, strangely, includes a 'sanitation ship': is this a garbage scow (as indicated in the 1978 terminology document) or, more worryingly, a sewage treatment vessel, and why would the Fleet need either of these as opposed to ejecting the waste into space or recycling it on a ship-by-ship basis?

Starbuck's romantic situation is further developed. Athena seems somewhat blinkered regarding Starbuck, apparently believing that she can get him to commit to a relationship, which is only making him run harder, where Cassiopea, again, seems to accept him for what he is; as he generally appears more comfortable with Cassiopea, there's a possible implication that he only continues to date Athena because she's the Commander's daughter (and thus in a position to make trouble with Adama), and won't take no for an answer. The draft script has Cassiopea still named as being a socialator rather than a medtech, exacerbating Athena's jealousy; when Adama says 'he [Starbuck] may be on to something', the script has Athena cattily interjecting 'probably a socialator'. To Athena's credit, however, she does show maturity when, after the Fleet believe Starbuck to be lost, she calls Cassiopea to tell her the news, acknowledging that the other woman also loves Starbuck and has a right to know what's happened to him.

As with the previous episode, another forgotten offshoot of the Colonies appears, on Proteus. While it does seem inconsistent that the *Book of the Word* should be accurate about stellar geography to the point of being usable as a guidebook to Kobol, and yet more recent colonies are lost to memory, it is worth remembering that the Colonies have been embroiled in a long and protracted war, and records do go missing in such situations. The Proteus prison asteroid has not had contact with the Colonies in seven hundred yahrens (the fact that there are said to be ambrosa bottles a thousand yahrens old on the loading dock suggests either exaggeration or that some bottles were being kept back for aging). There is a nice example of social allegory in that, while nobody on the asteroid knows the outcome of the war, the Enforcers do know that the Colonial shipments have stopped, and have been keeping this information from the Prisoners because the Enforcers only maintain power through being able to invoke the authority of the Colonies, and the Prisoners would rebel if they found out that this was no longer valid (as indeed happens when Starbuck turns up to tell them that the war has been lost). Robber and Slayer's daughter is named 'Tania', symbolising the way this particular family has broken free of the social controls on Proteus. At the end of the story, the Proteans join the Fleet, which makes sense as the Cylons definitely know where they are and are likely to come back for them (which is apparently not the case for the Equellans in the previous episode). While it is conceivable that there should be colonies on asteroids if some way could be found to provide them with atmospheres, as some known asteroids are the size of small planets, the origin of the abandoned buildings on the asteroid on which Robber's family hide is never stated; presumably they are the remains of another, failed colony.

The draft script again provides a few insights into production. The dining room of the *Rising Star* is stated to be the Council chamber set redressed; the script first states that the leisure lounge is 'the Astro Lounge on the *Edena*', reopened by the Scorpios with Council permission, but shortly thereafter this becomes the *Rising Star*, suggesting that production decisions were taking place even as the script was being written. The Recon Viper is named as the *Starchaser*, and indeed this is stencilled on the full-size prop in the filmed version. Starbuck's civilian clothing is not scripted, and he also swears 'in-bloody-credible' at one point. The script explicitly states that the action of Robber knocking Starbuck out should not be directly seen as per the censors' request, though this ironically winds up making the sequence appear even more violent.

We also have a slightly crammed-in reference to the search for Earth, in the sequence about The Silent One, a prisoner on Proteus some years back, who didn't speak but drew pictures on the walls of his cell, including one of Earth's solar system (presumably he was also into primitive Earth art, since he additionally drew replicas of the Lascaux cave paintings on the walls). While it seems incredible that Starbuck can remember the art on the cell walls in such detail after so little time spent in it, this is forgivable in that such feats of memory do exist. However, the idea that The Silent One originated from Earth, suggested in the story, contradicts the setup in *Galactica 1980* (although, as no idea how old the transmission of the moon landing seen in 'The Hand of God' is supplied, the latter episode cannot be taken as definite proof that the series takes place in the late twentieth century), which indicates that the Earth is not well enough developed technologically to have long-distance space pilots. The Silent One could perhaps have been a humanoid alien who had spent time on Earth, or similar, so the idea is excusable within the series.

LONG TIME PASSING: THINGS THAT DON'T MAKE SENSE IN 'THE LONG PATROL'

Unfortunately, the story does contain some material which isn't quite as excusable. The idea of a flight computer with a sultry human female voice which flirts with its pilot or captain (embodied here by CORA, being an acronym for the somewhat suspicious 'Computer, Oral Response Activated') goes back at least as far as the *Star Trek* episode 'Tomorrow is Yesterday' (and possibly even further), and is a bad idea in all its forms; it is dangerous to put anything that potentially distracting in front of a pilot, particularly one as testosterone-fuelled as Starbuck, and such a gimmick would take up valuable memory space best used on things more essential to the job at hand. When it comes to the crunch, also, CORA can't even stop the Viper being stolen by Robber (simply whining 'where's Starbuck?' as the ship is hijacked, rather than doing something sensible like locking down all systems till Starbuck returns). Both she and the gunless Recon Viper – clearly a recently modified Viper rather than a newly constructed craft – never appear after this episode, although Glen Larson would later borrow the idea of a talking computer on board a vehicle, in slightly less silly form, for reuse in *Knight Rider,* and stealth vehicles feature in Seasons Two and Three of the reimagined series. Although Rigel is normally listed as 'Flight Corporal' in the credits, however, the printout seen in this episode gives her rank as Sergeant. The Maitre d' on the *Rising Star* alludes to being able to remember 'the old days, before the war', which would appear to suggest either that he is over a thousand yahrens old, or that the Thousand Yahren War, like the Hundred Years War on Earth, was less a matter of continuous warfare and more a series of engagements broken by periods of détente (the draft script explains the discontinuity, by having Starbuck react with surprise to the Maitre d's statement, and the old man clarifies his remark by saying 'well, before it [the war] interfered with our annual run to Quatara'). While realistic astrophysics is never *Battlestar Galactica*'s strong point, the loose term 'star system' can be used to refer to any group of astral bodies, from a solar system up to a galaxy.

The worst, and silliest, aspect of 'The Long Patrol' comes in its portrayal of the Prisoners. The prison population of Proteus, who are entirely Irish (and scripted as such), are shown as drunken, criminal, ignorant, potentially murderous (since Robber only doesn't shoot Apollo in the back because Boomer finds Robber's wife and child at exactly that moment), and superstitiously confined by their beliefs about original sin. When unleashed, they promptly turn into a randomly violent mob. One could attempt to make a case for the story being social commentary about how humans are stuck in our social roles, whether as guards or as prisoners, and it takes a big shock to force people to change; while the Prisoners are obviously unhappy in their role, they carry on because it is the only life they know, and, although they are aware the cell doors are unlocked, their adherence to social taboos prevents them from going outside. Their collective ethnicity could be seen as indicating how some social groups are not only oppressed, but participate in their own oppression through accepting their designated role. However, all this is rather obvious and heavy-handed, and is highly defamatory to the Irish and all their various cultural, social and political achievements.

'The Long Patrol' is, like 'The Lost Warrior', a story which is less interesting, exciting and intelligent than the earlier multi-part stories. The sheer number of things which make little sense, however, as well as the relentless Irish stereotyping, destroys most of the credibility which it might have had.

5 • THE GUN ON ICE PLANET ZERO (PARTS ONE AND TWO)

US TRANSMISSION DATES: Sunday 22 October 1978 and Sunday 29 October 1978
TELEPLAY: Michael Sloan & Donald Bellisario & Glen A Larson (Uncredited: Leslie Stevens)
STORY BY: John Ireland Jr
DIRECTOR: Alan Levi
CREDITED CAST: Roy Thinnes (Croft); James Olson (Thane); Christine Belford (Leda); Richard Lynch (Wolfe); Denny Miller (Ser 5-9); Britt Ekland (Tenna); Dan O'Herlihy (Doctor Ravashol); Alan Stock (Cadet Cree); Curtis Credel (Haals); Jeff MacKay (Komma); Larry Cedar (Cadet Shields); Alex Hyde-White (Cadet [Bow]); Richard Milholland (Killian); Walt Davis (Vickers)

SYNOPSIS: The Cylons force the Fleet into a narrow corridor past a small icy planet. Starbuck and Boomer, patrolling with a group of cadets, discover a large gun on its surface, which a garrison of Cylons use to kill two cadets and force down and capture a third, Cadet Cree. Adama proposes a mission to the surface to destroy the gun, forming a team out of a group of criminals with relevant technical specialties, along with Apollo, Boomer, Starbuck and three other warriors. Boxey stows away on the mission shuttle with Muffit. The shuttle is forced down, and the team take the snowram into the wilderness. In an altercation with the warrior, Haals, the criminal Wolfe damages the snowram, and the team are trapped in an immobile vehicle in a deadly storm, until they are found by a hunting party, who take them back to their village. The crew learn that their rescuers are Thetans, a clone race created by Doctor Ravashol, inventor of the gun; they are enslaved by the Cylons, and supposedly sterile, but have in fact been having children in secret. Apollo contacts Ravashol; he refuses to help them at first, but learning about the Thetan children, his sense of responsibility is piqued. A two-pronged attack is planned, with Starbuck taking the garrison station (rescuing Cree in the process) while Apollo tackles the gun itself. The gun is destroyed, and Ravashol is reconciled with his 'children'.

ANALYSIS: 'The Gun on Ice Planet Zero', while not a bad story, is also not a very interesting or exciting one, and comes over as contrived, which is surprising, given how much time and effort went into its genesis. It does, however, provide some interesting material regarding the development of

Lucifer and Baltar's situation after the events of 'Lost Planet of the Gods'.

THE FLEET MUST GET THROUGH:
ROOTS AND DEVELOPMENT OF 'THE GUN ON ICE PLANET ZERO'

As the cumbersome title of the story suggests, this two-parter is largely an amalgam of the well-known adventure films *The Guns of Navarone* (1961) and *Ice Station Zebra* (1968). There are also some elements of *The Dirty Dozen* (1967), in that this, like the latter film, features a motley band of criminals tasked with a crucial mission, and a brief reference to the gold-theft wartime black comedy *Kelly's Heroes* (1970) when it is explained that Croft's crime involved unofficially raiding a Cylon platinum mine and refusing to share the proceeds with his commanding officer. In particular, *The Guns of Navarone* features a group of fairly unsavoury characters (albeit not actual criminals, as here) engaged on a mission to destroy a pair of guns on a Greek island in WWII so that Allied boats can get through. They are aided by members of the local resistance, one of whom turns out to be a traitor (see below regarding the deleted scene with the treacherous Planner), and who is said to have been whipped by the Nazis (as Ser 5-9 is whipped by the Cylons offscreen). *Ice Station Zebra* is about a Cold War mission to rescue the stranded crew of an arctic weather station, which similarly involves the assembling of a team of specialists, some of whom have less than moral ulterior motives.

The development of the story, one of the earliest in production, is known to be fraught. While it is frequently said to have been second in filming order (although, as indicated in the essay for 'The Long Patrol', production appears to have overlapped extensively on episodes of the series), the story seems to have been rewritten during the development of 'Saga of a Star World' and 'Lost Planet of the Gods', and reshoots of a number of scenes continued into mid-September 1978. These scenes were chiefly the Baltar-Lucifer ones, indicating the decision taken not to kill Baltar but retain him as the main villain, and others meant to accommodate changes in the series' setup from 'Lost Planet of the Gods' (for instance, the computer-bank sequence, with its reference to new female Viper pilots), which can be identified through observing Dirk Benedict's hair length (as it is decidedly longer in the reshot scenes).

The earliest available version of the story is an hour-long script by John Ireland (whose credits include being an actor on the film *Wham Bam Thank You Spaceman* [1975] and associate producer on *Slumber Party '57* [1976]), dated 30 November 1977 (with a note saying 'First Draft Teleplay, Acts One and Two Revised'), called 'The Nari of Sentinel 27'. A copy of the draft which was circulated online has this title crossed out and the new title of 'Crossfire' handwritten on it (and the story marked with a handwritten indication '1st Draft Teleplay December 8 1977'; the title appears to be justified only by a twenty-second sequence in Act Four in which the Cylons attempt to catch the *Galactica* in a crossfire), plus changes made in writing to the script itself. Apollo is referred to as 'Skyler', and Lyra (later Serina) is alive and a member of the Quorum of Twelve. Cree is given a first name, 'Terry'. Boomer and the other semi-regulars are missing, and are replaced by three other named pilots, Capa, York and Kang, the latter of which is, somewhat regrettably, a black man who dies in the third act. There are also some differences in terminology, with the characters referring to 'hours' and 'minutes' as units of time measurement, the Cylon base stars as 'battle stars' (sic) and the warriors' hand weapons as 'carbines'. Skyler's combat gear is described as 'mylar coloured … [looking] like a cross between football and boxing equipment'. At one point Starbuck says 'fly now, pay later', in a reference to the famous Pan American Airlines slogan (how the Colonials learned it is something of a mystery).

In this version of the story, the clones, here called the Nari, are the result of a longevity experiment, and outlived their (female) creator by centuries; they show Starbuck a book, written in a language which they can't read (the script indicates that it is in fact Hebrew), which they believe holds the secret of manufacturing armies of slaves (with consequent overtones of the legend of the Golem), and which the Cylons are after. They also show Starbuck a gallery of reproductions of Earth artworks (by, among others, Magritte, van Gogh, Rembrandt, Renoir and Warhol), indicating that they have some connection with Earth. Later, their leader, the First Nari, makes a speech about Columbus and his first contact with the Indians, all of which suggests that the series must at this point be intended to take place in Earth's future. This draft also contains a fairly silly subplot involving the Colonials dressing in Cylon 'uniforms' (the Cylons still being humanoid lizards at this point) to infiltrate the garrison, rescue Cree and reach the gun, and a climactic situation where Starbuck sets out to destroy the gun, following which Adama contacts Skyler with a change of plans – to capture the gun instead, so that they can train it on Cylon ships – leading to a race to the gun between Starbuck and Skyler's teams of warriors (Skyler wins, and, somewhat bizarrely, berates Starbuck for not knowing about the change in plans). The Cylons are, predictably, much more emotional in this version than in later ones, and also are seen to have beaten up Cree in a quite savage fashion (as he is described as bloody and having a broken arm).

Other points of note include a scene in which Cree's Viper approaches the gun at some speed, without prior permission, and Adama orders Starbuck to stop him, shooting him down if necessary, as his actions endanger the Fleet by revealing their location (indicating that the idea of the survival of the collective being placed over that of the individual goes back quite a long way in *Battlestar Galactica*'s conception). Adama comes across as something of a fascist in this draft, where Skyler actually comes across as more humane and sensitive than in the early draft of 'Saga of a Star World', telling his father he loves him at one point. There is also a scene where a Quorum member asks Adama the question which viewers have been asking themselves ever since, i.e., why they don't simply change their course to avoid the gun (Adama's answer is that doing so would cause them to run into a fleet of Cylon base ships to be discussed later). The science is generally pretty atrocious, with references to the pilots landing 'as close to the rim of the horizon as possible' (the horizon simply being an optical illusion related to the curvature of spherical bodies), and the script is also riddled with spelling mistakes, the most inexcusable being the fact that 'cannon' is spelled 'canon' throughout. Starbuck also, towards the end of the story, deploys a 'mushroom bomb' which stupefies the Cylons (saying as he does so 'don't tell me drug warfare is against the rules'), and later reveals that he had intended to spike Colonel Tigh's birthday cake with some of the bomb's contents, none of which would have endeared the programme to the censors. Although there are allusions to Starbuck's many girlfriends, he also seems to be the target of some gay innuendo in the stage directions (including one unfortunate description of him 'exposing himself' as he leans out a window) and dialogue, culminating in his being kissed on the cheek by a male Nari.

A later version of the script, entitled 'Ultimate Weapon', exists, which is closer to the finished version, but which shows some noteworthy differences (this script indicates fourteen revisions, suggesting that, counting the changes to the 'Crossfire' draft, the script underwent no less than eighteen revisions that we know of, including the transmitted version). The title of the story was apparently 'Ultimate Weapon' until fairly late in the day; Paxton notes that this script contains September 1978 reshoots, suggesting that it may have been very last-minute indeed, as the story was first screened in late October of 1978, and it is actually a much better title than the one the story wound up with, which is somewhat counterintuitive in that the name of the planet is not 'Zero', but, as indicated by Lucifer, Arcta (the name of the mountain, 'Hekla', references a real life mountain of that name, an active volcano in Iceland) and the temperature is presumably a good deal below the freezing point. Baltar is described as 'rubbing his stiff leg' in the reshoots (and seen to do this on screen), a reference to the events of 'Lost Planet of the Gods' (and, indeed, in the finished version of part two, Baltar can be seen to have a distinct limp when he walks). Doctor Ravashol's first name ('Benel') is given. Although the

Cylons are clearly stated to be robots (with Cree at one point telling Vulpa 'go rust yourself'), the Imperious Leader is described as having a 'reptilian' face, indicating again the idea of having him resemble the original Cylon species. There is a cut scene where Thane attempts to rape Leda, but she successfully fights him off, and another where Vulpa attempts to get Cree to talk through showing him Thane on the execution platform on the monitors, but this is less effective than Vulpa hopes, as, contrary to Vulpa's belief that Thane is an associate of Cree's, Cree does not know the man.

One point to note about the 'Ultimate Weapon' draft is that it appears to be a work in progress, containing a number of inconsistencies. Baltar's name is missing from the cast list (as he was only added at the time of the reshoots) and two mysterious characters, 'Mira' and 'Stafford', are present. The script is unclear whether two warriors died in the shuttlecraft or not (and, indeed, whether these two warriors are Vickers and Voight, who have little to do in the final version after the shuttle crash, or whether they are, possibly, Mira and Stafford), with the Cylon patrol indicating that they have found dead humans in the shuttlecraft, but the scenes with the human party do not have any of the characters dying under these circumstances. The prison barge is designated as such in the set list, but it is referred to as the 'grid barge' in dialogue (some of these references survive in the final). Athena alternates between appearing on the *Galactica* and in the shuttlecraft as part of the expedition (a line where she implies she believes Starbuck to be a coward, saying to him as he goes to meet the prisoners, 'hang around as long as you can. Maybe a little bravery will rub off', was also excised, for obvious reasons), and there are two scenes, designated 188a and 188b, in which first the Imperious Leader, then Baltar, give near-identical orders to initiate random firing (in a 16 June copy, which does not contain the insert scenes with Baltar, only the scene with the Imperious Leader is given). There are also two versions of the scene in which Wolfe and Croft fight, one in which Wolfe is killed by falling off the mountain, another in which he runs off into the wilderness, with the second clearly designated as 'alternate version' (both appear to have been filmed, as they are highlighted in yellow by Roy Thinnes in his copy of the script).

Certain sexualised elements of the story were added as the script was revised, but cut from the final version, particularly the sensual banter between Tenna and Starbuck (in one amusing exchange, he asks her to help him with an experiment of his own in 'human engineering'), and two very similar scenes, one in which Lucifer says of Cree 'his brain is quite confusing … many random thoughts … mostly dealing with the female of your species', and Baltar replies, 'that is logical', and another in which a Cylon involved in Cree's mind probe complains that his brain is full of 'these female images' (Vulpa, the bronze Centurian, dryly remarks 'strange'); images of Brie, Athena and other women are said to be playing on the monitors, and the Cylons to be 'adjusting knobs' as this takes place. Some of the Tenna-Starbuck banter did make it to the filming stage, including a scene in which Tenna offers to 'warm Starbuck up', and another, later, where he learns that the 'warming' will take place in public (as there is no private space in the Village), an idea which is natural to the clones, but which he is reluctant to go along with. This scene was annotated in the script with 'to be shot so the following two lines [which are the ones which make the implication of sexual activity clearest] can be cut from the TV release', indicating that the production team were both a) keeping a careful eye on the network censors' parameters for a 'family show' (but, as the entire scene rather than the two lines was cut, perhaps not as careful as they might have been) and b) looking to future cinematic releases, in which they might be able to include slightly more adult material. On a less racy front, the 'Ultimate Weapon' draft has Croft being reinstated to the rank of Commander by Adama at the end of the story, and it is a pity that this scene was expunged, as, the way the story stands at the moment, it is left ambiguous whether Croft is reinstated or not, leaving the subplot with no resolution.

There are also a number of directions, notes and cut lines which give an insight into the series' production and intentions of the writers. Three sets (the 'Cylon Crew Quarters', the 'Pulsar Control Room' and the 'Brain Probe Room') are designated as either *Buck Rogers* set' or 'possible *Buck Rogers* set' (the *Buck Rogers* pilot was filming at the time), and one exterior scene is annotated with 'Everest (stock)' indicating that it was planned to use stock footage of Everest for the mountain scenes. The 'Colonial Movers' ship is described as such in the script directions. Vulpa is named as an 'elite Centurion' (sic) and is indicated to be the Garrison Commander. The directions make it plain that Starbuck flirts with three Tennas in the story while believing them all to be the same woman, which is less clear in the final version, and the children are specified as having 'individual features', as distinct from their identical parents. The script describes the Cylons as 'a highly advanced mechanised culture', as contrasted with their portrayal as rather stupid reptiles in the 'Crossfire' draft. Wolfe and Croft are said to have been from the same snow garrison, and thus, presumably, involved in the same crime (this survives in the final on the printout which Athena holds, which further indicates Leda as also being from this garrison, named as being on the planet 'Kalpa'). The Cylons are described as having 'turbo laser rifles', and Baltar's reception room on the base star is named the

'Imperious Chamber'.[14] There is said to be Cylon armour, marred with scorch-marks, hanging on the walls in the clones' caves, indicating that the clone guerrillas have successfully withstood clashes with the Cylons previously.

The setup with Ravashol and the clones is given a curious series of subtexts by the script directions. Ser 5-9 and Tenna are described in almost suspect terms of Aryan perfection: Ser 5-9 is called 'noble, blue-eyed, blond and heroic proportions. Almost superhuman in his looks ... a classic Norse warrior', where Tenna is a 'Nordic goddess', and they are also said to resemble Vikings. Ravashol, for his part, is described twice as resembling Lenin (his picture on the wall at the Planners' meeting is likened to Lenin's portrait being at a Party Committee meeting, and he himself is said to resemble Lenin in having 'a quality of abstract thought'), and his clothing as 'Maoist', suggesting that the rigidly structured society is meant to have Communist parallels. However, he is also described as 'subtly deformed, as though his spine were twisted by the forces which flow through his being' (in the final version, he walks with a cane), and this is said to give him a 'vulnerable' quality. The script likens him in this regard to Toulouse-Lautrec. This, then, ties in with the idea not only of the Soviets trying to develop ideal societies, but with the stereotype of the crippled or ugly mad scientist creating a race of beautiful, healthy slaves to dominate as a form of psychological compensation. The fact that the Cylons consider them subhuman (and they are specifically described in the script as resembling a slave labour force under Nazi occupation) is taken as an indication of the Cylons' prejudice and wrongness, lending the odd, and presumably unintentional, implication that blonde, blue-eyed Nordics are, in fact, a superior form of human. The casting of the final version has both Ravashol and all the male clones played by bearded actors, giving them a slight resemblance suggesting a faintly narcissistic aspect to Ravashol's motivations. The Planners, for their part, are described as looking different from the other clones, with an 'intellectual, fragile' cast; in the draft script, they get more dialogue, which indicates, firstly, that they are not an undifferentiated group but one holding a variety of opinions and positions, and that the Planner who

---

14 Humorous observations have been made about the fact that Baltar appears to spend rather a lot of time sitting staring into space on the pedestal-mounted chair in this room, which must be a rather boring occupation (John Colicos, in an interview for *Starlog* #138, said that, when asked by a fan what Baltar did when the chair was not facing the camera, he asserted that Baltar was reading Marvel comics). In fairness to the logic of this, it has to be said that the chamber is constructed to be occupied by Cylon leaders, who presumably don't need the distractions that human ones do. It should also be noted that the audience normally sees him in situations in which he is trying to make an effect, and that otherwise we often see him walking about the base star, and thus visibly he does not spend *all* his time in the Imperious Chamber.

betrays the group (known as 'Planner Two') is doing so out of fear. Ser 5-9 says to the Planners, when he meets them, 'don't betray us', indicating that similar incidents have taken place before.

Other scenes of note which were filmed but deleted include one in which Apollo accuses Adama of rigging the computer selection so that he will not be chosen for the mission despite his qualifications for it (Adama insists that Apollo is not expendable, being their best warrior, and Apollo counters that if the mission fails, the entire Fleet is at risk of destruction, winning the argument), which at once explains how both Apollo and Starbuck wound up on the mission, continues the idea that Adama's pragmatism is tinged by a desire to protect his son, and also adds to the theme of collective survival being prioritised above the needs of the individual. A scene also was filmed in which Croft (addressed as 'Colonel' Croft by Adama, explaining why the belief persists in fandom that this was his rank despite the finished episode calling him Chief Commander; Ray Thinnes' copy of the script, dated 16 June 1978, has the word 'Colonel' handwritten over the word 'Commander' in this scene) asks if he will get his rank reinstated, and Adama asserts that he will, but only for the mission, and if he succeeds they will consider reinstating it permanently. There are also two crucial scenes which were recorded but, irritatingly, deleted: one in which the Planner class of Thetas are asked by Apollo for help and they say that they will consider his request at the next Council session, and another in which one of the Planners tells Vulpa that the fugitives are in the Village, drawing parallels with the cowardly and, sometimes, treacherous Quorum of Twelve in the Colonies. Both scenes lack sound effects, meaning that they never appeared in any of the various TV or movie forms that this story took.

On the production side, the story stands up well. The model work is impressive, particularly the Viper crashing into a snowbank, and the snowram was a redressed landram from 'Saga of a Star World'. The Galactica's computer, a mainframe bank in a room, is pleasingly retro. Richard Lynch, who played Wolfe, would return later as Xaviar, the Baltar-lite main villain in Galactica 1980. A well-known American character actor, he gained his distinctive scarred looks through an incident in the late 1960s in which he doused himself in petrol and lit a match while under the influence of LSD. Although one can point to visual and thematic similarities between 'The Gun on Ice Planet Zero' and the early scenes of The Empire Strikes Back (1980) (desperate rebels living in ice caves and fighting against armoured enemies through snowfields), that movie came after this story. The unit of measurement 'metron' first appeared in the serial Flash Gordon's Trip to Mars (1938). Vulpa, the bronze Centurian (although Vulpa's colour is not indicated in this script, a Centurian of this type is described as such in the script for 'The Living Legend', though the script for 'The Hand of God', refers to them as 'gold'), was originally intended to be the continuing main villain in the series, and the decision to reprieve Baltar has a sound production basis, in that the Cylon Centurian voices are fairly monotonous, while Baltar can provide a human face for the series' antagonists, making them easier to relate to as villains.

BRINGING BACK THE BAD GUYS: THE RETURN OF BALTAR AND LUCIFER

This story gives us, belatedly, an idea as to the follow-on from the events of 'Lost Planet of the Gods' regarding Baltar and Lucifer. Their relationship is strained from the outset, and, when the plan fails at the end of the story, Lucifer says to Baltar that, as they are both responsible for this, they need to come up with some mutually plausible explanation for the failure and to present a united front to the Imperious Leader. By implication, and following on from the scene in 'Lost Planet of the Gods' in which the Centurian says to Lucifer that they haven't heard from Baltar yet, one can assume that Lucifer's explanation to Baltar was that, having failed to hear from him, he assumed that he had been captured or killed, and launched an attack on his own initiative. Although Baltar is unlikely to have believed such a story, he wouldn't be in a position to challenge it, and he has no real choice bar continuing in an uneasy alliance with Lucifer, as, if he tried to complain about Lucifer to the Imperious Leader (who, Baltar suspects, is only keeping him alive because he is their best chance of getting at the *Galactica*), Lucifer could equally say a lot of very damaging things about him. Lucifer, for his part, also would not want to be seen by the Imperious Leader as having failed in his duty of helping Baltar to secure/destroy the *Galactica*. This situation is reflected in the characters' behaviour. Baltar is clearly not complacent around Lucifer, reflecting that he is likely to be more cautious and not to underestimate Lucifer's powers of deduction, or capacity for going behind his back, in the future, and Lucifer, while continuing to be smoothly polite, shows a certain facility with sarcasm. Baltar has also changed tactics regarding the *Galactica* since 'Lost Planet of the Gods', choosing to attack them rather than talk of peace, presumably trying to drive Adama to the negotiating table through force.

There is also a brief indication that the Cylons are perhaps not quite such an undifferentiated robotic mass as the humans believe. When Baltar orders the Cylon ships to attack the *Galactica*, and Lucifer observes that if they do this, they will not have enough fuel to return, Baltar retorts that they are only machines, and Lucifer points out that we are all machines, of a sort. When Baltar replies that he'd do the same if they were human pilots, Lucifer counters,

'I believe you would'. This clearly indicates that the Cylons do have regard for each others' existence as individuals, supporting the idea raised in 'Lost Planet of the Gods' in Lucifer's line 'I think I can assure you with some sense of pride, you will inherit the most capable Centurians in all the Empire', that Cylons possess different skill levels and attributes, and are capable of learning and development.

ICY HEROICS: CHARACTERISATION AND DEVELOPMENT OF THE REGULAR AND SUPPORTING CHARACTERS

The regular characters again show development between stories. Starbuck's worries about leaving Cadet Cree behind, such that he takes risks outside the mission parameters to rescue him, stem from three sources: that Cree was an inexperienced pilot who was lost on Starbuck's watch; as is later explained in 'The Man With Nine Lives', Starbuck's childhood as an orphan has given him feelings of anxiety about losing other people; and, more immediately, he still appears to be getting over his grief over Zac and his feelings of guilt about letting Zac fly what should have been his patrol (Apollo seems to have come to terms with it, reinforcing the impression that he is generally the better adjusted of the two). Boomer apparently spent some time on Thule, a planet clearly named after the region supposed in the Classical world to be north of Britain, and possibly including Greenland and Iceland, in the past. There are also references to battles and events which have not previously been seen or mentioned, indicating time passing for the characters between stories. The squadron at the start is evidently made up of cadets (a line in the draft script from Tigh indicates that they are low on manpower and are reduced to using cadets on patrol), which explains their impetuosity. Cree attempts to deceive Vulpa unsuccessfully by claiming he is from the battlestar *Columbia* (which Vulpa retorts was destroyed at the peace conference), which, added to the five named in 'Saga of a Star World', implies that there were at least six battlestars present at the peace conference. There is another reference to female Viper pilots which again suggests that they are an unusual and new development (in that Starbuck and the computer technician refer to 'new' and 'female' Viper pilots interchangeably), and reused footage from 'Lost Planet of the Gods' means that three are seen launching with Blue Squadron. According to Boomer, Blue Squadron is 'Commander Adama's Strike Wing'.

The characterisation of the criminals is, however, fairly one-note and predictable. There is a warrior who wants to redeem himself and return to his career, an apparently-cynical man who dies in a heroic act of self-sacrifice, and a plot to use the mission as a cover for a jailbreak. Leda takes a bullet for her man, somewhat inexplicably, as she hasn't shown the slightest sign of becoming reconciled to him throughout the story, aside from a brief admiring glance when Croft disarms Wolfe. The viewers never actually learn what happens to Wolfe; presumably he dies in the wilderness, though there is an outside chance he might have escaped in a Cylon fighter. While the main strength of *The Dirty Dozen* is the development it affords to its characters and the way in which their different quirks and agendas render the situation thoroughly unpredictable, 'The Gun on Ice Planet Zero' mostly consists of war-film clichés. We do get another indication of the stark nature of life in the Fleet, in that the encouragement for the prisoners to complete their mission successfully is not an actual reward, but the fact that, if they don't complete the mission, the whole Fleet, them included, will likely be destroyed by the Cylons, and Croft is afforded some development, if only in that Apollo's saving Croft from an avalanche appears to motivate Croft saving Apollo by disarming Wolfe later. Between the sanitation barge referred to in the previous story, and the prison barge referred to in this one, it seems that the Fleet is not a great neighbourhood.

The storyline revolving around Doctor Ravashol and the use of his pulsar communicator device as a weapon (and, of course, the clones as well, since the Cylons are using them to aid their war effort) addresses the moral issue of scientific discoveries intended for peaceful purposes used for military ones, as in the case of dynamite or nuclear physics. This is an ongoing and still current issue, as, it seems, if someone invents an item, someone else can almost inevitably find a way to use it to kill people. Apollo takes the stance that a scientist must take responsibility for the uses of his creation, and Doctor Ravashol does seem to come round to this point of view after meeting the Colonial warriors. However, the story unfortunately does not highlight the grey areas surrounding this issue, as scientists often have no choice in what happens to their research. The only way Rutherford could have stopped the creation of the atomic bomb was by not publishing his work on the atom, which would have deprived people of the peaceful use of nuclear fission to generate power, whereas here, although the idea that scientists should at least confront the negative implications of their work is valid, Ravashol's situation is portrayed as a much more black-and-white one. Disturbingly, the fact that Tenna says that their sterility is 'a Cylon mandate' indicates that the occupation predates the genesis of the clones, and that Ravashol created them for the purpose of acting as slave labour for the Cylons.

The setup, with a patriarchal leader, a small council of Planners and a large population of hunter/workers (explicitly stated to be divided as such in the

'Ultimate Weapon' draft script, though the final simply indicates it through dialogue and visuals), although in this case it is a deliberately bioengineered setup, has strong parallels with that among the Cylons (with the Imperious Leader, the IL-series Cylons, and the Centurians) and, perhaps disturbingly, the Fleet itself (with Adama, the Quorum of Twelve and the ordinary citizens). Ser 5-9's self-identification as 'Series 5, culture 9', suggests that the clones are normally grown in test tubes or through other artificial means (Tenna's name might also derive from a designation, presumably '10-A'). The Planner who actually speaks during the cut sequence where Apollo seeks their help appears to be trying to affect an English accent, in keeping with the trend in the series to use British accents as a sign of treacherousness or at least corruption (for instance casting Ray Milland as Sire Uri and Patrick Macnee as the voice of the Imperious Leader, and having Jonathan Harris voice Lucifer with an English accent). Apollo says in the draft script, when he learns that the Planners have sold them out, 'what did you expect?' indicating that he believes treachery to be the norm among the governing elite. The Planners wear white hooded costumes which superficially resemble the Enforcers' white helmets and uniforms from 'The Long Patrol', continuing the trend of white-clad bad or treacherous characters.

THE FOOL OF THULE: PROBLEMS AND INCONSISTENCIES

The story is dogged by a number of errors and questionable points. The most obvious one is the issue of why, if space is three-dimensional, the *Galactica* and its Fleet do not simply fly around the other side of the planet, and avoid the gun altogether. Whereas, in *The Guns of Navarone,* a ship sailing on a flat ocean surface can't go over or under a gun, in the case of the *Galactica,* even if they are, as stated, being 'herded' into a small corridor by the Cylons, it can't be small enough to prevent them from taking an alternate route; the 'Crossfire' draft actually indicates that the Cylons are pursuing them, rather than attempting to perform a flanking manoeuvre – and even if this were the case, Arcta revolves, meaning that the gun does not stay in the same position at all times. The gun itself is also said to have powers of total destruction within two hectars; although the 1978 writer's guide and the 2 October 1978 terminology document define a 'hectar' as nine million miles, or one-tenth of a parsec, the term sounds close enough to the modern word 'hectare' to cause viewers to wonder why space-going vessels are making that much of a fuss over weapons with a range of a mere 20 kilometres. There is also the nagging technical question that, if diethene reaching 'death point' turns air into liquid, this should apply to all the air on the planet rather than just that over the plateau, as turning the air into liquid over the plateau would cause more air to rush in to fill the vacuum, which would then itself be turned to liquid, and so forth, in a fatal chain reaction.

There are also some technical inconsistencies, for instance that the body on which the gun is built is variously said to be a 'planet', a 'small moon' and an 'asteroid', all of which are quite different things. On the printout that Athena holds which gives the background and qualifications of the mission specialists, Leda is said to be a warrior, decorated for service at the Battle of Caprica; when she appears, she is actually a medic (and a Cassiopea-style change of career would seem unlikely in her case, as the Fleet would presumably be keen to retain as many warriors on active service as it can). The nature of the editing, and the progressive script rewrites, lead to the impression that there are two bronze Centurians around the place, as, while the stage directions make it clear that it is Vulpa who kills Leda and is killed by Starbuck, this is less clear onscreen, due to the fact that a bronze Centurian also appears subsequently. On the terminology front, Cylon base ships or base stars are referred to onscreen as 'battlestars' twice, apparently in a holdover from the 'Crossfire' draft.

On the narrative front, while Boxey stowing away with Muffit on the expedition is a little contrived, it could be excused in light of the frequent use of such conventions in the 'boys' own adventure' story genre. However, unlike in that type of story, the pair contribute little to the action. Although Muffit does find the hunting party and bring them to the expedition, that could have been easily achieved without the daggit's help (by sending another character, for instance, or having the hunting party find the snowram on their own). The concept of a bearded patriarch with a horde of identically-dressed dependants is unfortunately altogether too reminiscent of that other late-70s set of icons, Father Abraham and the Smurfs (more disturbingly, the 'Crossfire' draft describes the Nari village as having 'a touch of gingerbread' and an 'old world charm', and the Nari themselves, in a crossed-out note, as having cobalt blue skin). While the clones' overalls are just about tolerable, their tan flat-caps make the whole thing look extra silly. The criminals, when discussing fleeing to another planet and abandoning the Fleet to its fate, consider one called 'Starlos', which, it is tempting to suggest, might have been named after the legendary 1973 telefantasy failure *The Starlost*.

Most problematic, though, is the question of why the Fleet deems it necessary to actually destroy the gun, as opposed to simply leaving it for the clones. The Fleet is, after all, unlikely to come back this way to be placed at risk by it, and, as the clones themselves argue: 'when news of our revolt reaches a Cylon outpost or base ship they will come here in their fighters to destroy us. You will have gone; we will be alone here and defenceless, unless we have the pulsar to repel them'. Although Ravashol hints that he has other potential weapons which the Cylons don't know about ('I didn't give the Cylons everything I created'), conveniently, it is never explained what they are. It is possible that the destruction of the gun takes place because they do not have enough time to capture it, and blowing it up is faster, but this is not really conveyed in the story, and one is left with the impression that the destruction serves merely to provide an exciting climax.

'The Gun on Ice Planet Zero' is the first multi-part story to be anything less than excellent in scripting and character development terms, even if the production is up to the usual impressive standard.

6 • THE MAGNIFICENT WARRIORS

US TRANSMISSION DATE: Sunday 12 November 1978
WRITER: Glen A Larson
DIRECTOR: Christian I Nyby, II
CREDITED CAST: Brett Somers (Siress Belloby); Dennis Fimple (Duggy); Eric Server (Dipper); Barry Nelson (Bogan); Olan Soulé (Carmichael); Rance Howard (Farnes); Ben Frommer (Nogow)

SYNOPSIS: Cylon raiders destroy two of the Fleet's three agro-ships and damage the third, resulting in crop failure. As the Fleet needs more seed, Adama plans to send a mission to the nearby planet Sectar, to trade an energiser for the necessary supplies. However, the only available energiser is owned by Siress Belloby, who insists on accompanying the expedition. On the planet, Starbuck and Boomer are sent into the town of Serenity to initiate the trading process; they find no takers, but are ambushed on the way home and their energiser stolen. Starbuck returns to the town to investigate, and is tricked, through a Pyramid game, into becoming Serenity's constable, before learning that the population face persistent raids from aliens called Borays, who have killed all the previous constables. Belloby is kidnapped in a Boray raid, but the Colonials use Muffit to track her to the Boray lair. Starbuck trades his constable's badge to Nogow, the Boray leader, for Belloby, making Nogow the local law enforcement officer and resolving the situation between the Borays and the villagers.

ANALYSIS: The title of 'The Magnificent Warriors' visibly references *The Magnificent Seven* (1960), and, while there are some similarities, revolving as both do around seven strangers (if, in the *Battlestar Galactica* story's case, one discounts either Muffit for being a mechanical daggit or Jolly for staying at the ship and not actually riding into town) who ride into town and chase off a group of bandits, the connections are vaguer than those of 'The Gun on Ice Planet Zero' to its source stories *The Guns of Navarone* and *Ice Station Zebra*. Like all the one-shot stories thus far, it is a curate's egg: not an unmitigated classic, but not an out-and-out disaster either.

CARRY ON COWBOY: 'THE MAGNIFICENT WARRIORS' AS WESTERN AND COMEDY
'The Magnificent Warriors' is the first *Battlestar Galactica* story which could honestly be described as a 'comedy episode', being light in tone and played for laughs. The story's resolution, in which the Boray chief is made the

town constable, is the sort of denouement one might expect from a comedy Western. There is also humour in how it comes about, in that Starbuck gets the idea through identifying himself with Adama's description of the chief Boray as greedy, lazy, and selfish, which sounds like an outsider's description of Starbuck's pose as a hedonist (which is, as has already been demonstrated several times, not true, as Starbuck has an altruistic streak a mile wide), so it appears to be Starbuck knowingly alluding to the way others see him. The denouement is quite a shrewd win-win situation, as the Borays aren't likely to try to endanger their new chief's position by raiding the village, and the humans aren't likely to cause trouble for the Borays lest the new constable exact retribution.

While Boxey and Muffit are once again shoehorned into the plot, it is better dealt with here than in 'The Gun on Ice Planet Zero', firstly because Muffit actually serves a useful function which could not have been fulfilled by another character (i.e., tracking down Siress Belloby), and, secondly, because the reason for them being there makes sense in plot terms, as Apollo, finding out that his father is bringing Siress Belloby along on the mission, decides to bring along his son as a bit of mischief-making. The inhabitants of Serenity appear to be comedically thick, as Dipper is apparently startled by the full moon, and nobody at the bar appears to have realised that one was due tonight (and they are also surprised when the moon is full again the following night), which, as moons go in cycles rather than suddenly appearing as full, suggests that nobody actually keeps track of the lunar cycle, which seems unlikely under the circumstances.

This story is also, like 'The Lost Warrior', one which continually references its Western roots. While there are no silver cowboy hats this time around, the same Western backlot is used, and the costumes are clearly trying to evoke a Wild West atmosphere. The plot, with the Borays raiding the human village, is a generic Western plot, in which 'Indians', 'bandits' or 'cattle rustlers' could be easily substituted as the antagonistic force. The idea of calling the besieged town 'Serenity' is an irony of a type often found in Westerns and Western-influenced telefantasy (as in Ian Rakoff's Western-set episode of *The Prisoner*, 'Living in Harmony', which was based on a Western comic about a violent town named 'Harmony', and Joss Whedon's space-Western *Firefly*, featuring a ship named 'Serenity'). There is an obvious joke when a townsperson refers to recruiting as constable a drifter passing through 'before the next high moon', although otherwise there is very little resemblance at all between this story and the classic film *High Noon* (1952).

The comedy aspects of the episode make it difficult to know how to take the subplot revolving around Siress Belloby, portrayed as a grasping, sexually rapacious woman who has designs on Adama and, if he won't come willingly, will use her possession of an energiser to obtain his sexual favours through barter. The draft script provides further backstory, explaining that she and Adama had a relationship before he met his future wife, and that Belloby subsequently became the owner of a successful salvage company. On the one hand, the character is portrayed as brave and, generally speaking, sensible; rather than cringing away from the attacking Borays, she grabs a gun to fight them off (admittedly getting kidnapped in the process), it is she who identifies where the powersled has been taken and, by the end of the episode, Adama has actually started respecting her, rather than treating her as a nuisance and imposition. On the other hand, though, the character is clearly being played for laughs and, while seeing an older woman expressing her sexuality openly was acceptable as a staple of comedy in the 1970s, the modern viewer might find it patronising to imply that a decently-preserved, intelligent and well-connected older woman can only obtain sex (with a man in a similar stage of life) through coercion or payment.

GOING WEST: THE STORY'S CONTRIBUTION TO THE BATTLESTAR GALACTICA UNIVERSE

'The Magnificent Warriors' is interesting, however, in that it contains a few more hints of the wider universe around the *Galactica*, casting light on some of the revelations of 'Saga of a Star World' and 'The Long Patrol'. It is indicated that humanity is not as united as they sometimes appear to be: not only do the crew not know about the lost farming colony of Sectar prior to discovering it here (as in 'The Long Patrol' and 'The Lost Warrior'), but they are concerned that if they reveal themselves to be Colonial, they will be betrayed to the Cylons, suggesting that not all humans are friendly to the Colonies, and some might even be sympathetic to the Cylons. Another group, from Orion, are mentioned, who are evidently neutral (though it's unclear whether or not they are human). Apollo says that Siress Belloby's energiser won't arouse suspicion as to their allegiances because it's from Orion, and Starbuck, when visiting Serenity, carries Orion as well as Colonial currency, as if a mix of the two is the sort of thing one might find out on the periphery.

This is particularly significant as, in cut scenes in 'Saga of a Star World', it is stated that the Colonies have only recently united against the Cylons, but, in 'The Long Patrol', the Prisoners and Enforcers clearly think in terms of a united Colonial force, even though they haven't had any contact with the Colonies in seven hundred yahrens. In practical terms, this might be an inconsistency due to the rapid speed of the writing process on the series. However, in story terms, it can be easily explained by the not-unreasonable idea that the Colonies have been more and less united at different periods in history. It would be easy enough for a formerly-united force to fall apart and come back together, perhaps even several times, over seven hundred yahrens, and for different breakaway groups to form.

The origins of Sectar are thus unknown. They have had some contact with the Colonies in the past, as they recognise Colonial money and weapons, and use similar words, like 'yahrens', 'quadrants', and 'lexons' (apparently a unit of weight), and play Pyramid, but they also recognise Orion currency and can use Orion-made energisers. The writing on the constable's badge, said by Bogan to be in the 'ancient tongue' of the people who colonised the planet, is not recognisable, and they are said to have 'moved on'. Adama speculates briefly in voiceover that the inhabitants of Sectar might be the descendants of the Thirteenth Colony, but this is not developed, and seems to be another example of the tendency the writers have to shoehorn gratuitous references to the search for Earth into non-arc stories.

This episode also sees the introduction of another alien species, the Borays, a piglike race with a name possibly derived from the word 'boar'. They, or something like them, have appeared before in the series: in 'Saga of a Star World', the casino supervisor (referred to in drafts of the script, and the novelisation, as the Pit Boss), who has some dialogue in a cut scene and can be seen wandering around in the background of the finished production, looks similar to the Borays seen here, but is taller, bald, and capable of articulate speech, so he may be either from a different but related species, a subspecies (as with the Borellian Nomen, a differently-evolved group of humans which will be encountered later in the series), or perhaps simply from a less primitive group of Borays. A Boray also appears in the background of the first-season *Buck Rogers* episode 'Unchained Woman'. There does, however, remain the lingering question of why the Borays are so keen to carry off human women, who must seem as ugly to them as the Borays do to humans.

MAKING A SILK PURSE: THE PRODUCTION

The episode first aired on 12 November 1978, which, according to Paxton, was originally supposed to have been the airdate for 'The Young Lords', suggesting that 'The Magnificent Warriors' was hastily rescheduled when 'The Young Lords' was held up in the production process. The episode sees the brief return of Greenbean, the Colonial warrior with the least character development ever (Jolly at least has a single defining character trait, even if it's only that he's fat). Another Colonial vehicle, the 'powersled', a kind of open-topped variation on the landram, is seen. Aside from a few model shots done specifically for *Battlestar*

Galactica, most of the agro-ship footage was lifted from the film *Silent Running* (1972), also to play a key role as the basis for Universal's countersuit to Fox's copyright-infringement suit regarding *Battlestar Galactica*, but it does provide a plausible explanation for how the Colonial Fleet is managing to feed itself.

The Boray makeup is really quite good, giving the whole society the feel of a sort of porcine version of *Planet of the Apes* (1968). They are clearly meant to have alien-creature mounts like the settlers in 'The Lost Warrior', but here, the result is more effective, in that the production team have mixed camels in horned headdresses and furry neckpieces with horses, and have shot them quickly, at angles and in a group, so that the viewer never gets a direct glimpse at the Borays' mounts and one is left with the impression of a kind of alien riding beast (provided one isn't watching with the DVD player on the 'slow advance' setting). There seem to be few changes over the writing process, with the major one being the loss of a sequence where the warriors scan the recovered powersled with a device which reads hand- and footprints, identify the owners of the prints as the three villagers who gambled with Starbuck, and force them to come out and join the stakeout against the Borays (meaning, as a stage direction makes plain, that we now have seven 'magnificent warriors' standing up to the raiders, although, as noted above, the *Magnificent Seven* metaphor reads even without this sequence). The draft also has rather more innuendo about the terrible fate awaiting women captured by the Borays, and a couple of good stage directions, for instance saying that when he confronts Belloby, 'everything about the usually stoic Adama is limp', and, later, when Adama fends off Belloby's advances by pointing out Apollo's presence, it is said that Belloby 'looks at Apollo as if he were a case of pox.' The draft script also provides in-text pronunciation keys for the made-up words.

The story's production contains a rather expensive anomaly. Apparently, hiring crews to shoot at night costs extra money in California, which, while it partly explains where the series' budget went, makes it rather odd that three episodes featuring the Western backlot were shot entirely at night (with the exception of a brief scene in 'The Long Patrol'). This might have been an attempt to make the towns seem more alien and less like a Western backlot, but it would have been easier, and cheaper, to shoot in the daytime, and the heavy referencing of Westerns in the costuming and characterisation makes one wonder why the team bothered.

'The Magnificent Warriors', like the other one-off episodes so far, contains some good ideas which are let down by some bad decisions in other areas. However, compared to the episode which follows it in screening order, it is practically Shakespearian.

7 • THE YOUNG LORDS

US TRANSMISSION DATE: Sunday 19 November 1978
WRITERS: Donald Bellisario and Frank Lupo and Paul Playdon
DIRECTOR: Donald Bellisario
CREDITED CAST: Charles Bloom (Kyle); Bruce Glover (Megan); Audrey Landers (Miri); Brigitte Muller (Ariadne); Jonathan B Woodward (Robus); Adam Mann (Nilz)
KNOWN UNCREDITED CAST: Felix Silla (Specter); Murray Matheson (Voice of Specter)

SYNOPSIS: Starbuck crash-lands on the planet Attila during a skirmish with Cylon fighters. He is captured by Cylons, then rescued by the last remaining humans on the planet, a group of children whose father is being held captive by the Cylons, led by an IL-series Cylon named Specter. The oldest boy, Kyle, conceives a plan to exchange Starbuck for their father. Starbuck, learning of this, persuades them to try and deceive the Cylons with a dummy in his clothes, and Kyle discovers that the Cylons were planning a similar deception on them. Starbuck plans a raid on the castle which the Cylons occupy, and he and the children successfully rout the Cylons and rescue their father; the Cylons flee the planet, Specter having concealed the fact of their defeat from Baltar.

ANALYSIS: 'The Young Lords' can be easily summarised as: 'it looks very good until some skinny fellow turns up on a unicorn, and then it all goes downhill fast'. Arguably the weakest of the original series episodes, 'The Young Lords' is an exercise in what *not* to do with a *Battlestar Galactica* story.

GET OFF THE UNICORN: PRODUCTION AND BACKGROUND

Originally called 'The Young Warriors' (making one wonder if the team are capable of coming up with a single-episode story title without first including the words 'lost' and/or 'warrior'), this story actually stands up fairly well from a production point of view. The opening sequence of Starbuck crashing on the planet is good, the scenes of the downed Viper well staged and atmospheric, and the battle sequences are well-shot. The images of the Cylons wandering around what appears to be a medieval castle are also appealing, like that of Red-Eye mounted on his horse in 'The Lost Warrior', reinforcing the knights-in-armour look of the robots. There is some very impressive Cylon stuntwork throughout. Interviews with Dirk Benedict indicate that the Cylon who falls down the stone steps really took some punishment in doing so, and that one of the Cylon performers tripped and fell in the swamp and nearly drowned as a result. There is also some nice direction as the camera follows Baltar through the flashing banks of computer mainframes out into the control chamber, recalling earlier shots following Lucifer into Baltar's presence. Baltar also acquires a new command post from this episode onwards, which is smaller than the Imperious Chamber and has a chair much closer to the ground. Footage and some dialogue from the scenes of Boomer and Starbuck in space were reused in the *Galactica 1980* episode 'The Return of Starbuck', making this the only instance of footage from *Battlestar Galactica* being actually used in a better story in *Galactica 1980* than in the original. Writer Frank Lupo would go on to co-produce *Galactica 1980,* and Paul Playdon, who worked as an uncredited co-producer on some episodes of *Battlestar Galactica*, was also known for co-producing *Kolchak: The Night Stalker*.

Like other stories, 'The Young Lords' borrows heavily from well-known adventure movies. The idea of the protagonists memorising and reciting a doggerel rhyme or song in order to make sure everybody knows what they're supposed to be doing at which point in the action comes from *The Dirty Dozen* (1967). However, in this case, the doggerel comes across as a silly children's rhyme: plus, it seems to come in two versions, a short one spoken by the group at the beginning, then a longer one recited in voice-over while the deeds are actually being done, making one wonder what the point of the short version was to begin with. There are also resemblances to the people-occupying-castles genre of WWII film, such as *The Colditz Story* (1955) and *Castle Keep* (1969). The title does bear a resemblance to the WWII film *The Young Lions* (1958), but the only connection between the two appears to be that neither of them are very good. The naming in the story is somewhat inconsistent: 'Miri' appears to reference a well-known *Star Trek* episode of that name (which also featured a planet of feral children living without adults), and 'Ariadne' has another of the generic Greek-myth names chosen at random which occasionally characterise this series (since she doesn't resemble the mythological Ariadne, Theseus' lover, at all), while the other children have generic names which sound a bit Scandinavian (Kyle, Nilz and Robus). One wonders whose idea it was, however, to name the patriarch of the family 'Megan', which, being a girl's name, is the sort of thing which would get him teased at school.

The first-draft script, dated 9 October 1978, differs very little from the final version; indeed, even Kyle's awful cod-Viking costume is scripted. The only major differences are that the scene where Tigh, Apollo and Boomer visit Adama originally also involved Athena (who has been cut out of the story altogether) and a brief final or 'tag' scene of Adama coming to the bridge, observing Tigh in command, and then being ordered back to bed by Cassiopea, was deleted. In the original, Boxey manages to sneak in to see Adama because Cassiopea is distracted by the fact that Tigh is insisting on seeing the Commander (when she refuses, he says that she ought to be put 'in charge of the gridbarge [sic]'). Robus does not appear in the original version, and gets so little to do in the story that one wonders why a second male child was included. Many of the changes are also for the worse: the planet is named 'Trillion' in the draft, which is a marginal improvement on 'Attilla', and there are a couple of good lines which are cut (for instance, after Starbuck introduces himself, Miri remarks 'you're well-named,' and later, after Kyle orders the other children about, she remarks 'you'll have to excuse Kyle. He thinks he's so ... grown up since we let him play leader'. Specter's strange reference to the children as 'those little sclime' was originally 'those little Borays'. Several references to the children in the original as 'guerrillas' are moderated in the final to terms like 'renegades' and 'warriors', which suggests another intervention by the censors. There is also a wonderfully appropriate typo in the script where Kyle is referred to as looking 'like Error Flynn'. At the end of the story, Starbuck gives Kyle his Star Cluster, echoing Apollo's gift to Boxey in 'Saga of a Star World'.

The setup of the narrative follows that of two out of the three single episode stories thus far, in which either Apollo or Starbuck is marooned on a planet and promptly makes contact with a family group of locals, and then becomes embroiled in politics before being rescued by an ad-hoc mission from the *Galactica*. This story is rather unusual in the *Battlestar Galactica* universe, however, in that the downed pilot actually expects rescue, which seems rather at odds with the series' general attitude, and contrasts with the self-sufficient approach of both Apollo in 'The Lost Warrior' and Starbuck himself in 'The Long Patrol'.

THE ANNOYING WHINY CHILDREN OF GOR: NARRATIVE AND DEVELOPMENT

In defence of 'The Young Lords', it has to be said that it isn't an unmitigated disaster. The sequence where Starbuck is chased through a swamp by Cylons, clearly having assumed that they wouldn't be able to follow him through water, is good, and there is a fun bit of dialogue where the captured Starbuck remarks to a Cylon Centurian 'at least I don't rust', and the group leader, somewhat reproachfully, exclaims 'silence!' The scene where Boxey climbs into bed with the ailing Adama to tell him a bedtime story is really rather sweet, being the sort of thing real six-year-olds get up to (his grandfather tells him stories when he's distressed, now he's reciprocating for his grandfather), and the story being exactly the sort of thing a kid of his age and background might make up, being rambling, surreal, and obsessed with mushies and daggits. Megan explicitly says that they are of Colonial ancestry, building on the impression of a universe full of lost Colonial colonies.

The problems come around about the time when Kyle, Miri and their siblings are introduced into the narrative. Leaving aside the groanworthy coincidence of a planet named Attila being home to a race of pantomime Huns, the one-off characters consist of a family of blonde children dressed in bits of dead animal and costume-party helmets: Kyle's headgear with its seagull-wing adornments is reminiscent of some of the costumes in Fritz Lang's *Die Nibelungen* (1924) but what is acceptable in German Expressionist silent cinema is ridiculous when perched on the head of a skinny microcephalic teenager. Kyle himself is given a massively irritating portrayal, with the actor delivering every line in a monotone which sounds both stilted and earnest, providing no impression that he's feeling any of the emotions he claims to be feeling. The unicorns are also ridiculous-looking, with the horses being visibly uncomfortable with their horned headgear.

There are serious inconsistencies in characterisation. Kyle is apparently intelligent enough to keep his siblings from being wiped out by the Cylons, and yet is so stupid as to not see the obvious flaws in his plan to trade Starbuck for Megan. Nobody in the family, also, notices that the Cylons have substituted a straw dummy for their father, even when it is only a couple of feet away. Starbuck's remark to Miri that he has been waiting a long time to meet a woman with brains as well as beauty is a massive insult to the women he's been recently involved with (Athena, an efficient bridge officer and, as will be shown in 'Greetings from Earth', part-time schoolteacher, and Cassiopea, intelligent enough to successfully retrain as a medtech in a short space of time), and is rather surprising given that Starbuck generally seems to respect the women he's with.

The plot is equally full of holes. It is never explained how Miri knows so precisely where the Cylons are keeping Megan prisoner (as well as where Miri manages to obtain her green eyeshadow and orange lipstick under such primitive conditions). Nor why, since the existence of the colonies on Equellus and Proteus was a surprise to the Fleet, everyone seems to know what this planet is called. When Starbuck and Miri creep into the Cylon control area, which is deserted except for IL-series Cylon Specter and the bronze Centurian, they neither of them do the obvious sensible thing and take the opportunity to gun them both down. 'Petro', rather than tylium, appears to be the fuel of choice; while it is not inconceivable that more than one type of fuel is used, it seems a rather abrupt change, and the name is too much like 'petroleum' to be properly evocative of an alien society. Finally, as has been frequently noted, there is the ridiculous fact that the family insist on staying behind, despite being the only humans on the planet (and containing two pubescent or shortly-to-be-pubescent girls, the consequences of which hardly bear thinking about); what is even more amazing is that nobody points this out to them, or suggests that they, like the Proteans of 'The Long Patrol', could put their abilities, such as they are, to far better use aboard the Fleet.

CASTLE KEEPERS: DEVELOPMENT OF THE CYLONS

The Cylon forces suffer particularly during this story. While there is a nice bit of continuity in that Baltar is no longer limping but is moving a little stiffly, particularly during his first scene, Baltar appears to have checked his brain at the door, going from the intelligent, shrewd and suspicious man seen in earlier episodes to someone so susceptible to flattery that he believes every single one of Specter's lies about the situation on Attila. Lucifer has also abandoned his dignity, muttering 'Felgercarb' every few minutes (since this is the *Battlestar Galactica* equivalent of the words 'crap' or 'bullshit', this seems rather out of character for the smooth, polite Cylon). Specter (played, like Lucifer, by Felix Silla, who visibly has trouble going up and down stairs in his costume, and voiced by an actor using yet another English accent) looks like a candy cane with a gumdrop stuck on top in his red-and-silver striped gown. The Cylons spend all their time in the castle polishing their guns, and presumably each other, perhaps explaining why they are so shiny. There is also the question of why, since the Cylon Centurians are presumably also filing reports, these do not expose the holes in Specter's story. Perhaps they are rather ashamed of the fiasco, and are just desperate to get off the planet.

The Cylons also look particularly bad as a military force in this story. Although they are shown in the sequences in which they hunt Starbuck down to have great resourcefulness and strength, in later sequences they go down fast without firing a shot, and are held off by a twelve-year-old-girl with a makeshift catapult and a few hand grenades. In a 1979 interview, Donald Bellisario complains 'they [the network censors] took the balls out of the Cylons … And so they became rather laughable. Since we are an 8 o'clock show, the network is very tough on us about violence. We had some leeway because we said, "look, we're only killing machines." But when you have 150 Cylons against three humans and the humans always emerge without a scratch, the audience won't take them seriously. We just couldn't take them seriously. We just couldn't make them believable as adversaries', which is rather cheeky coming from the man who co-wrote and directed this story. The effect is also, paradoxically, to make the rest of the human population of Attilla look singularly pathetic, if all of them bar one family were incapable of holding off such an incompetent force.

There are, however, one or two interesting points in the story regarding the Cylons. Although Lucifer claims he isn't programmed for jealousy, he clearly experiences the emotion from the way he behaves, and Specter appears to physically jump at explosions, suggesting that Cylons, or IL-series ones anyway, have something like an autonomic nervous system. Specter is said by Lucifer to be an earlier IL-series model to himself, and yet he looks very much like Lucifer, whereas the Imperious Leader, also an IL-series Cylon, looks nothing like either of them, suggesting that the Imperious Leaders who have appeared in the series are both from an even earlier model of the IL-series, given their generally lizard-like structure.

Battlestar Galactica approaches the absolute nadir with 'The Young Lords', in story and character terms at least. However, for the viewer who has yet to top themselves in order to escape the agony, things do take a turn for the better from this point on.

8 • THE LIVING LEGEND (PARTS ONE AND TWO)

US TRANSMISSION DATES: 26 November 1978 and 3 December 1978
TELEPLAY: Glen A Larson
STORY: Ken Pettus and Glen A Larson (Uncredited: Terrence McDonnell and Jim Carlson)
DIRECTOR: Vincent Edwards
CREDITED CAST: Jack Stauffer (Lieutenant Bojay); Rod Haase (Colonel Tolan); Lloyd Bridges (Commander Cain); Junero Jennings (Launch Officer on *Pegasus*); Ted Hamaguchi (Helmsman)

SYNOPSIS: Apollo and Starbuck encounter unidentified spacecraft, which prove to be Vipers from the lost battlestar *Pegasus*, governed by Commander Cain. The two battlestars are reunited, precipitating conflict as Cassiopea is an old girlfriend of Cain's, and his daughter, Sheba, is jealous of her. Cain informs the *Galactica* that the Cylons control the planet Gamoray; he tries to enlist Adama in an attack on it, but Adama is more concerned about the fact that the Fleet is running out of fuel. A plan is made to capture Cylon tankers, but Cain secretly shoots down the tankers, meaning that the battlestars must now attack Gamoray. Meanwhile Baltar, learning the *Galactica* has been sighted near Gamoray, launches an attack, but is repelled when the *Pegasus* enters the fray. Cain suggests a plan whereby a commando squadron would take out the control centre for the anti-assault batteries on Gamoray, while the *Pegasus* attacks the Cylon base stars as a delaying tactic, leaving the *Galactica* to attack Gamoray itself. Both Sheba and Cassiopea come along on the commando mission, and are reconciled. The ground squadron and Vipers take out the Gamoray-based air defence and secure the fuel depot. Baltar wishes to engage the Fleet, but is compromised by the fact that the Imperious Leader is on Gamoray and thus he must protect the planet rather than focusing on the Fleet. During the battle, the *Pegasus* fires its missiles at point-blank range at two of the base stars; when the debris clears, the base stars are destroyed but there is no sign of the *Pegasus*.

ANALYSIS: 'The Living Legend' is one of the best-known and best-regarded stories of the original series, for the introduction of a new regular character, Sheba, the portrayal of Commander Cain, and the way in which the battles in this story cast new light on the very premise of the series itself.

A LEGEND IN HIS OWN MIND: COMMANDER CAIN
The main focus of the story is the battle of wills between Adama and Cain.

Cain, who is played by Lloyd Bridges (the two-parters generally tend to have well-known film stars in them, and the one-parters not, suggesting that the idea of aiming for a cinematic release for the two-parters took place early on, but the decision to cut together the one-parters for further releases came later), is the titular 'living legend'. Bridges plays the character in a 'folksy' way, reminiscent of George W Bush and other American politicians who try to cover up underlying problems with bluff charm. Cain also visibly boosts his own legend, particularly in the sequence where he claims that he can feel the presence of Cylons. He is clearly too intelligent to rely solely on instinct, and so he must actually be using his experience of Cylon tactics in similar situations, but, in saying this, he is implying that he has a special instinct so as to increase his status and appeal. The script states that the light in his cabin is subdued, which, as well as enabling him to see the stars outside the window more clearly, would have the added effect of looking very dramatic.

Cain owes a lot in his characterisation to General Patton (and specifically George C Scott's portrayal of him in the 1970 film *Patton*), the American military commander in WWII who was a brilliant, innovative thinker and inspiring figure, but also difficult to work with and inclined to make enemies. In the film, he is seen making use of inside knowledge to gain the advantage, and letting his feelings get in the way of the job, like Cain. At one point, Patton says that he can identify a battlefield by smell, much as Cain said that he could feel Cylons. Larson, in the documentary *Remembering the Stars of Battlestar Galactica*, compares Cain to Patton and likens his relationship with Adama to that of Patton with Eisenhower, in that both men had very different ideas of how to run the war.

While Cain clearly shows himself to be intelligent, his status as a 'legend' means that he is also a risk-taker, engaging in spectacular feats and never running from a fight if he can help it. He wears a pilot's uniform (and is stated as doing so in draft scripts) where Adama wears a bridge officer's uniform, in a bit of macho posturing on Cain's part. While Adama is equally intelligent, it is in a different way: he is cautious, sometimes to the point of paranoia, and constantly puts the welfare of the civilian fleet first. When Cain learns of the survival of the *Galactica*, his first thought is that he could attack the Cylons with greater force, where, when Adama learns of the *Pegasus'* survival, his first thought is that it will join them on their quest for Earth. While Cain ultimately defers to Adama's authority in the scene where Adama relieves him of command (after having cleverly forced Cain into admitting that he blew up the Cylon fuel tankers himself), it is unclear whether this is because Adama formally outranks him (by being, as well as the Commander of a battlestar, the commander of the Fleet and a member of the Quorum of Twelve), or because he broke with an agreed battle plan, or because the incident takes place on the *Galactica,* which is Adama's territory, or whether it is because Cain is intelligent and self-aware enough to realise that, as he states, he made a serious tactical error in his handling of Adama. In some ways, Cain is kind of an anti-Adama, and, politically, is an indictment of military dictatorship. As is shown in this episode, people under autocratic rule take on the characteristics of the person in charge, which can be dangerous if that person is Cain.

Cain, whose name has connotations of criminality, sin and being an outcast, can also be quite selfish. It takes a while for him to really register the implications of having a civilian fleet, and, while he is concerned to protect his daughter and Cassiopea, he is less concerned about others who may have loved ones (a cut piece of dialogue between Cain and his helmsman – which has no sound effects, meaning that it was never included in any of the versions of this story – indicates that Cain hasn't told the officers on the *Pegasus* that he intends the trip to the Cylon base stars to be a suicide run). His blowing up the Cylon tankers indicates that he is willing to put the entire Fleet at risk just to get his own way. While he does show that he's capable of admitting he's wrong and adjusting his tactics, his goals continue to be egocentric; although he acknowledges the fact that he's been having an easy time of it against the Cylons because they've all been attacking Adama's fleet, he is willing to ignore this until Adama really hammers it home, and, though he does then change his tactics, it's still all in aid of his stated goal of attacking Gamoray. He is also very charismatic, which can be a danger; when Adama relieves him of command, on the grounds that his arrogance has put the Fleet at risk, Cain's crew practically (and, in some cases, actually) mutinies, despite the fact that they must realise the logic of Adama's decision. By the end of the story, even intelligent and reserved officers like Apollo are, by their own admission, starting to 'think like Cain' and take Cain-style risks, suggesting that Cain's influence over the Fleet is pernicious.

NEW GIRL IN TOWN: THE INTRODUCTION OF SHEBA

This story sees the introduction of a new regular character, Cain's daughter Sheba, played by Anne Lockhart. Lockhart's father had shared a university residence with Lorne Greene, and she had gone to school with Lloyd Bridges' daughter Cindy. In an interview on her website, Lockhart says that she was approached to play a regular female role very early on in the proceedings, but she turned the part down because she didn't like the role as written, saying that at the time, 'the show was about a lot of men and one gal who occasionally came in and said, "don't run off without your laser-guns, boys!'" Over six months later, Larson contacted her to ask if she would be interested in playing Sheba, a role he had written with her in mind, sending her the first twenty-five pages of 'The Living Legend'; this time, she found the role acceptable, though she wasn't allowed to tell anyone that she was expected to be a regular on the programme during the filming of 'The Living Legend', because her agent was still negotiating the contract.

Sheba is clearly at least partly intended as a move to court the adult female viewer demographic through introducing more strong women of action into the series. While Cassiopea is a strong character, she is also one in a conventional female role and thus not one who could frequently go out and have adventures with the male regulars. Her name relates to the Biblical Queen of Sheba (which refers to her home country rather than her name). However, since the original is best-known for reportedly being King Solomon's lover and possibly the co-author of *The Song of Songs*, a book in the Hebrew Bible, the use of this name again suggests that the writers are opening a dictionary of Classical and Biblical figures at random. Sheba is clearly the equal of Apollo and Starbuck in skill and bravery terms, and, like her father, is capable of admitting she's made a mistake (in this case, allowing her jealousy for Cassiopea to blind her to the woman's good points). Some have noted that in certain ways she is like a female version of Apollo, being the daughter of a battlestar commander and the best pilot in his force, and being both a risk-taker and someone who is very loyal and devoted to family.

Sheba is also plainly jealous of Cassiopea, for the reason that, as Cassiopea herself points out, when her mother died, she subconsciously wanted to take over her mother's role as her father's caretaker and companion. Cain, hearing this, retorts 'she's my daughter', and Cassiopea replies 'I could be your daughter as well', indicating both that Sheba is jealous because Cassiopea is trying, in her eyes, to take over her mother's role, but is close to Sheba herself in age, and that, while Cassiopea's relationship with Cain is recreational, she could, if he would allow it, take on a more familial relation to him. In a cut scene, dialogue between Apollo and Sheba indicates that Apollo thinks that Cassiopea's former job as a socialator is the reason behind Sheba's objections to her (though clearly it is much more than that), and in this scene Sheba also seems surprised that Cassiopea has retrained as a medtech, indicating, as she later admits onscreen, that she was stereotyping Cassiopea based on her jealousy of her.

THE MARK OF CAIN: DEVELOPMENT OF OTHER CHARACTERS

More details about Starbuck's backstory are provided. He explains that he had a lonely childhood, as contrasted with Apollo's upbringing in a large family, and so, though he surrounds himself with people, he tends not to cultivate close relationships. Cut dialogue between Cain and Cassiopea exists in which Cassiopea compares herself to Starbuck, saying that she too had a lonely childhood, but unlike him reaches out to people rather than pushing them away (hence, by implication, her choice of fairly people-focused jobs, first as socialator and then as medtech). At the same time, Starbuck also clearly wants to reach out to people; he is visibly jealous of Cain's attention to Cassiopea, though at the same time respecting her right to make her own choice between them (and also makes a play for Sheba, to underline the fact that, as Boxey points out, he's not the sort to tie himself to only one woman). Starbuck also seems to have lost some of his attitude towards female pilots, as he doesn't patronise Sheba in the slightest. At the end of the story, Starbuck offers to take part in Cain's suicide mission, indicating that his lonely nature has caused him to be drawn to a powerful figure; the fact that Cain refuses has the interesting implication that he wants Starbuck to survive so that Cassiopea will have someone to turn to should Cain fail to return, but also, that there should be people to tell the story of his heroism to future generations.

As well as Sheba, this story also sees the addition of Bojay, a pilot who is a friend of Starbuck's from before the attack on the Twelve Colonies, as what was intended to be another new regular character. However, actor Jack Stauffer was due to film a two-hour episode of *How the West was Won* immediately after 'The Living Legend', and, as Stauffer puts it in an interview with the fanzine *FRACK*, 'I was scared to death I was going to lose the other job I had. So Glen looked at me and said, "you know what? That works just fine. Go off and do your *How the West was Won*. We'll write some dialogue in, then when you come back, we'll put you in a couple more episodes in sort of cameo appearances, and then in the second year we'll really develop your character."' While Bojay does get a cameo appearance in 'War of the Gods', his absence from the series is only noted in dialogue in 'Take the *Celestra*', and, as the second season never materialised, the promised character development never came through.

HIGH SOCIETY: THE CYLONS ON GAMORAY AND ELSEWHERE

The action in this story revolves around Cylon activities on the planet Gamoray, formerly home to the Delphian Empire (another Greek mythological name, as Delphi was the home of the oracle of Apollo; 'Gamoray' also recalls the Biblical city of Gomorrah, destroyed as punishment for the wickedness of its citizens). It is said to have been a society of fifty million individuals (although there is no evidence whether these were human or alien) before the Cylons turned it into their Southern capital, which is said by Cain to be a model of machine efficiency. The *Pegasus* is in this area because, when the Fifth Fleet was destroyed, Cain decided to head to Gamoray, presumably to use the Colonies' connections with the Delphians to obtain supplies. It is never explained whether he arrived before the Cylon takeover, was supplied by the Delphians, and remained after the Cylons came, or whether he arrived after the Cylons took it over, and changed tactics accordingly.

Some indication of the political situation among the Cylons is also given. Adama observes that if the Cylons control Gamoray, they must wield power across half the universe, showing the extent of their influence at this point in the series (as well as indicating why Baltar is so keen to make a good impression there). It is very clearly shown here that the Cylons are not a unified and uniform species; multiple types of Cylon are seen and, for the first time, Cylon civilians who are identified as such are featured (they appear to be short mechanical creatures in shiny gold robes). The scene where the Colonial forces attack Gamoray thus has significant parallels with the Cylons' own attack on the Twelve Colonies, particularly since, like the Colonials in 'Saga of a Star World', the Cylons are assembling on Gamoray for what they believe will be a significant political occasion. Indeed, elements of the footage of Zac and Apollo's discovery of the tanker were reused for the scenes of the pilots finding the Cylon tankers here, albeit with the cloud effect removed. The fact that Baltar did not know about the second battlestar suggests either that the Cylons were attributing the *Pegasus'* destructive attacks to the *Galactica* (which must have been very confusing for them), or else that they were aware of it, but did not tell Baltar, either expecting that the *Galactica*-focused nature of his mission made other data irrelevant, or out of concern for the impact which the information might have on his loyalty.

There is also an interesting sequence of cut dialogue between Cain and Cassiopea regarding the Cylons, as follows:

CASSIOPEA:
I can't believe that God would let these hateful creatures take over the universe.

CAIN:
Maybe it's our own fault. Where did these machines learn war? From living creatures that programmed them thousands of yahrens ago. Creatures like us.

CASSIOPEA:
No … not like us. We have the capacity to love. They have no idea what it's like to feel and care and love.

This is noteworthy because, for the only time in the series, it is explicitly stated that the differences between Cylons and humans could be fairly minor. It also contains an element of irony, as Cain himself is not a particularly caring sort, where the Centurian 'Cy', in the *Galactica 1980* episode 'The Return of Starbuck', demonstrates that Cylons themselves can care, even for those of other species. Colonial prejudice against Cylons is attested to in the transmitted version, when Cain says 'as you know, Cylons have no independent initiative', and Adama does not correct him, even though Cylons have clearly demonstrated individual initiative throughout the series.

More than this, it is strongly highlighted in this story that there are, not just antagonisms between different individual Cylons as in 'The Young Lords', but also that there are different political factions, who are not necessarily inclined to support the Imperious Leader at all times. The dialogue between the two IL-series Cylons (who yet again speak with English accents, aside from the moment where one exclaims 'uh oh!' in a decidedly Bronx accent as the hall is attacked), indicates this, as well as that most of the Cylon resources are being devoted to their aims of universal conquest. In a piece of cut dialogue, they remark that they'd heard the humans were all but extinct, and speculate that either the Imperious Leader has been misinforming them or that someone else has been misinforming the Imperious Leader, again indicating that the Imperious Leader is not trusted by everyone in Cylon society.

The Cylons also seem to have an understanding of aesthetics, referring to 'this lovely hall' and otherwise giving a sense of art appreciation, as well as another example of Cylon sarcasm during the part one cliffhanger when Baltar, urged by a Centurian to look at the *Pegasus* coming in to attack, exclaims 'that's impossible!' and the Cylon replies, 'no, it is a battlestar'. Elsewhere, in a scene cut from the transmitted version, one Centurian remarks 'I understand the scouts came back with exciting news', and his companion replies that he hopes they found the humans, again indicating that Cylons do feel emotion. It is unclear at the end of the story whether the Imperious Leader survived the attack on Gamoray, as the audience never actually sees him die.

A FUNNY THING HAPPENED ON THE WAY TO GAMORAY: BALTAR AND LUCIFER

Although Baltar and Lucifer are still strongly allied with one another, personal relations between them are clearly deteriorating, and they are barely making any effort to hide their mutual antagonism. Baltar plays on Lucifer's jealousy by pointing out that other IL-series Cylons would be keen to be at Baltar's side (perhaps referring to the Imperious Leader himself as well as developing Lucifer's own antagonism towards Specter in the previous story). In a cut scene, in which Lucifer says to Baltar 'I'm sorry your victory didn't work out quite the way you had planned ... Even the Imperious Leader, in one of his most difficult moods, could hardly blame you from running from two battlestars', and Baltar retorts, 'I did not run. I executed a tactical retreat, you imbecile', Lucifer outlines their situation as such (ellipses included in the original): 'There's no reason to be abusive ... You forget ... I am on your side. I have placed my fate in your hands ... My rise to a position of supremacy over my fellow IL-series is completely dependent on your success ... or lack thereof ...' As outlined by Lucifer, then, he has to work with Baltar, but he is not happy about the situation.

Baltar is also here seen to be following a new plan. He is no longer attempting to encourage, or force, Adama into attacking the Cylons' homeworld, but is engaging in a personal power bid. He is clearly aware that there are different factions among the Cylons; Baltar intends to attack the *Galactica* and become a hero by being seen to wipe out the last remnant of the Colonies. He speaks of wanting to make a big impression on Gamoray by showing himself as personally leading the final assault on the humans. He wears a Cylon-style helmet during the attack on the Fleet, which is presumably symbolic of his embracing of Cylon culture and politics (although it does look unfortunately comical in the execution). However, he still continues to put his own interests first, being willing to sacrifice the other two base stars in order to ensure his personal safety. Baltar thus seems to be trying, through his attack plan, to become a 'living legend' himself, in order to achieve significant power among the Cylons.

WAR IN THE AIR: THE BATTLES AND TACTICS OF 'THE LIVING LEGEND'

One thing to remember before tactics are discussed in detail is that *Battlestar Galactica*, like many space-set telefantasy programmes, is treating space as an ocean and the spaceships like sea-going vessels, and ignoring the three-dimensional nature of space. This isn't a problem in this story from a narrative point of view, as it is all more or less consistent and gives the audience something to work with. However, it does throw up a couple of odd-sounding ideas, specifically that, as well as getting references to the Cylon Empire as having a 'Southern capital' (as cardinal points would be largely irrelevant in space), the Fleet are said to have to come to a dead stop due to lack of fuel, whereas, in a situation with no friction or resistance, they would only need fuel to change direction, and, if they cut their engines, would simply continue to drift in the same direction at the same speed, rather than slowing or stopping as on water. Nonetheless, in doing this, the story evokes memories of films of air and sea warfare, setting a narrative stage which is easily grasped and assimilated by viewers for its battle sequences.

This is another story which owes much to actual WWII air warfare, and specifically to elements of the Battle of Midway, where the aircraft carrier *USS Yorktown*, which the Japanese thought they had sunk, had in fact survived, leading to a situation in which the Americans had one more aircraft carrier operative than the Japanese expected; the Japanese also had received inaccurate reports of American positions, and so were taken by surprise by the opposing forces, much as Baltar is here. One could also see elements of Pearl Harbour, again, in the Colonials' attack on Gamoray, in that it is a strategic position taken by surprise whose defenders do not have the chance to mount an effective counterattack.

During the initial engagement between the Colonial Fleet and Baltar's forces, in a cut scene, Adama points out that the Cylons are using the same tactics on them which they normally use on the Cylons, namely, destroying their ability to land their fighters to refuel, and then running them out of fuel and ammunition; he and Omega both agree that this set of tactics must mean that Baltar is leading the force. Baltar then retreats when the *Pegasus* arrives, because, having expended fuel on the sustained attack, where the *Pegasus* has a full complement of fresh battle-ready fighters, the Cylon force are the ones at a disadvantage.

For the final battle in 'The Living Legend', Adama approves an initial plan whereby, while the *Galactica* is attacking Gamoray, the *Pegasus* will approach the three base ships and, when the Cylon fighters are launched, will draw them off and lead them away. Cain's plan, however, is to fly straight through the fighters and go for Baltar himself. Baltar, when he sees the *Pegasus* approaching, gives instructions that it should be destroyed, and, indeed, this nearly comes to pass as the Cylon forces are overwhelming; when the *Pegasus* does not engage the fighters, but continues on to the base stars, Baltar sees this as a decoy, meaning that the original plan would not have worked. However, Cain's alternative plan only succeeds because of the presence of the Imperious Leader on Gamoray, which Cain could not have foreseen, meaning that he wins through sheer luck alone.

The precariousness of this victory is brought home in the scene where Baltar and Lucifer discuss the attack on Gamoray. Initially, Baltar proposes reverting to his original plan as outlined in 'Lost Planet of the Gods', leaving Gamoray to its fate and attacking the undefended Colonial Fleet instead, with the obviously intended consequence that, without the Fleet, the *Galactica* and *Pegasus* will be free to strike at Cylon itself. However, when Lucifer indicates that the Imperious Leader is on Gamoray, he changes tactics again to attack the battlestars (in a cut exchange, Lucifer says 'if you succeed, Baltar, you will be greeted on Gamoray as the greatest military leader in the history of Cylon …. That is, if there still *is* a Gamoray'; of course, there is also the incentive that, should the Imperious Leader be killed through Baltar and Lucifer's failing to come to the rescue, the next Imperious Leader is not likely to look too kindly upon them). When Cain attacks Baltar directly, Baltar withdraws his base ship purely because he realises that the man behind the attack is Cain, and, therefore, a ruthless lunatic who will stop at nothing to kill him (a move which Cain, knowing Baltar's tendency towards self-preservation above all else, no doubt anticipated). Had Baltar and Lucifer stood their ground with the other two base ships, they could still have won the day; even though Starbuck puts the victory down to Cain's brilliance, it is purely Cain's legend, with a certain amount of sheer dumb luck, which actually saved them.

FRIENDS REUNITED: CONTINUITY AND WORLDBUILDING

There is also some more progression in the series' development. It is stated that the Fifth Fleet perished at the Battle of Molecay over two yahrens ago, and, according to Bojay, the *Pegasus* only survived through Cain pulling off a decoy manoeuvre; the huge size of the Cylon forces ranged against them is indicated when Bojay says that Cain knew that the Cylons would be 'lined up from Molecay to the Colonies waiting for us', hence his decision to turn out into deep space and keep going. This also suggests that the Battle of Molecay took place relatively close to the time of the armistice, which would mean that two yahrens have passed since the destruction of the Colonies, raising questions of how it is that Boxey still appears to be the same age as when the Colonies were destroyed (possibly, Colonial children develop at a slower rate to Earth children).[15] We also learn that the entire Colonial Fleet was wiped out during the Battle of Caprica at the time of the proposed armistice, meaning that the ships which we actually see engaged in battle at the peace conference in 'Saga of a Star World' were only a portion of the Colonial forces. Cain later learned that there was a rebel fleet in space through intercepting Cylon communications, but, as he couldn't break the code, not that it was the

---

15 As a side point, this timescale is supported by the unfilmed script 'The Mutiny', in which Apollo says that it has taken them 'yahrens' to lose the Cylons and provide the Fleet with some breathing space.

Galactica and its dependants specifically, indicating that the Fleet's survival is a source of discussion. The question of how Cain managed to get supplies from Gamoray despite it being so well-defended is never answered, but it would seem likely that the planet was originally lightly defended, and the recent rise in its combative capabilities is because of Cain's raids on it.

On the subject of gender equality in the Fleet, Brie and other women are seen launching in footage reused from 'Lost Planet of the Gods'; it is indicated in the draft scripts that women should be specifically seen among the pilots launching (although the draft specifies that one of them should be Deitra, who does not appear). At least six women pilots are seen in the background when Cain comes aboard the Galactica. However, among the *Pegasus* crew, the only female pilot seen is Sheba, suggesting that female Viper pilots were in fact not totally unknown before the loss of the Colonies, but equally that they were rare.

There are also further references to the religion and politics of the series. In a partly cut sequence of dialogue between Tigh and Adama, Tigh comments that Cain's appearance is providential, and Adama remarks that he believes there is a benign providence out there causing such things, tapping Tigh playfully on the chest as he does so, and he and Tigh share a grin, indicating again that Tigh is an agnostic, Adama a believer, and that the two of them manage not to let this get in the way of a good working relationship. Cain's arrogance is highlighted by his reference to his crew having the right to decide their own destiny, when in fact he really means for them to follow his plan for them. There are also a couple of interesting lines likening the *Galactica*'s activities to holy war, for instance when Adama exclaims 'Cain! By all that's holy', and Cain replies 'nothing holy about me. Except maybe what I'm doing to these Gol-Monging Cylons …' and, elsewhere, in a cut line when Apollo emphasises to Sheba that Cassiopea's past as a socialator shouldn't matter to her, he says 'we've all been through a cleansing fire, it's stripped every one of us of those things that brought down our world – only the strong have survived', an explanation with distinct overtones of rebirth and religious transformation.

BEHIND THE LEGEND: THE STORY'S WRITING AND PRODUCTION

The story which became 'The Living Legend' originally began as a one-part script, described as a 'Patton-in-space type episode', which was given to Jim Carlson and Terrence McDonnell to write by Donald Bellisario, who asked them in the late afternoon to come back with a complete first act the next morning. They did, entitling the draft 'The Last Legend', and Bellisario asked them to write a subsequent act by the next morning; however, he then called

Carlson at home and said that, on the strength of their work, he would like to invite them onto the series as story editors, but that Glen Larson had decided to write the 'Patton' story himself as a two-parter.

The second draft of the story differs relatively little from what was transmitted, aside from the changes noted above; the episode cliffhanger is different, ending after the first battle, with Adama agreeing to meet with Cain in Adama's quarters in twenty centons, whereas the finished version ends on Baltar's surprise as the *Pegasus* emerges. A few lines are also changed (including yet another instance of the word 'sealed' being changed to 'married'), with the most amusing difference being the change of Cain's scripted line from, in the 24 October 1978 draft, 'what are you running on the bridge … a braisserie [sic]?' to 'what are you guys smoking on the bridge?' by 2 November, to, as finally screened, 'what are you guys cooking on the bridge?' presumably to avoid implications of drug use (or of the anachronistic presence of French restaurants in the Colonies).

The story also exists in slightly altered form as a 108-minute movie entitled *Mission Galactica: The Cylon Attack*. This version cuts out most of the character-related material (which is a shame, as it is that which makes the story really interesting), and fills in the time with cut-in bits from 'Fire in Space', making a tenuous link with the *Galactica's* damaged landing bays in 'The Living Legend', and removing the Boomer, Boxey and Athena subplot which was what gave 'Fire in Space' its dramatic thrust (and also adding a few shots from 'Saga of a Star World' and 'The Hand of God' to the battle sequences). The ending of the story also, with the aid of dubbed-on material, explicitly states that Cain survived. Patrick Macnee's opening voiceover is cut from the transmitted version of the story for some reason; however, a new voiceover by Patrick Macnee is included on *Mission Galactica*, which is quite different both to the normal voiceover and to that which appears on 'Saga of a Star World', stating that the story takes place 'in the seventh millennium of time' and recapping the human-Cylon battle and the creation of the Fleet briefly, concluding that it is searching for 'a distant shining planet, a planet known as Earth'.

There are one or two points of note in the story's production. The horselike insignia of the *Pegasus* pilots' helmets is described in the script, and the script also states that the Imperious Leader's robe and hood obscure us from getting a good view of him, reflecting Larson's dislike of the costume's mask. A draft script states that the decoration at Cain's throat is the Gold Cluster, the only time we actually see this award in the series. An earlier version of the scene where Cain first meets Cassiopea has Cain asking after her mother and brother, and several lines of Cain's dialogue were amended to change his references to the pilots as 'boys' to more gender-neutral terms. According to Laurette Spang, actor Richard Crenna, later to play Colonel Samuel Trautman in the *Rambo* films, was originally approached to play Cain. A clip featuring explosions from *Operation Crossbow* (1965), a film which will be later recycled elsewhere in *Battlestar Galactica* and *Galactica 1980,* appears. This is a particularly good story for people who like to spot the reuse of *Battlestar Galactica* and *Buck Rogers* props, costumes and sets in the two series: while the Cylon control centre on Gamoray was actually a redressed part of the Draconian ship from the *Buck Rogers* pilot, *Buck Rogers* later returned the compliment by reusing Cylon robes from this episode in the first-season story 'A Dream of Jennifer' (which guest starred Anne Lockhart).

There were also one or two difficulties with the production. Jonathan Harris, who recorded his dialogue separately, mispronounces 'Gamoray' in one scene (as 'gamma ray' rather than 'gah-MOR-ay'), but has corrected his pronunciation by the next scene. Jack Stauffer, recalling the sequence in which a team parachutes onto Gamoray in the *FRACK* interview, notes that the fact that the black leather outfits had trousers based on female dimensions, coupled with the harnesses which the actors had to wear while being hoisted thirty feet into the air by a crane for close-up shots (the team being doubled in long shot by an Army parachute team), meant that the experience was a very painful one for the male actors. In an interview for *Starlog* #138, John Colicos remembers the red lamp in his Cylon-look helmet 'burning a hole in [his] forehead'.

NO MORE HEROES: THE STORY'S ENDING

One question which the episode raises is whether it should have been made clearer whether Cain survived or not, as in the original version of the story, which has him perishing (which the network felt was too downbeat), or as in the *Mission Galactica* cut (in which he is stated as having survived). On balance, the decision to leave it ambiguous, as in the transmitted version, seems to have been the right one; although it would take a miracle for him to have survived, given the battle damage to the *Pegasus,* the implausibility of surviving the explosions of two base stars at close range, and the fact that, even should he have survived all this, there is a mass of Cylon fighters and one base star waiting to take him out, we never get direct proof of his death, tying in with the 'living legend' theme of the story. Legends do not really die, and the idea of disappearing facing fearful odds is part of legends; Butch Cassidy and the Sundance Kid could never logically have survived the final showdown, but, because the audience never sees them killed, viewers can always entertain the possibility that they will return. Similarly, there is no rational reason to assume that the *Pegasus* was not destroyed, but it has also been stated by Apollo that Cain has survived impossible odds before.

However, it is also worth considering the circumstances of Cain's supposed victory. If Cain hadn't blown up the Cylon tankers, the Fleet would have refuelled and carried on; as it is, Cain's manipulation and the actions of the people who buy into the myth throughout the story result in a lot of death, destruction and material loss for both the humans and Cylons (although, since there are far more Cylons than humans, the impact is ironically greater for Cain's own people, making it a tactical success but a strategic defeat), while Baltar only fails to win through sheer good fortune on the Fleet's part. The idea is thus that, while legends may be attractive, they tend to bring destruction to those who come too close to them, even if only for a short while.

9 • FIRE IN SPACE

US TRANSMISSION DATE: Sunday 17 December 1978
TELEPLAY: Jim Carlson & Terrence McDonnell
STORY: Michael Sloan
DIRECTOR: Christian I Nyby II
CREDITED CAST: William Bryant (Fireleader); Jeff MacKay (2nd Crewman)

SYNOPSIS: The *Galactica* is attacked by a kamikaze squadron of Cylon ships, loaded with solonite explosive. Although Blue Squadron successfully destroys most of them, one explodes close enough to the bridge to cause considerable damage, seriously injuring Adama (who urgently requires surgery), and the other crashes into the port landing bay, causing a fire which spreads throughout the *Galactica*. Boomer, Boxey, Muffit and Athena are trapped in the ship's Rejuvenation Centre. Boomer successfully opens the door to a storage compartment and escorts the people in the Centre to temporary safety; affixing a note to Muffit's collar, Boomer sends Muffit through the ventilation system to seek help. Apollo suggests fighting the fire in the landing bay by equipping three Vipers with megapressure pumps that will enable them to spray a fire suppressant called boraton. The Fireleader backs this idea and also intends to use a megapressure pump to boost the power of the ship's internal hose system; however, the megapressure pump blows a seal and fails. Apollo and Starbuck then fight the fire by placing explosive charges on the outside of the hull, using the vacuum of space to put out the flames. Muffit reaches the bridge and is sent back to the storage compartment with life-saving air masks; he then returns along the ventilation shaft to rescue a stranded firefighter. Adama's family are reunited in the life station, including the burned but still functioning Muffit, and Apollo assures Boxey that Doctor Wilker will repair the daggit.

ANALYSIS: 'Fire in Space' is an episode which appears to be frequently excoriated by fans of the series, but this seems a little unfair ('bad science', the most often cited reason, is hardly sensible given that the science is no worse than that in any other episode of *Battlestar Galactica*, or, indeed, any other space opera; one might speculate that it may actually be down to irrational prejudice against Boxey and Muffit on the part of some people). The story is, if anything, more internally consistent and more entertaining than any of the one-parters so far.

GETTING FIRED UP: BACKGROUND AND PRODUCTION

This story is one with a fairly lengthy genesis. Originally, 'Fire in Space' was a two-parter by Michael Sloan (dated 22 June 1978), a producer who would work on *The Equalizer* among other programmes. Jim Carlson and Terence McDonnell, who wrote the final version, have stated in interviews that they never saw the original script, but based their version on Larson's account of what the story was about. Carlson has said in an interview on Susan J Paxton's website that he recalls Sloan, who was working at Universal at the time, giving him the cold shoulder, and later learning that he felt they had infringed on his territory (and Paxton also reports that Sloan has said to her that he did not like the rewrites to 'Fire in Space'). Carlson and McDonnell, of course, were originally tasked in October 1978 with writing the one-part 'Patton in Space' story which later became 'The Living Legend', and were offered a replacement episode when Larson said he would like to do the 'Patton in Space' episode himself. This is clearly the replacement which they were offered.

Sloan's original script was far removed from the final version. Briefly, the story features Starbuck, Boomer and Apollo disguising themselves as aliens to go to an alien bar and seek information under the guise of being bounty hunters tracking the Fleet (Starbuck's disguise is of a piglike alien, although, since he asks 'why am I disguised as a pig?' this is evidently not another reference to the Borays, for more on which see the review for 'The Magnificent Warriors'). They learn of a Cylon plan called the 'Delta Factor' before being forced to flee in the company of a human slavegirl called Helatia. Meanwhile, Orion, the presumed-dead husband of Starbuck's girlfriend Rachel, turns up and acts in a rather abusive fashion, and is then killed. Starbuck is accused of his murder; though Starbuck admits to shooting him following an altercation, he claims the gun he shot him with was set to stun and thus could not have killed him. Similarities between this storyline and the later Carlson and McDonnell episode 'Murder on the *Rising Star*' led to Sloan being given a 'story by' credit on this story as well; to be fair to Carlson and McDonnell, the idea is a generic one and the trial scenes in the two stories very different, with Sloan's version featuring the Council of Twelve sitting in judgment and a device being used which both forces its victim to tell the truth through causing pain (which seems to be essentially torture) and acts as a mind-probe showing records of people's memories. Starbuck's guilt is assumed because, as he did not look down when resetting his pistol to stun, the visual record in his mind is simply of Starbuck shooting Orion. A doctor examines Helatia and learns that she has a Cylon transmitter in her brain, and that this is the abovementioned 'Delta Factor'; that humans are unwittingly serving as Cylon agents (in a twist not too far removed from one of the premises of the reimagined series). A fire breaks out on the *Galactica* due to the Cylons staging suicide runs, and Adama is injured and needs surgery; Apollo leads a team to find the necessary equipment for this (which is on the burning Beta Deck), while Starbuck pilots a Viper loaded with 'detergent' to spray the flames from the outside. Callon, a Council member, who is the real murderer of Orion, and who has been trying to kill Boxey due to the boy having witnessed the murder, takes advantage of the confusion to set fire to Apollo's room (where Boxey, Muffit and Helatia are sheltering), but Muffit saves the day by biting Callon's leg. Apollo arrives just in time to knock Callon out with a hypnotic ray device invented by Doctor Tolkay (who plays the role which Doctor Wilker plays in the transmitted series) and Boxey reveals that he saw Callon kill Orion, clearing Starbuck's name. Cadet Cree from 'The Gun on Ice Planet Zero' also appears in this script, suggesting he was originally intended to be a recurring minor character.

The story is an early draft and might have been improved, but it has to be said that the televised version is much better paced, and focuses on the fire in space itself rather than using it as a side plot (in the draft, the fire does not start until page 81 of a 118-page script). The universe is again the multispecies one seen in, for instance, 'The Beta Pirates', with Thalians, Slavians, Cosatians and a multi-armed alien called a Dalon appearing as well as another Ovion (who again appears to be working for the Cylons); it is still rather close to the *Star Wars* universe, with another alien cantina appearing and the Cylons apparently now employing bounty hunters to track the human fleet. Although the Cylons are described as mechanical, the Imperious Leader is described as a living reptile, and one which can apparently extend a subtle telepathic contact to Adama; Baltar does not appear. 'Sodium juice' and 'elixir-wine' are the drinks of choice on the Fleet, and the name of the leisure ship is the *Starlight Cruiser* rather than the *Rising Star* (and it is said to resemble the *Concorde*). Cassiopea appears to be still a socialator, though she does act as part of a first aid team at the climax. There are a couple of continuity references to earlier stories when Starbuck suggests that he may receive the Gold Cluster 'this time for real', and a doctor extends condolences to Apollo over the death of Serina. There are some continuity and plot problems: although Starbuck has a steady girlfriend, Athena and Cassiopea are still apparently fighting over him, and Callon's motivation is only given in a brief line towards the end of the story (apparently Orion killed his son, though under what circumstances is not explored). Boomer's rank is variously given as Flight Sergeant, Wing Sergeant and Lieutenant. We are also introduced to a Colonial law whereby a murderer is made responsible for the family of the man he murdered, which would seem to be designed to raise more problems than it solves. There is also a telling discrepancy between Starbuck's memories of shooting Orion (in which Orion's gun is unholstered) and Jolly's of finding the corpse (in which the gun is holstered) which the Council do not pick up on as significant; Starbuck's memories appear to be, strangely, perceived in the third person rather than from his point of view, judging by the description in the script, and the playback of the memories also omits Starbuck's interjection to the unconscious Orion, 'you can sleep it off here', which would further cast doubt on the idea that he murdered his rival. The trial is also apparently being conducted before the doctors have completed tests on the corpse which would verify the truth of Starbuck's story about stunning Orion. While the draft is an interesting glimpse into the way in which the series' conceits were worked out, it has to be said it would have made a fairly uneven and unengaging story.

As far as the transmitted story is concerned, the writers are again borrowing from well-known movies, in this case principally the disaster films which were a particular craze in the mid-1970s, such as *The Towering Inferno* (which, having been released in December 1974, would have been fresh in the minds of both the production crew and the audience). The continuous switching between the daring rescuers and the plight of the trapped individuals is a constant theme of such stories. The WWII motif also returns in that we see Cylons using kamikaze tactics, smashing their explosive-packed ships against the *Galactica*'s hull. McDonnell has complained in an interview with Susan J Paxton that he was dissatisfied with the ending, having originally scripted one involving a wave of Cylon kamikaze fighters closing on the ship as Apollo and Starbuck try frantically to set the charges, rather than, as shown, Apollo drifting into space and being saved by Starbuck, and blames the network for the toning-down of the climax.

The episode may, according to Paxton, have been the last episode shot before the production team went on Christmas hiatus, as the series changes in tone, with the Cylons being largely sidelined as an enemy and the Fleet's quest for Earth, and the spiritual aspects of their journey, being emphasised after this point. The production makes use of cut-in explosion footage from *Operation Crossbow* (which, since it fits the material, isn't a problem), and again lacks the Patrick Macnee voiceover introduction. A female pilot is seen launching her Viper in the initial battle, and we see several female pilots in the Rejuvenation Centre. The scenes of the Vipers firing boraton at the launch bay are effective, but do have a disturbingly Freudian appearance.

YOU'RE FIRED: CHARACTER DEVELOPMENT AND WORLDBUILDING

This story is unusual in giving almost every one of the regular characters, even fairly minor ones like Doctor Wilker, something to do; the two exceptions are Jolly, who is absent from the action, and Bojay (according to Jack Stauffer in the *FRACK* interview, Glen Larson had promised to script an explanation for Bojay's absence; however, a close viewing of the episode indicates that none appears, and Stauffer may have been thinking of 'Take the *Celestra*' instead). Lorne Greene gives an exceptionally good performance as the injured Adama, really sounding like he is at death's door. His dialogue about Boomer, Boxey and Athena when giving the order to plant explosives in the launch bay indicates that not only does he believe that they are dead, but he knows that, even if they could be alive, he has to sacrifice them to save other lives.

Unusually, this is a story which puts Boomer very much at the focus of the action, with Boomer being the one who is ultimately responsible for the rescue of the trapped crew, leading in part to this episode being nominated for an NAACP award for its positive presentation of black characters. However, it is a little dodgy that the one *Galactica* pilot who turns out to have a past as a petty criminal (in this case, one spent 'hotlinking hover-mobiles', evidently the Colonial equivalent of hotwiring cars) just happens to be black, and also, Herb Jefferson Jr has to share the stage with Maren Jensen, who is outacted by a six-year-old and a chimp in a fursuit. However, Boomer is such a brilliant character that one can let minor difficulties pass.

Boxey and Muffit are also strongly featured. This time, no contrivance is needed to wedge them into the plot, as it makes perfect sense that they would be spending their free time in the Rejuvenation Centre, playing a game which looks suspiciously like air-hockey. Muffit's heroic self-sacrifice at the end of the story is deeply touching, as is Boxey's reaction when he believes that his pet has been destroyed (and Apollo once again demonstrates that real men *do* cry, and are no less manly for it). The implication is, following on from the discussion in the cut scene of 'The Living Legend' regarding whether Cylons can care, that a metal dog can certainly show love and be loved in return.

FIRING SQUAD: THE STORY'S PROBLEMS AND ADVANTAGES.

First of all, it should be noted that many of the items stated popularly to be 'problems' with the story are in fact no such thing. The title does make sense, as it revolves around a fire, which takes place in space. Furthermore, the charge that the writers overlook the fact that fire cannot burn in a vacuum is mooted by it being a plot point that the *Galactica* crew put out the fire (burning in the landing bay, which is supplied with oxygen and whose access point is evidently protected from space through some kind of semi-permeable forcefield) by exposing it to the vacuum, although the issue can be raised of why they do not simply switch the forcefield off, or, indeed, why the forcefield has not failed due to the colossal damage in the landing bay area. There is an in-story explanation for why the boraton is, as critic John Kenneth Muir puts it, 'fired like laser beams', in that the lasers on the Vipers have been replaced by pumps taken from a damaged energiser operating in the manner of fire hoses (and, since both energisers and Vipers are fictional, they can be deemed compatible if it suits the plot). Muir's claim that boraton is water is perplexing, as it seems clear from the script and execution that it is some kind of smothering chemical, as used in, say, CO_2 fire extinguishers, and, since it is a fictional substance, the way in which it performs as an extinguisher is entirely up to the writers. There is also no reason why, Muir to the contrary notwithstanding, Tigh should not handwrite, rather than type and print out, a note to send with Muffit – in fact, since writing is faster than printing out a document, it might be more desirable to handwrite the note given the urgency of the situation (and the fact that the note is in English cursive is simply part of the overall convention of telefantasy that signage should be understandable by the audience). Complaints about Adama's injuries seeming rather light considering the alleged seriousness of his condition overlook the fact that no network would allow a realistic portrayal of a man with shrapnel wounds in the family viewing time slot, and again can be easily put down to TV conventions being observed.

This is not to say that there are no problems with the story. There is a small continuity error in that there are only two energisers on the battlestar in 'Fire in Space', where there are said to be many of them in 'The Magnificent Warriors'. It is unfortunately very easy to tell when footage of Anne Lockhart in the Viper sequence is reused from 'The Living Legend', as she wears a helmet with a Pegasus insignia in the reused shots and a Galactica insignia in the new ones. There are visible wires in some of the scenes of Apollo and Starbuck laying charges in zero-gravity, and there are a few too many scenes of firemen using hoses and uttering macho phrases (after a while, they cease to be dramatic and become repetitive). Mushies feature heavily in the story, which is a problem as, if you happen to have missed the one single line in 'The Long Patrol' (six episodes previously) explaining that mushies are a popular Colonial foodstuff, you would be in some confusion as to what they are and why they are important.

Despite this, the story does have a number of good moments. The look on Tigh's face, and his body language, as he places a tray of mushies in front of the air duct to lure Muffit to the right location are absolutely priceless: the series' in-house gag reel contains a mini-sketch of Terry Carter, during the filming of 'Fire in Space', doing a mock-commercial for mushies, pantomime-eating several with relish and then doing a realistic impression of throwing up off-camera. Unusually, this is one episode in which the lack of friction or resistance in space is not only acknowledged, but a plot point (as Starbuck uses his momentum to push Apollo clear of the explosion). The idea of Apollo propelling himself along the *Galactica*'s surface using magnetic charges is also a good one, and there are some good lines, particularly Adama's dramatic 'the Vipers will be our eyes' after he learns that the scanners have been knocked out. The attack on the bridge, and the destruction of the Rejuvenation Centre, are very well done, with explosions and parts of the bridge ceiling falling in, and stuntpeople flying all over the place.

'Fire in Space' is a rather good narrative, and a particularly outstanding single-episode story, certainly worthy of reassessment for its cohesion, drama and characterisation, as well as for its treatment of disaster-movie conventions.

10 • WAR OF THE GODS (PARTS ONE AND TWO)

US TRANSMISSION DATES: Sunday 14 January 1979 and Sunday 21 January 1979
WRITER: Glen A Larson
DIRECTOR: Daniel Haller
CREDITED CAST: John Williams (Statesman); Janet Louise Johnson (Brie); Jack Stauffer (Lieutenant Bojay); Patrick Macnee (Count Iblis); Kirk Alyon (Old Man); Paula Victor (Old Woman); Paul Coufos (1st Pilot); Chip Johnson (3rd Pilot); Bruce Wright (Guard); Leann Hunley (Girl Warrior); Olan Soulé (Carmichael); Norman Stuart (2nd Statesman)

SYNOPSIS: When a Viper patrol goes missing, with the disappearance being accompanied by readings of a seismic event on a nearby planet, Adama orders Apollo, Starbuck and Sheba to investigate. They find a crashed ship and an apparently-human man, who introduces himself as Count Iblis, and take him back to the Fleet. Sheba develops an attraction for him, and he tells Adama he has been to Earth and can take the Fleet there. Brought before the Quorum, he suggests that they test his powers by giving him three challenges, and he also apparently causes plants on the agro-ships to grow large and abundant fruits. The Quorum asks for Iblis to deliver Baltar to them (which he does) and to take them to Earth, with the third test to be decided on later. A second patrol, sent out to investigate mysterious balls of light flying near the Fleet, vanishes. Falling under Iblis' influence, the Fleet abandon themselves to hedonism, and Boomer also vanishes after firing on one of the lights. Becoming suspicious of Iblis' powers, Adama asks Apollo to investigate the planet again; he and Starbuck examine the crashed ship, and are shocked by what they find. Apollo confronts Sheba and Iblis, accusing Iblis of being demonic. Iblis tries to kill Sheba, but Apollo takes the blast in her stead, and this fully breaks Iblis' hold over her. Iblis vanishes, and, as they return to the Fleet, Starbuck and Sheba are drawn into one of the mysterious lights, this one proving to be a giant Ship of Lights, crewed by angelic beings. They restore Apollo to life when Starbuck and Sheba offer their own in his place, and say that they will return the missing pilots; they also say that as they are now, the Colonials may become. Sheba, Starbuck and Apollo return to the *Galactica* with no memory of these events, but, when Earth is mentioned, they suddenly recall a series of coordinates which appear to indicate its position.

ANALYSIS: 'War of the Gods' is a story which sees *Battlestar Galactica* at its best, using space opera and dramas of battling aliens to explore philosophical and political issues, and to question the nature of good and evil, as well as the purpose, or lack of purpose, of humans in the universe.

GOD OF THE WARS: COUNT IBLIS

The story revolves around the appearance of Count Iblis, who is powerful and charismatic, played with a charmingly sinister edge by Patrick Macnee. Iblis seems to be a devil or evil god; the name is an Arabic word for the primary devil in Islam; early drafts of the script render his name as 'Prince Diabolis' (which makes the connection unfortunately rather obvious; at least a name like 'Iblis' is likely to make the average 1970s American television viewer do some research). Apollo's line referring to Iblis as 'Mephistopheles, Diabolis, the Prince of Darkness …' is largely the same in this version (albeit with the order changed, so that 'Diabolis' comes first), meaning that the connection would have been explicit in that version. He appears to have supernatural powers, including telekinesis, teleportation, walking through solid objects, the ability to be perceived as human, and the power to withstand close-range laser fire. A direction in the script says of Sheba and Iblis 'his power clearly draining her of her own identity', suggesting demonic possession. He is described in the script as 'standing in regal splendour … his robes made of white velvet, its collar standing high above his head' (the finished version has him wearing a similar outfit to Adama's uniform, but in white, appealing to the trust of both the military and the – themselves mainly white-robed – civilian Council) and he has an English accent, which, as has been noted before, is frequently shorthand in *Battlestar Galactica* for treachery. He originally describes himself in the draft script as 'not of your world, your time', making his origin more mysterious.

However, it is clear as the story progresses that Iblis is more of a clever charlatan than a god. We learn that he has psychic powers, when, for instance, he looks into Sheba's mind and sees what she truly wants (adding that all people are capable of this with time and experience), and, when Adama says to him 'my son told you that?' the draft script has him responding 'not exactly', implying that he read it from his mind. Iblis uses the fact that he has superior psychic powers to humans to make it seem like he's reading the future or having preternatural knowledge, through reading people's minds and acting quickly on the information (casting doubt on his claim to possess 'infinite knowledge' of the universe), and exploits his understanding of phenomena which the humans don't comprehend (in his seeming 'miracle' of the increased food supply, which Doctor Wilker later theorises is actually down to the lightships' influence, suggesting that Iblis' amazing physical abilities may also have a scientific source), as well as simple psychology. It doesn't take much to guess that food is of concern to a refugee fleet, or that Sheba is looking for a father figure, and it is debatable whether Boomer wins the Triad game because of Iblis' influence, or through being given extra confidence through his conversation with Iblis.

Iblis' philosophy is based around that of influential English occultist Aleister Crowley (1875-1947), focusing as it does around the idea that people should engage in pleasure provided it hurts no one, conveniently glossing over the fact that such hedonism can have long-term, unforeseen consequences (as here, where essential personnel become scattered, unable to defend the Fleet, and giving Iblis ammunition to attack Adama's leadership). Iblis' followers give themselves to him through selfishness; Boomer's simple wish to win a game against Apollo and Starbuck puts him under Iblis' spell, and after that, he is the only pilot on patrol to actually fire on one of the small lightships (although this is not the reason why the Ship of Lights takes him; a cut scene exists where Apollo suggests that he, Starbuck and Boomer get a proper scan of the ship by, rather than chasing it, slowing down as the ship passes such that each Viper gets a partial scan, and then amalgamating them, and Boomer was the last one, meaning that he was the one captured in the process).

Iblis seems also to present himself as a father figure, playing on the paternal themes of the series. In a cut scene where Adama debates with the Council whether to take Iblis as a leader, the Council members describe themselves as lost children (Adama deliberately plays up to this, emphasising his own role as benevolent father to the Fleet in his subsequent impassioned speech to them); Iblis is described as watching 'his children' in celebration in the night club in the script, and also to be staring at Adama during the Triad game in a way which suggests that the real contest is between him and Adama. Sheba, in a cut line, says 'I am at peace, I want to follow Count Iblis', implying that one can best achieve peace through following a leader (echoed in Starbuck's line in the finished version, 'it seems everyone was looking for someone to believe in'). There is thus a kind of paternal competition throughout the story regarding Iblis and Adama.

There is also, however, a connection between Iblis and Cain, which is set up early on when a reference to Sheba's father's disappearance is made. Both are charismatic older men, with a slightly creepy edge to them, who attract people willing to follow them blindly (including, in both cases, Starbuck). Sheba's attraction to Iblis is at least partly that he reminds her of her father, and she explicitly says to Adama that she is following Iblis because he said he would find her father, where Adama, for reasons never made clear to the audience (although probably involving not wanting a charismatic lunatic with a death wish in any sort of position of power in his Fleet), won't even search for him. Cain, though, was more personable, explaining perhaps why Apollo is slower to warm to Iblis than to Cain (Cain was a warrior, where Iblis is more of a politician, also explaining the appeal to Apollo). Cain engaged in the same sort of manipulation in the guise of offering a free choice as Iblis; again, recall that he did not tell his officers about his plans to stage a suicide run, but did encourage a cult of personality aboard the *Pegasus*. Sheba's line to Iblis, 'you have a very dark side to you. There's something about you that reminds me of my father, of his love of war and conflict', and Iblis' reply, 'that's a very perceptive observation', and her response, 'And this war of yours, Count Iblis, is it of your choosing?' recalls a cut line from 'The Living Legend', where Cassiopea says to Cain 'I don't know ... there's just a side to you I see sometimes that frightens me ... what would you do without all this fighting?' Significantly, what Iblis actually said to Sheba is 'I will bring you together... your father... the legendary Commander Cain. You'll see him again', which is rather ambiguous and could even be taken as implying that Cain is in Hell, and Iblis will lead Sheba to him there. A sinister light is thus retrospectively cast on Cain's charisma and influence over the Fleet's warriors.

YOU'VE GOT TO HAVE FAITH: RELIGIOUS METAPHORS IN 'WAR OF THE GODS'

There are significant parallels with the story of the Fall of Man. As in the Garden of Eden, the first person to fall under Iblis' spell is a woman, Sheba (significantly, this takes place in a garden aboard an agro-ship, and Iblis' battle with the lightships becomes associated with miraculous fruits, referencing other aspects of the legend). There is also a strong sexual overtone to Iblis' relationship with Sheba, even after Standards and Practices, the censors of the day, cut some of the more problematic lines (including one where he says he will be 'inside' Sheba; later he says a similar sort of thing, but with fewer connotations, when he says he would like to play a Triad game 'through' Boomer). Sheba and Iblis end up kissing in the garden (and, in a cut sequence, being spotted by one of the gardeners doing so). While the original script has Sheba calling Iblis 'the only man who truly knows me', the final version puts it as '... who has truly known me', adding a further sexual connotation. This is perhaps a little unfortunate as, while Starbuck acknowledges at the end of the story that they are all to blame somewhat, it still plays into the stereotype of women as vulnerable to temptation, particularly of a sexual kind, and that they corrupt men through this (as it's after Sheba is corrupted that Iblis turns his attention to the men of the Fleet). In the second-draft script, Starbuck and Sheba are described as waking up on the Ship of Lights naked (seen from the waist up, and Sheba only from the rear), with obvious echoes of Adam and Eve in Paradise, rather than in pure white versions of their own uniforms, as screened.

It is perhaps interesting to note that, although she admits that she finds him attractive, Cassiopea does not fall under Iblis' spell as Sheba does. This might be down to their different emotional situations regarding relationships. Cassiopea is an ex-socialator, and still appears to prefer casual relationships; for her, a bit of flirtation with a handsome older man is simply a diversion from her job for a few minutes. Sheba, however, still hurting from the loss of her father and not sure about her feelings towards Apollo, is vulnerable to someone offering what seems to be a strong relationship.

There are other Biblical allegories within 'War of the Gods'. There are again connections with the story of the Golden Calf, as the Colonials turn their backs on Adama and follow someone who seems to offer them more tangible rewards, and Glen Larson, on the documentary *Looking Back at the Future*, says that he was explicitly inspired by the story of the fall of Lucifer, and the idea that we have a choice whether to follow him or not. A line in the draft script which refers to 'the limits of your evolution' was later changed to '... of your flesh', referring to the limitations of carnality and putting the story in a more religious than scientific frame.

While the image we get of the Colonial faith in this story is very Old Testament, with its ideas of universal rules which neither people nor angels should break (in a cut line after Apollo's death, Sheba says 'in all the universe, are there no balances ... rules ... and counter rules [sic] ... Even for an advanced race, there must be a greater law'), there is also something very New Testament in the plot of Apollo sacrificing himself to save Sheba (a sinner, who is referred to in the script as Iblis' 'disciple'), and she is redeemed through his act, and then she and Starbuck follow his example, offering their lives for his, and this causes him to be brought back to life. If Iblis had succeeded in being elected President, this would have made him the thirteenth person around the council table, referring to Christian superstitions about the number thirteen being unlucky. Sheba says that after Iblis' arrival 'we're all saved', but Adama, in a cut scene, says to her 'you belong to him ... he can do with you what he will. Now cast him out before it's too late', implying demonic possession.

There is also an influence from Mormon beliefs in the story, in that the idea that human beings can achieve godhood is a (somewhat controversial) Mormon tenet; here, the inhabitants of the lightships are human beings who have become gods, and this is held out as a possible future for the humans of the Fleet. In a cut line, Iblis says to Adama: 'man in his evolutionary development has reached many levels … some far greater than others … as you are, I once was … as I am … you may become', a line also spoken by the people on the Ship of Lights (although they say 'we' rather than 'I') implying Adama, and indeed the people of the Fleet, could become godlike (or perhaps also that he/they could become evil and corrupt). The idea of deities being powerful aliens, with miracles being scientific facts which people too primitive to grasp the sciences misinterpreted, is also distinctly von Däniken (and the title of the story reads like that of one of von Däniken's sequels to *Chariots of the Gods*); again, this seems to be an actual part of Colonial belief as well. Adama's psychic powers (which provides another link between him and Iblis) also pick up on the 1970s belief about psychic powers being real and potentially cultivatable by ordinary people, as exemplified in such television programmes as 1979's *The Omega Factor* (Adama's reference to 'bending eating utensils' is yet another nod to the contemporary Uri Geller craze).

UNSOLVED MYSTERIES: IBLIS AND THE DEMON SHIP

Much speculation has also emerged regarding the fact that we do not see what is inside the crashed ship, leading some to suggest that it was the wreckage of the *Pegasus*, and that Starbuck warned Sheba against looking inside so that she would not see her father and former shipmates' corpses. However, we know that the intention was for the ship to contain the corpses of demon creatures, as in this excerpt from the second-draft script, stating that Apollo and Starbuck see: 'a piece of metallic surface, highly scorched but out of which protrudes a foot-like extremity, except that its tip is clearly in the shape of a cloven hoof … [lifting the metal sheet] They grimace in horror … Under the wreckage is the figure of a devil … a demon'. Story editors Terence McDonnell and Jim Carlson have stated that the scene was cut because ABC thought it was too frightening, but in an interview quoted on the www.colonialfleets. com forums, Anne Lockhart suggests it might have been on quality grounds: 'It was supposed to be something malevolent and deadly looking when I go in there. Apparently it was on short notice and this was the best they could come up with to suggest this Mephistopheles character – but they couldn't show anything so they had to cover it. It looked like a dead sheep under a blanket with its feet sticking out. It was about the most unthreatening thing you have ever seen. It was far more effective to not ever show what we saw because for 25 years people have been asking about it'. Lockhart has a good point in that, despite the network's intentions, removing the clip seems to have led to unrestrained speculation.

The ship is unlikely to have been the *Pegasus* in any case, due to the nature of its commander. Cain is not the sort of person to make deals with the devil, and is also not easily threatened, as a glorious death is as appealing to him as a victory, and thus the idea that he would sell his soul to Iblis, even to defeat the Cylons, is rather out of character. In an interesting coda, when Iblis reappears in the 1995 Maximum Press Comics *Battlestar Galactica* series (with a backstory which sometimes contradicts the screen version), there's a nod to the controversy over the demon ship's appearance when Iblis convinces Sheba that the crashed ship on the surface contained the remains of Cain, while Apollo and Starbuck insist to her that it was a ship full of demons.

What exactly happened on the ship is not known for certain. It is possible that they were shot down or forced down by the lightships, but it is also possible that there was a mutiny among Iblis' followers. As we see with Sheba, some pressures can induce them to break away, and, if Iblis had crossed a line while they were pursued by the lightships, a struggle for control, followed by a crash, might have ensued. Although we will see a strong tendency to interventionism on the part of the lightship people in 'Experiment in Terra' (suggesting that its crew did, in fact, manipulate the situation such that the Colonials would encounter Iblis, and might well have shot him down right at this point), the accidental scenario does seem more likely in terms of the lightship people's general reluctance to take punitive action against Iblis unless he is 'breaking the rules', as it would be more of a coincidence for Iblis or one of his followers to have transgressed the rules right at that point than for the *Galactica* to have come across Iblis and the lightships by happenstance. This would also explain why the Ship of Lights started picking up Colonial Vipers right after the crash; Apollo's suggestion that they were trying to understand the humans and find a weakness is partly right, in that, although they were not trying to attack the Fleet, they were trying to gather information from them, to find out what was going on, where Iblis was, and whether there was a connection between them and him. A Council member says, in a cut scene, that Iblis has lost his people and is looking to lead the humans as a substitute. Iblis says that his ship was destroyed by 'the Great Powers', which would suggest that the ship was shot down; however, he does not always tell the truth, and also could have used the phrase to mean that they had indirectly caused its destruction.

FREE TO BE YOU AND ME: POLITICS AND PHILOSOPHY IN THE COLONIAL FLEET

'War of the Gods' is a good story for *Battlestar Galactica* philosophy. An express conflict is set up between good and evil (with the lightship inhabitants, frequently called 'angels' in extracanonical literature and in a handwritten note on the 2 March 1979 draft of 'Experiment in Terra', and Iblis, representing either side), with the humans winding up caught in the crossfire. The lightship people, are, broadly speaking, good, opposing Iblis and encouraging the Colonial Fleet not to be controlled by outside forces. They do not appear to attack anyone in the story, and do not hurt the pilots (a cut scene explains that the pilots were put down on the planet with Vipers out of fuel and no memory of their experiences on the Ship of Lights, but instead a plausible alternate explanation involving navigational 'pilfering', by which Larson appears to mean having had their navigational equipment interfered with). They respect and reward self-sacrifice and seem to regard love as redeeming. Iblis, equally, is bad, with a totalitarian and deceptive philosophy and followers manipulated into believing him through his playing on their weaknesses.

However, the lightship people's ways are at odds with conventional ideas of good as coming from compassion and fellow-feeling; they would not have intervened had Sheba died, because she was a follower of Iblis, even though it's arguable that she isn't a bad person, just rather emotionally vulnerable, and yet intervene at Apollo's death not because of his worth as a person, but because his dying is 'against the rules', and because of Sheba and Starbuck's willingness to sacrifice themselves for him, as they see Apollo as the right person to follow. They give the coordinates to Earth to the Fleet, not as a reward, but, a cut line indicates, because they wish to penalise Iblis by providing 'something distressing' for him, perhaps occasionally offering Adama some 'added wisdom in his quest for Earth'. Although Iblis wears white robes, which is often a symbol of a bad person in *Battlestar Galactica*, the lightship people also wear all white clothing, indicating perhaps that, although they may seem to wish us well, their idea of 'good' may be at a different angle to ours, and impossible for us to understand, or perhaps that, as per the harsh philosophy of the *Galactica*'s warriors, that 'good' can involve people making morally problematic choices, like putting the safety of the Fleet ahead of that of one's own family.

The story also revolves around the issue of free will, and the idea that everyone in Colonial society has a free choice in their actions. This, again, recalls the neoconservative philosophy that people, given free choice, will mostly tend to choose the morally correct option; although Starbuck, Sheba and Boomer are all initially seduced by Iblis' charisma, Apollo and Adama are not, and the three who are eventually recognise Iblis as evil. One could argue that this is a hypocritical or contradictory philosophy, as people in the series are continually having to sacrifice their individual freedoms for the common good of the Fleet; however, this then references the Enlightenment discourse over the nature of freedom, and how people may have to sacrifice some liberties (the freedom to steal, to kill, to behave in an antisocial manner) for the greater freedom provided by a legal system, under which the rights of all citizens are protected.

Another neoconservative ideal is very strongly referenced in this story, namely, that beings which have achieved some form of enlightenment, should help less enlightened beings to achieve it, in a kind of divine interventionism. The people on the lightships want to help the Colonials become more like them, and say that they wish the Colonials to do the same to less evolved groups than themselves (an idea which will be returned to in 'Experiment in Terra' and *Galactica 1980*). However, there is a slight sinister element to the lightships' people, which, coupled with some of the implications of 'Experiment in Terra', might suggest that the authors are aware of the dangers of pursuing an interventionist philosophy too naively.

FAUSTUS OF STEEL: THE CYLONS, BALTAR AND IBLIS

Although the Cylons themselves make only a brief appearance, the audience here receives a crucial expansion on the Cylon backstory given in 'Saga of a Star World', through the dialogue between Baltar and Iblis. It is directly stated that the robot takeover took place at the outset of the Cylon-human conflict[16], and the Imperious Leader speaks with Iblis' voice (Larson says that Iblis' voice was 'transcribed into' the Imperious Leader), suggesting that, as Baltar realises, Iblis must have made a major impression on the Cylons at the point of the robot *coup d'état*, which, in a cut line, Iblis (then still known as Diabolis) refers to as a 'diabolic takeover'. The obvious implication is that the Cylons, fearful of the humans, asked Iblis for his help, and the price was, as a species, transformation into a robot society, twisted demon versions of themselves. The fact that the robot Cylons resemble humans, as noted in 'Saga of a Star World', may be down to Cylon fears of human power and abilities. Larson, on the *Looking Back at the Future* documentary, says 'the Cylons were well converted, and so when he [the Imperious Leader] spoke, he spoke with the voice of the Devil', and it is suggested that, although the Cylons may have forgotten the initial reason for it, they have unwittingly been serving Iblis all along, with the contact surviving in remnants such as the Imperious Leader's

---

16 Which would seem to contradict Apollo's assertion in 'Saga of a Star World' that the lizard Cylons died out 'thousands of yahrens' earlier, and the cut line in 'The Living Legend' where Cain refers to the mechanical Cylons as having been programmed 'thousands of yahrens ago', but then, neither man is in a position to know the details of Cylon social history.

voice (if the Imperious Leader acts as Iblis' agent, this suggests that the Cylons and Baltar have both been his unwitting pawns throughout), and names such as Lucifer, Specter and so forth. In a cut line, Baltar whispers 'my God', as Iblis vanishes, leaving it ambiguous as to whether he is swearing or acknowledging Iblis as his unwanted spiritual leader. On a side note, the Cylons are referred to as an 'empire', but Iblis also mentions 'the Cylons and their allies', indicating that, although the Cylons may be the dominant power in the alliance, they have not actually obliterated their partners as yet.

Baltar's behaviour is also highlighted in the story. Although clearly the impetus for his going over to the *Galactica* is Iblis' mental influence, Baltar thinks he is acting of his own free will. We know that he is at heart insecure, and that he fears, and is attracted to, those more powerful than himself – including Adama, who has been defeating him regularly since the loss of the Colonies, and the lightships, whose behaviour is inexplicable. When the Cylons encounter the lightships, Baltar speculates that it is some new technological breakthrough on Adama's part, and Lucifer says 'let us hope so … the alternative is that we have encountered a new and more powerful form in the universe than our own'. Baltar demonstrates this fear/respect of the powerful, and especially Adama, throughout the story, being continually drawn to Adama: when he says to the Council 'you need me', he addresses Adama directly, and he appeals to Adama (in an ad-lib) when being forced to kneel by Iblis. Significantly, though, he does not attempt to side with Iblis, and, when Baltar says 'there is a power greater than yours … greater than the Cylon Empire … it will destroy us all if we do not unite', he indicates that he also only wishes to side with those familiar to him (whether Adama or the Cylons), and fears and rejects powerful things which he does not understand.

Iblis is thus pushing at the open door of Baltar's fears and insecurities to induce him to come to the *Galactica* of what he believes to be his own free will. Starbuck speculates that Baltar and Iblis are working together, to get inside their defences; in a way, this is partly true, because Baltar has given himself freely to Iblis through his association with the Imperious Leader and is thus under Iblis' power, but not quite in the way that Starbuck thinks. Interestingly, when Baltar says he wishes to go to the *Galactica*, Lucifer's response indicates that he suspects that Baltar is up to something, such as making a secret deal with Adama, as he finds the idea completely illogical.

On a side point, this story makes it most likely that the opening voiceover is being spoken by Count Iblis, as he says he has been to Earth (and, since the lightship people know where it is, there is no reason to assume he is lying), and it is more plausible that he would know who the Toltecs and Greeks were than that the Imperious Leader would. It is unknown if the voiceover was removed from the transmitted version of this story, the one which precedes it, and almost all of the ones which follow it, to avoid confusion over which character was speaking, or for time reasons, or some other reason, but, if Iblis is the one introducing the story's premise, then there is an element of irony from the outset.

MEN IN SPEEDOES: COLONIAL POLITICS AND LEISURE

This story focuses to some extent on the nature of Colonial politics. Adama seems to be acting as leader of the Council as well as being officially the leader of the military, though he does not seem to have been formally elected President; however, they are visibly not under martial law, as the Council of Twelve (as they are referred to here, as an alternate to 'Quorum') appear to have final deciding power, and Iblis' conversation with Adama indicates that he can be overruled. It is unclear if Adama's power comes from a formal line of succession (such that, if the President dies, the leader of the military is automatically pro tem leader until a proper election can be held), a formal or informal decision (a Council vote, for instance) appointing him leader on a temporary basis, or whether he has not had any sort of actual confirmation but simply governs through the respect the other Council members have for him. Each time we see the Council, or Quorum, they appear to have changed many of their members, but it is worth remembering that time passes between stories, and the changes can be put down to elections, resignations, and other happenstance. Baltar seems to have been tried in absentia, and sentenced to life imprisonment, indicating that the Colonies do not have the death penalty even for treason; however, the fact that, although he comes aboard *Galactica* under 'the universal sign of truce', he is arrested the moment he sets foot in the Fleet, does not make them look very diplomatic.

One weak aspect to the politics is that the Council seem willing to hand over power to Iblis rather quickly and without putting up a fight (reinforced in the cut scenes, where a councillor extols his virtues), even though Iblis indicates that some of the Council are sceptical of him. Politicians are generally very bad at handing over power, and so it seems rather out of character for the most powerful individuals in the Fleet to willingly surrender that power to an outsider, whatever he may be offering. While Iblis' mind control might explain some of it, it does not explain why those who Iblis identifies as sceptics don't put up more of a fight, bar Adama. The politicians' behaviour is just about excusable in this instance due to the introduction of the mind control element, but it will not be long in the series before it becomes more caricatured.

Among the ordinary people, it is clearly indicated in the script and on the screen that the Fleet's inhabitants are living in squalid, close-packed quarters. We only see the conditions aboard the *Gemini* freighter, but Sheba's dialogue indicates that there are other freighters in a similar state. The people's words to Iblis indicate that they bear resentment towards the military and the politicians, believing (and apparently with justification) that they are getting better rations and treatment than the ordinary people, who feel trapped and desperate. There is an acknowledgement that if people are in despair, they will follow anyone who seems to offer hope, even if, as with Iblis, they believe (as they state in cut dialogue) that he is mad. It should also be noted that it is not the speed of the growth of the fruit which is noteworthy (as Colonial science being able to make plants grow faster is seen in a cut sequence from the early draft of 'Saga of a Star World', and returns as a plot point in 'Space Croppers'), but the size and abundance of the produce in question, as Wilker notes that the fruit from the agro-ship is 'unusually large'. Adama says of Iblis that 'his promises are giving our people the first real hope they've had in a quarter yahren', although what the last incident which gave them hope was (Cain's arrival perhaps?) is never articulated.

On the leisure front, the Colonial sport of 'Triad' is seen here for the first time, with Apollo, Boomer and Starbuck being keen players. This is a sport broadly based on basketball, but with two-man teams, a small court and football-style padding. Detailed rules for it can be found in the draft script. However, the description differs from the final version in that the court is described as three-sided, a member of each team stands facing each other across a line during the 'face off' (the hand-grasping-and-circling manoeuvre seen in the final instead of this was apparently made up by Richard Hatch, Herb Jefferson and Dirk Benedict when they would stand together waiting for shooting to begin), and the offensive team have to get past the defending team to get to the ball, with which the teams then score points by hitting lighted circles on the walls, which flash at random, must be hit while lighted to score, and have different point values depending on how long they stay lit. Passing is also said to be only permitted on a ricochet (though the finished version sees at least one direct pass between the Gold Team players). These differences lend credence to Richard Hatch's claims in interviews that the game was largely made up on the fly by the players.

The players wear decidedly brief uniforms (consisting of helmets, swimming trunks and gladiatorial webbing) in a blatant attempt to boost the programme's adult female audience. In the 1970s, with *Cosmopolitan* publishing male centrefolds and feminist writers engaging in discourses on sexuality and power, networks and publishers were grudgingly coming to realise that women do rather enjoy sex as well, and that there is money to be made in acknowledging this.

We also see an instance of Colonial popular dancing (large amounts of footage of which were cut). This appears to be a cross between disco and Morris-dancing, and anyone noting the resemblance to the notorious 'future dance' sequence in the *Buck Rogers* pilot will not be surprised to learn that there is a note on the script at this point reading 'we might get our B.R. [*Buck Rogers*] choreographer to come up with spacy disco-dancing'.

FRIENDS IN DIFFICULT TIMES: CHARACTER DEVELOPMENT

Apollo features strongly in this story. Although he denies it outwardly, he clearly has a mutual affection developing with Sheba, and is jealous of her attraction to Iblis. Starbuck is, however, not totally fair in suggesting that Apollo is only going after Iblis for this reason (although it certainly does inform his behaviour). He has put aside personal concerns for the good of the Fleet before, and his primary reason for going on the mission is because of his conversation with his father about Iblis' motivations, plus what he has learned from Doctor Wilker and his father which suggests that Iblis may be a charlatan. Given Apollo's reputation for sensitivity, it is amusing that, when Sheba accuses him of being insensitive, he reacts with surprise (the original script has her accusing him of lack of refinement, which is less entertaining). Starbuck himself, although he claims more selfish motives, is actually being selfless in accompanying Apollo back to the planet, to support his friend, and weeps openly at Apollo's death. He once again swears 'for Sagan's sake'.

This is also a good story for the series' minor characters. Jolly, Brie, Bojay and Greenbean all make appearances (although they are promptly sucked into the Ship of Lights; squadron assignments appear to be flexible, for example, Jolly is currently flying with Silver Spar and Brie with Red Squadron, despite the fact that both normally fly with Blue Squadron, where Sheba changes after 'The Living Legend' from Silver Spar to Blue Squadron). Having Brie return is a nice piece of continuity, as well as, perhaps, compensation for the repeated reuse of the clip of her launching. The script spells her name 'Bris', which bears an unfortunate resemblance to the name of the Jewish circumcision ceremony. Paul Coufos, who had a minor speaking role as a pilot in 'Lost Planet of the Gods', has a few lines as a pilot in this story. Doctor Wilker, the thoroughly singleminded scientist, makes a welcome reappearance, and the fact that the Colonials are capable, in theory at least, of building lifelike androids which can pass for human is mentioned (and bits of the same are seen lying about his workshop).

CREATION MYTHS: PRODUCTION AND PRESENTATION

One of the more noticeable features of this episode is the colour effects on the planet. Despite Anne Lockhart and Terence McDonnell's recollections about using 'infrared film' to record the location sequences, and Lockhart claiming that the actors had to wear special 'mint green' makeup for these, there are a number of alternate takes of the sequences on the planet which are in ordinary colours on normal film (with the actors' makeup looking no different to usual), suggesting that the colours were actually an effect added in post-production (the authors of this book have discovered that it is possible to achieve a similar effect through experimenting with a 'War of the Gods' publicity picture in Photoshop). The idea of the planet looking unusual goes back to at least the third-draft script, where it is described as having 'soft red grass', and Starbuck has a line 'you should see yourselves', indicating that there was intended to be some kind of lighting or other effect on them (though the specific reference to the light, from Apollo, is not in the third-draft script, where it is called in the notes 'an oddly coloured red planet'). The reason why the effect suddenly disappears in the scenes around the crashed ship was likely because it would have caused problems with the selective inversion of colour used in the sequence where Apollo shoots Iblis and we briefly see Iblis' demonic form, but the result is to make viewers wonder where the strange colours went every time the actors are up by the wreckage.

Outtakes also indicate that some of Apollo, Starbuck and Sheba's lines from the external filming were reshot using back projection; while it is true that there is a lot of external noise from wind, airplanes and so forth in these sequences, this could have been dealt with through redubbing the dialogue, so the reason for doing this is probably because the originals, which were mostly done in long shot, were not very dramatic, and they were better able to work in close-ups in the reshoots. There is a note on the script regarding the wreckage of the spacecraft reading 'a large skeletal remains of a burned-out ship (possibly some of the Hindenburg framework might serve us well here)'; as Universal had released a film entitled *The Hindenburg*, about the famous zeppelin disaster, in 1975, reuse of props from this film is probably what was intended here, although in the end the ship wreckage was apparently in fact recycled pieces of set from the Universal telemovie version of *Brave New World* (released 1980), which would have been in production at the time. A cut sequence in which Apollo, Starbuck and Sheba fly through and describe the planets of the system would later be used in 'The Hand of God'; while another piece of footage, in which Starbuck chats up one of the lightship people, was visibly filmed as a joke, there is an interesting connection in that

Starbuck's line to them in the finished version, 'I don't know who you are, but whatever you want from me, you can have', was originally intended to have later consequences in 'Experiment in Terra'.

'War of the Gods' also reintroduces the idea of Adama keeping a 'captain's log' style voice diary (as in 'Saga of a Star World', albeit with a different microphone), which will return as an introductory motif for all but one of the rest of the series' episodes. This is also the first time Anne Lockhart appears in the title sequence, rather than the list of guest stars. There appears to be some influence from *Close Encounters of the Third Kind* in the appearance of the Ship of Lights and the lightship people. The ending, with Apollo, Starbuck and Sheba eidetically reciting the way to Earth, is distinctly like the ending of the 1979 *Blake's 7* episode 'The Keeper', which is very odd as there is no way the two production and writing teams could possibly have been aware of each other's activities at the time. The story is also noteworthy for showing the first use of pistols which fire laser beams in the series.

There are a couple of minor continuity errors in 'War of the Gods'. In the second Triad game, we see two Shebas in the audience, one in a pilot's uniform cheering, and one seated next to Iblis in a purple dress. After losing two out of three agro-ships in 'The Magnificent Warriors', the Fleet suddenly has multiple agro-ships again. Although Tigh's reference to 'Agro-Ship Nine' need not necessarily indicate that there are nine agro-ships in the Fleet, dialogue, namely Iblis' reference to 'agro-ships' in the plural, suggests there is at least more than one out there (and, since they are now in another galaxy, it is unlikely that they have built or picked up new ones since 'The Magnificent Warriors'). While it is tempting to speculate that 'The Magnificent Warriors' was meant to come after this story, the fact that there is no place for Sheba in it suggests that this is most likely an error due to the speed at which the series was being written. We again get the idea of Vipers needing lots of fuel to travel long distances, rather than an initial boost. More amusingly, two alternate takes exist of the pilots waking up after the party, in one of which Dirk Benedict ad-libs 'I'll never drink that shit [again]' just after the director shouts 'cut', and in the other, he ad-libs instead 'anybody got an aspirin?'

There is also some confusion about the number of ships which disappear. Five ships are visible in the first scene, though Adama refers to there being four in that squadron (confirmed by the fact that the script calls for four fighters in its stage directions to be seen at this point), and there are four ships launched in the next squadron; Adama then tells us that eight ships have gone missing. After Boomer goes missing, Starbuck says in the script that they have lost nine Vipers, however, in the story as transmitted Benedict says 'eight', all of which suggests a certain amount of confusion between actors, director, and writer.

Leaving aside minor errors and discrepancies which are largely down to the circumstances of the production, then, 'War of the Gods' is easily one of the strongest stories of *Battlestar Galactica*.

II • THE MAN WITH NINE LIVES

US TRANSMISSION DATE: Sunday 28 January 1979
WRITER: Donald Bellisario
DIRECTOR: Rob Holcomb
CREDITED CAST: Anne Jeffreys (Siress Blassie); Lance LeGault (Maga); Robert Feero (Bora); Anthony De Longis (Taba); Fred Astaire (Chameleon); (Bruce Wright (Cpl Lomas); Dan Barton (Crewman); Patricia Stich (Zara); Frank Parker (Zed); Leann Hunley (Female Pilot); Alex Hyde-White (Male Pilot); John Holland (Maitre d'); Lynn Halpern (Dealer)

SYNOPSIS: Starbuck, Apollo, Boomer and Jolly go to the *Rising Star*, on furlon (furlough). Also present are a trio of Borellian Nomen, desert nomads who are on a 'blood hunt', and an older man named Chameleon. Chameleon contrives to meet Starbuck while gambling and, through discussing their past histories, Starbuck comes to believe Chameleon might be his father. The pair go to *Galactica* for genetic testing, and the Nomen follow, signing up as Colonial warrior recruits. The less precise test suggests a genetic relationship between Starbuck and Chameleon, and, as they wait for the results of the more accurate test, Starbuck angrily rejects his friends' concerns that Chameleon may be deceiving him, and vows to resign his commission to spend time with the old man if he does prove to be his father. The Nomen escape the recruits' quarters, and track Chameleon down to launch bay Alpha where Starbuck is showing him how to operate a Viper. A battle ensues in which Chameleon routs the Nomen by firing the Viper's lasers into the launch bay. Chameleon explains that the Nomen's blood hunt was against him, as he had once posed as 'Captain Dimitri' of the livestock ship and had been paid to provide them with black market livestock. Cassiopea informs Chameleon that the genetic test is positive, but Chameleon asks her to lie to Starbuck about the result, saying that he does not want to see Starbuck give up everything to spend his life with an old con-artist.

ANALYSIS: 'The Man with Nine Lives', after the dramatic, world-affecting events of the previous five episodes, is a welcome shift to the small-scale and personal, focusing not on gods or heroes or life-threatening disasters, but simply on a drama in Starbuck's life.

ONCE UPON A TIME IN THE DESERT: WESTERN AND [MIDDLE] EASTERN THEMES
This story is one which, like earlier one-parters, draws on Western elements,

although it is more subtly done than 'The Lost Warrior' and 'The Magnificent Warriors'. The sequence where the Nomen walk into the bar, the music stops, and Boomer stands up to let them know that they're welcome to drink but he has his eye on them, and the Nomen sit at a table whose occupants clear off quickly is an almost exact take on the familiar Western scene of the villains walking into the saloon and being warned to behave by the sheriff, and the idea of a posse after a gambler has a lot in common with the gambling-man subgenre of Westerns, such as *Maverick*.

However, the Nomen actually have less in common with Indians than they do with Arabs, or at any rate with American stereotypes of Middle Eastern Arabs. They are desert nomads, with a strict socio-religious code, who don't mix with outsiders. They wear earth-tone robes and thick beards, and the draft script describes them as wearing 'Tureg (sic) -style burnooses'. Their blood hunt has a parallel with Albanian blood-feuds (which can obsess clan groups for generations), and, although the context suggests that they may well be making this up in order to take advantage of non-Borellian ignorance of their culture, they claim to have a religion requiring them to pray in private, like modern Muslims. They are described in the ship as eyeing Sheba and Athena in the docking lounge 'like pieces of meat to be auctioned off', playing to the Western stereotype of the lascivious Arab. Curiously, in the draft script, Boomer says 'they're used to the freedom of the steppes of Borella', adding a Russian element, and their heavy-browed makeup suggests Neanderthals. They are a minority, and there is the implication that they face prejudice because of it; when Maga accuses Apollo and Boomer, effectively, of discriminating against them, there is no indication that the warriors find the idea ridiculous. The story has a blending of Western and Middle Eastern elements with sci-fi elements, which is more satisfying than a straight Western pastiche.

Although the concept of 'political correctness' was several years in the future at the time this story was written, the Nomen subplot reads rather like a modern anti-PC rant, in that the Nomen take advantage of the warriors' willingness to accommodate their cultural differences. When challenged by Apollo on the *Rising Star*, they retreat behind accusations of discrimination, and use claims of religious prejudice to manoeuvre Corporal Lomas into a position where they can whack him over the head and chuck him in a closet, with a subtext to the effect of 'if you respect other people's cultures they'll take advantage of you'. They in turn are not willing to accommodate the Colonials, dismissing their culture and beliefs as 'weak'. At the same time, though, the Nomen indicate that they perceive respectful behaviour as a sign of weakness, and that they would respect the warriors more if they were antagonistic to them. Their Code is also a sensible thing to have in a harsh desert environment, encouraging as it does loyalty, obedience, respect for elders and responsibility for family members, as well as curbing the hot-headedness of youth.

THE MAN WHO GOT NO SIGN: STARBUCK AND CHAMELEON

'The Man with Nine Lives' revolves primarily around Starbuck and his relationship with Chameleon. We learn that Starbuck was an orphan found wandering the thorn forest near Umbra on Caprica after a massacre, and knows little about his origins, explaining why he is drawn to father figures. He also indicates that he cares much more for Cassiopea than he has hitherto admitted, principally that he'd actually think of getting 'sealed' to her (the script here refers to 'sealed' throughout, rather than 'married'), though the fact that he keeps putting conditions on the circumstances suggests he's not quite serious yet. Starbuck also shows an idealistic side when he says that he doesn't regard his work as a warrior worthwhile, and that he'd consider the job of genetic tracer more valuable, suggesting that his orphan upbringing means he idealises families and views his own military career, which he associates with death, as not being of value. Although Starbuck states that he doesn't know how old he is, the episode suggests that he is between 22 and 25 years old, if the incident which orphaned him took place twenty years ago (as, if he was younger than two at the time, he wouldn't have been able to wander around the forest, and children older than five are usually fairly certain when their birthdays are and are capable of reasoning, remembering, and so forth; Benedict was in his early thirties at the time of filming). The draft script pinpoints his age at 24, as a cut line has Chameleon recalling that his son's birth was in 7318, and we know that the massacre took place in 7322.[17]

Chameleon, Starbuck's father, is a lot like Starbuck in many ways. They are both rogues, anti-commitment, good gamblers (who came up independently with the same scheme for winning at cards), plausible but a bit slippery, and, if the final scene is real and not Chameleon playing a game, they both have an idealistic and self-sacrificing side. There is of course the question of whether, at the end of the story, he wants to keep Starbuck's paternity secret from the warrior for idealistic reasons, or more selfish ones (namely, so that Starbuck doesn't act as a restraining influence on his schemes); depending on how one views it, the idea is either deeply touching or deeply exploitative.

---

17 As pointed out in the book *Somewhere Beyond the Heavens,* there is a minor inconsistency with 'Saga of a Star World', in which we learn that the Colonials are entering the seventh millennium, and 'The Long Patrol', in which Starbuck refers to a 'sixth millennium fighter' as if it were an artifact of the distant past, and yet the dates given here clearly refer to the 7000s, or the *eighth* millennium.

The revelation that he really is Starbuck's father is a massive coincidence – such a coincidence, in fact, that it does make the twist at the end genuinely surprising, as the whole thing seems like a con-artist setting up a vulnerable victim (as the fact that Starbuck does not smell a rat at any point when Apollo and Boomer have clear suspicions suggests that he wants truly to believe). As stated in the episode, the odds are astronomical of them finding each other and yet, inexplicably, it happens.

Chameleon does, however, seem to have been deeply affected by the loss of his son. Despite his reputation, Chameleon never actually lies in any of the backstory he provides about losing a son on Caprica, and when he mentions that the number of lost children in the attack on Umbra is 'burned into his brain', this would be quite plausible if he had lost a child there. He is genuinely interested in the results of the tests, as he hastens the process rather than ensuring his security by delaying them as long as possible, and the fact that he knows enough about genetic tracing to be able to pass this off as his profession suggests that he may have investigated the possibilities of using it to try and find his child at some point. The name 'Dimitri' could be symbolic in that it is a derivative of 'Demeter', the Greek goddess of fertility who searches the Earth for her lost daughter, although it might simply have been a case of selecting an interesting-sounding name. We never at any point in the story learn what Chameleon's real name is, though his pseudonym (pronounced 'shameleon', either as a means of disguising its obvious association or as a pun on 'sham') suggests either that Earth chameleons are of Kobollian origin, or that the Earth lizard was named after a similar animal on Kobol.

DAUGHTERS AND DUCHETS: DEVELOPMENT AND WORLDBUILDING

On the character front, this is another strong story for Boomer; with Starbuck enamoured of Chameleon, he takes the role of Apollo's primary sidekick and foil, and plays the responsible lawman while the pilots are on the *Rising Star*, taking charge of the situation with the Nomen. Sheba, meanwhile, is convinced from the start that Chameleon is Starbuck's real father, and is angry at suggestions that he may be a con artist, which can be read as her being understandably irrational about the possibility of people finding their long-lost fathers, or, alternatively, as more evidence that she's easily taken in by smooth-talking older men.

The episode also produces some good examples of the *Battlestar Galactica* external vocabulary, as we hear a selection of gambling slang terms: 'build me' for 'deal me in', 'hover' for stay or hold, and the game of Pyramid seems to operate on a pyramid-building metaphor, involving 'capstone' cards, in the same way that modern card games use the feudal European nobility as a metaphor. We also get another example of *Battlestar Galactica*'s alternative slang, when Apollo says that he feels like an 'equinises' atrum' (clearly, a horse's ass).

We learn more about civilian life on the Fleet in this story. Shuttles seem to run more or less like buses within it, and are paid for using 'duckets' (pronounced, and in some sources spelled, like 'ducats', a genuine currency in our world), which seem to be the equivalent of bus tokens (the draft script describes them as plastic discs). In the waiting area of the shuttle, a Triad game plays on the TV monitors. One might perhaps question whether having an interfleet TV station might attract unwanted Cylon attention through its broadcasts; however, if it is simply a short-range station, then it would presumably blend in with the normal inter-ship communications traffic. On the *Rising Star*, we see another example of the bad dancing which seems to plague Glen Larson's science fiction output of the late 1970s, crossing the worst bits of disco and figure-dancing, as well as some kind of dance performance involving women in bodysuits which Jolly and Apollo appear, bizarrely, to find appealing. A planet named 'Borallus' has been mentioned in 'Saga of a Star World', which may well be the homeworld of the Borellian Nomen (the draft script refers to them as coming from 'Borella', but this may well be due to the writer misremembering under the time pressure which the series was facing). We also get a visual reference to 'Fire in Space' when we see two landing crewmen pushing around tanks marked 'Boraton' in the background as Tigh and Omega harangue the recruits.

The Fleet apparently has an orphan ship and a 'seniors' ship' (named in the draft script as the *Crucible*), on which, according to the draft script, nobody is under sixty yahrens of age (the idea of colonials living well past a hundred yahrens appears to have been forgotten; the recruitment advert specifies that candidates must be between sixteen and forty-six yahrens of age, whereas, if lifespans were longer, one would expect a later cut-off date). Colonials appear to self-classify into 'tribes' in the same way that Earth humans classify themselves into ethnic groups or nationalities. Not only do we see more female pilots (as well as several female candidates for warrior, and the recruiting advert doesn't specify gender), but Siress Blassie mentions them in the context of, with some jealousy, suspecting Chameleon of wanting to 'interview' some.

The idea of a genetic tracer is interesting to modern audiences in that, although it is presented here as a strange and complicated idea, it has become commonplace in the intervening time since the programme was broadcast; in fact, DNA testing is even simpler than this, as one is not confined to neural cells when making an identification. The science of the genetic tracer is all over the place. Initially they need a neural cell, then only the 'image' of that cell, and there is also the question of why the cell must be taken from the brain as opposed to another, less-hard-to-access spot in the nervous system. The original script actually has the science more consistent, as it does not contain the line about making an image of the neural cell.

DAY OF THE BORAY: THE STORY'S PRODUCTION

'The Man with Nine Lives' is best known less for its plot or character and background revelation than for being 'the one with Fred Astaire'. Although Astaire's presence might seem like gratuitous celebrity casting, he is actually an inspired choice, and really gets a chance to show off his skill as a serious actor; the story was reportedly written specifically for Astaire after he told Glen Larson at a party how much his grandchildren enjoyed *Battlestar Galactica*. The character of Chameleon is also strikingly similar to the one Astaire plays in *The Towering Inferno* (1974), a charming conman who proves, in a crisis, to have a heart of gold. He got on well with Dirk Benedict, with Benedict recalling him in a number of interviews. In one, on www.schooldisco.com, Benedict says 'he was from a different generation back when celebrity was based on a career of achievement, not over-night [success] and he was also very humble, an extremely hard worker, he wanted to rehearse … We became good friends and used to sit and talk after the show was over, I learned a lot by watching him. He was a beautiful human being'. In *Starlog* 247 (1988), he says that Astaire 'was an incredible person. We chuckled a lot at each other's silly sense of humour and developed a friendship that continued after filming. I remember he was very much in love with his girlfriend, soon to be his wife, and she was many decades his junior!' Most recently, in the *Remembering Battlestar Galactica* DVD documentary, he has recalled that, while a technical crew were fixing the weapons on the full-size Viper during the filming of the launch tube scene and began testing the gun effect mechanism by 'firing' it in an irregular rhythm, that Astaire, waiting for the next take, began to improvise a dance to that rhythm, and told Benedict that this had given him an idea for a dance show with an outer space motif. Although, according to Terence McDonnell and episode director Rod Holcomb, Astaire was reluctant to dance during the programme, he was persuaded to do the brief dance sequence with Anne Jeffreys, making this episode, according to many sources, the last time he danced onscreen.

Otherwise, the laser-bole effect in the story, while very much of its time, still stands up well today, as does the Nomen makeup, though Lance LeGault, who played Maga (and also played Bootes in 'The Lost Warrior') recalls that it took two and a quarter hours to put on and an hour to take off, and likened the beard to a Brillo pad in terms of its lack of comfort. A story circulates that writer Don Bellisario came up with the name of 'Nomen' for the characters when, during an after-work session with Jim Carlson and Lance LeGault in which Bellisario was complaining about being unable to come up with a name, Carlson suggested that if they had originated from an ice planet, he could have called them 'snowmen', and then suggested that, since they came from a hot planet, they should be called 'nomen' (although the similarity between 'nomen' and 'nomad' suggests that this may be all or partly apocryphal). Leann Hunley, who plays the unnamed female warrior who pilots the shuttle with Sheba, also previously appeared in 'Lost Planet of the Gods' and 'War of the Gods' as a female warrior; Lynn Halpern, who plays a dealer, was Don Bellisario's wife at the time.

An earlier draft of this story, entitled 'The Furlon', latest revision dated 2 January 1979 (which differs only from the first draft, dated 19 December 1978, in that it contains a glossary sheet giving pronunciations and definitions for Colonial terms and character names), is also available and contains some interesting points of difference from the finished version. Adama's opening diary entry is not present in the draft version, and, while Bojay features extensively in Act One, he is completely excised from the final, and his surviving lines are given to other characters. Athena also is a strong presence in the original (in which she pilots the shuttle with Sheba), but in the finished version, she is not, and her surviving lines are largely given to Sheba. The original story has the Nomen running a black market, rather than simply hoarding, and implies that the Nomen were killed (whereas in the final, they survive). The draft script also gives an unusual insight into an aspect of the series' production when the monitors in the departure lounge are said to be showing a programme about the galaxy they are in, and the script indicates: 'perhaps we can pick up on a NOVA-type show for this' – NOVA is an award-winning documentary series running on the American PBS network since 1974.

The draft script also elaborates on the *Battlestar Galactica* universe in several areas worthy of mention. The script indicates that the shuttle is full of pilots from Blue and Silver Spar squadrons, meaning that, although this is not directly articulated in the episode, Red Squadron are on patrol. Blue Squadron are said to be a crack squadron by the television interviewer. We learn that the gaming deck will accept cubits, 'Orion checks' and 'warrior script' (sic – probably 'scrip'); Bojay says 'what … no Cylon krael? I stole a sackful on a raid', which not only evokes Croft's crime in 'The Gun on Ice Planet Zero', but indicates that the Cylons have a formal currency system. The

Rising Star restaurant Maitre d' from 'The Lost Patrol' is specified as appearing in the script; although his lines have been cut, the same actor who played the character, John Holland, is clearly visible in the background of some scenes.

More Colonial vocabulary appears in the draft script, with 'grog' being a drink (as in 'Saga of a Star World'), and 'voltons' a unit of power; the line where the Nomen refer to Captain Dimitri as 'that jackal' calls him 'that Boray' in the original. The body-suited dancers are called the 'Virgo Quad dancers', and, in the original draft, Bojay tries to chat one of them up by claiming that his father was a 'stager' and that he grew up with dancers and artists. When she fails to respond to his charm, Jolly remarks, 'you think we should have told him the Virgo Quad dancers are deaf?' and Boomer replies 'some things a man just ought to discover for himself … it's maturing'.

The *Canarius* shuttle, the civilian carrier, is described in the script in terms evoking the shortage of materials in the Fleet: 'from the worn seats and bulkheads, we can tell the ship has seen better days. Every seat is filled with civilians dressed in their best attire, and representing a cross section of the survivors of the colonies', suggesting that life is gradually settling down to a routine in the Fleet. The script specifies that the crewman collecting the duckets is dressed in yellow (presumably, given the ship's name, this is a pun on canary yellow). The crewman also says that the ship is kept flying on 'hand me down parts', which, together with the scripted dilapidated appearance of the vessel, continues the theme of privation and scarcity in the Fleet indicated in other stories. More ships are mentioned, the *Aquarius*, the agro-ship (singular), the *Trinian*, the *Pisces*, the freighter *Borella* and the Comm-Tel ship, from where broadcasting is done (the final script instead mentions the *Tauranian*, the *Pisces*, the agro-ship, the Comm-Tel ship and the freighter *Borella*); the fact that two of these are the names of Zodiac signs (and thus related to the names of Colonial tribes), and a third is a known planet name, makes it tempting to speculate that some ships contain only people from particular planets. The 'livery ship' is again mentioned, though changed to 'livestock ship' in the final. The 'scanners [monitors] inserted into the back of all the seats' are mentioned in the script; the idea of this as a futuristic concept is curious to modern viewers, accustomed to seat-back televisions in most large airliners and some trains.

There are also a few added instances of characterisation or new backstory for the regulars. Starbuck is said to be the winner of the Gold Cluster at the battle of Rigus (since he was to be given this for clearing the minefield in 'Saga of a Star World', this is presumably another award of the same decoration), with three stars for gallantry in the rear action at Carillon, the raid on Molekay (sic) and the rescue at Otarrius, in an evocative mix of names familiar and unfamiliar to the regular viewer. In a cut line, Apollo says he inherited his cautiousness from Adama (Adama retorts 'you can't blame your mother or I for everything you do'). When Starbuck discovers Apollo asked Tigh to conduct a security check on Chameleon, the script describes him as 'really pissed', which is apt, if rather colloquial.

'The Man with Nine Lives' is arguably the best of the one-parters, being a charming character piece which reveals much about Starbuck, as well as of the loss and loneliness which the Fleet's personnel, separated from home and family, must often feel.

12 • MURDER ON THE RISING STAR

US TRANSMISSION DATE: Sunday 18 February 1979
TELEPLAY: Donald Bellisario and Jim Carlson & Terrence McDonnell
STORY: Michael Sloan
DIRECTOR: Rod Holcomb
CREDITED CAST: Brock Peters (Solon); W K Stratton (Barton); Ben Frank (Chella/Riftis); Lyman Ward (Pallon/Karibdis); Frank Ashmore (Ortega); Newell Alexander (Elias); Ted Parker (Zed); Patricia Stich (Zara); Ted Noose (Official); Paul LeClair (1st Guard)

SYNOPSIS: Starbuck is accused of the murder of his old rival Ortega, and all the evidence appears to point to his guilt. Apollo agrees to defend Starbuck, and he and Boomer investigate, learning that Ortega had another enemy, named Karibdis, who was once Baltar's pilot, and was the man who sabotaged the defence computers on Caprica at the time of the holocaust. They learn that Ortega was blackmailing three men, Chella, Elias and Pallon, who had all bribed him to let them on to the Fleet during the evacuation of the Colonies. While Boomer defends Starbuck in court, Apollo conducts a ruse to ascertain Karibdis' identity by picking up the suspects to take them to the *Galactica* to testify, then informing them that they have identified the real murderer as Karibdis, and that after he drops them off, he will be going to the prison barge to pick up Baltar, who can identify him. As Apollo predicted, Karibdis stows away on the shuttle with the intention of killing him and Baltar, meaning that he is able to identify Karibdis positively as Pallon. Boomer opens up a channel to the shuttle in the courtroom, so that the tribunal is aware of these events. Karibdis attempts to take control of the shuttle but is thwarted when Baltar knocks him down , and Starbuck is acquitted.

ANALYSIS: 'Murder on the *Rising Star*' is one of the most banal episodes of the series, as contrasted with the entertainingly-bad nature of earlier poor episodes. However, it can be partly forgiven due to the rushed nature of its writing.

TEN LITTLE WARRIORS: WRITING AND PRODUCTION
'Murder on the *Rising Star*' was written by Jim Carlson and Terence McDonnell under serious time pressure, exacerbated by the fact that, according to Carlson in an interview with Susan J Paxton, they had sent several story ideas to Glen Larson and Larson took his time getting back to them over which idea he

wanted them to develop. He then remembers a marathon thirty-six hour writing session to get the story out by the next day. McDonnell, in another interview with Paxton, recalls 'we were told on a Wednesday to write that particular script, we didn't even have the story worked out, and it had to be in mimeo[graphics] at 7 o'clock on Friday morning, and we stayed at the office and wrote all Wednesday night, all Thursday, all Thursday night, and Friday morning'. Regarding the fact that Baltar is referred to in this story, but nowhere else in the series, as 'Commander Baltar', McDonnell has said that this is a mistake, and commented that if they had been able to rely on a series 'bible', it would have made it easier to avoid inconsistencies (the 2 October 1978 terminology document is certainly not a comprehensive one). However, it does actually make sense, as the person addressing Baltar as such is Karibdis, who was Baltar's pilot.

This story is also one which, as noted in the review for 'Fire in Space', had to have a 'story by' credit for Michael Sloan, due to it having strong similarities to a storyline in Sloan's original version of 'Fire in Space' (the 16 January 1979 draft, strangely, credits the whole script to Sloan, but by the 17th the credit has changed to Bellisario, McDonnell and Carlson, with a 'story by' credit for Sloan). In defence of McDonnell and Carlson, however, this idea is a staple of many television programmes: one of the series' heroes is accused of having committed the crime (even though the audience knows he isn't capable of such a deed) and the prosecution's case is seemingly watertight, but at the eleventh hour information is discovered which links another person to the crime and exonerates the hero.

The problem with this story is less the generic nature of the plot, however, but that, although *Battlestar Galactica* is a fairly continuity-heavy series, we now suddenly meet characters and hear backstories which have never even been hinted at before. Although we have been following Starbuck's friendships, romances and enmities over the eleven previous stories, we are suddenly introduced to an arch-rival who he's known since the Academy, and who has been at his throat constantly over everything from gambling to Triad to women, and yet we have never heard Starbuck or any of his friends so much as mention this man before. Similarly, we learn that Baltar had an assistant, Karibdis, who performed an act of treachery every bit as extreme as Baltar's (sabotaging the defence computers on Caprica), and yet nobody seems to have been looking for him, reviling his name, or even mentioning him before. All of this unfortunately gives the episode a rather contrived air.

While the 17 January 1979 draft is quite close to the final version, give or take a couple of deleted scenes and changes in terminology, the 16 January draft has a very different ending. In this draft, Apollo thinks first of checking the computer, on the assumption that, of the three men, only Karibdis' new identity would be recorded there, but finds that all three are recorded. He asks Boomer to continue to search the computer for anomalies, and Boomer learns that both Ortega and Pallon logged into the computer at the same time, suggesting Pallon's guilt. Apollo then asks Boomer to look for a photograph on file of Baltar with one of the three men, which will prove which one was Karibdis; Boomer appears to do so, arriving in court and showing the tribunal a photograph purporting to be of Baltar with his pilot, and Pallon attempts to run, and, upon capture, admits he killed Ortega. We then learn that in fact Boomer had not found such a photograph, and was bluffing, but the tactic has worked. In both early drafts, Chella is not an administrator, but was 'serving brig time' when the attack on the Colonies came, consequently was not given priority to board a rescue ship, and bribed Ortega for this reason. Both of the early drafts also contain an extra scene, opening Act Three, in which Adama accuses Solon of trying to play the trial out on television and it becomes clear that Solon had planned to get Adama, who he knows to be sympathetic to Starbuck, to withdraw from the tribunal by questioning his impartiality during his interview – a tactic which plainly fails, as Adama is on the tribunal in all versions. In both drafts, all three suspects discover Ortega's body, rather than just Chella, but significantly, Pallon is the one who points to the corpse.

On the production front, McDonnell and Carlson have said that they wrote the role of Solon with Brock Peters specifically in mind, having worked with him on an episode of *The Six Million Dollar Man*. The shuttlecraft interior can also be spotted, in redressed form, in the *Buck Rogers* episode 'Planet of the Amazon Women'. Laurette Spang sports a new, and very flattering, haircut from this episode onwards. The three 'suspect' characters are all clad in identical sets of black vinyl or leather boots, which means that, in theory, we should not be able to tell which set of boots is the one returning to the shuttle after Apollo docks; unfortunately, in practice, the trouser fabric above the boots keeps getting into the shot, meaning that, since their trousers are all different, the sharp-eyed can figure out who Karibdis is before Apollo takes off for the prison barge.

This is also the episode with the famous 'wedgie' incident, where, in the final sequence, as Hatch and Benedict prepare to go out onto the Triad court, Anne Lockhart grabs the back of Hatch's Triad shorts and pulls sharply upwards; although it's said that Laurette Spang did the same to Benedict, this is not supported by the surviving outtake footage. In some of the shots which made it into the finished episode, Lockhart is visibly trying to suppress a case of the giggles, which works within the story, but takes on an added meaning when you know the outside context.

A STUDY IN SCARLET: THE NARRATIVE ITSELF

In fairness to the story, it does have good points. This is another episode where Boomer gets to take the role of Apollo's sidekick (due to Starbuck being in prison), which is again fun to watch, and we also see another black actor, Brock Peters, playing a character in a position of power (Opposer Solon). Although the character doesn't get to do much, what he does, he does well, coming across as a tough but fair lawyer. He argues his case, but accepts Apollo's evidence, and, although he paints his opponents negatively in the interview, he is a lawyer who thinks he is going to win the case. Starbuck mentions knowing him socially, and he nobly does not rise to the bait when Starbuck adds that he does not want to know him professionally. Adama's opening speech, which speculates that *Galactica*'s arrival on Earth might induce culture shock should the people of Earth prove more primitive than the Colonials, both recalls 'War of the Gods' and looks forward to the premise of *Galactica 1980*. Finally, Cassiopea comes across as a very strong and resourceful woman throughout the story, and she and Starbuck finally confess their love for each other.

Unfortunately, the episode contains a number of problematic elements. Why, for instance, are so many people on the prison barge (according to Baltar) out to kill Starbuck? He wasn't involved with law enforcement, but was simply a warrior. It is possible that his gambling habit has got out of hand and he is now having trouble with the local equivalent of the Mafia, but if that were the case, we would surely have seen some indication. It is true that celebrities in prison can get unwanted attention, but this does not generally involve murderous vendettas. There is also the question of why there is no comeback for Starbuck's prison-break; he should at least be charged with attempting escape from prison, assault, hostage-taking, threat and putting two individuals in fear for their lives, but none of that seems to be mentioned again (is Adama pulling strings on his behalf?). Starbuck's defence team only have ten centares (which appears to be equivalent to ten hours) to prepare their case, which seems an unfeasibly short amount of time.

The murder plot also contains nonsensical elements. Chella/Riftis' story about how he feels guilty because, since he got on the *Rising Star* (which, at the time of the holocaust, was only carrying children and nursery attendants) through bribing a warrior, a child had to stay behind, and that he still thinks of the child, is ridiculously melodramatic (and also, since the number of passengers on a spacecraft would have been an issue of weight, two children at least would have had to remain, and probably pretty fat ones at that). Ortega's wingman Barton says that Ortega said that, of the possibility that someone might kill him, 'only one person in the Fleet has nerve enough to try … Karibdis', which begs the question of why, if he knew Karibdis was a danger to him, he continued to blackmail him, rather than trying to kill him before he did anything fatal (especially when you consider that Karibdis is working as a waiter and thus not making a great deal of money, unlike Chella, who is a Pyramid dealer). Karibdis is at one point said to have been responsible for 'nearly a million' deaths on Caprica (which would make it a rather small society), and later, for 'millions' of deaths there (the 16 January draft also cites the figure 'hundreds of thousands'). It also raises the issue of why, if only Caprica's defence computers were sabotaged, the other planets also were overwhelmed (was there a traitor on every planet? If so, why has nobody remarked on it thus far? Or did none of the other planets have defence computers?). There is also the question of how it is that the Fleet personnel don't know Karibdis' name, or what he looks like, but somehow they do know his codename ('Proteus'), and also of how anyone found out about the nature of his involvement in the destruction of the Colonies without also learning of his real identity. We again get another computer with a CORA-like girly voice, the Fleet Personnel Computer, though this one is at least less ditzy.

Finally, it is worth noting that the denouement as screened does not in fact exonerate Starbuck of Ortega's murder, as the bulk of the evidence is still against him, and Karibdis' entire 'confession' consists of him saying 'terminating Ortega was easy', which doesn't necessarily mean he did it (it could even mean that he didn't have to do anything, just left it to Starbuck, where the 17 January draft has the line as 'killing Ortega was like swatting a buzzer', making Karibdis' guilt explicit), and he is largely convicted based on his previous reputation and his attempted murder of Apollo and Baltar. Whatever the Colonials may think, the jury is thus still out on Starbuck's innocence.

DEATH IN THE AFTERNOON: CHARACTER AND WORLDBUILDING

The episode develops the series' central characters. Athena now appears to have accepted that Starbuck's primary relationship is with Cassiopea, and doesn't seem to be exhibiting any more jealousy. Apollo studied law ('the codes') at the Academy, but didn't graduate in it. Adama is clearly not a sports fan, where Tigh is, given that Tigh is visibly enthusiastic about the Triad game and suggests that they go to watch it in the arena, where Adama, though his son is playing, is less enthusiastic about the prospect, and even seems unsure what the score is. Baltar appears to have settled down on the prison barge, in that he is no longer a frightened man on the back foot, but trying to figure out a way of escaping; if people are inclined to kill celebrity prisoners, then Baltar surely must be under some kind of special security protection, since a lot more people would have grounds for trying to kill him than Starbuck. Two out of the three suspects appear in the first scene (Elias and Karibdis, the former of whom is picking up empty glasses and the latter of whom serves Tigh and Adama their drinks), in a clever bit of foreshadowing which is only apparent on second viewing.

We also learn more about Colonial culture. The Triad game we see here is much rougher than the earlier ones, indicating that it can be a serious contact sport. The legal system is very much like the modern American one, though it seems any person can act as defence lawyer ('protector') in a criminal case without prior qualifications or even official sanction. We have a tantalising hint that the military are becoming more powerful in the Fleet in that it is said that Adama's mere presence on the tribunal could influence it in Starbuck's favour; since at this point in the story Starbuck looks guilty as hell, the implication is that the military could, through Adama, pull strings to keep him out of trouble. As in the previous episode, we see Colonial television; there is only one channel, Inter-Fleet Broadcasting (first mentioned in 'The Man with Nine Lives'), and it seems to broadcast interviews, news programmes and sports (presumably, what they are able to achieve on their present limited resources). It also seems that court cases are openly discussed on television by the participants; Opposer Solon's interview would, by modern Western standards, be seen as prejudging the trial's outcome, but not only does nobody complain, Starbuck's insistence to the guards that he wants to see the televised discussion of his case suggests this is a routine practice.

THE ORIENT EXPRESSIVE: CLASSICAL AND OUTSIDE REFERENCES

The story also contains more classical allusions. Solon is named after the famous Athenian archon, whose name has passed into English as a euphemism for politician, thus implying wisdom and political ability on his part. Karibdis' name is a misspelled version of that of the Greek monster Charybdis; since one can only draw the most tenuous connections between the man and the monster, this is again probably a matter of randomly selecting names. His codename, Proteus, has more relevance, being that of the old man of the sea who could change his shape (as well as being the name of the asteroid in 'The Long Patrol'). Ortega may be a reference to Jose Ortega y Gasset, the Spanish philosopher who argued that ordinary people are incapable of self-government; however, considering that conservatives of the 1970s might have approved of his message, it is surprising that his name is given to such an unsympathetic character, and one who is in no way a philosopher. Finally, classicists might well wonder if Zed, the television announcer, is any relation to Omega, the bridge officer.

'Murder on the *Rising Star*' contributes to the *Battlestar Galactica* mythos. However, the fairly predictable plot, plus the numerous problems, make it a story with more points against it than in its favour.

13 • GREETINGS FROM EARTH (PARTS ONE AND TWO)

US TRANSMISSION: 25 February 1979
WRITER: Glen A Larson
DIRECTOR: Rod Holcomb[18]
CREDITED CAST: Randolph Mantooth (Michael); Kelly Harmon (Sarah); Murray Matheson (Geller); Lesley Woods (Aggie Moreland); Frank Marth (Josh Moreland); Curt Lowens (Krebbs); Lloyd Bochner (Commandant Leiter); Bobby Van (Hector); Ray Bolger (Vector); Gary Vinson (Doyle); Ron Kelly (Security Officer [Reece]); Alex Rodine (Lanceman); Lester Fletcher (Donner); Michele Carol Larson (Charity); Gillian Greene (Melanie); G Eric Larson (Todd); Kimberly Woodward (Loma); David G Larson (Baby Walker); Donald Mantooth (Med Technician)
KNOWN UNCREDITED CAST: Paul LeClair (Guard)

SYNOPSIS: The *Galactica* encounters a shuttle containing two adults and four children in suspended animation, and brings them aboard. A battle of wills ensues between Adama, who is concerned about the dangers of interfering with the sleepers, and the Council of the Twelve, led by Sire Geller, who wish them to be revived. One adult, Michael, is woken, but cannot live normally in *Galactica*'s atmospheric pressure. The sleepers are, it transpires, from a divided society called Terra; they are refugees from the planet Lunar Seven, fleeing the totalitarian Eastern Alliance, and are planning to build a new life on the planet Paradeen. The warriors resolve to send the ship on its way, engaging in various subterfuges to this end until it is eventually dispatched with Apollo, Starbuck and Cassiopea as escorts. On Paradeen, Michael, his companion Sarah and their respective children try to build a new life, while the *Galactica* crew try to find clues to the way to Earth. Starbuck explores a nearby deserted city, but becomes lost in its archives and must be rescued by the others. When the crew of an Eastern Alliance warship, led by Commandant Leiter, take advantage of their absence to attack and take Sarah prisoner, Apollo and Starbuck, with the help of Michael and their new neighbours the Morelands, retaliate, capturing the Alliance members and taking them back to the *Galactica*.

ANALYSIS: 'Greetings from Earth' does not have a particularly bad premise, if a little derivative, but, as some reviewers have pointed out, the execution views like a dry run for *Galactica 1980*, full of gratuitous interchangeable children

---

18 Some sources credit Ahmet Lateef/Ahmer Lateaf, however, Rod Holcomb has stated in an interview with Marcel Damen that this is incorrect, and he has no idea who Lateef is.

147

(three of whom would actually go on to appear in the latter series), pointless infodumps, and a story which only gets sillier as it goes on.

FAREWELL TO EARTH: PRODUCTION AND TRANSMISSION

Unusually for *Battlestar Galactica*, 'Greetings from Earth' was screened not as a two-part story but as a complete telemovie, starting at 7pm – which meant that it had to adhere to designated regulations about children's programming, including a requirement for educational content and controls on the amount (and kind) of screened violence, explaining the story's slow, information-heavy first half and general lack of action. The story is far too long; while the first hour is better than the second, even it feels dragged-out, with the same facts reiterated several times, and Michael spending most of the episode declaiming that he can't trust the Colonials before experiencing a sudden change of heart at the crucial moment.

The Paradeen deserted city sequences were filmed at the Expo '67 site in Montreal (the first, but definitely not the last, time that Canada would double for an alien location in *Battlestar Galactica*), which can still be visited. Michael and Sarah's ship looks like a futuristic version of the space shuttle (and indeed is described in all draft scripts as 'a simple shuttle ship, circa 1980-2000') both the model and full-size mockup were redressed and repainted props from the *Buck Rogers* pilot, and, returning the compliment, the hovercraft (also variously referred to in the script as a 'hovercar' and 'shuttle'), appears, with a blue paint-job, in the *Buck Rogers* episode 'Unchained Woman' (which also saw the reuse of the six-sided Pyramid cards), while Leiter's uniform reappears in the episode 'Planet of the Amazon Women'. Within the series, the decompression tubes are recycled props from 'Lost Planet of the Gods' (where they were cryo tubes), and the guard, played by Paul LeClair, whom Starbuck holds hostage in 'Murder on the *Rising Star*,' reappears in the background. Apollo's weapon is once again beamless, as earlier in the series.

The hovercraft seen in the story appear to have been particularly unpredictable. The sequence where Apollo shouts 'Vector, where'd you learn to drive?' as Vector careens the hovercraft into boxes and barrels appears to be an overdub to cover an accident, as Hatch's onscreen reaction suggests he wasn't expecting the collision, his lip movements don't match the statement (he seems to be saying something along the lines of 'watch out!'), and the outtakes suggest the travel machines weren't easy to control – particularly one for the 'hit it, Hector' scene, in which Bobby Van drives off, nearly runs over Richard Hatch (who exclaims 'Jesus Christ!' as he leaps out of the way), and audibly hits something with the machine off camera.

One of the 'name' guest stars of the episode was Randolph Mantooth, who had a leading role on *Emergency*; his brother Donald Mantooth, who was also Laurette Spang's boyfriend at the time, appears as a medtech. The other two guest stars are Bobby Van and Ray Bolger, the latter listed as 'special guest star'. Both are vaudeville performers of long standing, but Bolger is of particular note for having played the Scarecrow in the 1939 film version of *The Wizard of Oz* (explaining, perhaps, why the Hector and Vector makeup includes Scarecrow-like gold noses and arched eyebrows), and Bobby Van, while perhaps less of a well-known name, appeared in the 1953 film version of *Kiss Me Kate*. According to Rod Holcomb, Van complained of headaches during filming, and not long thereafter died of a brain aneurism. The child performers all have connections with the series, with Gillian Greene being the daughter of Lorne Greene, and Michelle (here credited as Michele Carol), G Eric and David G Larson all being children of Glen Larson. This is also the last appearance of Athena and Boxey in the original series.

Once again, draft scripts and a number of cut scenes exist for this episode. The first draft, dated 26 January 1979, and another dated 29 January are both only a single hour long. Boxey and Muffit are completely absent from both, and Sire Geller does not appear in the first draft (which is singularly uneventful, suggesting that the Geller subplot was added to provide some much-needed dramatic tension). There are only five refugees in the earliest drafts, and Michael is said to be 23 or 24, while Sarah is seventeen; the younger children are her siblings. Doctor Wilker, in the earliest draft, is somewhat out of character, whinging nervously about the resuscitation project and going to the lounge for a drink to steady himself; by 29 January he is once again the psychopath we all know and love. Hector and Vector are considerably more violent towards each other, with Hector shooting Vector's arm off at one point. In the first draft, the shuttle is accompanied by Apollo, Cassiopea, Sheba and Boomer, and in the second, Starbuck has replaced Sheba; in both, Hector and Vector, who are not yet designated as father and son, assume the newcomers to be the children, grown up through an accident with the slumber chambers; as in the final version, they believe Starbuck, with his long hair, to be Charity, calling him 'a beautiful big girl', but apparently realise their mistake when they see that Boomer is black. The first draft contains a marauding race of dwarves on Paradeen, called Banji's or Benji's (sic), who are the main antagonists, and Sarah and Michael's new neighbours, learning that none of the men is the father of the children and Sarah is unmarried, assume them to be setting up some kind of free-love commune, with one saying 'this may be the last stop before Hell, but if that's the kind of place you kids are thinking of starting …

you didn't go far enough'.

The most significant change, however, is that Sarah and Michael's origin planet is explicitly stated to be Earth, not Terra, in the earliest drafts; Lunar Seven is even said to be out beyond Jupiter in the first draft (the second changes it to 'beyond Callais'), Michael makes a reference to Adam and Eve which goes over Apollo's head, and Hector and Vector have a Smith and Wesson gun. The Eastern Alliance are not mentioned, but rather, there is said to be war between factions on Earth which has spilled out into the colonies, with Michael and Sarah fleeing when they discovered Lunar Seven was being sabotaged from within. There are said to be caste-like differences between farmers and technologists on Lunar Seven, and Sarah, as the child of technologists, considering Michael, a farmer, as not worthy of her. The first draft ends on a cliffhanger as a group of Benji's kidnap Sarah's siblings; the second ends with Boomer and Cassiopea staying behind to help the group settle in on Paradeen, and the rest of the Fleet going on to Lunar Seven.

While the 9 February 1979 draft script is much closer to the finished version, it does contain some interesting insights. There appear to be a few late additions to the story, such as Apollo's line to Boxey, 'you're going to get it', and Boxey's cheeky smile in return, or Hector hitting the dashboard of the machine in response to the line 'hit it, Hector'. Michael's 'silver suit' is scripted, and, inexplicably, Hector's face is said to 'flush' at one point. Boomer's rank is incorrectly given as 'flight sergeant' in the 9 February script (which is, interestingly, the rank he is given in the 27 February 1978 draft of 'Saga of a Star World'), but corrected to 'Lieutenant' by the final. On the other hand, Jolly is also described in the script, as per 'Lost Planet of the Gods', as a 'flight sergeant' but is a 'Lieutenant' in the final, suggesting that he has been promoted. Michael's line 'what do you mean, we're all human', continues in the draft script '... you mean there's someone out there who isn't?' evoking the spectre of the absent Cylons as well as indicating that the Terrans have never met any aliens. Most of the cut material is redundant dialogue, but there is an interesting deleted scene where Adama and Tigh discuss whether it would be proper to have a member of the Council of the Twelve present when they meet what they believe to be a shuttle from Earth, and Adama effectively says that he would like to keep the whole operation strictly in military hands. One extensive cut from part two is a long scene where Adama explains atmospheric pressure to Boxey, which was no doubt deleted because it is rather tedious, and, if the two episodes are edited together, redundant (given that the concept was thoroughly explained in part one), as well as because neither Greene nor Hathaway are giving particularly good performances. Finally, in an amusing outtake of the confrontation between Apollo and Starbuck and the Civilian Security officers, Dirk Benedict ad-libs 'get on your motorcycles and get out of here', a quote from *The Wild One* (1953).

EARTH DEFENCE DIRECTORATE: GOOD AND BAD PARTS OF 'GREETINGS FROM EARTH'

To be fair to it, 'Greetings from Earth' is not unmitigatedly bad. The our-heroes-picking-up-space-travellers-in-suspension premise is a tried and true space-opera motif, best known from the *Star Trek* episode 'Space Seed', but appearing in quite a few telefantasy programmes of the 1970s. The family with children roaming around space and being pulled off course is also slightly *Lost in Space*, complete with comedy robots and silver spacesuits. It's also nice to see another blended family appearing in the series, and generally being accepted as a normal family by the other characters.

While the abovementioned 7pm start did result in more tedious factual exposition, it did also mean that the science in this serial is actually more accurate than usual: the idea of people raised in a low-pressure atmosphere having trouble breathing at a higher pressure, and people from a high-pressure environment having less trouble breathing in a low-pressure one (provided they have oxygen to hand) is scientifically documented, and the idea of first contact bringing plague is well-referenced in the colonial history of Earth (as well as being a direct steal from 'Lost Planet of the Gods').

The sequence where the family are smuggled off the *Galactica* and Boomer and Jolly cover for the deception is hilarious, with Boomer exclaiming 'Jolly, you forgot the kids!' when Reese, the leader of the Civilian Security forces, uncovers the decompression chambers and discovers that they do not, in fact, contain the children as he was told; later, when Geller turns up and demands to know who is in charge, Reese, not wanting to relinquish his authority, exclaims 'I am!' without thinking the implications through, and ultimately winds up having to support Boomer and Jolly's story about the ship being jettisoned for fear of contamination out of sheer self-preservation. The Leiter/Starbuck exchange 'We are the most advanced military force in the Galaxy!' 'Oh, I believe it, that's what's so encouraging', is also a great line.

Unfortunately, leaving aside the superficiality of the plot, there are also some problems and discontinuities. In part one, 'Terra' is stated by Adama to be a Gemonese word for Earth, but by part two, Apollo says it is 'a word used by an ancient race' to mean Earth, though the Gemons don't seem any more ancient than anyone else in the system (though it is interesting that once again the Gemons are associated with mysticism). Another discontinuity occurs due to the fact that what is a complete scene in the draft is cut into two and part of it placed earlier, meaning that one of the destroyer's crew, Donner, says that the homing signals have stopped before the device is actually switched off in the episode. Sarah and Michael's families also sleep fully clothed and under fur, suggesting that they must reek. Ironically, also, the Colonials have attracted unwanted attention to the very people they wish to protect, as Leiter is not particularly interested in the refugees' flight so much as he is in the Vipers; also, by delaying their journey, the Colonials cause Sarah and Michael's ship to be picked up by the destroyer, and because the unexpected circumstances cause Hector and Vector to not switch off the homing device immediately, they allow Leiter to track them down.

COLONIAL CONCERNS: CONTINUITY, WORLDBUILDING AND POLITICS

This episode sees the portrayal of politicians finally cross the line into unbelievable territory. It is true that politicians can be silly, impulsive and ignorant, as portrayed here, and the idea of politicians dismissing scientific and military advice and paying the price for it has a real-life basis (for instance British politicians dismissing well-substantiated warnings about bovine spongiform encephalitis out of fear of losing votes and/or alienating the farming lobby), and the idea that Sire Geller would suddenly change his tune when Adama tells him the ship is a threat, rings true. However, it is difficult to believe that politicians would do something quite so stupid as demand the opening of an unknown ship whose inhabitants may bear bacteria, viruses or other threats, as it would be impossible for them to deny that they were responsible should plague subsequently break out on the ship. Sire Geller is yet another naïve and cantankerous Englishman (and is specified as having an English accent in the script), with a name suggesting a connection to Sire Uri. The portrayal of politicians thus ignores the fact that they generally have a good sense of self-preservation.

It is, however, worth pointing out that the Fleet is still not under martial law; a vote by the Council of the Twelve (as they are called here) overrules Adama, and the military must step aside when this happens. However, Adama does ensure that he regains control of the shuttle through declaring its inhabitants to be hostile and a threat, thus putting them in military jurisdiction and giving him effective carte blanche over their fate.

We also hear more statements of Colonial philosophy. When Adama says 'Doctor Salik has just reaffirmed that we are a race worth saving', this evokes the repeated idea of people having to prove that they are worthy to a higher power, and of humanity having bad and good aspects. The ending of part one and beginning of part two present us with the idea that mutiny is acceptable, provided it is against an immoral order. There may seem to be a discontinuity between the fact that Apollo says initially 'the lives of those six people do not belong to us', but later accuses Michael of 'trading six lives for six thousand', but in fact, this expresses the tension between the individual and society, and the idea that, while individuals must make sacrifices for the good of society, it is ultimately up to the individual whether or not to make that sacrifice, and no one should constrain them to do so. Apollo also remarks that 'the quality of a civilisation is determined by the values placed between extremes', criticising Starbuck for seeing everything in absolute terms. In two cut lines, Apollo and Starbuck, encountering the shuttle, speculate that the inhabitants might not have met anybody from beyond their planet before and might be hostile as a result, referencing the culture shock idea mentioned in 'Murder on the *Rising Star*'. A 'might makes right' theme is also articulated, with Apollo shooting barrels on the ranch to demonstrate why he should be in charge, and Starbuck touting their military superiority over the Alliance, continuing the idea that people gravitate towards the strongest force.

On the character front, Doctors Wilker and Salik see a welcome return, squaring off on opposite sides of the issue of reviving the humans on the shuttle: Salik refuses to do so on the moral grounds that he has a medical responsibility to the people, whoever they may be, but Wilker does, it seems, view them as (in Adama's phrase), 'human testing drones', high-handedly informing the warriors that the sleepers' fate is 'out of their hands'. Boxey, in his brief final appearance, is still well-characterised, innocently repeating his father's remarks, using his visit to see the shuttle's inhabitants as a way of boosting his status among his classmates, and trying to wriggle out of detention through sheer charm, which unfortunately shows up the characterisation of Sarah and Michael's virtually interchangeable children (though, to be fair, they are not played by professional child actors as Boxey is). While Boomer has less to do in this story than the previous two episodes, he does figure out quite quickly that Apollo and Starbuck are up to something in the scene where they smuggle Michael and Sarah back on to the ship.

In terms of the Fleet in general, Security have developed over the series from private security guards stationed on luxury liners, as seen in 'Saga of a Star World', to an official civilian police force, with jurisdiction over civilians only, who report to the Council, as seen here, which makes logical sense, as there would be a need for such a force and trained security professionals would be the obvious choice for the role. A Civilian Security member is referred to as a 'blackshirt', with obvious connotations of fascism for viewers, and one cut line from the draft script has Starbuck remarking 'I love sticking it to Civilian

Security ... They're mostly washed-out warriors who love to stick it to us'. We are also given at least an approximate survivor number in this story, when Apollo states that there are six thousand people on the Fleet.

We also receive an answer to the lingering question of where the other human groups that the Fleet has encountered come from, why the Colonials are not surprised to see them, and why they do not settle down on one of these human-inhabited planets, in the sequence where Apollo, Starbuck, Sheba and Boomer have a drink together. As Boomer and Starbuck note, up until now everyone they have encountered is of Kobollian origin, either from the original exodus from Kobol or else secondary expansion from the Twelve Colonies, they have been kept from settling by the fact that their forces are too weak to allow them to successfully fight off the Cylons, hence their quest for Earth and the lost Thirteenth Tribe (who, they hope, might help them withstand this force), and the shuttle is the first evidence of human culture that is distinct from this. Michael, Sarah and Leiter, unlike all the other humans we have encountered, do not understand words like 'centon' or 'centare', and measure distance in kilometres (although, for some unexplained reason, they and the Colonials appear to speak a mutually intelligible language). The same scene has a moment of postmodern awareness when Starbuck says to Apollo 'I'm the hotheaded, impulsive one', as if the character is aware of the archetype he represents.

More problematically, the series seems to be falling into a formula whereby Apollo is never wrong, in that even his hunches turn out to be correct; while this isn't true everywhere, it does seem to be rapidly developing into the series' default mode. The scenes with Athena teaching the children are fairly unbelievable: none of the children are fidgeting, whispering, or doing any of the other things children normally do in classrooms, and the fact that she leaves a classroom full of under-twelves unsupervised for several minutes is criminally irresponsible, as is the fact that she then goes on to discuss with Apollo the very issues that she was concerned about him mentioning in front of the children despite the fact that Boxey is standing there and listening to them. Athena's lack of genuine shock at Boxey's use of the word 'frack' (which does not appear in the 9 February 1979 draft script) suggests either that it's a much milder expletive in the original series than it will be in the reimagined one, or else is another example of her dubious classroom manner.

Finally, we learn a few more details about life aboard the Fleet. Viper pilots can actually sleep in their ships with an autopilot enabled, a mode called 'sleep period' which is apparently used for long flights (this first appeared in a sequence at the start of 'The Living Legend' which was omitted by the 2

November 1978 draft), and the word 'metrics' is used as a unit of distance. While a reference to 'a year' in the draft script is changed to 'a yahren' in the final, suggesting that the producer views 'year' and 'yahren' as approximately equivalent, a cut line from the 9 February 1979 draft script also has Vector stating that a centon is roughly equivalent to a minute, and a sectar of an hour, though adding that where the Terrans divide their time into sixths, the Colonials divide theirs into tenths, suggesting that there may be cumulative differences between the measurements. The draft script has Apollo giving a 'universal sign of peace' to the shuttle, which appears to involve flashing his outboard wing, 'giving a star filter effect', in red, white, and red in succession. The schoolroom sequence is described in the 9 February 1979 script as taking place in the '*Galactica* School Bay', and the children to be sitting at tables normally used for training Viper pilots, which is a nice touch, suggesting the adaptation of pre-existing systems to fit the new, post-holocaust case.

THE REIGN OF TERRA: THE INTRODUCTION OF THE TERRAN STORYLINE

Beginning with this story and continuing through 'Baltar's Escape' and 'Experiment in Terra', the series abandons the Cylons for the most part in favour of a storyline focusing around the planet Terra and its outposts. In a contemporary interview, Don Bellisario asserted that he felt this was a good idea, but whether he was right is rather more questionable with hindsight.

Terran politics are a deeply unsubtle metaphor for Cold War Earth. All of the Western characters who we encounter here are the good guys (although Sarah, Michael and the children were born on Lunar Seven, they appear, from their dialogue, to be Westerners; the implication is that Lunar Seven was taken over by the Eastern Alliance), where the Eastern Alliance are portrayed as a kind of cross between Soviets and Nazis, with names like Leiter (German for 'leader') and Krebbs (which is a misspelling of the German for 'crab' or 'cancer'), and officers who sport what look like cod-SS uniforms (the draft describes Leiter's uniform as 'Prussian-looking') on a spaceship which has visibly been modelled on a Nazi U-boat, blatantly deploying clichés of evil. The idea of bombs which destroy people but leave the buildings intact is a staple of Cold War science fiction, reflecting fears that the governments involved consider the buildings more important. In the scripts from 29 January onwards, the shuttle is described as 'bearing a combination of strangely familiar flags, including a flag similar to the American flag, yet with a UN variation on the dark blue field'. Michael swears 'what in the name of God', suggesting that some Terrans, at least, are monotheistic, and use swear words more familiar to us than the Colonials' vocabulary. Sarah's anti-technology mindset, however,

155

is somewhat in keeping with the cut reference in 'Lost Planet of the Gods' to the people of Kobol destroying their technology as part of their colonial dispersion, suggesting that there is some sort of connection between the two.

Even the sympathetic Terran characters do little to endear themselves to the audience. Sarah is a hypocrite, whinging about hating technology while not seeming too upset about the fact that she escaped on a spaceship wearing machine-made clothes and has android servants at her new home; in a cut sequence, when Michael points out to her that her own father was a scientist, she rationalises the discrepancy by saying that he only became one in order to find a place to live for his children (although she seems somewhat conflicted over this; in a sequence which survived to the final version, she also berates her father for it, and blames his death, for no good reason, on science). Moreover, she comes across as something of a bunny-boiler, stalking Apollo (who, shrewdly, sics Cassiopea on to Michael in order to cause him to be more desirable in Sarah's eyes) and smashing the Viper controls to ensure that he doesn't leave, which is understandable when the character is a seventeen-year-old girl, but not when she is a widow in her mid-twenties. The situation is actually not too far removed from 'The Lost Warrior' (note that 'Greetings from Earth' also employs a few Western tropes, with its ranch-like settlement, horses, and hostile neighbours who band together with the heroes when an outside force threatens everyone); unlike in the earlier story, however, Apollo does not mention the fact that he has a child and a (reasonably) serious relationship back on the *Galactica*. Apollo is something of a natural psychologist, though, and appears to be stringing Sarah along here in order to encourage her to help him, while at the same time gently pushing her to transfer her affections elsewhere, rather than rejecting her outright. Lunar Seven (which, despite the name, is described as a 'planet'), their place of origin, is a Terran colony world with a low-pressure atmosphere, meaning that the families cannot go on to Terra, but are confined to planets with similar atmospheres; however, it is unclear whether this is a natural phenomenon or because, like Paradeen, it was terraformed.

HECTOR INVECTIVE: IRRITATING ANDROIDS

The Terran storyline also introduces us to two of the most hated characters in *Battlestar Galactica*: Hector and Vector, two comedy dancing robots who aren't particularly funny. While Fred Astaire managed to refuse all but the briefest dancing sequence, Bobby Van and Ray Bolger wind up having to do an inexplicable and badly shoehorned-in vaudeville number in the middle of the show (this is designated simply as 'Hector and Vector dance and sing a small ballad' in the 9 February draft script, suggesting that the performance was worked out later with the pair, which Rod Holcomb confirms was the case; the 26 and 29 January draft scripts do not have this sequence, suggesting that the casting of Bolger and Van occurred sometime in early February). The actors all laugh quite gamely at the performance, but at the end of it one can briefly see what looks like Dirk Benedict physically forcing the small blonde girl to clap her hands together. If the standard of entertainment at the Royal Theatre on Terra is this bad, it is no wonder people want to escape. Behind-the-scenes footage suggests that the problem is with the script rather than the performers; when ad-libbing after errors, the two clown around in a saucy way which is much funnier than anything actually screened (Bolger, for instance, changing the line 'carry out Master Michael's order', which he had fluffed, to 'carry out Master Michael's daughter', the last word said in a lascivious voice), and, in the DVD documentary, Dirk Benedict diplomatically notes that the performers were very funny 'in real life'. Out-takes also suggest that even Van and Bolger weren't completely sure which of them was supposed to be Hector and which Vector.

There are nonetheless a few interesting points in the androids' portrayal. Their dialogue is actually quite savagely violent under the jokey tone, with Vector threatening to break his own son down into spare parts; they also lack the usual Asimovian telefantasy-robot prohibition against threatening or killing humans. Like Muffit and the Cylons, they seem to feel emotions, which unfortunately makes a mockery of Starbuck's remark that he'd like to replace politicians with robots like Hector on the grounds that they'd rule by logic (accusing politicians of 'passion, greed, jealousy ...'), since Hector isn't exactly a model of logical thought. The androids appear to have absorbed their masters' values, wanting females to interact with even though sexual drives are not likely to be an issue with them.

'Greetings from Earth', the last of the two-part stories, is thus not entirely without redeeming features, but unfortunately is for the most part a tedious and faintly ridiculous outing for the characters, which sets up a weak ongoing plot revolving around the planet Terra.

14 ● BALTAR'S ESCAPE

US TRANSMISSION DATE: Sunday 11 March 1979
WRITER: Donald Bellisario
DIRECTOR: Winrich Kolbe
CREDITED CAST: Ina Balin (Siress Tinia); Lloyd Bochner (Commandant Leiter); John Hoyt (Sire Domra); Robert Feero (Bora); Anthony De Longis (Taba); Lance LeGault (Maga); Bruce Wright (4th Guard); Ron Kelly (1st Guard [Reece]); Mitchell Reta (Control Operator); Paul Tinder (5th Guard); Paul LeClair (2nd Guard)

SYNOPSIS: The Council of Twelve, wearying of martial law, vote to end the emergency, and assign a Council advisor, Siress Tinia, to observe Adama. The Council orders the Eastern Alliance prisoners brought to the *Galactica*, to open negotiations with them. Meanwhile, Baltar plots an escape attempt with the Borellian Nomen and the Eastern Alliance prisoners, proposing that they hijack the shuttle intended to take the Alliance Enforcers to the *Galactica* and then flee in their ships to Lunar Seven. The plan succeeds, with Boomer, Sheba and a Council Security team being taken hostage. Baltar insists that the expedition proceed to *Galactica* in order to neutralise it and recover the Eastern Alliance destroyer. Adama suspects a trap, but Tinia blocks his efforts to increase security, and the Council are taken hostage. Baltar demands the return of his Cylon fighter and its crew as well as the destroyer within a centare, and Adama and Tinia offer themselves as hostages in exchange for another centare. Apollo and Starbuck discover that the Cylon crew have been dissected by Doctor Wilker. Although Wilker reassembles them, they can only function on a limited level, punching through a scanner when asked to press a button, which gives Apollo an idea. When their demands are met, the Enforcers and Nomen escape, but Baltar is trapped in his fighter when the reassembled Cylon punches through the console upon being ordered to take off. Apollo and Starbuck, hidden within the craft, take Baltar prisoner and prevent him from pressing a detonator which will blow up the shuttle containing the hostages. The Council vote to restore Adama's authority over the Fleet.

ANALYSIS: 'Baltar's Escape' is generally a good and pacy single-parter, with many points to recommend it. Its main problems are a fairly substantial continuity error regarding the governance of the Fleet, yet more silly portrayals of politicians, and the fairly obvious recycling of elements from 'Saga of a Star

World' (the Council decorating Adama to distract from the fact that they're pushing through a measure they know he'll oppose, much as Apollo was decorated under similar circumstances earlier, as well as the idea that Adama senses a trap where the Council sense none and 'unofficially' increases security against their wishes).

ESCAPE FROM REALITY: POLITICS ON THE FLEET

In this episode, it is stated as an explicit fact that the Fleet has been under martial law since the Cylon holocaust when Apollo says to Adama 'we're operating under martial law', and Starbuck adds 'the Fleet's been under your command since we fled the Colonies'. This is later echoed by Siress Tinia. Unfortunately, the events of 'Greetings from Earth' present an unresolvable continuity error. While, up until 'Greetings from Earth', one could perhaps consider that this is the case – even though Adama defers to the Council throughout, he is said to be in charge of it in 'War of the Gods' (although the fact that the Council can overrule him rather suggests that martial law has not, in fact, been declared) and he states in 'Baltar's Escape' that 'my warrior oath holds me responsible to the Council', and he may also be deferring to them as a political strategy, to maintain civilian support, or out of a moral and ethical belief that even martial law should not mean dictatorship. However, in 'Greetings from Earth', had the Fleet been under martial law, Adama could have overruled the Council on the subject of where and when to open the shuttle; he clearly felt strongly enough that the act would be dangerous to engage in subterfuges to get the shuttle under military control, but the very fact that he has to do so indicates that they are not under martial law. Indeed, the dialogue in 'Greetings from Earth' shows a clear differentiation between civilian and military spheres of influence. Furthermore, if it were not for the fact that martial law is said to have been declared soon after the destruction of the Colonies, there would still be no error, as it would just be assumed that martial law had been declared sometime between 'Greetings from Earth' and 'Baltar's Escape'. As it stands, however, it is a problem.

On first glance, also, the story reads as hypocritical. It takes a fairly broad swipe at opponents of might-makes-right policies: the Eastern Alliance are clearly villains, so the Council's suggestion that they should have been approached diplomatically strikes the viewer as ridiculous. Although Adama seemingly acknowledges that the military should defer to civilian interests and martial law should only be a temporary measure when he says 'when two of my best warriors forget their oath to obey the civil government, we've been under martial law too long', the rest of the episode is pro-military, with the politicians admitting at the end that their pacifist approach is incorrect and going meekly back under martial law. At the same time, however, the very reason the Eastern Alliance are shown to be wrong is because of their simplistic belief that the strong should dominate the weak, which appears to be the very line this episode is pushing. However, the unspoken point is that the *Galactica* warriors show compassion, where Leiter and his men do not; the Colonial system contains the provision that the Council can vote to terminate martial law, suggesting that strength unchecked is a bad thing. There is thus a logic to the story's philosophies of power, contrasting compassionate conservatism to totalitarianism.

The politicians continue their downward spiral in intelligence terms. They firstly dismiss a report on the events of 'Greetings from Earth' by announcing that they 'disagree' with it, secondly propose to make peace with the Eastern Alliance without first ascertaining whether this is possible or desirable, and thirdly refuse extra security on the landing bay after communications from the prison ship cease. While the third instance might be understandable as a move to try and distance the new civilian regime from the previous military one, and the first does ring true given the repeated instances, in the run-up to the second Iraq War, of governments ignoring intelligence which did not say what they wished to hear, the second is completely implausible, since, again, there is no politician who would walk cheerfully into an alliance without considering the costs and benefits to themselves. The Council are led by Sire Domra, yet another craven Englishman (are there no non-craven Englishmen in the Fleet? Indeed, are there any Englishmen in the Fleet at all who are not on the Council?), and the Council are constantly set up as antagonistic, with Starbuck saying of the hostage situation 'Baltar, Nomen and the Enforcers – at least we've got all our enemies in the same place', and Apollo replying 'Including the Council!' The fact that Adama draws parallels, in his diary, not only between the Eastern Alliance and the Cylons (who, of course, also are sometimes said to have an Alliance), but between the Council's behaviour towards the Alliance and their earlier attempt to make peace with the Cylons, flags up the fact that the Council do not learn from experience. Adama's passive-aggressive game with Tinia on the bridge, obeying the Council knowing full well that there is trouble brewing and that they will come crawling to him once the situation has got out of hand, is utterly predictable.

To be fair, it must be said that Tinia (described in the 2 February 1979 draft of the script as 'competent, intelligent and liberal') shows herself to be far cleverer than her position as a Quorum member would suggest. She figures out immediately that Tigh's request to leave the bridge means that he will go down to the landing bay to increase security unofficially, and, in later offering herself as a second hostage, she reveals that, under the right circumstances, she has a pretty shrewd grasp of military strategy (suggesting that Adama's turning up at the officer's club with her on his arm might be a genuine rapport rather than, as Tigh suggests, simply an attempt to wind him up). She does have an American accent, which might be taken, on this occasion, to imply that she's less corrupt than the usual round of craven Britons. However, it is also odd that, although little time has passed since 'Greetings from Earth', Sire Geller is neither present nor even mentioned; the draft script refers to Geller in Adama's opening monologue, but the character has become Domra by his first appearance, suggesting that the production team wanted the character to return, but discovered during writing that this was not possible.

ESCAPE FROM THE WORLD: TERRAN SOCIETY AND POLITICS

We also have more development in this episode of the Terran storyline. We learn that the Eastern Alliance's opposite number are called 'the Nationalists', and also the writing team are doing a clever job in stringing out as long as possible the question of whether Terra is Earth. Although it is technologically in advance of twentieth-century (or indeed twenty-first century) Earth, it is not known when, relative to Earth's timeline, the series takes place, so the question is ambiguous at this point.

Although Leiter is still very much a pantomime Nazi, he does get a better deal on the characterisation front in this episode. He goes in for wolf-pack metaphors and refers to his 'homeland', and embraces a philosophy that the universe is divided into the strong and the weak, and the strong should rule by right of destiny (conveniently glossing over the fact that the *Galactica* is stronger than anything that the Alliance has to offer, and thus that, by his logic, the Colonials should rule over his people, by rationalising that the Alliance will eventually defeat them, thus putting them in the realm of the weak). He is initially prepared to believe that Adama would, in fact, let them go in order to save the hostages' lives, and only believes otherwise when Maga explains the situation to him, suggesting that his passionate belief that his enemies are by definition 'weak' blinds him to the possibility that they may be more ruthless than he thinks.

BALTAR'S FAILURE TO ESCAPE: THE BALTAR AND NOMEN STORYLINE

The crux of the story is, as the title suggests, Baltar and the Nomen's attempt to escape from prison. In planning his jailbreak, Baltar is living up to previously seen character traits: now that a potentially more powerful force than the

Galactica is on the horizon, he will betray the *Galactica* and ally himself with them; learning little from his betrayal of the human race to the Cylons, he assumes that if he betrays the Fleet to the Alliance, they will welcome him with open arms. When Baltar proposes this plan, Maga remarks 'your record to date does not exactly inspire confidence', and Baltar retorts 'I had incompetent followers', which is, unfortunately, an excuse which implies that only stupid people will follow him.

Baltar's plan is somewhat flawed in its consideration of the people involved and their motivations. Leaving aside the question of why the escapees don't simply take over the prison barge and quietly fly it away, his justification for why the escapees have to go to the *Galactica* – to take useful hostages, and also because it must be disabled or else it will prevent them from escaping (although the fact that his Cylon fighter is on the *Galactica* also means that he can, if he needs to, abandon his collaborators and continue the escape attempt on his own) – overlooks the fact that they already have suitable hostages with Boomer, Sheba and the two security men, with more, if they want them, aboard the prison barge (guards, pilots, and prison personnel). He is also taking a risk in that, while he might assume that Adama would not object to imperilling the lives of a few hostages, even people he cares deeply about, to stop the escape, making the disabling of the *Galactica* a necessity, he is overlooking the fact that Adama might be having to defer to the Council over the situation (indeed, even under martial law, Adama might be reluctant to make himself unpopular with the civilians by deliberately engineering the deaths of their family members or friends, and killing Council Security members might just induce the Council to vote to end martial law). On the other hand, the hostage-taking strategy is flawed in and of itself, as, even with the entire Council as hostages, Baltar's allies believe that they will be attacked, because Baltar's reputation as a ruthless traitor suggests that he would not be above killing the hostages once the authorities have given in to their demands and they are safely under way, and it is only when Adama gives himself up as a hostage that the escape attempt can go ahead. Baltar's desire for revenge against Adama thus blinds him to the problems with his plan.

The Nomen, by contrast, come over quite well. Even in prison, they are intimidating, chasing two prisoners out of their seats in the mess hall (recalling their entrance into the bar in 'The Man with Nine Lives'). The scene where Maga outthinks both Baltar and Leiter by showing a shrewd understanding of Adama's mind is not only brilliant, but a nice subversion of the usual television drama cliché of the good guys setting up the bad guys by pretending to give in to their demands and the bad guys buying it hook line and sinker. The ability to induce temporary death at will is also a believable development for a human subspecies living in a hostile physical environment, much like opossums faking death to fool predators.

We also learn more about justice on the Colonial Fleet. It is implied that all prisoners rotate duties, so Baltar's working in the kitchen is not the privilege of a 'trusty'; however, it seems odd that the Colonial equivalent of public enemy number one is allowed to dish up food without any comment on the part of guards or prisoners (particularly since if, as stated in 'Murder on the *Rising Star*', Starbuck would be a target for hostility from other prisoners, Baltar must be even more so). Security generally seems lax on the prison barge, since Baltar and the Nomen can openly discuss their escape plans in the mess hall without arousing suspicion.

ESCAPE TO JUSTICE: CONTINUITY, CHARACTERISATION AND WORLDBUILDING.

This episode sees the development of various ongoing threads in the *Battlestar Galactica* universe. Hostilities continue between the civilian force, here called Council Security, and the military, as indicated by the scene in which Boomer and Sheba have an altercation with the security guards on the shuttle going to the prison barge. We see the welcome return of both the Nomen's laser-boles and the Cylons: having not seen the latter for three stories, it's good to have them return, in whatever form. The explanation for why the escapees are trying to get to Lunar Seven rather than Terra itself comes in Adama's opening monologue, when we learn that it is the nearest Terran outpost; shuttles are presumably not built for long-distance travel. The Star of Kobol is an award which has not been bestowed to a living individual for over a millennium, and Tinia echoes earlier assessments of Adama's character, even a few given by himself, when she accuses him of paranoia.

Regarding characterisation, Tigh gets another good deadpan-comedy sequence, from his sarcastic request of Tinia's permission to retire to the officer's club, to his casually letting it slip to Starbuck and Apollo what the situation on the landing bay is, knowing full well that they will investigate. Following the military structure, when Tigh is officially in command, even Adama, his superior officer, must obey without question. Reese returns, as does Wilker, who is revealed to have dissected two Cylons (which, when one realises that they could technically be considered sentient beings, has some rather suspect moral implications), and is nerdily excited about the idea of reprogramming them. Comparisons to Mengele are tempting, and yet this is the man who built Muffit.

On the production front, Anne Lockhart is not in the opening credits despite being in the episode (and Maren Jensen, Tony Swartz, Laurette Spang and Noah Hathaway, who aren't, are all credited); the credit sequence also alters the usual order of names, reversing Laurette Spang and Tony Swartz's positions. Paul LeClair's security guard also reappears in this episode, and the long-haired security guard on the shuttle, played by Bruce Wright, appears to be the same one who tried to break up Apollo's bachelor party in 'Lost Planet of the Gods', explaining his antagonistic attitude to warriors here (Wright is a regular bit-part actor on the series, whose *Galactica* roles also include Lomas in 'The Man with Nine Lives' and a German soldier who aids the SS officer in the *Galactica 1980* pilot 'Galactica Discovers Earth'). The 2 February 1979 draft of the script has it that Starbuck and Apollo were to dress in the Cylon armour; the version we have is rather better in that it subverts this well-known telefantasy cliché. The draft script also has a continuity reference to 'The Man with Nine Lives', when the Nomen retrieve their laser boles; Taba, who had been castigated by Maga for misusing his weapon, is reluctant to take his until Maga gives him permission, and then he assures him that he will not fail him again. Director Winrich ('Rick') Kolbe is a German who would go on to work extensively in the *Star Trek* franchise, directing, among others, the *Deep Space Nine* episode 'Blood Oath', featuring John Colicos as the Klingon warrior Kor. The prison barge is said to have a 'grid deck', which links back to references to the prison barge as a 'grid barge' in the later draft script for 'The Gun on Ice Planet Zero' and elsewhere. Lunar Seven is misspelled as 'Luna Seven' throughout the draft script, which survives in the computer transcript of Adama's monologue as transmitted. While it is not a continuity error, there is a certain amusement in learning that Colonial idiom for a toilet is 'turbo-flush', and the draft script, when referring to Tigh as 'red faced' after his encounter with Tinia, adds the encouraging notation 'do your best, Terry'.

Finally, the escape attempt is, actually, a partial success, in that the Nomen and Enforcers manage to flee in the destroyer, even if they are being tracked, and only Baltar, ironically, remains behind. It also, subversively, suggests that even villains can have their admirable traits, in that Baltar, the Nomen and the Eastern Alliance Enforcers can put aside their differences and work together for a common goal. Leiter even, at one point, remarks that he and Adama think in similar ways (although, of course, he is overlooking the compassion element discussed above). 'Baltar's Escape' is, overall, a reasonably enjoyable episode.

15 • EXPERIMENT IN TERRA

US TRANSMISSION DATE: Sunday 18 March 1979
WRITER: Glen A Larson
DIRECTOR: Rod Holcomb
CREDITED CAST: Melody Anderson (Brenda Maxwell); Peter D MacLean (President Arends); Edward Mulhare (John); Nehemiah Persoff (Eastern Alliance Leader); Logan Ramsey (Moore); Ken Swofford (General Maxwell); Sidney Clute (Stone); Kenneth Lynch (Dr Horning); Jordan Rhodes (Brace); John de Lancie (Officer); Russ Marin (Alliance Member); Milt Jamin (Alliance Leader)

SYNOPSIS: While on patrol, Apollo is brought aboard the Ship of Lights. Its representative, 'John', informs him that he must stop an all-out war on the planet Terra, by going there in the guise of a Terran warrior of the Nationalist political bloc, named Charlie Watts. Apollo makes contact with Charlie's girlfriend Brenda, but she is troubled by his strange behaviour and turns him over to the authorities. Brenda's father, General Maxwell, is dismayed. He opposes the President's pacifist policies, and Charlie would have been able to provide proof that the Eastern Alliance were taking over Lunar colonies. However, Maxwell and Brenda are also taken into custody due to Maxwell daring to question the President. Starbuck and Boomer identify Apollo's distress signal, and Boomer goes to inform the Fleet while Starbuck tracks Apollo to Terra, and, after a meeting with John, springs Apollo and his allies from prison. The leaders of the Eastern Alliance plan to attack when the President announces the formation of a peace treaty with them (incurring an automatic retaliation from the Nationalists' defence systems). Apollo, however, addresses the President and Precedium, warning them of the dangers of pacifism, and the *Galactica* arrives in time to prevent the missiles from reaching their targets. The Eastern Alliance sue for peace, and the *Galactica* returns to the Fleet to continue the search for Earth.

ANALYSIS: 'Experiment in Terra' is one story which really shows the definite dumbing-down of the series in its latter half, due to the lack of time to write the stories and to the decision to switch formats from a humans-versus-Cylons space Western to a humans-versus-other-humans political 'thriller' format. While 'Baltar's Escape' was hardly a pinnacle of television drama, 'Experiment in Terra' is like watching neoconservative paint dry.

The story, a fairly dull episode with plot holes you could drive a Colonial

Viper through, allegedly derives its title from the 1962 film *Experiment in Terror*, a psychological thriller which bears no resemblance whatsoever to the *Battlestar Galactica* episode. Like 'Greetings from Earth', the story foreshadows *Galactica 1980*, this time in the way it involves two young warriors running around an Earth-like planet, accompanied by a faintly annoying young woman who is alternately a help and a hindrance, engaging in a number of so-called comedy moments revolving around the warriors' lack of local cultural knowledge, with the *Galactica* itself featuring only as a *deus-ex-machina* at the end of the story. Although the idea appears to have been Larson's, it also bears some curious resemblances to Donald Bellisario's later series *Quantum Leap*, featuring as it does a young man trying to solve a problem while wearing the 'aura' of someone else's appearance, and being advised by a savvy older man who is invisible to everyone but him.

TERRA NOVA: POLITICS ON TERRA

The political situation on Terra is another reiteration of that in 'Saga of a Star World', albeit with less subtlety even than the earlier reiteration in 'Baltar's Escape'. The President of the Nationalists is making peace with a fairly obviously evil enemy, and ignoring or suppressing everyone who gainsays him on this, but is forced to go crawling back to the people who disagreed with him when the enemy turn out to be treacherous. The fact that the Eastern Alliance strike right when the President is announcing the peace treaty (with a speech that is 100% pure Neville Chamberlain) draws further parallels with the Cylon attack on the Colonies, and, yet again, the military suspect that something is up and have been flying extra patrols against the President's wishes (in parallel with Adama's fortuitous paranoia). The President does have an American accent, which makes a nice change from all the craven Brits, although this might have been an attempt either to echo Adar in 'Saga of a Star World', or make a broader parallel with Carter and/or Lyndon B Johnson. Maxwell's description of him as 'worn down by wars, public opinion and God knows what else' does suggest Johnson more than it does Carter (the 2 March draft contains lines where Maxwell also calls the President a coward and a 'lying … old man'); however, an extended version of the President's speech in the telemovie cut has explicit references to disarmament (and Maxwell directly accusing the President of 'appeasement'). A conversation between Apollo and Stone in the 2 March draft also makes the President look an even bigger bastard, making it clear that he was aware of the loss of the Lunar colonies but covering it up out of fear of war to the point where he was imprisoning members of the military who tried to expose this, to prevent the Precedium learning what was going on. The fact that the main dissenting voice to the stupid politicians comes from intelligent and sympathetic military men should also come as no surprise by this point.

The scenario as presented here is actually a simplified iteration of that in pre-WWII Europe. The Eastern Alliance's strategy (which is made clearer in the 2 March draft than it is in the final version) is to capture all the Nationalists' supply worlds, taking advantage of the fact that the President is too afraid of war to retaliate, and then take out the Nationalists themselves while they are thus without allies who might come to their aid (which explains why the Alliance are going through with the charade of the peace treaty; at the point at which we join the story, all the supply worlds have been taken over, and thus, if mutually assured destruction does occur on Terra, the Alliance, with their population safely in bunkers, have won). The President's lack of retaliation is clearly based on the passive response by Britain and other powers to the Nazis' annexation of nearby countries, and again the result of this is shown to be destruction. However, this overlooks the fact that there were clear reasons for the European powers to act as they did in the 1930s (chiefly, the fear of the Soviet threat from the East, against which an expanded and remilitarised Germany was considered a bulwark), and this complexity is missing from the *Battlestar Galactica* version.

The Eastern Alliance come across as rather like a non-satirical version of *Doctor Strangelove* (1964), planning on isolating the elite in bunkers and thus ensuring that everyone else, their own 'undesirables' as well as the Nationalists, are annihilated by the mutually assured destruction programme. They comment that 'overpopulation is one of our worst problems', in an echo of Mao's casually sophistic responses when confronted by his ministers about the high death rates caused by his economic advancement programmes (which, since little concrete information had emerged to the West from China at that point, is likely unwitting). The Elite, however, appear to have failed to think their plan through, as there is no explanation as to how they will deal with the horrific aftermath of nuclear war; even assuming that the bombs used here are the same kind as used on Paradeen, which (it is stated in 'Greetings from Earth') leaves the cities intact while killing their population, the amount of disease borne by the corpses of the slain, and the total lack of a medical, technical or subsistence infrastructure would be difficult to cope with.

One further point worth noting is that the Nationalists seem to be as much a fascist state as the Eastern Alliance. Their army has the slightly Maoist title of 'the People's Nationalist Force', Brenda sees nothing unusual in armed guards turning up to take her boyfriend off for medical treatment, and the President has been locking up or exiling to the Lunar colonies everyone who has the ability to oppose his plans. The President appears to have the Precedium (the local parliament) in his pocket. Despite this, the Nationalists are given more in the way of characterisation and sympathy than the Eastern Alliance (who speak with cod Eastern European accents and come across as pantomime Nazis or Soviets), which is somewhat contradictory.

The Nationalists we encounter, principally Brenda and her father, General Maxwell, are also not exactly engaging characters. Brenda shops her boyfriend to the security forces simply for acting peculiarly, and then, when her father takes her to task for this, she whinges that she didn't know about the true state of affairs in the Nationalist regime, which doesn't make much sense, since one would think that, even if her father was keeping the specifics of his suspicions about the President quiet in order to protect his plans to oppose him, at least some impression of his discontent might have filtered through to her. The story about Charlie being held captive on Lunar One, then escaping when the base was attacked by the Eastern Alliance and everyone else was killed (with the President thus believing him dead as well) fits in with the implication in 'Greetings from Earth' that the Eastern Alliance have been taking over Nationalist Lunar colonies (and a line of dialogue in the extended version of the President's speech confirms it).

This story also finally concludes the Terra arc, and makes it plain that Terra is not Earth. John states so explicitly, and, while he calls himself and Apollo 'brothers', does not consider the Terrans in the same fraternal light. This begs the question of where Terra came from; the usual explanation, that it is another offshoot of the lost Thirteenth Tribe, does not hold in this case as they use Earth measurements like 'kilometres' which were unknown in ancient times and Earth names like 'Charlie' and 'Brenda' rather than the vaguely Classical ones which permeate the Colonies and their offshoots. If Terra is not Earth, the most likely scenario is that Terra is a 'lost' colony world of a future Earth, which has a pleasing narrative symmetry in that, as the Fleet moves further away from Colonial space and closer to Earth space, they cease to encounter their own lost colonies and begin to encounter those of the other planet, and since, at this stage, we do not know when *Battlestar Galactica* takes place relative to Earth's history (and indeed, 'The Lost Patrol' and the draft of 'The Nari of Sentinel 27' suggest that it takes place in Earth's future), there is nothing as yet to rule this out.

ANGELS WITH DIRTY FACES: JOHN AND THE LIGHTSHIP PEOPLE

'Experiment in Terra' sees the return of the Ship of Lights and its people seen in 'War of the Gods', as principally here represented by John. Again we have the suggestion that they may not be wholly good, or at least not 'good' in the sense that we understand it. John has an English accent (though he is played by an Irish actor, Edward Mulhare) and is dressed in white, thus bearing a slight resemblance to Count Iblis. He is a manipulator, continually keeping Apollo and Starbuck in the dark about various things. There is also the fact that being dragged into the Ship of Lights is apparently a painful experience. John indicates that he has no physical body as Apollo would understand it, saying that his appearance is 'a reflection of intelligence; my spirit, if you will'.

Although John states that he cannot interfere in Terran politics, he does do so through getting others to do it for him (perhaps in an echo of CIA activities in contemporary world politics). The question is begged of why the lightship people did not intervene at the Cylon invasion as they do in a similar situation with the Terrans (even if they cannot interfere directly, all they would have to do is send someone to convincingly prove Baltar's treachery to the Council). The unstated answer is that they didn't know about the Colonials beforehand, and, as mentioned in the review of this episode, only had direct contact with them in 'War of the Gods' (which would suggest that they are nowhere near as godlike as they claim). In the 1 March 1979 draft, when asking Apollo to call him 'John', his guide says, 'is that sort of name familiar to you?' and, when Apollo indicates that it isn't, he continues, 'You're right. I was thinking of Terra', showing that he is familiar with Terran, but not Colonial, culture. The idea of a character who is continually shadowed by a secret advisor who is invisible to everyone but him will return, albeit with more sexual content, in the reimagined series.

TERRA INCOGNITA: PHILOSOPHY AND WORLDBUILDING

Again, this episode develops the series' overall philosophical threads. The idea of everything being interconnected is raised; the lightship people can be affected by events on Terra, even though the Terrans are no relation to them. The idea of Apollo being protected by a 'pure white aura' is very late-1970s new-age in its formulation. We see again the idea of minimal intervention: that outside parties should interfere to provide freedom for oppressed peoples, and that subsequently the people should be then allowed to make their own choices, which will ultimately be the right ones (as John puts it, he 'helps people to help themselves'), although in this case, the Colonials are at no point seen to warn the Terran people about the encroaching Cylons or offer to help with their defence against this enemy, suggesting that their intervention could, and probably should, have gone further.

There are also echoes of the deleted scene in 'Saga of a Star World', in which Apollo tells Boxey that the opposite of war is not necessarily peace.

Initially, Maxwell inverts the statement by saying of the President 'maybe he believes that the alternative to peace is not necessarily war', and, later, Apollo argues that 'the opposite of war is more often slavery', and 'strength alone can support freedom', again supporting the series' anti-détente philosophy (there's also an interestingly prescient foreshadowing of Regan's Strategic Defence Initiative in the *Galactica's* space-borne planet-wide anti-missile shield). However, the 'Saga of a Star World' scene was more sophisticated, in that the subsequent conversation (in which Apollo acknowledges that fighting the Cylons is making the humans very much like their foes) challenges Apollo's certainty and forces him to admit that there are no easy answers to these questions. Here, however, there is a disturbing similarity to Leiter's might-makes-right line in 'Baltar's Escape', particularly when coupled with the story's denouement, in which the Alliance, confronted with a superior power in the form of the *Galactica*, simply cave in and sue for peace (which is actually less sophisticated than in the previous episode, when Leiter's rationalisations allowed him to justify his continued faith in the Alliance despite the Colonials' visibly superior strength).

In world-building terms, it is stated here that the *Galactica* does not go to light speed often (even though it is well established that she can do so) because she is protecting the Fleet. Adama is seen making executive decisions without consulting the Council, suggesting that the Fleet is still under martial law. He's also fairly relaxed about the prospect of Cylon attack, leaving the Fleet with only two squadrons of Vipers to protect it, no doubt reflecting the fact that the Cylons haven't been seen for several episodes. Further to the information given earlier in the series that Viper pilots can sleep in their ships, Apollo refers to believing himself to be in 'a state of flight slumber'. The escape of the Nomen is mentioned in Adama's opening monologue.

TERRA INSANA: THINGS THAT DON'T MAKE SENSE

The most obvious problem with the episode is the fact that, as the 28 February draft of the script makes clear, Starbuck was meant to be the pilot sucked into the Ship of Lights and sent to Terra. Not only would it make sense to have Starbuck acting in the role of Charlie Watts, who is said to be a bit of a rogue and who has a girlfriend who looks a lot like Cassiopea, but the line 'Amnesia, that's a pretty name', would work better if said by Starbuck (as Benedict's joking delivery would suggest that Starbuck was taking the mick, but Hatch's more serious manner makes it seem as if he really believes Brenda's name to be 'amnesia', which makes him look like an idiot). To have had Starbuck in the role would also have picked up on Starbuck's statement in 'War of the Gods' that he would do anything the lightship people ask, making it seem as if they are taking him up on his offer.

There are a number of additional problems with the narrative. The fact that the Nationalists lock Brenda and Apollo, and Maxwell and Stone, together in the same cells (which are right opposite one another) is massively convenient for the plot. When Apollo introduces himself to the Precedium as Captain Apollo, the President doesn't say 'no you're not, you're Charlie Watts', even though the fact that Apollo's uniform is still white must mean that he still looks like Watts, and thus must seem completely insane to anyone in the audience who might know him, with his talk of coming from another galaxy. While it is a common telefantasy feature and thus not specifically a problem, the idea of having a deadly forcefield door on a prison cell is a stupid one: a suicidal prisoner would throw themselves at it, a psychopathic one would throw his cellmate at it, and a bored one would just sit in the cell spitting at it to watch the explosions and getting on everyone's nerves. There is also the fact that a Nationalist soldier, giving a cursory glance at a Viper, says 'whoever or whatever flew those craft in are not from Terra. Their technology is too advanced', when what we've seen of Terran technology thus far suggests that a one-man jet-type spacecraft isn't beyond them. While the Colonial units of measurement simply sound like clever world-building when everyone is using them, they sound contrived when all but two of the characters are using normal Earth units like hours and minutes.

There are also a few continuity errors. In the President's speech to the Precedium, he alludes to it being night, and Starbuck and Brenda are seen at the same time driving around in the night; and yet the Precedium's exteriors are seen to be in broad daylight. When the President, his aide, and Maxwell discuss the fact that the Eastern Alliance has launched its attack, the rest of the Precedium, even those close enough to hear, are remarkably calm about the announcement, but a mass exodus then appears to take place between scenes. There is another visible continuity error when the *Galactica* lays down the force shield over the planet: in the first shot the shield is there, in the next it isn't, and then we see the *Galactica* laying it down. Starbuck's (again beamless) gun has an interesting stun setting, knocking out nine men with three shots and then blowing up two vehicles (the 2 March 1979 draft has him adjusting his gun settings between stunning the men and blowing up the vehicles). Although John says that when Apollo's uniform returns to its former colour, he will be back to normal and not under the aura, at no point does it ever do this (although, again, it does so in the final scene of the 2 March draft).

TERRA FIRMA: PRODUCTION AND CASTING

The haphazard crediting continues on this story, with Lockhart, Spang, Hathaway and Jensen all being credited despite not appearing. On the casting front, Edward Mulhare was best known at the time for playing an interfering ghost in the television series *The Ghost and Mrs Muir*, Melody Anderson (Brenda) is better known for playing Dale Arden in the Dino de Laurentiis film version of *Flash Gordon* (1980), and John DeLancie, who appears here as a Nationalist soldier, would later go on to international fame as Q in *Star Trek: The Next Generation*. Regarding the Apollo-Starbuck character swap on the episode, Richard Hatch has said in an interview that he, upon seeing the original, Starbuck, version of the script, had complained to Larson that his character was being sidelined and that he would like to see an Apollo story – only to find that Larson had responded to his request, not by writing a new Apollo-focused story to follow later, but by largely transposing the names of the two characters in the extant script, leading Hatch to seek out Benedict and apologise for the situation.

The sequences with the Vipers on Terra were filmed at Vasquez Rocks, which has been a popular external location for filming companies since 1931, including four episodes of *Star Trek* and several episodes of *Bonanza*. The Precedium on Terra was represented by external shots of the French Pavilion in Expo '67, which still stands at the time of writing (having been redeveloped into Le Casino de Montreal), and the same shots were reused for the establishing shots of the Earth Defence Directorate headquarters in *Buck Rogers*. The 26 February 1979 draft's version of Starbuck's confrontation with the Nationalist soldiers identifies their leader as 'General Deering', in an obvious reference to *Buck Rogers'* Colonel Wilma Deering. Unconfirmed rumours suggest that Charlie Watts was named after the drummer of the Rolling Stones, when Larson discovered that Watts was a fan of the series. The drafts of the script state that Terra should be represented by a satellite shot of Earth from space, which, as well as drawing out the mystery of whether Terra is Earth, foreshadows the reimagined series' conceit of there being two identical planets, both called Earth, in different parts of the universe.

Although the 2 March 1979 draft is quite close to the broadcast version, an earlier draft, dated 28 February 1979, has some significant differences. The opening has a squadron of Vipers in pursuit of the fleeing Eastern Alliance destroyer, which contains not only the Alliance crew and the Nomen, but also Baltar, and, it transpires, Boxey and Muffit, who stowed away on the destroyer and are subsequently held hostage by the escapees. Starbuck/ Charlie's relationship with Brenda is also somewhat racier; rather than his steady girlfriend, she is a woman with whom he has had a casual fling in the past, who appears rather free with her affections. When we first encounter her, she is not driving out to the desert to pick up Charlie after receiving a phone call from him, as in the final, but comes across him by accident as she drives tearfully, ruminating on a fraught encounter with a married man, and, when he asks if she knows anyone named John, she replies 'I know lots of Johns'. Both this and the later draft have Starbuck/Apollo pulling a gun on Brenda when she hesitates over taking him back to her flat, which makes more sense of her decision to call Security later. Stone also assumes Charlie's apparent detachment from the Nationalist cause (referring to 'your half of the planet', for instance) to be a sign that he has sold out. Continuing the paternalism theme, John, when explaining why he can't intervene on Terra, likens himself to a father whose children are going astray, but he can only advise them. Apollo's line in the final, 'I've got to give up night life or have my oxygen checked', continues, as Starbuck's line in the original '… I'll start with having my oxygen checked', providing some genuine humour.

The telemovie version of this episode differs from the broadcast one in that it has some extended sequences and is incorporated with a cut-down version of the *Galactica 1980* episode 'The Return of Starbuck' (albeit with the sequences involving Angela and the baby removed, and the ending reedited to imply that Starbuck made it back to the Fleet in the improvised craft). It also has an opening which differs significantly from those of others in the series: beginning with a variation on the 'there are those who believe life here on Earth began out there …' voiceover, spoken by Patrick Macnee, but then developing into a story, accompanied by specially-shot new footage, of an astronaut finding a fragment of Adama's log, which then follows, in the form of paintings of the development of the Cylons (actually reused concept art by Jerry Gebr, done when the series was being pitched to the network in 1977), and visuals from the series, accompanied by a narration track by Lorne Greene, which gives a potted version of the creation of the mechanical Cylons (called 'Cylon Centurians' throughout), the machines turning against their creators due to, according to this version, a 'slight error in their programming' of the Imperious Leader, the war with the humans, the destruction of the Colonies, and the exodus of the rag-tag fleet towards Earth, ending just prior to their journey through the minefield to Carillon.

This log provides a few, occasionally controversial, additions to the series' continuity, in that, first, the lizard Cylons (referred to as 'serpents' here) depicted are tall, thin creatures which look nothing like the Imperious Leader (contradicting the implication in the screened version of 'Saga of a Star

World' that the Imperious Leader most resembles the original lizard race), and also implies that the whole Cylon War was down to a technical error, not to political conflict and/or the interference of Count Iblis. Furthermore, the prologue goes on to say that after the Battle of Molecay the Colonies were left with a single fleet with only five battlestars, and implies that this is a weak situation, whereas, not only do we have evidence of at least six being present according to 'The Gun on Ice Planet Zero', in 'The Living Legend', Adama states that 'they didn't use more than three base ships when they wiped out our entire fleet at Caprica', which, since six battlestars were at the peace conference and thus involved in the Battle of Cimtar, means that the six battlestars only formed a small portion of the overall Colonial force. Furthermore, the humans do not see themselves as negotiating from a position of weakness in 'Saga of a Star World'. Indeed, the cut dialogue about the uniting of the human colonies against the Cylons suggests otherwise. The narration also refers to the *Galactica* as being the flagship of this fleet, and the *Pegasus* as the flagship of the Fifth Fleet, which is not indicated elsewhere. Finally, a good portion of Macnee's voiceover is from the point of view of Earth humans, referring to the people of Earth as 'we', which would suggest that the speaker is neither Iblis or the Imperious Leader. This document can thus be taken to be of debatable canonicity.

'Experiment in Terra' brings a welcome end to the 'Terra arc' of the series with all its accompanying problems, returning us for the final two episodes to more Fleet-based and Cylon-focused stories.

16 ● TAKE THE CELESTRA

US TRANSMISSION DATE: Sunday 1 April 1979
TELEPLAY: Jim Carson & Terrence McDonnell
STORY: David S Arthur & David G Phinney and Jim Carson & Terrence McDonnell
DIRECTOR: Daniel Haller
CREDITED CAST: Paul Fix (Kronus); Nick Holt (Charka); Ana Alicia (Aurora); Randy Stumpf (Damon); Richard Styles (Hermes); James R Parkes (1st Mutineer); Michael Horsley (2nd Mutineer); Ted Hamaguchi (3rd Crewman); Robert Murvin (Duty Officer)

SYNOPSIS: During a ceremony on the *Galactica* to honour Kronus, commander of the Fleet's electronics ship, the *Celestra*, Starbuck sees an old girlfriend, Aurora, whom he had thought killed during the holocaust. Aurora, and her new lover Damon, are involved in a mutiny plot, and, when Kronus returns to the *Celestra*, they begin their takeover attempt. Starbuck, hoping to meet Aurora again, goes to the *Celestra* with Apollo, and is caught up in the mutiny. The attempt is suppressed, and the mutineers are taken under Kronus' charge to the *Galactica* to face trial, with Apollo and Starbuck piloting the shuttle. Kronus' second-in-command Charka, however, stages his own mutiny, giving the shuttle the wrong coordinates, and then shutting down all systems so that the *Celestra* is undetectable, stranding Kronus. Kronus learns from the mutineers that Charka was abusing his authority, and, in exchange for the promise of a fair hearing, the mutineers agree to alter the shuttle's computers so as to track the *Celestra*. The ship is retaken, with Kronus being killed in the process. Starbuck is reconciled with Aurora and her new relationship, and Kronus is given a space funeral.

ANALYSIS: 'Take the *Celestra*' is a fairly good episode, with its main strength lying in the fact that it is a character piece, and thus a welcome relief from the crudely drawn political thrillers of the 'Terra arc'. It has an interesting twist regarding the double nature of the mutiny, and also some nice character development in the presentation of Kronus as a plausible man who gets results but is really a rather bad manager.

THE FISH ROTS FROM THE HEAD DOWN: CHARACTERISATION AND WORLDBUILDING

The mutiny plot is the key driver of the story, and one of the most interesting things about it. It seems initially to concern a mutiny on the part of the

Celestra's workers, against the rule of both Kronus and Charka, but then, once the mutiny is suppressed, Charka stages his own attempt to get rid of the mutineers and the commander at the same time.

Although Kronus appears to talk a lot of sense, he is also clearly a poor manager; his focus on the rules is a source of friction even away from the *Celestra,* as witness his berating of Tigh for remaining at the ceremony rather than, as he is supposed to, proceeding directly to the bridge. Kronus is unaware of the situation that has developed below decks on the *Celestra,* and it seems that his authoritarian, get-results attitude is partly behind Charka's development into a petty dictator, and thus ultimately responsible for the uprising. When Charka attempts to get the officers on his side, he offers them not assumptions of loyalty, but money, promotion and, he emphasises, respect, implying that Kronus takes loyalty for granted and does not respect his underlings.

The other main focus of the story is Starbuck's complicated personal life. Apollo, not without justification, accuses Starbuck of having double standards: he dumps Cassiopea to go chasing after Aurora, but still worries about the possibility of Cassiopea going to the concert with another man. He also hits the nail on the head when he accuses Starbuck of not running to Aurora so much as away from Cassiopea, saying 'I think you and Cassiopea were getting so close you're scared'. The idea that Starbuck didn't come looking for Aurora, not because he didn't love her but because he genuinely believed she was dead, is in keeping with Starbuck's character as someone who is a bit of a rogue but never deliberately insensitive, and the fact that he patches things up with Damon when Damon gets jealous of his former relationship with Aurora is also in keeping with Starbuck's well-established sense of self-sacrifice, giving up the possibility of renewing his relationship with Aurora so that she and her partner can be happy. Cassiopea, meanwhile, won't chase after Starbuck, ostensibly as she doesn't want a possessive relationship, but, given the fact that Starbuck has a tendency to run when pursued, this is probably the best approach. Rather than find a new man to go to the concert with, she changes her concert duckets for ones for the next night, shrewdly realising that Starbuck would be coming back to her. Apollo admonishes Starbuck for lying about needing to go to the *Celestra* for an electronics maintenance scan of his Viper, saying that if he wants to see Aurora he should be honest about it, and then promptly uses the same excuse on Tigh himself, suggesting perhaps that he does not quite apply the same standards universally.

There is a certain amount of recycling from 'Saga of a Star World' in this episode: the scene where Starbuck's attempt to make things up with Aurora is interrupted by Cassiopea turning up with the concert duckets, and, in the resulting farrago of explanations and recriminations, he winds up with neither woman, is reminiscent of the scene in the casino with him, Athena and Cassiopea. The idea that the workers are oppressed, and the warriors are thought by them to be living the life of Riley, unaware of the suffering of others in the Fleet, has come up in both 'Saga of a Star World' and 'War of the Gods', but is here developed further, with specific reference to the *Celestra*'s workers.

In terms of Fleet politics, we learn that the Council of Twelve voted to decorate Kronus and give him executive command of the three industry ships, suggesting either that martial law has been rescinded, or that Adama is letting them have a long leash. The three ships in question – 'the parts ship, the textile ship, and the *Celestra*', suggest increasing specialisation among the Fleet. There is also a telling moment where Kronus observes that 'this collection of moving derelicts isn't a fleet, it's a convoy', elaborating on this by saying that a convoy is held together by mutual dependence, of necessity rather than to practical effect, and that a fleet, by contrast, is held together by force and discipline, and does not move, but performs; he then concludes that he doesn't think that Adama (who, we learn, used to be Kronus' aide) is aware of this distinction, suggesting that there are officers in the Fleet who think that Adama's use of military language and pomp is simply a failure to grasp that they are not engaging in a bold manoeuvre so much as an undignified retreat.

In continuity terms, Bojay is briefly mentioned as being on deep patrol, explaining his absence, and Greenbean gets a namecheck. Another boraton tank is visible in the *Galactica*'s launching bay, 'duckets' is again used as a synonym for tickets and, as Paxton notes, this is the only occasion where we see female warriors in dress uniform. We also learn that Kronus was the commander of both the battlestar *Rycon* and the Fourth Colonial Fleet, that he was the hero of the Battle of the Cosmora Archipelago during the war, and that he retired shortly before the destruction of the Colonies. Philosophically, it is again asserted that mutiny is a good thing if it is against an evil regime, with the mutineers getting off with probation where Charka and his supporters are sent to the prison barge.

DAWN OF AN ERA: PRODUCTION AND DEVELOPMENT

This is another episode which draws heavily on Classical mythology for its nomenclature. Kronus' name is drawn from Kronos, the Titan, who was the father of Zeus and various other gods, of whom it was prophesied that one of his children would destroy him, so he swallowed them (with Zeus, who was hidden by a trick, growing up to fulfil the prophecy); the idea of draconian father figures being killed by son-figures has some resonance here. Hermes was the messenger-god, and the god of language and travellers, for the Greeks, so there is a tenuous connection here in terms of naming the bridge officer on the *Celestra* after him; however, in the case of Aurora, who shares her name with the Roman goddess of the dawn, it would seem to be another instance of selecting classical names at random, and why 'Dianapolis', one of the security guards on the *Celestra*, was given a name translating to 'Diana City', is unknown. The idea of a rebellion against unfair authority on a technical ship would return in the reimagined series, albeit as industrial action rather than mutiny.

The draft script (dated 12 March 1979) shows few changes from the transmitted version. Most of the significant differences have to do with fleshing out the Starbuck-Aurora-Cassiopea love triangle: for example, the sequence where Sheba urges Cassiopea to pursue Starbuck, but the latter refuses because, she says, she doesn't want a relationship based on possession, is a late addition, as is the revelation that Starbuck went to Aurora's house to try and save her when the Cylons attacked Caprica but found it destroyed (which gives a concrete reason for why Starbuck did not try to track down Aurora on the Fleet but simply assumed she was dead). The sequence where Aurora tells Damon that she no longer loves Starbuck is not present in the original script, only the subsequent scene where Starbuck himself tells Damon this is the case; the addition of the first sequence makes the love story much more about Aurora's personal choice, and Starbuck's respect for this. The brief sequence where Kronus assures Damon that he has his word that the mutineers will have a fair hearing replaces an earlier version where Apollo, instead, assures Damon that since Adama is his father, he will see to it that they get their case heard. Charka's line where he tells the *Celestra*'s officers that if they follow him, they will gain respect as well as status and money, is a late addition; in the draft, also, Damon's mutineers were let off without charge at the end of the story, rather than found guilty but given probation due to the mitigating circumstances.

According to Terence McDonnell, the episode was shot as a budget-saving exercise. Although this is well disguised, it is clearly filmed on only a few sets, with no locations, few new special effects, and the bridge, landing bay and corridors of the *Celestra* being redressed extant sets, while the hall where Kronus receives his awards is draped in black curtains, again suggesting saving money by not constructing a whole ceremonial hall. This aside, however, there are some great overhead shots in the ceremony honouring Kronus (though the ceremony itself is very *Star Wars*) and the scene of the full-sized Vipers taxiing on the landing deck of the *Celestra* is also well done. The *Celestra* model is lovely (although the schematic ship seen on the shuttle's screen purporting to represent it looks nothing like it), and can be seen again, redressed, in part one of the *Buck Rogers* story 'Time of the Hawk'. This is another rare episode in which the Colonial weapons are seen to fire beams (which, in this case, serves to make it clear that Kronus was shot, and by which side, as otherwise it can be hard to tell what has happened). The anthem played at the ceremony is a variation on the *Battlestar Galactica* theme tune. McDonnell has complained in an interview with Paxton that budgetary constraints prevented him from, as he wanted, showing Kronus' coffin drifting away into space, saying that 'as far as I know it would have been the first space burial on film'.[19]

On a less positive level, Aurora's boyfriend Damon looks like Leo Sayer, whose perm appears to be compensating for his lack of height. The Patrick Macnee voiceover returns, suggesting that this episode is underrunning. This is yet another story which ignores the fact that one doesn't need fuel to travel in a straight line in space, and the *Celestra*'s steering mechanism consists simply of a joystick on a column (this is clearly down to budgetary constraints, as the draft script describes it as 'a large complicated console board with stylised levers, twinkling lights and many switches'). In an outside environment with no gravity, also, one wouldn't need to desperately seize control of the steering mechanism, as the ship would simply drift in the same direction until stopped, rather than being pulled off course as would a plane or a boat.

Both McDonnell and Jim Carlson also have vivid memories of a battle which ensued with Standards and Practices over the level of violence in the story during the vetting of the script. The Standards and Practices guidelines allowed only a certain number of 'acts of violence', as designated by their criteria, and, according to Carlson, a new member of the Standards and Practices division decided, rather than counting the entire firefight sequence as a single act of violence (which was apparently the norm under their guidelines), to count each time the story cut away from the firefight and then cut back as indicating a new act of violence. Carlson recalls that he had to go over her head to her superior to ensure that the episode was broadcast as written.

'Take the *Celestra*' is another of these rather good small-scale character pieces at which *Battlestar Galactica* excels, giving us insight not only into the major characters, but a familiar scenario of bad leadership with which the audience can empathise.

---

19 Actually, *Doctor Who* beat them to it by over twelve years, featuring a space burial in 'The Ark' (12 March 1966) and another in 'Planet of Evil' (11 October 1975).

17 ● THE HAND OF GOD

US TRANSMISSION DATE: Sunday 29 April 1979
WRITER: Donald Bellisario
DIRECTOR: Donald Bellisario

SYNOPSIS: While showing the *Galactica*'s Celestial Chamber to Starbuck, Sheba and Cassiopea, Apollo picks up what seems to be a transmission from Earth. A planetary system is found in the direction of the transmission, and Adama orders it to be investigated; the pilots do not find a human civilisation, but rather a Cylon base star, strategically positioned so as to force the Fleet to take a long detour if they want to avoid it. Adama, tired of running, proposes that they attack the base star. Apollo and Starbuck come up with a plan to sneak aboard the base star using Baltar's captured Cylon craft and knock out their scanners, giving *Galactica* the initial advantage. Boomer gives the pair an identification transmitter, which will prevent the pilots from shooting them down by mistake. The plan works, but the transmitter is lost, however, Starbuck 'waggles the wings' of the craft so that it is identified as Colonial. The base star is destroyed, but the *Galactica* also sustains damage, including the loss of the recording of the original transmission; however, at the end of the story, another comes through, unseen by the Colonials, showing the Apollo 11 moon landing.

ANALYSIS: 'The Hand of God' is generally a good, solid and enjoyable episode; nothing overly clever, deep or difficult to understand, but, on the other hand, no inept politics or clichéd pantomime Nazis, making it a strong way to end the series.

SCRIPT TO SCREEN: WRITING AND PRODUCTION

Unlike the earlier draft scripts discussed in this volume, almost all of the contents of the available draft script (which has a single revision date of 21 March 1979) for this episode makes it into either the final version or a filmed out-take, with the differences largely being ad-libs or changes in chronology (Baltar and Adama's dealmaking scene comes later in the draft than in the final version, for instance), which is no doubt down to the fact that the production team were operating at some speed at this point (the episode was transmitted just over a month after the cited revision date) and were also very familiar with the show's characters and format. A few noteworthy changes involve the fact that Cassiopea's line in the opening scene visibly evolves through the production process, initially running 'what's this bubble used for ... besides scaring me?' then, in three existing takes of the scene, saying instead 'what's this bubble used for ... besides *that!*' (in visible anticipation of a lewd response from Starbuck), however, in the final version, all material after 'used for' is cut. In the opposite vein, Boomer's line that he had dreamed he had met a beautiful girl and was 'just about to make ...' is not in the script, in an unusual example of suggestive dialogue being added to, rather than removed from, the episode. Starbuck's shining the bedside lamp in Boomer's face to wake Boomer also appears to have been added during the production, but, amusingly, his brief pause to consider the possibilities of encountering a female prisoner on the base star (as Cassiopea suggests), is actually in the original script.

A few scenes also change subtly, but significantly. The original scene of Adama outlining the battle plan to the pilots runs:

ADAMA:
You'll be outnumbered two to one.

STARBUCK:
Better odds than we had at Caprica.

BOOMER:
We lost at Caprica.

ADAMA:
But you're used to that.

In the final version, however, Adama's lines are run together, and then Starbuck and Boomer's lines follow as a sarcastic coda, with the change probably being because the original version implies that the pilots are used to losing. In the original version of Apollo and Sheba's meaningful conversation, Apollo is the one who says 'I've begun to realise that two people who snap at each other for no reason ... do it to avoid their real feelings', and Sheba replies, 'I've realised that for quite a while now', whereas in the final, Sheba says it all, suggesting that Apollo is less in touch with his own feelings than he thinks. In the draft script, Apollo, Sheba and Starbuck cheer when Adama announces that they will attack the base star, whereas in the transmitted version their reaction is more subdued, in keeping with the seriousness of the endeavour.

There is also a filmed but cut sequence in which Starbuck remarks 'everyone wishing us luck is making me nervous', and Apollo replies 'Yah, (sic) I know what you mean' (as well as a little more dialogue about Apollo's fondness for Sheba). This adds more significance to the pair's double-take at Baltar's wishing them luck later, which, as it stands, simply looks like they are cynical about the arch-traitor's good wishes. There are also a couple of extra bits of dialogue deleted from later in the episode, one in which Starbuck and Apollo reiterate their situation and the importance of the transmitter as they reach the cockpit of their Cylon fighter, visibly intended to bring late-arriving viewers up to speed, an establishing scene of the Cylons in their control centre at the start of Act Four (again, presumably to quickly set the scene for new viewers), and some dialogue between Viper pilots to underscore the destruction of the base star in Act Four. After saying 'seal all compartments', in the draft script Tigh says 'laser pumps to full charge', which was lost as it is a little too suggestive of the well-known nautical phrase 'man the pumps'.

The script also casts some light on the nature of the series' production. The scenes where the warriors listen to the recording of the NASA footage, in the draft, contain generic broken-up dialogue visibly meant to suggest the Apollo 11 mission (the word '...eleven' appears in the text). In alternative takes of this scene someone can be heard offscreen reading in the lines as they appear in the script, but the final version uses actual excerpts from the real Apollo 11 recordings, as obtained from NASA. The Cylon landing bay is described in the script as follows: 'INT. CYLON LANDING BAY – (FRONT PROJECTION) with a partial Cylon fighter mock-up (I hope) in the f.g. as Cylon pilots rush to their fighters', with the interjected 'I hope' indicating the pressure under which the team were working and the idea that they might not be able to complete such a mock-up in time (which was fortunately unfounded).

The script also designates the onscreen footage of the lunar module as 'NASA footage' and the base star core set as 'Skylab set' (the base star core sequences were indeed filmed in the interior of the mockup or backup vehicle of Skylab, the first American space station; two flight-ready Skylabs were built, with one being used for training, and this vehicle currently resides at the National Air and Space Museum in Washington, with the mockup being at the United States Space and Rocket Centre in Alabama). The script also designates the base star computer corridor and control centre with the annotation 'Note: Computer Corridor and Central Control are old sets used in shows with Baltar on Stg. 27'. The bronze Centurian is designated 'Commander' in the script, and is also, strangely, referred to as 'gold'.

An alternative take on the scene where Adama and Baltar strike their deal has them shaking hands rather than doing the usual Colonial forearm clasp (as in the final version). Two outtakes of the scene where Boomer gets out of bed exist, one where Herb Jefferson accidentally throws his blanket over the two women and they corpse. In an unusual case of recycled footage, the sequence of the three Vipers overflying the planets is one cut from 'War of the Gods' and slotted in here.

The direction on this episode is generally good, with particularly memorable sequences including the overhead shot of the bridge, the bronze Centurian's journey down the ladder, and the slow-motion shootout between the warriors and a Cylon guard. The Celestial Chamber set is excellent, and Starbuck and Apollo's poses as they sneak onto the base star are very Han Solo. An alternative take of the base star core sequences shows that the ladder/tube was quite short, but Bellisario cleverly lengthens it using a wide-angle lens, low-angle shots, and cutting back and forth between overhead, underneath and side shots of actors climbing along it. There is a great sequence (which is described in full in the original script) where the scene cuts from the base star model in space, representing the Cylon base star, to what is likely the very same base star model, and then, after a beat or two, revealing that it is not in fact a base star in space, but a model on the *Galactica* being used to plan the attack. The Patrick Macnee introduction is again missing (and some instances of trimming of recorded scenes suggest the episode was overrunning), and Jensen and Hathaway are again in the title sequence despite not appearing.

HAND IT TO THEM: CHARACTER DEVELOPMENT AND WORLDBUILDING

There is some development of the regular characters here, particularly Apollo and Sheba. Starbuck comments that Apollo would have loved living in the past, knocking about space in a sublight rocket, and Apollo agrees, saying he thinks life was more fun then (and, considering that his entire life has been spent in wartime, this is not likely to be simple nostalgia). This, coupled with his likening of the Apollo vehicle (suggesting a less Classical antecedent for Apollo's own name) to the primitive spacecraft of the Colonies, indicates that he's got an interest in Colonial history. In Apollo and Sheba's meaningful conversation, she accuses him of signing up for every high-risk mission since Serina's death, suggesting that his actions since 'Lost Planet of the Gods' have been at least partly driven by guilt and grief. Adama's decision to take on the base star is slightly reminiscent of 'The Gun on Ice Planet Zero' (albeit making more sense, as, while 'The Gun on Ice Planet Zero' begged the question of why the ship didn't simply fly around the obstruction, the base star is mobile), but with the added psychological element of wanting to confront, rather than simply flee, the enemy.

We also learn that Boomer is a 'whiz' at long-range communications and capable of cobbling together gadgets at short notice; this character trait is not really signalled elsewhere in the series (his electronic skill in 'Fire in Space' is said to be down to a misspent youth rather than a general fondness for technology), but might lend credibility to the second season document (discussed later in this book), which includes the idea that Boomer would become a technological wizard in the Doctor Wilker mould (perhaps significantly, at the end of this story Wilker's lab is destroyed and there is no word of Wilker himself). There is also some improvisation from Benedict in the scene where Cassiopea goes up the ladder before Starbuck, and he looks up her skirt and then looks rather smug about it. Considering the 1970s' reputation for sexual experimentation, also, it is amusing that Colonel Tigh asks what the four of them were doing up in the Celestial Chamber, with the visible implication that he believes it to have been something immoral.

Elsewhere, we learn that the *Galactica* was built over five hundred yahrens ago, at a time when navigational coordinates were double-checked using manual observation (although, if lifespans for Colonials are about two hundred yahrens, this just makes it the equivalent of, say, a WWI gunboat for us). The military have also begun to assume that, since the Cylons weren't present, they had lost them for good, and the Cylon practice of making suicide runs is mentioned. The script says that the stock footage during the Viper-launching sequence should be of 'male and female pilots', and, indeed, the reuse of footage from 'Lost Planet of the Gods' means we see a couple of shots of Deitra as well as another female pilot. We learn that each Cylon base star carries about 300 fighters, meaning that Cain went up against almost a thousand fighters during his suicide mission in 'The Living Legend'. Silver Spar squadron appears to have been disbanded, as when the call comes to launch all fighters, Omega calls for the launching of Red and Blue squadrons only, and Jolly is seen as part of this mission. A boraton tank is again seen in the landing bay, and the weapons are back in 'no-beam' mode.

On the subject of Earth, there is an ambiguity as to how old the recording of the Apollo 11 mission that the *Galactica* intercepts is: it is stated that it could be millennia old, placing the series in Earth's far future (which fits with everything we have seen thus far in the series, although *Galactica 1980* drives several carts and horses through this chronology). The planetary fly-past also leaves it initially ambiguous as to whether the system in question is Earth's or not, until Starbuck's visual display reveals that there are only five planets in the system, and we then learn that the third planet from the sun is a gas giant.

On the problematic front, the series concludes with another difficult-to-overlook error, in that the idea of checking a starship's coordinates by eyeball, in what is essentially a space crow's nest, would be impossible in reality. The question has also been raised of why the Colonials do not back up the recording, to prevent it from being lost, but it has to be said that the concept of backing up data, while commonplace now, was not particularly well known in the late 1970s, with personal computers being largely a novelty. It is also worth noting that Baltar has been wearing the same outfit since 'Lost Planet of the Gods', suggesting either that he has several identical suits (which he brought with him to the *Galactica* in 'War of the Gods'), or that his personal hygiene leaves much to be desired.

HAND IT OVER: THE END OF THE SERIES

In her online guide to *Battlestar Galactica*, Susan J Paxton indicates that this was likely written deliberately to be the series' final episode; it was shot nearly a month after 'Take the *Celestra*', and aired the Sunday after the series' cancellation was announced. The episode does seem to have a sense of concluding the narrative: there are a lot of references back to earlier episodes, including 'Take the *Celestra*' (Wilker is said to be on the 'electronics ship'), 'Lost Planet of the Gods' (Apollo and Sheba's discussion about Serina's death and its aftermath), and 'The Living Legend' (in references to the *Pegasus*' disappearance, and Sheba's allusions to her father's apparent death when reminding Apollo that he is not the only one who feels lonely). Baltar's excited initial reaction when Adama tells him that they have made contact with the Cylons might suggest that he is thinking that Adama has brought him there to discuss attempting Baltar's original plan of attacking the Cylon homeworld.

The story also aims at resolving, albeit not concluding, some of the running plots seen throughout the series. Apollo and Sheba finally have a long talk about their relationship, and conclude that they do love each other. The Baltar arc also approaches resolution, in that Adama offers to maroon him on a habitable planet in exchange for his help (which sounds rather lonely and dangerous, though Baltar evidently considers it a better prospect than the prison barge, and he does negotiate shelter, adequate provisions and a short-range communicator to allow him the possibility of rescue). Adama also gets Baltar's help through answering his question, 'what if they destroy you and me along with you?' with 'that's the risk you will have to take', indicating to Baltar that Adama plans to go through with his scheme regardless, and so Baltar had better help him or he is putting his own life at risk.

The episode is also a celebration of the warrior ethos. Adama, Cain-like, decides to fight the base star rather than going around it because, effectively, the Fleet must assert itself as a martial force, in what he accurately describes as a 'toe-to-toe slugging match' with the Cylons. Cassiopea's assertion that Starbuck is going on the mission in the hope of impressing a 'female prisoner', equating the mission with sex, is interesting in that it indicates that for Starbuck, fighting is as important to him as the pursuit of sexual adventure (although Apollo's reference to the first planet they overfly as 'pretty' and Sheba's describing the second as 'beautiful but deadly' are innocuous in themselves, Starbuck's 'trust me to get the ugly one' immediately places the whole exercise in a sexual context). Apollo's wish that he could simply explore space in a sublight rocket underscores the fact that this is not, actually, what he does, and that he is rather defined by his choice of a military occupation. The series thus culminates in an almost Classical assertion of military virtues, giving the lie to critics who derided *Battlestar Galactica* as cowardly.

The choice of the moon landing footage as their first communication from Earth works well in the episode because, first of all, it establishes without question that the transmission is from Earth, while still leaving some ambiguity as to how far away the Earth is at this point and how long ago the transmission was sent, and, secondly, it has an iconic quality, suggesting humanity's first steps out into space and American early space triumphs, linking in with the idea that Earth humanity is showing progress, but that they can still learn much from the Colonials.

The first *Battlestar Galactica* series thus ends on an ambiguous but optimistic note: the Fleet has not yet found Earth, and the character plotlines are all left on cliffhangers (will Apollo and Sheba, and/or Starbuck and Cassiopea, get sealed? Will Baltar be rescued, and by whom?). There is also a poignancy to the fact that the Colonials miss the actual moon landing broadcast, again indicating the perilous and delicate nature of their mission. Adama's increased belligerence and willingness to risk the Fleet simply because he is tired of running also strike a warning note, indicating that the remnant of humanity is capable of degenerating into self-destructive and dangerous behaviour under continued pressure. On the whole, however, the episode looks forward to a positive future in which the Fleet will find Earth someday, in keeping with the generally optimistic and forward-looking tone of *Battlestar Galactica* in the 1970s.

UNMADE STORIES 1 • THE BETA PIRATES

BY LESLIE STEVENS

SYNOPSIS: The Colonial Fleet travels through the outer reaches of the Beta Triangle, an area beset with turbulence and storms. The *Gemini* freighter is damaged, and Athena and Starbuck are dispatched to help it (with Boxey and Muffit stowing away). The freighter is attacked by pirates, led by Xanon, who strip the gold fittings out of the ship's computers and kidnap Athena, Boxey and Muffit. Meanwhile, the Imperious Leader dispatches a death-force, led by Baltar, to the Triangle to track down the Fleet. Skyler, searching for the lost Colonials, finds an unconscious Starbuck aboard the *Gemini* freighter, and later, stranded and adrift in an escape pod, a man who claims to be a trawler captain named Aleph, whose ship was hijacked by the pirates. Back on the *Galactica*, Aleph reveals that Athena, Boxey and Muffit were taken to Cordugo Pit, a refuelling base on a dead moon, along with his ship, which contains star-charts that he can use to guide the Fleet safely through the Triangle (in fact, Aleph is secretly Xanon, who has been double-crossed by his crew, and this is all a ruse to regain his ship, the *Bluestreak*). Arriving on Cordugo Pit, Skyler, Starbuck and Aleph learn that Athena and Boxey have been taken to the Pleasure Dome to be sold as slaves. They attempt to buy them, but, when they are purchased instead by Voyar, the Pleasure Dome's owner and the local chief magistrate, they follow him to his Governor's mansion and stage a rescue attempt. Aleph succeeds in releasing Boxey and Muffit, but Skyler, Starbuck and Athena are arrested by the Ovion police. Aleph, having located his ship, wants to leave, but finally has a change of heart, and instead helps Boxey and Muffit break the others out of jail, and escape in the *Bluestreak*. The Cylon death-force attempts pursuit, but is lost to the turbulence inside the Triangle and the black hole at its apex; Baltar escapes in an emergency pod. Aleph reveals that he is in fact Xanon, but says that he has realised that humans must help each other, and will guide the Fleet through the Triangle.

ANALYSIS: 'The Beta Pirates' is an early example of an unmade script which, given its length, might conceivably have formed one of the initially-planned series of telemovies. It is therefore interesting in terms of what it reveals about the directions which the series might have taken.

The script is dated 31 October, 1977; the title of the series is given as 'Battlestar Galactica: Saga of a Star World'. As in other early episodes, Apollo is still Skyler, and is again rather more of a cold fish than he would be in the final version; Starbuck is more or less as he is in the televised series, though he refers to Athena as 'my girlfriend' in a way that the commitment-phobic later version would never do, and the terminology does not appear to have settled into its finished form (the term 'years' is used alongside more Colonial terms such as 'centons' and 'millitons', and the guns are 'laser carbines'). Both Cassiopea and Serina/Lyra are absent. An early version of the 'fleeing from the Cylon tyranny …' speech appears as part of the opening monologue (which is to be spoken by Adama), which refers to Earth as a 'land of Zion' (a phrase also used to describe Earth in the dialogue; interestingly given the Old Testament references, 'Aleph' is the first letter of the Hebrew alphabet). Muffit is again a 'droid' rather than a 'drone', and there is a reference to 'Cylon Centurions (sic) in black armour', suggesting again the lizard rather than robot Cylons. Boomer's rank is given as Sergeant, Skyler's as 'Wing Captain' and Starbuck's as 'Flight Lieutenant'. There is also evidence that the Ovions were considered as an ongoing antagonist race, as they are the key figures of law and order in Cordugo Pit; as in the early draft of 'Saga of a Star World', they speak clear (if 'sickly-sweet') English, where Voyar, an alien of another species, has to use a translator device. Baltar again features as the key human antagonist, suggesting that this story was drafted during one of the periods when the writers had decided to keep Baltar alive.

The script is visibly an early draft, with some things left undecided (Boomer, for instance, sometimes appears to be on the mission to Cordugo Pit, and sometimes not), and some things left vague, such as where the pirates manage to get explosive tylium fuel packs from after Aleph breaks them and the Colonials out of jail (which they then throw at their Ovion pursuers). There are certain similarities to 'The Gun on Ice Planet Zero', with Boxey and Muffit stowing away on a mission, and the Carillon sequences of 'Saga of a Star World' (as well as the scenes of Michael Sloan's 'Fire in Space' draft script featuring Starbuck, Boomer and Apollo infiltrating an alien bar disguised as bounty hunters). Some of the stage descriptions verge on the racist (the Pleasure Dome contains 'Space Arabs' playing 'four-dimensional Mah-Jongg'), and sexist (when, as the slave auction starts, we hear that 'the auctioneer slides on and displays an obese "beauty"'). Although Athena does get some good scenes, there is a slightly fetishistic focus on the idea of her being sold into slavery and, later, threatened with torture.

The scenario is clearly predicated on an ocean-going metaphor throughout. The Beta Triangle, with its 'heavy storms', is clearly based on the Bermuda Triangle, and there is a reference to the *Galactica* 'listing and rolling, almost capsizing', which seems an odd thing for a spaceship to do. Later, the Fleet slows to 'trolling speed'. Aleph claims that pirates forced his crew to 'walk overboard without their helmets', a futuristic version of walking the plank. Areas of turbulence are indicated by 'space buoys' (when a Centurian remarks that seven buoys are out of commission, Baltar notes 'that's a hole big enough to pass the entire colonial fleet'). The science is generally fairly dodgy to the point of double-entendre (when we learn that the Beta Triangle has a black hole at its apex, Athena warns Starbuck not to go too deep), which is perhaps not surprising when one remembers that Leslie Stevens also wrote the innuendo-laced 'The Nari of Sentinel 27'. Baltar, fleeing in an emergency pod at the end of the story, manages to avoid being sucked into a black hole even though the Cylon warship he is escaping from is lost to it.

Certain of the story's elements bear a slightly too close relationship to *Star Wars* to pass muster. The architecture of Cordugo Pit is described as 'Algerian-Mexican-otherworldly', with Starbuck, Skyler and Aleph disguising themselves as traders to move around in it, and later, after stealing ID from police officers, posing as bounty hunters. The descriptions of the Pleasure Dome owe a lot to the Mos Eisley Cantina sequences. Some of the scenes actually anticipate *Return of the Jedi* by several years, for instance by describing a 'fat-form' alien playing 'wraparound keyboards' (like Max Rebo in the abovementioned film) in the Pleasure Dome, and the scenes of Athena and the suggestively-named Voyar have her sitting at his feet adorned in gold chains, reminiscent of Princess Leia and Jabba the Hutt (though Voyar seems rather more of an egocentric dolt than a vicious crime-lord; he 'lives in a Lawrence of Arabia tent decorated by Yves St Laurent out of Salvador Dali', and one of his chat-up lines to Athena is 'please believe me, I am truly wonderful'). There is a general feeling of a multispecies universe in which humans are far from the only players, and indeed are almost extinct, which makes more sense than the finished series' continually encountering lost human colonies, but would have been expensive to realise as well as incurring further ire from Fox over similarities to *Star Wars*.

The early parts of the story also resemble *Silent Running*, with the *Galactica* possessing a number of chirping and bleeping 'work robots', known as 'fix-it robots' or 'fix-its', who appear to be rather like Huey, Dewey and Louie from the film. The sequence with Skyler piloting his 'fighter-bomber' craft through storms recalls the sequence in *Silent Running* in which the *Valley Forge* passes through the rings of Saturn. Given Stevens' later involvement with *Buck Rogers*, it is interesting that we have a pirate race of humans called the 'Dragonids', which is not a million miles from the Draconians of the *Buck Rogers* series.

The story starts off fairly poorly, with a tedious runaround about an attempt to rescue the damaged *Gemini* freighter, and also ends fairly unbelievably, with Aleph/Xanon suddenly experiencing a change of heart regarding the *Galactica*'s mission (though not a total one, as he strands his crew on Cordugo Pit at the very end), pronouncing 'there's a better leader than me. Out there trying to save what's left of the human race. His name's Adama', and his crew suddenly forgetting their mutinous urges and supporting him in this, although an explanation – that Xanon and his crew were originally political rebels before turning pirate – is provided. The pirates are also generally a little too cosy and child-friendly to be credible (with Aleph resembling a cross between Han Solo and Long John Silver). The narrative is also overpadded, with lots of repeated capture-escape runaround. However, the middle sequences are actually quite hilarious, with a sort of *Carry On* film feel to them, particularly the scenes in the Pleasure Dome, in which Starbuck arouses the suspicions of the authorities by confusedly bidding more for Athena and Boxey than humans are said to be worth, and indeed rather more than he possesses, and then eliminates the competition (a trader from the somewhat Biblically-named world of 'Bablion', who will, according to Aleph, 'buy anything') by sneaking around behind him and shutting off his breather tube.

The space pirates who are the catalyst for action in the episode are effectively described as resembling a cross between Vikings, pirates and Hell's Angels. Their ship is 'a hybrid, a souped-up monster made out of parts salvaged from fighters-bombers-cutters'. Aleph/Xanon is largely well characterised; the fact that the supposed victim of the pirates is actually their former leader is disguised for the characters by having him initially appear wearing a 'Dragonid helmet and breather tubes', and his plan in assisting the Colonials is clearly to get into a position where he can steal his own ship back and flee (although once Skyler and Starbuck pull their guns on him he has little choice but to cooperate with them); the 'star charts' he makes so much of turn out to be in his head. He also gets some good lines (Skyler: 'whose side are you on?' Aleph: 'I'm on the side of not getting killed'). The Dragonids generally are said to have rebelled, although against whom (Ovions or Colonials) is not quite clear (foreshadowing the idea in 'The Magnificent Warriors' that there are multiple factions of humans, not all of which are sympathetic to each other), and are now almost the last remnant of humanity, tolerated by the Cylons and their allies simply because they are elusive.

There are also some more entertaining examples of worldbuilding in the script. Baltar's initial encounter with the Imperious Leader has the latter promising to Baltar that he will not kill him after he has eliminated all the humans, as he plans to keep some humans as a source of slaves, and will let Baltar rule them. As an added incentive, he tells Baltar that if he doesn't comply with him, his Centurians will kill him, which Baltar refers to as 'a typical Cylon bargain'. 'Scanner-heads' is used as a nickname for Centurians, and motion-sick space-travellers are referred to as 'greensick'. As well as space pirates, 'space gypsies' are also namechecked. As in the finished series, Adama reiterates that the Fleet cannot be risked to save a freighter, or a lost crewmember, several times; there is a slight difference, however, in that any ship which falls behind, by Adama's standing order, must be abandoned and considered lost, whereas, according to a line in 'Lost Planet of the Gods', in the series the convoy stays at the speed of the slower vessels. The *Gemini* freighter and *Tauron* tanker are referred to, with the former ship being spectacularly destroyed. Ovions apparently regard carbohydrates as a sort of drug, and a trader in Cordugo Pit tries to sell Starbuck a diamond as a 'carbon deposit'; there are also references to a 'pit daggit' with scales (Aleph's amusingly vague explanation for this physical peculiarity is 'it's not a nice neighbourhood') and to an illegal 'bork fight' taking place (a bork is, apparently, a 'four-legged chicken with hair', which can be orange or blue; Starbuck is intrigued by the practice and suggests acquiring a pair of borks for the *Galactica*), which lends some context to the scripted line in 'The Magnificent Warriors' where Siress Belloby insults the belligerent Nogow by calling him a 'bork', unless of course the script is referring, in misspelled form, to the piglike 'boarks' of 'The Mutiny'. A torture chamber is described as having 'evil-looking dentistry devices', in a possible reference either to *Marathon Man* (1976) or the Roger Corman *Little Shop of Horrors* (1960), and the bombing of the streets by the pirates in Cordugo Pit is said to '[resemble] the night bombing of London'. Boxey is able to reprogramme Muffit to 'solve problems' (in this case, to rescue the captured adults) using a set of calculator-like buttons behind a panel on the droid.

All that survives of 'The Beta Pirates' is a first-draft script, which unfortunately gives little idea of what the final version might be like (particularly when one considers the changes which 'The Gun on Ice Planet Zero' went through during the rewriting process). Although there are some weak points, there are certainly enough entertaining moments to suggest that a good story might have been made from it.

UNMADE STORIES 2 • SHOWDOWN

BY FRANK ABATEMARCO

SYNOPSIS: Apollo, Starbuck, Boomer, Deitra, Athena, Boxey and Muffit take the Explorer Shuttle to an asteroid. They have trouble landing due to technical problems, and Tigh punishes the three specialist crewmen responsible, Andor, Bule and Masi (a former pilot cadet) by confining them to quarters. The exploring party discover a crashed ancient starship on the asteroid, apparently of Kobollian origin. The specialists, meanwhile, break their curfew by visiting the Officer's Club. When bridge officer Rigel warns them that they are confined to quarters, they start a fight, and flee with a shuttlecraft and three land probes, jamming the launch tubes to avoid pursuit. Landing on the asteroid, the specialists discover a lost colony town, and go on a rampage through it; arriving too late, Apollo and the others bear the brunt of the colonists' anger. The *Galactica* is attacked by Cylons, but, being unable to launch the Vipers, fights back as best as she can with her turret lasers. Sending the women, Boxey and Muffit back to the *Galactica* in the shuttlecraft, Apollo, Boomer and Starbuck track down the miscreants and engage them in combat, winning, despite the specialists' superior firepower, through ingenuity and tactical superiority, and the help of the now-compliant colonists. Apollo appeals to Masi's better nature and fixes the launch tubes on their return. The Vipers launch and the Cylons are defeated.

ANALYSIS: 'Showdown' is a one-part script which, apparently, was almost filmed (the cover indicates four revisions, with the first being 5 July 1978 and the final 15 August 1978), with the 'land probe' space motorbike props actually having been built, and were later used in *Galactica 1980* (a story featuring them is also mentioned in the document outlining the supposed *Battlestar Galactica* second season). Overall, it is fairly derivative, but not more so than some that were actually filmed, and does keep in line with many of the series' themes.

The episode's author, Frank Abatemarco, is a scriptwriter/producer with credits on *Cagney and Lacey*, the 1988 revival of *Mission Impossible*, and *Star Trek: The Next Generation* (having been a writer on three episodes, and supervising producer on thirteen; one of the stories he is credited on, 'Chain of Command', has a teleplay by Ronald D Moore, showrunner of the reimagined series). The script appears to have been written during the rewrites on 'Lost Planet of the Gods' (the cover for "Showdown" is first dated

5 July 1978, and goes on to show that further revisions took place throughout July and August) as, although Deitra features and Athena is given a role as a Viper pilot rather than a bridge officer, Baltar does not appear (his role is taken by the Imperious Leader, who is said to have 'the ever-present lizard on his shoulder'). Cassiopea also does not appear, even though the decision to keep her had been taken by this point, as she appears in the 27 July draft of 'Lost Planet of the Gods'. Presumably her absence is down to a miscommunication to the writer that the new female character had been added to the roster. Why the story was never filmed is unknown; land probes aside, it does not seem to present any budgetary problems (the fact that the town of Croy is described as looking rather like Pompeii, and its inhabitants to be clad in togas, if male, and tabards, if female, suggests that the story was written with the idea of reusing extant Universal Studios sets and costumes), and, while the issue of actress availability (in the case of Deitra) or unsuitability (in the case of Athena) could have presented problems, the two women's roles could easily have been given to Brie and Cassiopea, or, indeed, amalgamated and given to either of them.

The episode has some interesting differences from the finished series. Athena plays a more extensive role than she would later do (though she and Deitra are both, it must be said, criminally underused, passively sitting around the landram and/or shuttle while the male characters have the adventures), and she and Starbuck are seen in a clinch at one point (again, recalling the earlier idea of having her as his primary love interest). Rigel and Omega are seen off-duty in the officer's quarters, something which never happens in the series. Boxey addresses Apollo as 'Daddy', which is perhaps a bit too twentieth-century-Earth to be credible.

The episode also continues some of the series' themes and trends, not always in a good way. The story reads like *The Wild One* (1953) crossed with *Gunfight at the OK Corral* (1957), featuring as it does the team of specialists running wild on land-probes in a small town where the authorities are powerless to stop them and the women all find them fascinating, and then culminates in a gunfighter-style showdown between the specialists and Boomer, Apollo and Starbuck with a chorus of frightened townsfolk looking on, in much the same way as many of the finished episodes reference well-known films with greater and lesser success. A character called 'Lea' has a name unfortunately a little too close to the female protagonist of the *Star Wars* series. The meeting of the Croytens (this being the accepted noun for 'inhabitants of Croy', apparently) is described as follows: 'everyone in the room is wearing a dark hooded robe with the exception of 12 men in white hooded robes seated off to the side of the front of the room in something resembling a jury box', and Selmar, as their leader, wearing a white hooded robe bearing the (unspecified) symbol of the mother colony. As well as sounding reminiscent of *The Prisoner* episode 'Fall Out', this again means that we have a group of twelve ruling figures in white, led by a thirteenth. They then turn out to be just as cowardly as the Council of Twelve, when Selmar advises 'it is my recommendation that we do not take sides- In the conflict of others – We must heed the warning of the intruder's (sic) and do as they say'. Despite their hostility to Apollo's party, they also wind up turning to them for help to get rid of the miscreants, much as the Council of Twelve alternately vilify and then plead for the help of the warriors in 'Baltar's Escape'. It is also unfortunately predictable that Masi, the specialist who, by his own account, had been a good pilot cadet before it was discovered that he had a computer speciality, turns into the moral voice of the specialists, again implying that people in the military are basically good eggs (and means the author is tacitly acknowledging Masi's earlier remark, regarding the pilots, that 'my sole purpose around here was to make … those hotshots look good'). Once again, the Colonials do not offer to rescue the Croytens, or even to help them build up their defences against a Cylon attack (admittedly, they *are* rather annoying, but that's no excuse for leaving them to die). There is also a minor continuity error in that Omega and Rigel are back on the bridge very shortly after they are seen off-duty in the officers' club, with the concurrent, enormously contrived, suggestion that their break ended just as the crisis on the bridge began.

There are more positive connections to the finished series. The Ovions are namechecked (Starbuck remarks, regarding the pre-flight check crew, that he is 'gonna feed them to the Ovions'). The Kobollian alphabet is described as resembling the Greek one; the Croytens' situation, having been forced to start over as a civilisation when their technicians were killed in the initial crash, recalls the case of both the Twelve Colonies after the Cylon holocaust, and the original settlers from Kobol when they arrived at the Colonies. Rigel's rank is given as Flight Corporal, and the crewmen are given the rank of 'specialist', an idea which would be extensively reused in the reimagined series. Starbuck and Apollo altruistically cover for the flight crew's mistakes, much as Starbuck covered for the cadets' problems in 'Crossfire'. The prison barge is again the 'grid barge', female cadets are namechecked, and a Croyten called Zara foreshadows the fact that a newsreader of that name appears later in the series (in 'The Man with Nine Lives' and 'Murder on the *Rising Star*'). The stage descriptions flesh out the situation in the officer's club more than we see in the finished series, explaining that it is open to all ranks, but that the different groups tend to socialise with each other rather than mix with other groups.

Andor contributes a new Colonial colloquialism, when he tells Apollo 'you can take the tube!', which appears to be the Colonial parallel of 'go take a running jump' (presumably, the expression is an abbreviation of 'go fire yourself out of a launch tube'). There is also a moment where Andor describes the regulars as 'the chosen few', which, of course, they are, giving a flash of insight into how the ordinary people of the Fleet view Apollo *et al*'s continued presence on the important and exciting missions.

The story is something of a mixed result. 1970s social trends get a look in, with the biker craze of the day featuring heavily (Andor and Bule, the flight mechanics, are even described as looking like 'Hell's Angels enforcers'). Tabletop and upright electronic games, then very much novelties, are described; the specialists are seen at one point playing a game which involves pitting Cylon against Colonial fighters (and Andor is described as playing the Cylon side, shooting Colonial ships, foreshadowing his later role in sabotaging the Colonial war effort). There are a couple of good lines, such as Selmar's words to the Colonials: 'we have nothing in common. We live in peace. You are the hunted. You're not wanted here', and Starbuck and Apollo's exchange as they sneak up on the rogue specialists: 'Think I should mention something about the pre-flight check they did on the shuttle?' 'I'd let it go'. On the other hand, not only are the female characters underused, but Boxey and Muffit might as well not have been in the story for all they contribute to it. It's also highly improbable that one technician would have the computer skills to jam all of the launch tubes such that no one else on the ship can fix them (as this exposes the *Galactica* to any number of risks even outside the scenario presented here of the technician in question going rogue), and also, considering the amount of time which passes between the start of the Cylon attack and the return of the heroes to save the day, the Cylons seem to have made remarkably little progress in the battle; realistically speaking, they should have been in a position to just pick off the Vipers as they emerge from the launch tubes.

'Showdown' is not a million miles from the scripts that were actually filmed, and is arguably better than some of them. However, it would not have been a particularly memorable or classic story, being more 'The Magnificent Warriors' than 'The Living Legend'.

UNMADE STORIES 3 • THE MUTINY

BY GUY MAGAR

SYNOPSIS: After a long period with no Cylon attacks, the people of the Fleet, led by the Council of Twelve and, specifically, Siress Orestra and Sire Hadar, rebel against Adama, insisting on starting a new colony on the planet Zarta. Adama and a few loyal crewmembers remain on the *Galactica*, while the others launch themselves into pioneering activities. Starbuck discovers that the planet is inhabited by a wild man, and tracks him to the ruins of a settlement. Meanwhile, as the Colonials degenerate into squabbling factions, Baltar, leading the Cylons, prepares to attack. Believing all to be lost, Adama decides to die in battle, and pilots a lone Viper out to meet the oncoming Cylon fighters. The wild man is found to be carrying a recording which reveals that the planet was once the home of a group which split off from the Thirteenth Tribe during their exodus to Earth, but which degenerated into factions and were picked off by Cylons. Thus warned, the Colonials abandon Zarta and return to space in time to fight off the Cylon attack.

ANALYSIS: 'The Mutiny' is an unmade single-part script which is fairly average, and whose main point of interest is that it appears to foreshadow certain themes of the reimagined *Battlestar Galactica*.

Guy Magar is best known in television as a director rather than a writer (on, among others, *Buck Rogers*, *The A-Team* and *La Femme Nikita*), and had been second-unit director on 'Lost Planet of the Gods', which explains the familiarity with the series' available stock footage which permeates the script for 'The Mutiny', even down to the detail of suggesting that Adama's damaged Viper should be represented by footage of Zac's from 'Saga of a Star World'. Rumours exist that 'The Mutiny' was a script written for the never-commissioned second season of *Battlestar Galactica*; however, the absence of Sheba and the date of the script (2 October 1978) suggest that it was written for the first season, although it may have been considered as a script for Season Two in rewritten form (as with, for instance, 'I Have Seen Earth'). It is tempting to speculate that the writer was influenced by *Space: 1999*, which focused around its protagonists trying, and failing, to find a planet to settle, and also in that it had a character named Maya (Jolly's girlfriend is here called Maia). However, the idea is a fairly obvious direction in which to take the characters (indeed, the presence of a savage, half-mad, marooned wild man whose name is variously given as 'Bengun' or 'Bengum', implies that Magar may have been drawing his inspiration primarily from *Treasure Island*), and 'Maia/Maya' is a generic science-fiction women's name.

The story contains much which is in keeping with the rest of the series. There is a thematic similarity with the Carillon sequences of 'Saga of a Star World', with the rest of the Fleet embracing life on an alien planet where Adama has justified doubts. Religious iconography is again used (the journey to Zarta is referred to as an 'exodus' in the stage directions, in quotes and underlined), and the consideration of military rank is referenced when Adama must defer to Apollo's orders during the battle, as Apollo is in command of this particular mission. The cowboy roots of the series are referenced in the description of what happens when the Colonials land on Zarta: 'A montage not unlike a "John Ford" pioneering sequence … as the people begin to build their new town … some men including Boomer (shirtless) are busy cutting down huge trees … others, with Omega (shirtless) are digging the large wells for water …' and so forth. When not shirtless, the warriors are said to be wearing civilian clothing, symbolising their departure from military life.

The Council of Twelve once again make a decision which Adama disapproves of, and wind up turning desperately to him for help the moment things start going wrong (Siress Oresta is explicitly stated in the script as wearing white robes, as well). Here, however, the interesting twist is that the military also support this decision, giving the episode a possibly anti-democratic subtext, in that it suggests that even the warriors (normally held up as paragons of virtue and wisdom) cannot be trusted to make the right decisions. Whereas episodes like 'Take the *Celestra*' imply that mutiny is a good thing if it is in the general interest, here, Apollo explicitly states that a mutiny, even with popular support, 'cannot be tolerated, now or ever'. When Oresta argues that what they have here is 'not a mutiny … but a democracy', Apollo backs down, but again the will of the people is shown to be flawed and the people in need of Adama's guidance, even if what ultimately prompts them to go back to the fold is the warnings contained in the wild man's recording. There is also a theme of great civilisations degenerating into primitivism, symbolised in the fate of the earlier colony.

The story also uses, and adds to, the Colonial argot. 'Sealed' is once again a synonym for marriage, and, when Apollo reminds Starbuck that 'this is not a space circus' when he performs a loop-the-loop with his Viper, we learn something about Colonial entertainment. 'Four hectons of flexite', evidently a foodstuff, is stolen at one point, and there are periodic mentions of a drug called 'noxkaine', apparently an inhaled euphoric. The Fleet contains a vessel called 'space bus *Delta-3*'. More problematically, the word 'clakton' is given as the Colonial equivalent of a day (a term seen nowhere else, and indeed contradicted on page one of the script when Starbuck refers to his 'graduation day' at the Academy) and Baltar at one point says 'don't count your cliggets before they hatch'.

The episode as written also contains a continuity point, in that it backs up the idea that, by the time of 'The Living Legend' (the first draft of which is dated July 1978) the fleet had been in transit for two yahrens. Apollo says, regarding the Cylons, that 'it took us yahrens to lose them'. The story has to take place prior to 'The Living Legend', due to the absence of Sheba, and the fact that the characters say that they haven't seen any Cylons for a hundred 'centons' (this term likely meaning a period of about a week[20]), which, since the Cylons appear in 'The Living Legend', would again place 'The Mutiny' before 'The Living Legend'. Since Hadar says that there is no evidence that they are on the right path for Earth, the story also definitely takes place prior to 'War of the Gods', in which this evidence is provided. Having said that, Baltar and Lucifer's conversation suggests that the Cylons' last encounter with the Fleet was fairly recent, so it may simply be that the writer is understandably unsure of the meaning of the terms 'yahren' and 'centon'.

Ironically, however, the main problem with the story lies in its relation to the rest of the series' continuity. The planet was supposedly settled during the exodus from Kobol, which would mean that it took place long enough ago for the rest of the exiles to arrive at the Twelve Colonies, rebuild their technology from scratch into a space-faring civilisation, and then hold a thousand yahren-long war with the Cylons (which, even with Colonial lifespans lasting two hundred yahrens, would take several generations). However, the ancient Hadar says, in a recording made about forty yahrens previously, that it was a 'short-lived' civilisation. The implication is thus either that the exodus from Kobol was relatively recent (which contradicts the rest of the series) or else that Hadar has a very strange definition of 'short-lived'.

This continuity problem provides a curious connection to the reimagined series. The story itself is very close to the latter's series two closing story, 'Lay Down Your Burdens' (with the difference that the planet here is much more hospitable than New Caprica). More than this, however, the presence of the recording, in which we encounter 'Hadar, son of Marduk', has echoes of the reimagined series' 'all this has happened before' theme, suggesting as it does that not only did an earlier group of Colonials have a near-identical experience

---

20 Although 'centon' is usually used to mean a short amount of time, somewhere between a few seconds and a minute, and 'secton' to mean a period of about a week, the meaning of the terms within the series is inconsistent, and 'centon' is indeed used in 'Saga of a Star World' to indicate a period of several days.

of settling on the planet and being attacked by Cylons, but also that earlier versions of the characters themselves (in this case, the roles are reversed, and the modern Hadar is the *father* of the modern Marduk) have existed. There are thus intriguing echoes in this story of the later *Battlestar Galactica* series.

There are some problems with the story beyond its continuity issues, some of which could have been remedied through clever script editing. The coordinates of the area (Beta 2 quadrant in the Swytar Galaxy), and even the name of the planet (Zarta) seem to be quite well-known, which would appear to contradict the idea that they have been in 'a whole new galaxy, one no human in this Fleet has ever seen before' since 'The Long Patrol' (broadcast 15 October 1978), although the area could have been charted but not often visited. Despite the extensive use of stock footage, the story is also rather expensive-sounding, with a comedy sequence in which Starbuck attempts to trap 'boarks' (described as a kind of pig-like creature, rather than some relation of the chicken-like 'borks' of 'The Beta Pirates'; they apparently yield 'boark chops') requiring at minimum two trained pigs, possibly in makeup. Athena is said to be in love with Starbuck, which is odd as the writers were playing down that idea by this point in the series.

There are more extensive problems. While the idea that, with the common enemy which holds them together gone, a group will degenerate into factions, is not unsupported, the Colonials here seem to split up disturbingly fast, considering that they still face a common obstacle in the form of the primitive conditions on the planet. Oresta implies that Adama does not respect her because of her gender, which seems an accusation rather at odds with his normal behaviour. Before Adama abandons the *Galactica*, he informs Tigh that 'after I'm gone … I want you to surrender the Galactica … and lead our people as best you can under Cylon rule …' , which contradicts the fact that Adama otherwise believes the Cylons to be bent on their extermination rather than their domination. At the end of the story, the *Galactica* somehow wins through against the combined force of three base stars, which seems miraculous.

That having been said, the characterisation of the regulars is generally rather good. Adama, in particular, shows a Cain-like streak in, effectively, mounting a solo suicide charge against the Cylons in a Viper (this is the only time in the original series that Adama is seen flying any sort of vehicle, let alone a combat craft, although the scene where he meets Tigh in the landing bay in 'Saga of a Star World' has him sitting in a Viper, and their dialogue implies that both men were Viper pilots at some point in the past). Jolly turns out to have been developing a serious relationship with Maia, who is a 'technocrat' (this appears to be the Colonial equivalent of technicians). The warriors, faced with the mutiny, are described as 'doubting, yet loyal', supporting Adama but at the same time seduced by the possibility of taking up a normal life; Apollo says that Starbuck has 'always wanted a crack at civilian life', recalling Starbuck voicing his ambivalence towards his military career in 'The Man with Nine Lives'. Greenbean and Giles make an appearance, and Jolly's rank is here given as 'Lieutenant'. Baltar also gets a good, albeit brief, showing, saying 'I always have a plan, Lucifer; great leaders always have plans', even though it's fairly obvious that he himself doesn't; he also says to Lucifer 'never underestimate the inspiration of human intelligence and courage … obviously lacking in machines … no matter how advanced', which Lucifer apparently doubts, but Baltar has been put in charge for a reason, namely, that the Imperious Leader evidently thinks he understands the human mind in a way that his mechanical followers don't. Baltar refers to Lucifer 'letting the *Galactica* escape your multiple quadrant sentries', and Lucifer replies 'I did not plan on Commander Adama taking such a risky escape route', which suggests prior unseen events. A more curious revelation is that Boxey goes down to Zarta with Athena, where Apollo stays on the *Galactica* and visits them occasionally, which seems to contradict the fact that he appears otherwise to be Boxey's main caregiver. Cassiopea appears only in a single shot, with no dialogue, which would have been a serious waste of Laurette Spang.

'The Mutiny' contains much which is problematic, but also contains, accidentally and otherwise, a few ideas which give the reader pause for thought on the Fleet's relationship to its earlier ancestors.

UNMADE STORIES 4 • TWO FOR TWILLY

BY JIM CARLSON AND TERENCE MCDONNELL

SYNOPSIS: Apollo and Starbuck travel to Agro-Three, bringing with them Zeena, the wife of their friend Twilly, a gyro specialist currently working there. Upon landing, Starbuck and Apollo learn that Twilly has another wife, Gayla, on Agro-Three. Twilly desperately contrives to keep the women apart (complicated by the fact that Zeena has been assigned as a hydroponics tech, assisting Gayla). When the pair finally learn of the connection, Gayla confronts Twilly with a gun and accidentally damages the ship's gyros in the process. A race is on to stabilise the agro-ship before it is drawn off course into a nearby mega-star, with Twilly sinking into self-pity and his wives engaging in recriminations against him. Starbuck and Apollo eventually persuade the women to patch things up with Twilly, in time for him to fix the ship. Crisis over, the two women divorce Twilly, who, we discover, has a third wife, Vella, elsewhere in the Fleet.

ANALYSIS: 'Two for Twilly' is self-consciously a comedy episode, explicitly based on the 1953 Alec Guinness film *Captain's Paradise* (featuring the captain of a ferry between Gibraltar and Morocco, who keeps a wife in each port and contrives to prevent them from meeting). It is competent but forgettable, with its central character being one of its worst aspects.

The most circulated draft of 'Two for Twilly' is dated 22 December 1978. Unlike other unfilmed scripts from the second half of 1978, it appears to reference the events of 'The Living Legend', with Sheba having a small role. However, this is explained by the fact that the two writers were the series' story editors, and thus more in tune with how the series was developing than commissioned freelance writers. References are also made to Starbuck and Cassiopea's relationship, and Athena, Boxey, and Baltar are all conspicuous by their absence (though the Cylons are briefly namechecked, as the stated reason for the Fleet to be doing a slingshot manoeuvre around a mega-star is to put some distance between them and the Cylons), which is again more in keeping with the series' actual setup in its latter half than the other unfilmed scripts. Also, the other stories appear to have been written so as to come, chronologically, before 'The Living Legend'.

The story did, in fact, get close to filming, with Carlson and McDonnell recalling auditioning Jamie Lee Curtis for a role in the story (presumably the fiery Gayla), and Anne Lockhart recalling that the cast and crew were given the script, and they were about to do a reading of it, when the story was pulled. The reasons for its withdrawal are unknown, with plausible suggestions being concerns that it was too close to its source story (with the Fox lawsuit still ongoing, the crew were conscious of plagiarism issues) or, more likely, that ABC's Standards and Practices objected to the story focusing on polygamy, despite the fact that Adama says that monogamy is 'the natural order of things' at the end of the story.

Much of the episode takes place on an agro-ship, Agro-Three, which apparently boasts a lake, and has a female captain in late middle age named Demeter, who was, of course, the Greek goddess of the harvest and fertility, suggesting more symbolic naming (the other officer we encounter is named Argus, the name of the many-eyed watchman in Greek mythology; as he does not seem to share any symbolic traits with him, this appears to be more random selection of classical names). Agro-Three is the only agro-ship mentioned in this script, which, if we take this to mean that it is the only such ship in the Fleet at this time, would be consistent with the situation following 'The Magnificent Warriors', but which might contradict 'War of the Gods' (with its multiple agro-ships, including one named Agro-Ship Nine). The name 'Vella' had previously been used for a different character in 'The Lost Warrior'. Compressed boraton is mentioned, forming part of 'fire suppressors', and we learn that Apollo has had some training in fixing gyros. New Colonial terms in this script include 'floatator', a boat, and the expressions 'son of an Orion klarn' (an insult) and 'what in Sagan's hole' (which invites dubious speculation as to its referent). Tigh is described at one point by a bartender as 'madder than a Cylon with welded elbows'. Polygamy is illegal in the Colonies, and divorce proceedings (called 'breaking the seal') usually take six months, though Adama is capable of legally divorcing people on the spot if necessary. The terms 'marriage' and 'sealed' are both used, interchangeably. Twilly's rank is 'chief', foreshadowing the use of the term in the reimagined series.

The script does have some rather good lines, to its credit. Starbuck, wrongly, describes Twilly as 'so settled down, that I'll bet Zeena has to dust him off every now and again'. Later, when it transpires that Twilly has been two-timing Zeena with Gayla, Apollo remarks 'doesn't look very dusty to me'. When Starbuck confronts Twilly over his behaviour with Gayla, exclaiming 'you said you weren't fooling around', Twilly retorts, 'I'm not! She's my wife!' In keeping with their established characters, Starbuck is more sympathetic to Twilly's situation than Apollo is. Twilly's two wives have quite different personalities (as is the case in *Captain's Paradise*), with Gayla being assertive and Zeena emotional and inclined to burst into tears. We learn something more of the agro-ship's operations, involving a hydroponic system where crops are grown in nutrient fluid. The idea that spacecraft would need gyroscopic stabilisers is scientifically justified, and the science/pseudo-science is internally consistent throughout. There is also rather a clever subtext in the idea that Twilly, an expert in gyroscopic stabilisers which keep the ship in a delicate balance, is similarly maintaining a delicate balance in his own relationships; when his relationships break down, the result is that Agro-Three also loses its stability, and it is only when some closure is achieved in his personal life that Twilly is able to restore balance to the ship.

The main weakness of the story is the character of Twilly. As with the same writers' script 'Murder on the *Rising Star*', in which we learn that Ortega, despite never having been mentioned before, is a longstanding nemesis of Starbuck's, here Twilly appears to be a major name in the Fleet, the only gyro specialist aboard the *Galactica* (having survived the holocaust by virtue of having been aboard an agro-ship, fixing it, at the time), and a longtime friend of Starbuck and Apollo's from Academy days. Despite Apollo and Starbuck's liking for the man, he comes across in the story as selfish, unpleasant, tedious and self-pitying, such that the reader just wants to give him a damned good kicking by the end of it; he is blatantly exploiting the fact that he is the only person left who can do his job. Considering that all of the trouble would not have taken place if it hadn't been for Twilly's hyperactive libido (to say nothing of the fact that he confesses to deliberately damaging equipment, which is difficult to replace in the fugitive conditions of the Fleet, in order to have excuses to go over to Agro-Three), it is also rather odd of Apollo to plead with Adama for clemency on his behalf on the grounds that he saved them by fixing the agro-ship. Other problems include that all the progressive aspects of having a female ship's captain are undermined by the fact that, in a crisis, she first demonstrates incompetence and then promptly hands over effective command to Apollo, and that the sheer amount of technobabble means the story reads like a fantasy in the mind of an oversexed autistic.

'Two for Twilly' is thus a mixed result, not because it is a comedy, but because the central character is too unsympathetic, and the dramatic tension of the repairing of the agro-ship is too drawn out, making the story seem rather thin once the wives discover the situation. Reports exist, however, that it is another story which might have been developed in the series' planned second season.

UNMADE STORIES 5 • I HAVE SEEN EARTH
BY STEVE KREINBERG AND ANDY GUERDAT

SYNOPSIS: Starbuck, Athena and Apollo, on patrol, rescue a small craft under attack from the Cylons. Its owner, Jaspar, is a prospector who quickly endears himself to Boxey through his bluff manner and tall tales. He learns of the Fleet's quest for Earth, and tells them that he has been there. He encourages them to go to the planet Opelon, where he claims there is an Earth colony. In fact, the planet is home to a Cylon mining operation, and Jaspar hopes to deliver the Colonials to the Cylons, then, in the resulting conflagration, steal the ore from the mine and flee. However, Boxey and Muffit stow away on his ship when he leaves the *Galactica* secretly to carry out this plan, and, when Jaspar lands on the planet, the child is discovered by the Cylons. Baltar contacts Adama and attempts to use the fact that he has Boxey prisoner as a bargaining chip. Meanwhile, Apollo leads a rescue mission to save the child. Jaspar stays behind on the planet and destroys the mine, after giving Boxey a medallion… which turns out to depict Earth.

ANALYSIS: 'I Have Seen Earth' is another unfilmed one-part episode which is firmly in space-Western territory, and again not too far removed from stories which actually were filmed (it is possible that the reason why many of the later unfilmed scripts were dropped was less a matter of quality and/or economics as that they could not be easily fitted in with the arc which develops after 'War of the Gods', with the Cylons largely absent and Baltar a prisoner on the *Galactica*). The story is average, marred slightly by the fact that the audience has to believe that the Fleet personnel would fall for a fairly obvious trick.

'I Have Seen Earth' is currently available in the form of a second-draft script (original dated 26 October 1978, revised 3 November 1978). Like 'The Mutiny', it fits with the series' setup prior to 'The Living Legend' and 'War of the Gods', with no Sheba and the Fleet having no idea of the whereabouts of Earth. Reportedly this script was in consideration as a second season episode, with revisions by Carlson and McDonnell; however, the presence of Baltar as the main antagonist and the heavy use of Boxey and Muffit is at odds with the second season document, suggesting that, if this document is in fact an indication of the way in which the series was developing, it would need heavy revisions. Kreinberg and Guerdat both have credits on a range of American television programmes, including *Mork and Mindy*.

The story itself is rather reminiscent of *Lost in Space* (which had an episode featuring a space prospector, 'Blast Off Into Space', and another featuring an old adventurer who charms the young boy Will with preposterous anecdotes which turn out to be lies, 'The Questing Beast'), involving as it does Boxey becoming fascinated by a folksy space prospector with a comic-relief pet which is clearly a monkey in makeup (Nugget, the 'simian', said to be an animal which 'looks like a monkey, except for one difference. Instead of fur, it has a brilliant coat of feathers, all the colours of the spectrum. Its tail, like a peacock's, is long, flowing and exotic'). Jaspar is also not too far removed from Aleph/Xanon of 'The Beta Pirates', particularly regarding his change of heart at the end, which is apparently due to his guilt over his inadvertently putting Boxey in danger.

The characterisation and development of most of the regulars are problematic. While Boxey is fairly well-drawn, engaging in his usual trick of stowing away, and innocently asking Adama why he doesn't like Jaspar while in full view of the man in question, Adama appears to have checked his brains at the door for this story, allowing Jaspar to take extraordinary liberties despite his doubts about the fellow, and the rest of the ship's personnel are similarly gullible. Athena is again acting as a Viper pilot, and it is a plot point that she has never shot down a Cylon raider, which, aside from contradicting 'Lost Planet of the Gods' (in which the script has her shooting down two raiders and the screened version, one) begs the question of why a fighter pilot with such a poor record hasn't been quietly taken off the duty roster. When Athena disingenuously asks Jaspar what Earth women are like, there is again the implication that she is pursuing Starbuck, which had been dropped by the latter half of the season (curiously, Cassiopea appears in the cast list, but not in the episode; she may have appeared in the 26 October draft and been written out). Jaspar is welcomed to the Fleet by Adama with an elegantly-set meal of exotic dishes, which seems selfish in light of the ongoing food shortages mentioned elsewhere. Baltar and the Cylons are a mixed result: Lucifer gets in some good lines like 'Baltar will devise a plan. He is a brilliant man … provided the plan works', but Baltar tends to sound rather more like Doctor Smith from *Lost in Space*, calling the Cylons 'tin-plated monstrosities' and one Centurian a 'mechanical haploid' (which, referring as it does to chromosomal anomalies, is inaccurate), and is subject to some rather undignified treatment, getting a kick in the shins from Boxey and a bite from Muffit.

Some of the story's conceits are also questionable. Jaspar is seen finding directions with 'an old betasextant' (implying a device which would not work in space). He suggests that they navigate by a particular 'constellation', when constellations are only visible at fixed points (all of this resulting in a surreal exchange in which Adama says 'Tigh, I'm allowing this Fleet, equipped with the finest navigational equipment in the universe, to be led through space by a stranger using nothing more than a primitive sextant', Tigh counters, 'You're afraid he'll make a mistake?' and Adama replies 'I don't know. I just hope I haven't already made one'). Adama voices suspicions about Jaspar's story on the grounds that the ancient writings do not mention an Earth settlement on Opelon, which begs the question of how he expects the people of Kobol, who authored the ancient writings, to know about a settlement which would come into being some considerable time later. The Cylons refer to Boxey as the 'sole inhabitant' of the *Golden Queen* when they find it, suggesting that (surprisingly for mechanical lifeforms) they don't consider Muffit worthy of mention. It apparently takes two Cylon guards to hold a primary school-age boy prisoner (the detention chamber door is also unlocked, begging the question of why they don't just lock the door and save themselves the effort). The Cylons in the mine have arms modified into pickaxes and scuttles, and their scanning-eyes replaced by lights like a miner's helmet lamp, which makes one wonder how they see.

Other aspects of the story are better. The fact that Jaspar uses vocabulary recognised by Colonials ('leonine' for a lion-like animal, for instance) suggests a common cultural origin. There is also some continuity with earlier episodes, with Jaspar referring to having travelled 'from Zanus to Carillon, from Palobar to Earth' and a reference to the Golden Cluster as being the Colonial warriors' highest award (presumably the writers are referring to the Gold Cluster, which is mentioned in 'Saga of a Star World' and the draft versions of 'The Man with Nine Lives' and 'The Living Legend'; the 2 October 1978 terminology document, as well as the March and April draft scripts of 'Saga of a Star World', all use the term 'Golden Cluster'). Athena acts as a teacher (as in 'Greetings from Earth'), although here it is apparently just on a one-to-one basis with Boxey, and the fact that she nearly shoots down Starbuck's party in their commandeered Cylon craft recalls the fact that she shot down Starbuck during the simulator exercises in 'Lost Planet of the Gods'. We get some new items of vocabulary, with 'gyroballs' as a child's game rather like marbles, and 'tinheads' as a new epithet for Cylons (Jaspar swears 'rusty-eyed tinheads!' at one point), as well as the more unbelievable expression 'the underdaggits'. Jaspar has a 'numo rifle', recalling the pneumatic weaponry of 'The Lost Warrior', and 'megon', a unit of measurement first used in 'Lost Planet of the Gods', reappears. Baltar here learns for the first time that Boxey is Adama's grandson. Adama is again willing to sacrifice the rescue party when waiting for them could pose a threat to the Fleet more generally, and Baltar again articulates the idea that he wishes to form an alliance with Adama to attack the Cylon Empire.

There are a few good lines, such as Tigh and Starbuck's exchange about Jaspar and Nugget: 'Is that him?' 'Yes, sir. The one without the feathers'. When Jaspar tries to defend Boxey's disobedience in being out of his quarters without permission, saying that it was his own fault, Apollo says 'but Boxey's still responsible for his own actions', flagging up the series' theme of individual accountability. There is also a nice bit of characterisation when Athena suggests to Adama that his mistrust of Jaspar comes from jealousy over Boxey's closeness to the prospector, and Adama assures her this is not the case, then immediately tells Tigh to congratulate Jaspar on his and the Fleet's behalf. Jaspar's plan to string along the Colonials and then hand them over to the Cylons on Opelon is actually breathtakingly evil. While the ironic ending – that, unbeknownst to the Colonials, Jaspar's medallion depicts Earth – is a suitable twist for the story, it is slightly obvious and also rather too close to the ending of 'The Long Patrol'.

'I Have Seen Earth', like most of the unfilmed scripts, would have likely made a well-crafted, if not too original or exciting, finished episode, although some aspects of it would undoubtedly need to change during the rewriting process.

BATTLESTAR GALACTICA: PROPOSED SEASON TWO

In recent years, a document has come to light which appears to be a promotional piece outlining a possible second season for *Battlestar Galactica*. Peter Noble, who describes the contents on www.cylon.org, obtained his copy from Chris Larson, son of Glen Larson, via an Ebay auction; other sources dispute its authenticity, pointing out that it contains illustrations known to have been made in the mid-1980s and 1990s (although these may have been added to the document at a later date as a way of making it more saleable), and that stories which we know were being reworked for inclusion in the second season do not appear in the list of proposed episodes. If (entirely or partly) genuine, the document suggests that, had the series continued, it would have changed radically, and not necessarily for the better.

The document starts off by aggrievedly pointing out that *Battlestar Galactica* was beset with scheduling changes and pre-emptions during its run (thus implying that any problems the series might have had are largely down to the network), and then outlining the changes which will be made to the series format, describing the characters, and summarising a few proposed scripts.

The document indicates that the revised series would have more of a focus on female viewers, saying 'the women of our crew will take more important parts in the adventures of the *Galactica* staff which will give the women in the audience more identification with our characters. Although the seriousness of the mission is never in doubt, we will introduce more humour into the show'. Whether *Battlestar Galactica* was in fact failing to attract female viewers, as the document claims, is debatable, as the series was aimed at families and had a number of strong female characters, and Benedict and Hatch reportedly had quite a following among teenage and younger women, but there was seen to be a need at the time for television networks to cater more to women, as evidenced by such late-1970s offerings as *The Bionic Woman* and *Charlie's Angels*, as well as the continual exploitation of Gil Gerard as a sex object on *Buck Rogers* and of David Soul and Paul Michael Glaser on *Starsky and Hutch*. The document indicates that there will be more of a focus on character-driven stories, which, to be fair, is what *Battlestar Galactica* did best (although the story synopses below rather give the lie to this). The document also says that Isaac Asimov, 'the world's most respected science-fiction author', had agreed to be the series' creative consultant despite, or perhaps because of, his condemnation of it upon its release, and Larson has confirmed in interviews that he was indeed in touch with Asimov on this matter. Asimov's involvement was unlikely to have been too close, however, given that Asimov lived in New York and had a fear of flying, and that it could take up to two weeks for a package to go from California to New York in the late 1970s.

The cast was also to be reduced, with Colonel Tigh, Doctors Salik and Wilker, Muffit and Baltar to go entirely, and Boxey to be 'reduced to an occasional guest appearance if required', which, although unfortunate, is not surprising given his diminished role in the latter half of the first season. More controversially, Sheba was also to have been killed off, which strikes a false note with the document's emphasising the need for strong female characters (and Anne Lockhart herself has said that had it come to that, she would have challenged it strongly). Athena would have instead taken on the main female role, but she would have been severely disfigured in the first episode and had her beauty restored by plastic surgery (suggesting that a recasting was in the air), though her body would remain scarred; she would have become more aggressive, replacing Apollo as Adama's main supporter in the command structure of the *Galactica*, which sounds unfortunately like the 1980s idea that in order for a female character to be considered 'strong' she must also be aggressive and masculine.

On the male front, Apollo, scarred emotionally by the loss of Sheba, would effectively swap characterisations with Starbuck, with the former becoming more fun-loving and less focused on responsibility, while the latter would be chosen by Adama for command, and would give up his relationship with Cassiopea. Cassiopea herself would replace Doctor Salik as the chief medical officer, while Boomer, manifesting a 'combination Einstein-Edison talent' would become the Wilker-substitute, being 'a fixture on the bridge and in the lab. His new role and ambition brings him into natural conflict with Athena, but Boomer's warmth and understanding eventually soothes these ruffled feathers'. Adama appears to have been more or less unscathed, but the synopsis adds a new character, Troy, Adama's cabin boy, brought in 'to further solidify our position with young girls', and to be 'cute, mischievous, well intentioned, a pain in the ass for Starbuck and Apollo', suggesting that the character would essentially be Boxey with added teenage appeal.

The proposed scripts are then summarised as follows:

Return of the Pegasus: In this story, the season opener, the *Galactica* would have faced a devastating Cylon attack, which would have killed Sheba and wounded Athena (as above). The Fleet is saved by the reappearance of the *Pegasus*, complete with Cain and a beautiful XO, Renata (described, somewhat improbably for someone in such a commanding position, as 'warm, almost subservient') for whose affections Apollo and Starbuck compete. The latter, wandering through the bowels of the ship, finds out that Cain has been replaced by a Cylon android, and the rest of his crew are gradually meeting the same fate, and Renata is their leader. If genuine, this story is interesting in its foreshadowing the use of humanoid Cylons in *Galactica 1980* and the reimagined series, and particularly the use of attractive female Cylon agents in the latter.

A Woman's Power: This episode is essentially Aristophanes' *Lysistrata* in space: the Fleet's women decide they have had it with military life and will withhold sexual favours and domestic duties until the Fleet achieves peace, with Athena becoming involved with them. Adama, understandably irked by their behaviour, throws the leaders in the brig, but one escapes and, strapping a bomb to her body, makes it to the bridge and threatens to blow everyone up unless the prisoners are released and given safe conduct away from the Fleet. Athena, realising that her support of the women is in fact due to her feelings about her disfigurement, talks them out of their course of action and persuades Adama to give the women of the Fleet more say in its day-to-day governance. This idea seems not only patronising and silly, but at odds with the first season, which gave us a Fleet filled with women warriors, politicians and, in the case of Siress Belloby, shrewd commercial negotiators, and thus no reason to agitate in this way.

Island in the Sky: As the previous story draws on *Lysistrata*, so this one is heavily indebted to James Hilton's *Lost Horizon* (which was also used as the basis for the *Space: 1999* episode 'Death's Other Domain'). Starbuck and Apollo crash-land on a planet with a severe gravitational pull, but are rescued by a group of beautiful young people, who live in a verdant valley where the gravitational effects are not felt, led by Prince and Princess Ling. Apollo is promptly smitten with the she-Ling. Starbuck, learning that the people are exiles from Earth, and have Earth's coordinates, wants to leave and bring the good news back to the Fleet; Apollo agrees and tries to bring along Princess Ling as well, but she reveals she is over a thousand years old and would die if she left. The warriors are imprisoned by her brother when he learns of their plans, but she helps them to escape, and ages to death in the process. While this story sounds derivative, it could well have wound up working in the execution.

The Bad and the Brave: After a battle, both the Fleet's orphan ship and a Cylon base star crash on a jungle planet. A trio of warriors, led by Starbuck and mounted on turboscooters (a kind of futuristic airborne motorbike;

presumably, it was planned to reuse the land-probe props from the almost-made 'Showdown') make sorties against the Cylons to try and prevent them from fixing their craft while the Colonials repair the orphan ship, in what sounds like a general race-against-time narrative. Athena is on the mission for some reason, and accuses Starbuck and his cohorts of grandstanding heroics. This story, with children and airborne bikes, foreshadows, or possibly resembles, *Galactica 1980*; the synopsis appears to have overlooked the fact that a Cylon base star contains 300 fighters and thus at least 900 Centurians, which would seem to be more than usually insurmountable odds.

A Plague in Space: This story would have featured Boomer bringing a sick crewmember into the life station, who turns out to be suffering from a cholera-like disease which once existed on Kobol. As more crewmembers fall sick, including Athena, Adama urges Boomer to find the carrier, who turns out to be Cassiopea herself. While again this story might have been successful in the execution, *Battlestar Galactica* has already done one space-plague story, and the twist here is not original enough to particularly distinguish it.

A Queen's Ransom: In this story, Apollo and Starbuck, seeking a crystal needed for *Galactica's* navigational systems, investigate the planet Sirenus, where, it transpires, gender roles are reversed and women rule where men serve. The presence of *Galactica's* all-male mining party incites a gender revolt, and they are ordered off the planet by its ruler, Areola, who will relent only if Starbuck becomes her concubine. It's usually a bad sign when a series does a 'gender-reversal planet' episode, and the fact that the planet's ruler is apparently named after the human nipple is not promising. A storyline in which a female ruler demands Starbuck's sexual favours in exchange for something the Fleet needs also appeared in the non-canonical *Battlestar Galactica* Marvel comic book series, albeit in a less anti-female context (the space pirate queen Eurayle offering the crew safe passage off of Scavenger's World).

While these are the only stories summarised in the document (and again, which if any of these are authentic has been questioned), well-substantiated reports also exist that certain of the unfilmed scripts of the first season were being rewritten for inclusion in a second, with Carlson and McDonnell confirming that they were working on 'I Have Seen Earth' with this aim in mind, and similar rumours circulating about 'The Mutiny' and 'The Final Flight' (which did eventually see the light of day as *Galactica 1980's* 'The Return of Starbuck').

In conclusion, it has to be said that this document, if we take it at face value, rather invites comparison with the second series of *Buck Rogers* and *Space: 1999*, both of which also took space series which were good but flawed, and, rather than building on their strengths and improving the problems, turned them into something entirely at odds with what had gone before. In this case, in the name of a perceived but nonexistent need to cater more to women, *Battlestar Galactica* would have gone from a casual portrayal of women (in both traditional and less traditional roles) as strong human beings to a set of patronising gender stereotypes, and with many well-loved central figures either being killed or written out, or changing their characters substantially in too short a time to be credible. The stories do not sound particularly promising as a whole, though, to be fair to them, many things which sound poor in synopsis can be good in the execution. It is also debatable whether, at the end of the day, this would have been really much worse than the actual follow up to the series, *Galactica 1980*, was.

GALACTICA 1980

Created by:
Glen A Larson

Executive Producer:
Glen A Larson

Supervising Producers:
David J O'Connell

Associate Producers:
David G Phinney (2 – 6), Tim King (2 – 6)

Story Editors:
Chris Bunch (2 – 6), Allan Cole (2 – 6), Robert W Gilmer (2 – 4)

Produced by:
Gary B Winter (1), Jeff Freilich (2 – 4), Frank Lupo (2 – 6)

Co-Producers:
Dean J Zanetos (1), David M Garber (1), Gary B Winter (2 – 6), Ben Kadish (2 – 6)

Music Score:
Stu Phillips

Theme:
Stu Phillips & Glen A Larson

Directors of Photography:
Frank P Beascoechea (1), Mario Dileo (2, 4, 5), Ben Colman ASC (3, 4, 6)

Art Directors:
Fred T Tuch (1), Sherman Loudermilk (2 – 4, 6), Bill Camden (2), William Taliaferro (4, 5)

2nd Unit Director:
Bob Bralver (1)

Set Decorations:
Leslie McCarthy (1), Morrie/Morey Hoffman (2 – 4, 6), Jennifer Polito-Puma (2, 4, 5)

Casting by:
Mark Malis (1), Phil Benjamin (2 – 6)

Film Editors:
John J Dumas (1), David Howe (1, 2, 4), Bill Parker (1), Michael Berman ACE (2, 4), Buford F Hayes (3, 5), John Elias (6)

Sound:
James F Rogers (1, 2, 4, 5), Earl N Crain Jr (3, 4, 6)

Titles & Optical Effects:
Universal Title

Educational Advisors:
University of South California, Department of Physics-History and Department of Cinema Television

Unit Production Managers:
John C Chulay (1 – 4, 6), Harker Wade (2), Charles E Walker (4, 5)

1st Assistant Directors:
Phil Cook (1), Pat Duffy (1 – 4, 6), Bob Bender (2), Gary Grillo (4, 5)

2nd Assistant Directors:
Ray Gomez (1), David Beanes (1), Doug Metzger (1), Dick Erickson (2 – 4), Charles Watson Sanford (2, 5), Louise S Race (4), Ryan Gordon (6)

Sound Effects Editors:
Dick R Wahrman (1), Samuel Reynolds (1 – 6)

Music Editors:
Ted Roberts (1), Herbert Woods (2 – 6)

Costume Designers:
Al Lehman (1), Jean-Pierre Dorleac (2 – 6)

Costume Supervision:
Mark Peterson

Special Photography by:
Universal Hartland

Miniatures and Special Photography:
Universal Hartland

Miniatures and Special Photography Supervisors:
David M Garber & Wayne Smith

REGULAR CAST
Captain Troy – Kent McCord (1 – 5 [credited for episode 6, but did not appear])
Lieutenant Dillon – Barry Van Dyke (1 – 5 [credited for episode 6, but did not appear])
Jamie Hamilton – Robyn Douglass (1 – 5 [credited for episode 6, but did not appear])
Commander Adama – Lorne Greene
Xaviar – Richard Lynch (1, 3 [uncredited, archive footage])
Xaviar – Jeremy Brett (3)
Doctor Zee – Robbie Rist (1)
Doctor Zee – Patrick Stuart (2 – 6)
Mr Brooks – Fred Holliday (1 – 3)
Colonel Jack Sydell – Allan Miller (2, 3)
Colonel Boomer – Herbert Jefferson Jr (1, 2, 5, 6)

The Super Scouts Alphabetically
Michael Brick, Jeff Cotler, Nicholas Davies, Ronnie Densford, Mark Everett, Georgi Irene [Sunshine], Tracy Justrich [Starla], Lindsay Kennedy, David Larson, Eric Larson [Moonstone], Michelle Larson, Jerry Supiran, Eric Taslitz (2 – 5)

GALACTICA 1980: BACKGROUND AND PRODUCTION

Six months after the cancellation of *Battlestar Galactica*, the sequel series, *Galactica 1980*, was commissioned, airing between January and May 1980. Although the premise is not totally without merit, being essentially a variation on *The Day the Earth Stood Still* (1951), the series was not popular with audiences or critics.

ROUND UP THE USUAL SUSPECTS: PRODUCTION AND DEVELOPMENT

The development of the series began, in concept, when Glen Larson was approached on 18 May 1979 to write a two-hour movie sequel which would reportedly involve *Galactica*'s arrival at Earth. By autumn 1979, Larson was being asked instead to do a sequel series to *Battlestar Galactica*; although ABC's motivations for this have never been officially clarified, it probably had quite a bit to do with the realisation, following *Mork and Mindy*'s failure in the 8pm Sunday timeslot, that *Battlestar Galactica* had in fact been a bigger hit than they realised. Furthermore, *Buck Rogers in the 25th Century* was proving very successful on NBC, which presumably also encouraged ABC to try and capitalise on the loss of their own Glen Larson-fronted science fiction series. Isaac Asimov was rumoured to be involved and to be writing one of the stories. However, Larson has confirmed that, while he did have contact with Asimov at the time, this was due to his trying to get Asimov on board for the, ultimately unproduced, second season of *Battlestar Galactica*, and that any association between Asimov and the sequel series is a misunderstanding of the facts.

As with the original series, Larson was given very little time: in this case, although he asked for a September 1980 release date, he had only four weeks to prepare the show. Thus, as on the original series, there was much last minute writing and rewriting, with, according to Chris Bunch and Allan Cole, two of the series' three story editors (the third being Bob McCullough), episodes frequently being rewritten actually on set and lines being given to the actors minutes before they were due to record. Neither Larson nor Bunch and Cole were enamoured with the project: Bunch, in an interview with Susan J Paxton, recalls that 'Larson … whored for the money with a bad attitude. We were literally blackmailed into the gig because of ostensible expertise in SF.' Both Bunch and Cole, having recently had another series greenlighted, were not keen on having to work on *Galactica 1980*. Cole, in an interview on battlestargalactica.com, recalls that production was particularly chaotic: 'the day I reported to work no one had the faintest idea what the series was going to be about. And it changed every day – even while the scripts were being written. Major characters disappeared. New ones appeared. Then were gone again'.

The budget of the series rapidly proved to be a sticking point. The concept was visibly intended to run on a smaller budget than *Battlestar Galactica*, with the Earth setting obviating the need for complicated sets and locations, and the studio being able to reuse effects shots from *Battlestar Galactica* and thus recoup some of their expenses. However, the series spiralled in cost, partly due to the short schedule, which meant that people were having to work on evenings and weekends (consequently incurring overtime); Larson remembers being called in to do some editing on a Sunday (which was unprecedented in itself) only to find that the crew were in doing some filming at the same time. In addition, according to Allan Cole, both Universal and Larson hated having to do the series, and were using it to recoup old obligations by giving people essentially useless, but lucrative, jobs as 'producers': 'every day we'd be introduced to another guy who had just joined the staff as a new producer. I don't know what any of them did – we rarely saw them again – but they sure were collecting the bucks. Can't blame Glen entirely for all the producers. Many of them were pushed onto the show by Universal, who figured if they were going to eat the big green slime anyway, they might as well take care of some obligations and dump all their losses into one (overflowing) bucket'. The two producers who, according to Cole, did actually do production work, Frank Lupo and Jeff Freilich, both have, it must be said, excellent credentials, with Lupo going on to *The A-Team*, *The Greatest American Hero* and *Walker: Texas Ranger*, and Jeff Freilich having previously worked on *The Incredible Hulk* and *Mrs Columbo*, and going on to *Falcon Crest* and *Freddy's Nightmares*.

A large portion of the budget was also wasted on unproduced scripts. As Cole, supported by Bunch, recalls: 'we went way over budget on the scripts … Very few of them were ever shot, because [Larson] just kept on writing. Sitting in his luxury condo overlooking the beach in Hawaii. Without an idea in his head he'd hit the typewriter, do a Fade In, then steam on until he had sixty pages. Then he's say, I'm out of time. So he'd type – End Part One. And then he'd go on to Part Two and so on.' This is attested to by the relatively large number of unfilmed scripts, some still only at the treatment stage, available from this series.

Ultimately, the show wound up, according to Cole, costing between $1.2 and $1.5 million per episode to make (the $1.5 million being for 'The Super Scouts', part one). As ABC only paid between $600,000 and $700,000 per episode, Universal Studios, ironically, wound up having to pay for the overspend themselves (the only episode which did not go over-budget was 'The Return of Starbuck', the episode with the strongest connections to the original series). Despite this, the programme's heavy reliance on *Battlestar Galactica* stock footage, and the fact that only a small set was constructed to represent the *Galactica* bridge, means that the series appeared cheap to viewers.

Of the *Battlestar Galactica* cast, only Lorne Greene and Herb Jefferson Jr reappeared in their original roles in *Galactica 1980*. Larson has subsequently said that he had not intended to cast Greene, but that Greene had rung him up and said that he was heartbroken that he was not in the series, but Larson has added that in hindsight he feels there shouldn't have been any original cast members in it at all. Richard Hatch, in an interview for *TV Zone*, has said that he was approached and turned the series down because he thought that it was going to be a cheap show. Dirk Benedict states in an interview quoted in *Battlestar Galactica: Somewhere Beyond the Heavens* that he was shown some scripts for the new series, and had thought they 'were bad', and that he believed the studio 'were going to cheapen the production values', and thus that to him, to do a lesser spinoff series after *Battlestar Galactica* would be 'like cheating on your wife'.

Rumours that the series' cast were replaced by largely unknown actors purely as a budget-saving measure are also untrue. While the cast would undoubtedly have been slimmed down for the new series, and although Allan Cole implies that Benedict's agents set a high price for his services, the presence of Apollo and Starbuck in early drafts of 'Galactica Discovers Earth' suggests that Hatch and Benedict were not considered too expensive for the show (as does the fact that both actors were approached). Indeed, the series' new regular male leads, Kent McCord and Barry van Dyke, were, at the time, arguably of more or less the same professional stature as Hatch and Benedict: McCord was well known in the 1970s for appearing in the TV series *Adam-12*, and, according to Paxton, had originally been considered for the role of Apollo in *Battlestar Galactica* (he would go on to appear in *Predator 2* [1990]). Barry van Dyke, the son of Dick van Dyke, would later appear opposite his father in the long-running series *Diagnosis Murder*. Robbie Rist, the original Doctor Zee, was also reasonably well-known at the time, having been in several episodes of *The Brady Bunch*. The most likely reason for the lack of most of the original cast was, as Allan Cole put it, 'schedules conflicted … One of the big problems when you cancel a show and let everyone go home, when you look for [the original actors] again, they aren't likely to be available'.

THE VOYAGE HOME: GALACTICA 1980'S CONCEPT

The premise of the series was fairly simple: that *Galactica* finally locates Earth, and, finding the people there primitive and bellicose, the Galacticans (as they are called in this series) plan to secretly infiltrate Earth and bring their technology up to speed for fighting the encroaching Cylons. This premise in itself is not a problem: the hugely successful film *Star Trek IV: The Voyage Home* (1986) appears to have lifted much of the concept and trappings of *Galactica 1980* (as well as having future humans infiltrating the Earth to carry out a desperate mission in secret, the film also features, like *Galactica 1980*, an invisible spaceship, a California setting, a contemporary American woman who attaches herself to the crew, and much fish-out-of-water humour), and manages to be at once entertaining, dramatic and charming.

More problematic, however, was the fact that the network gave the show a 7pm Sunday timeslot, which was earmarked for children's programming and put them opposite ratings giant *60 Minutes*. This time slot was a particularly irritating matter for Larson, as not only did it affect the budget (Cole notes that the budget for a prime-time series would have been $800,000 to $900,000), but also affected how many acts of violence (as defined by the network) could be shown and required them to have at least one educational moment per part (meaning a minimum of four per episode), with the result that the story frequently grinds to a halt as educational content is shoehorned in. Kent McCord has also said that he felt the introduction of large numbers of children to the cast was detrimental to the series' quality. It is also possible, though not directly substantiated, that the nature of the series was also affected by the Fox lawsuit (which was still ongoing at the time of production), in that the fact that *Galactica 1980* bears almost no resemblance to *Star Wars* made the series as it stood exempt from any legal proceedings.

Cole recalls also that the network caused problems for some of the concepts, noting that they disliked the time-travel idea introduced in 'Galactica Discovers Earth', and that they wanted the series to be less 'gritty' than the original, saying, according to Cole, that they wanted 'nice, clean-cut people … and lots of kids'. The series' continuity is also something of a problem, as in 'The Super Scouts' it is said to have been 30 years since the last Cylon attack, meaning that it is at least 30 years from the end of 'The Hand of God', which can take place no earlier than 1969, thus invalidating the rationale behind calling the series *Galactica 1980*; this will be discussed in more detail in the essay for 'The Super Scouts'.

STARBUCK'S NIGHTMARE: RELEASE AND REACTION

The series premièred 27 January 1980 on ABC, initially to strong ratings, which were probably due to the kudos which had accrued to the original series. However, the ratings gradually dropped off, and the final episode, only the tenth of the series, was aired on 4 May 1980, to an audience of 8.09 million households. Although the series is collectively known as *Galactica 1980*, and is named as such on the scripts, this title actually appears on the first two episodes only, with the remainder going out under the *Battlestar Galactica* title (although the opening voiceover of episode 3 still calls it 'Galactica 1980'), presumably in a move to boost the series' popularity by linking it to its more successful predecessor.[21] Allan Cole recalls: 'I remember that I posted a big sign on my office door with the number 13 on it. We had been told if the ratings dropped to 13 or below that we would be cut. Every morning my then partner, Chris Bunch, and I would chant "Come on, 13!"' The cancellation, which was reportedly due finally to the spiralling costs of the series (as Universal was asking ABC for more money), was so abrupt that production had actually begun on the eleventh episode, 'The Day they Kidnapped Cleopatra', at the time it was announced.

The series was not shown in syndication in the USA until 1996 (on The Sci-Fi Channel), although it has repeatedly been shown overseas, as part of a package with *Battlestar Galactica*. A film, entitled *Conquest of the Earth* and compiling 'Galactica Discovers Earth', 'The Night the Cylons Landed' and 'Space Croppers' (and also footage of Specter, Lucifer and Baltar from 'The Young Lords'), with voiceovers from Lorne Greene and others attempting to run the disparate stories into a continuous whole, was made, and, appropriately for tridextrophobes, released as the 13th *Galactica* movie. VHS copies are now unsurprisingly rare; however, among the film's notable points are the fact that, to explain the change of actors for Doctor Zee between episodes, voiceovers were added stating that they are the twin geniuses Doctor Zee and Doctor Zen, and that a voiceover was added in which Jamie Hamilton admits to a love for Dillon, but, with Robyn Douglass unavailable, the voiceover was recorded by an actress who sounds nothing like her.

Galactica 1980 has been almost universally derided since its release, with even Glen Larson repeatedly disowning it and describing it as 'Lieutenant Starbuck's nightmare'. The sole exception is 'The Return of Starbuck', which does generally get a positive press. John Kenneth Muir suggests that the

---

21 This fact has probably done more than anything else to damage the reputation of the former series; most of the criticisms leveled at *Battlestar Galactica* – excessive child-friendliness, obvious use of stock footage, and thin, jokey plots – apply more to *Galactica 1980*.

reaction may have been more negative than it would otherwise have been because the series' fans tuned in expecting *Battlestar Galactica* and were thus unprepared for the quite different show they got instead; however, it is questionable whether the series would have achieved much success on its own merits in any case. Many fans consider it of dubious canonicity, and its main legacy has been, first, that the idea that Boxey's real name is Troy and that he would grow up to be an excellent warrior has been continued in the later series of *Battlestar Galactica* original novels, and, second, arguably the introduction of the humanoid Cylon concept.

Galactica 1980 thus did not prove to be the popular sequel series which ABC had hoped it would be, becoming instead largely an embarrassment to all concerned. Nonetheless, it is an important footnote in the history of the *Battlestar Galactica* franchise.

1 ● GALACTICA DISCOVERS EARTH (PARTS ONE, TWO AND THREE)

US TRANSMISSION DATES: Sunday 27 January 1980, Sunday 3 February 1980 and Sunday 10 February 1980
WRITER: Glen A Larson
DIRECTOR: Sidney Hayers
CREDITED CAST: Robert Reed (Donald Mortinson); Pamela Susan Shoop (Dorothy Carlyle); Sharon Acker (Anne); Richard Eastham (General Cushing); Vernon Weddle (1st Cop); David Moses (2nd Cop); Brion James (Willy); Mickey Jones (Donzo); Duncan McKenzie (1st Pilot/3rd Guard); Douglas Bruce (2nd Pilot); Eddie Firestone (Derelict); Frank Downing (1st Guard); Don Maxwell (2nd Guard); Adam Starr (Willie[22]); Christopher Stone (Major Stockwell); Albert Paulsen (General Yodel); Louis Turenne (Colonel Werner); Michael Strong (Smite); Ted Gehring (Sheriff); Curt Lowens (German Commander); James R Parkes (Father); Bruce Wright (Aide); Missy Francis (Little Girl); Todd Martin (3rd German); John Zenda (3rd Cop); Erik Holland (2nd German Officer); Eric Forst (1st German Officer); Hank Brandt (Colonel); Jonathan Williams (2nd Guard); Paul Brown (4th Guard); Ray Duke (Newspaper boy); Doug Hale (Air Force Major); Billy Jocoby (Tucker)

SYNOPSIS: The battlestar *Galactica* and its fleet have arrived at Earth, in the year 1980, and found it to be a primitive place. The genius Doctor Zee suggests that, in order to raise the technological level and social cohesion of the planet, warriors will go down to Earth and infiltrate its societies, making contact with scientists and providing them with their expertise. Two warriors, Troy (formerly Boxey) and Dillon, go to California to meet Doctor Mortinson, a nuclear scientist, encountering as they do a young reporter named Jamie Hamilton. Troy and Dillon gain access to Mortinson's lab and amend the formulae he is using to develop a new form of safe nuclear power, but, in doing so, they are accused of being protesters out to sabotage his work and arrested. They escape and Doctor Mortinson contacts Jamie with a view to meeting them; she arranges this, as her network is interested in an interview with Mortinson, but Mortinson is reluctant and the situation degenerates into a car chase with the police when Mortinson allows Dillon to drive. Troy and Dillon return to the *Galactica*, with Jamie insisting on accompanying them. Once there, the trio learn that Commander Xaviar, a prominent member of the Galactican fleet, has travelled back in time in a Viper with a view to

---

22 Credited as 'Boy' in parts two and three.

augmenting Earth's development in the past. They pursue him to Peenemünde in 1944, where they thwart his plan to improve the weaponry of the Nazis, saving a group of Jewish refugees in the process. They return to the present to drop off Jamie, only to have their Vipers confiscated by the US Air Force. They ascertain the Vipers' location, and that Xaviar has also returned to Earth. Xaviar contacts Mortinson and tries, but fails, to persuade him that Troy and Dillon are the villains. Xaviar goes to the Air Force base, with the warriors in pursuit; all three (plus Jamie) regain their Vipers, but Xaviar travels back in time before they can stop him. The warriors vow to track Xaviar down.

ANALYSIS: 'Galactica Discovers Earth' sets the tone for Galactica 1980 with a three-part story which leaves much to be desired, compared to the parent series. Even the title sounds like an educational children's book (qv Doctor Who Discovers Space Travel). While it is generally good practice to be lenient to the flaws of a pilot episode, this one is difficult to excuse.

THE TRAINWRECK BEGINS: STRUCTURE AND PRODUCTION

The story, like 'Saga of a Star World', is divided into three parts (although they were never screened in one sitting as 'Saga of a Star World' was), and also falls into three more or less discrete storylines: the Galactica arriving at Earth and her personnel debating how best to contact their lost brethren; Troy and Dillon's search for Doctor Mortinson; and Troy, Dillon and Jamie's trip to 1944 to thwart Xaviar. In the case of 'Galactica Discovers Earth', however, the storylines aren't neatly separable into three hours: the first storyline takes up about two-thirds of the first episode, then it is followed by storyline two, which is interrupted about one-third of the way into the second episode by storyline three, before returning to storyline two at the end of the third episode.

The first draft script, dated 26 November 1979, is quite close to the story as transmitted up until the trip to Peenemünde (the episode ending with Adama ordering the warriors to time-travel back to Rome in 44 BC rather than WWII), but with a few notable differences: we first meet Jamie stargazing with her (reactionary and sexist) fiancé Walter in a car, Doctor Zee's simulation involves Starbuck and Apollo (who take the Dillon and Troy roles in this script) becoming celebrities prior to the Cylon attack on Earth (and while in Hollywood, the pair are taken unawares by the attack and killed onscreen), Doctor Zee is called 'Doctor Zero', and the role later taken by Xaviar is here played by Baltar (with no explanation as to how Baltar managed to rehabilitate himself and, by implication, to have rejoined the Council of Twelve, beyond a couple of vague references to his having 'paid the price' for his crimes). In this draft, Jamie has just taken a job as a secretary at 'Trans World Broadcasting' (later to become the United Broadcasting Company) but has ambitions to move into reporting, which makes more sense than her confused job situation in the transmitted version (explained in more detail below). Doctor Mortinson is explicitly said to be 'elderly' and to work for the 'California Institute of Technology' rather than, as transmitted, the Pacific Institute of Technology.

A copy of a later draft also exists, dated 13 December 1979, which is closer to the final version (although the narrative abruptly cuts off shortly before the rocket-launch sequence). Although Troy, Dillon and Xaviar are now present and correct, Troy is not identified as Boxey, though Troy does at one point say 'the opposite of war isn't always peace. More often it's slavery ...' in an echo of Apollo's earlier statements. Xaviar is explicitly identified as a member of the Council, where in the screened version he wears a blue officers' uniform. There is a slightly odd sequence where Adama orders Troy and Dillon to extend their patrol beyond the usual range to see if the Cylons are following them, which first begs the question of why Adama has apparently never done this before, and second, reveals that neither Troy nor Dillon have ever used the full thrusters on their Vipers outside of training. The German officers at the rocket test are identified as 'Colonel Werner' (possibly named for Wernher von Braun, though the screened version has him in a Luftwaffe uniform, where von Braun was in fact an SS-Sturmbannführer) and 'General Yodel' (possibly intended to be the real-life General Jodl, particularly as the script contains a note reading 'we will use names of real members of the German High Command at this point in the war'). In neither draft does the 'Little Willie' storyline exist; both drafts, however, contain an exchange between Adama and Baltar/Xaviar regarding the latter's plans to travel back in time and augment the Earth's technology, in which Adama points out that should a single individual be killed in the process this will wipe out all their present descendants, and Baltar/Xaviar asserts that this will not happen, but that the same people will all still exist in a technologically enhanced world.

The story was originally known as 'Galactica 1980', then, when the decision was taken to develop its premise into a series, this title was applied to the series as a whole and the present title applied to its première serial. In a clear sign that ratings are no indication of quality, the original screening of 'Galactica Discovers Earth' did very well with audiences, with the première ranking 30th for the week, and the World Almanac and Book of Facts 1980 citing Galactica 1980 as 20th out of the top 100 series in the Nielsen ratings.

The story is notable in production terms for its use of stock footage and sequences from films. The Cylons-attacking-Earth simulation has been derived from unused effects footage for the disaster movie, *Earthquake* (1976) which coincidentally starred Lorne Greene (and featured Donald Mantooth and George Murdock in supporting roles; the 26 November 1979 draft contains a note suggesting that footage from this film be used for this sequence). The 1944 storyline features footage from no less than four well-known WWII movies: *Operation Crossbow* (1965) supplied most of the rocket-testing sequences, *The Battle of Britain* (1969) many of the aerial sequences, *The Bridge at Remagen* (1969) the anti-aircraft guns, and there is a brief piece of unused footage of a German train going into a tunnel from *Von Ryan's Express* (1965). The new sequences were filmed on the Universal Studios backlot. Doctor Zee is also seen to watch stock footage representing Earth entertainment, which contains, among other things, stock-car racing, a vampire movie, a Western, a police drama, some stunt-bike riding (perhaps explaining how he came up with the wretched space motorbikes), Rod Serling (in an introduction to an episode of the series *Night Gallery*), and Hawaiian dancing (the 26 November 1979 draft suggests including a clip from *Mork and Mindy*, and footage of Johnny Carson and Lucille Ball). There is also a lot of effects work from the original series: reportedly the only new Viper-based special effect is the time-travel sequence.

The sequences featuring the 'turbines'[23], or flying motorbikes, mean that the crew finally get a chance to use the props which were originally built to serve as the 'land probes' in the unfilmed story 'Showdown', and which were reportedly also to have figured in the proposed season two story 'The Bad and the Brave'. The concept of the invisibility-field-generating bracelets recalls that of *The Gemini Man* whose protagonist was an invisible man kept visible only by the use of a special wristwatch-like device. Portions of the story were filmed at the Golden Oak Ranch. On the casting front, Richard Lynch, who plays Xaviar, had previously played Wolfe in 'The Gun on Ice Planet Zero' (albeit with less eye-liner), and Curt Lowens effectively reprises his 'Greetings from Earth' role as Krebbs when playing the SS officer. Robert Reed, who plays Doctor Mortinson, played the father, Mike Brady, on *The Brady Bunch*. Adam Farrar, the child actor who played Willie Griffin (under his earlier stage name Adam Starr), is the stepbrother of Leonardo Dicaprio, and apparently Farrar's childhood interest in acting encouraged his stepbrother to take up the profession himself. Farrar was arrested on suspicion of attempted murder in 2000, but released without charge.

The serial was also novelised (by Mike Resnick, who would go on to more high-profile work, eventually winning a Hugo Award), with a somewhat

---

23 This is what they are officially named as onscreen, but stage directions in draft scripts refer to them variously as 'turbocycles', 'turbobikes', 'flotation bikes' and 'space scooters' instead.

different story to the transmitted version. The main deviation from the story as transmitted involves Troy and Dillon pursuing Xaviar through the past, building on the never-resolved cliffhanger of Adama ordering Jamie, Troy and Dillon back to the eighteenth century to track the fugitive, including to Ancient Greece, Europe during the Crusades, and the time of the American Civil War. Some sources suggest that the novelisation was based on an earlier script treatment, as story editor Allan Cole has remarked that, during the filming of the series 'there was a mad scramble to find footage of old sword and sandal movies', (and that the network censors objected to the blood and gore of the stock footage to be used in the historical sequences); however, this could also have been down to the fact that the earliest draft of the script ended with the heroes travelling to ancient Rome. They then conclude that Xaviar has returned to present-day Earth to influence it.

ALL CHANGE IS NOT GROWTH: DIFFERENCES AND DEVELOPMENTS FROM BATTLESTAR GALACTICA

'Galactica Discovers Earth' introduces a new orchestration of the Battlestar Galactica theme tune, accompanied by exciting footage from the original series of casinos, mountains, pyramids, Cylons attacking cities, and so forth, setting the viewer up for disappointment when nothing remotely that exotic appears in the actual story. Adama provides an opening voiceover, which, in part one, runs: 'The great ship, Galactica; majestic and loving, strong and protective, our home for these many years we've endured the wilderness of space, and now we near the end of our journey ...'; episodes two and three, mercifully, have the voiceover slightly shortened and without the line 'majestic and loving, strong and protective', and it is this abbreviated voiceover which we hear for the rest of the series.

The character of Adama has changed somewhat. In the process of growing a full beard, he appears to have lost some intelligence; whereas before he was irascible, articulate, paranoid and continually weighing up every situation, he defers constantly to Doctor Zee here. In fact, everyone on the Galactica appears to be failing to consider the obvious these days, with no one apparently having given any thought to the potential negative consequences of their encounter with Earth before the moment they arrive. The character list has also been reduced: while the original series did focus mainly on Apollo, Starbuck and Adama (adding Sheba in the latter half of the season), there was also a large and well-developed crew of regulars and semi-regulars supporting them, whereas here the personnel have been reduced down to Adama, Troy, Dillon, Doctor Zee, Boomer and Jamie, with no chorus of pilots, medtechs and bridge crew to back them up. Although female as well as male warriors are seen, none of them become actual characters.

The familiar Colonial terms, 'yahrens', 'hectares' and so forth, vanish for part one, replaced by other, more Earthlike terms, such as Adama's reference to 'a billion star miles'. While this could be seen as a good decision, as 'Experiment in Terra' demonstrated that the Colonial argot sounded contrived in an Earthlike setting, 'star miles' is hardly an improvement, and, since the old expressions return in part two, makes the viewer wonder why they periodically change units of measurement. The continued references to the Lords of Kobol have also disappeared (although religious references are not absent; Doctor Mortinson likens Dillon and Troy's arrival to the coming of the Messiah, and Jamie misquotes the Book of Ruth when she jumps into the car saying 'whither you go, I will follow'. One of the few good lines in the story comes when Jamie, getting ready to time travel in the Viper, says 'don't bother me, I'm praying'). The invisibility fields are called 'force fields', which normally refers to a quite different pseudoscientific phenomenon. The term 'Galactican' is used as a name for the Colonial fugitives for the first time (by Jamie in part two, but the others don't challenge it and later in the series seem to use it as a self-designation). While this makes some sense in that, after thirty years in space, they might well give up thinking of themselves as Colonials (Troy and Dillon do say that *Galactica* might be considered their planet), and the writers also might have wanted to find a name which has fewer implications of colonialism (generally regarded with suspicion by modern Americans), but it is still a new development for the series. The Galacticans are said to have no fingerprints.

By far the most irritating new development is the character of Doctor Zee, who comes across like some kind of juvenile nerd power fantasy. He is said to be a child genius, born in space, and is possessed of scary-looking rimless glasses and a rather forced attempt at an English accent (which continues even when another actor takes over the role and the glasses are mercifully abandoned). Everybody on the Fleet defers to him continually; even if he is, as Adama says, 'a cerebral mutation far in advance of our own intelligence', it is unbelievable that nobody in the episode bar Xaviar so much as appears tempted to give him a clip round the ear at any point. By contrast, Adama says 'the Council has never overruled Zee, and he is never wrong', which, in the first place, makes one wonder what happened to the Council of Twelve's continual challenging of every decision made by Adama, second, suggests that the Fleet is now an absolute dictatorship, and third, overlooks the fact that Zee is revealed to be wrong in the very first scene, when he informs Adama that he had assumed (based on no visible evidence) that Earth would have the ability to help them fight the Cylons. Doctor Zee also seems to have some decided character flaws, as he mocks up a simulation of a Cylon attack on Earth seemingly for no reason at all (bar, perhaps, his own sadistic pleasure), shows it to the assembled senior warriors and Council, and then only afterwards tells them that it is not real. His reasoning that the warriors should approach Earth scientists for first contact because they are more likely to be open-minded and receptive to the idea of alien life is crushingly naïve. The scenario of a prescient genius predicting disasters and contacting top scientists based on his predictions is one which goes back to Larson's original idea for *Adam's Ark*.

Galactica 1980 does have some points of continuity to its parent series. The warriors all wear the same uniforms as before, albeit with the jackets done up (bridge crew uniforms also remain unchanged). We briefly see a pair of mechanical daggits playing with each other (although, aside from a 2007 episode of the reimagined series, 'A Day in the Life', this is the last time they will be seen in this or any other *Galactica*-related series). Adama is again depicted keeping his voice diary, for the last time (the 13 December draft identifies the transcription device he uses as a 'voicescriber'). The Cylons are referred to as an 'alliance'. Troy and Dillon come across as pale imitations of Apollo and Starbuck, with a dark-haired serious one and a blonde, cute and slightly roguish one, although Dillon a) also recalls Robin Williams in his *Mork and Mindy* period, and b) keeps the roguery toned down for the moment. It is rather depressing to learn that a charming child like Boxey grew up to be such a humourless, boring adult. Since Terry Carter, who played Tigh, was originally cast as Boomer, it is mildly ironic to see Boomer (promoted to Colonel) now taking Tigh's role on the bridge, with some grey at the temples. The Council of Twelve are namechecked (although they appear more useless than ever), and Troy's gift to Willie of a warrior's badge echoes Apollo's similar gesture to Boxey in 'Saga of a Star World'. The two-man Vipers seen throughout *Galactica 1980* are not, in fact, new to the series, as the Viper which Apollo and Adama use to go to Caprica in 'Saga of a Star World' must necessarily have space for both men. Apollo is referred to in the past tense in the televised episode, and in the novelisation Adama states 'my sons are dead. Zac was little more than a boy, Apollo lived to become our greatest warrior'; the compilation film 'Conquest of the Earth' features an alternate version of Adama's introduction in which he has a photo of Apollo in a glass crystal clearly visible on his desk. Athena's absence is not remarked on, other than possibly in Adama's opening voiceover when he says 'too many of our sons and daughters did not survive to share the fulfilment of our dream'; the 13 December 1979 draft makes the connection clear in that, when Adama speaks this line, his eyes are said to turn to a 'mini-mural' of pictures of Athena, Apollo, Zac and Ila.

There are in particular connections between this story and 'War of the Gods', as well as 'Experiment in Terra'. The time-travel storyline, like 'War of the Gods', involves an evil person who goes to a less developed civilisation and offers to help them, arouses their suspicions in doing so, and is recaptured by his counterparts, and the general idea that more advanced civilisations should help the lesser-advanced ones to improve also runs through not only that story, but also 'Experiment in Terra'. Troy's explaining to the American, Stockwell, in 1944 that 'we're brothers' recalls John's similar words to Apollo in 'Experiment in Terra'. The fact that the warriors' uniforms go white when travelling back in time, as when they are on the Ship of Lights, also references this; while Doctor Zee's connection with the Ship of Lights will be made clearer later on, he is an advanced being dressed in white, who created the time-travel process.

However, there are also some problems in that the ramifications of this ethical position, while they were at least implicitly debated in the original series, are not in the least explored in 'Galactica Discovers Earth'. The idea of a moral duty to help the less able, or the politics of intervention, or the complex nature of the opposite of war, are not considered; it is simply an uncomplicated premise for the story. On the opposite tack, it seems hypocritical of the Galacticans to make such a fuss about Xaviar's plans to advance Earth in the past, as they plan to do exactly that in the present; one might even raise the problematic moral issue that it would actually be to the *Galactica*'s advantage to support the Nazis, as, with assistance from a technologically-advanced party, they certainly had the ambition to develop the central world government which the Galacticans need, with a strong military force. However, although the drafts do briefly touch on the problematic morality of the situation, Xaviar is never given a chance to raise these issues in the transmitted version, and we are left with the implication that his time-travel plan is wrong not because of the nature of totalitarianism or the ethics of development, but just because Adama says so.

A particularly problematic note is struck when Doctor Zee says to Adama that the fact that they haven't encountered Cylons does not mean that the Cylons have gone, but that they are using the Fleet to lead them to the last humans in space, and Adama's reaction clearly shows that he has not considered this. In the first place, the idea that this would come as a shock to Adama rather strains credibility (as well as making one wonder why the beings on the Ship of Lights were willing to put the Fleet on the path to Earth, considering that in doing so they have unleashed a trail of destruction upon the human populations of the universe), and suggests that the Cylons have been casually exterminating all the little colonies which the *Galactica* encountered in the original series, making the Colonials seem criminally irresponsible in retrospect.

AND A LITTLE CHILD SHALL LEAD THEM: CHILD-FRIENDLY THEMES IN 'GALACTICA DISCOVERS EARTH'

The impact of the timeslot-mandated necessity to contain child-friendly content is apparent right from the early scenes on *Galactica*, with gratuitous children all over the Fleet. Even the 1940s sequences contain a number of children, with the subplot about the little Jewish girl escaping the German roundup being milked for pathos for all it's worth.

On contemporary Earth, we also have the rather contrived subplot involving the unfortunately-named 'Little Willie's' discovery of Troy and Dillon's spaceships in his father's field. Willie is utterly charmless, with a default expression which involves gaping with his mouth open, and he and his dog Skipper wind up mostly inviting negative comparisons with Boxey and Muffit. The fact that he appears to be the only child on the school bus suggests that he is as popular with the other children as with the viewer. Finally, there is the case of Willie's problems with the school bullies. Although they seem to be fairly feeble as bullies go (pushing him over rather than beating him to a pulp), this is clearly meant, from Troy's homilies about not emulating bullies, as a point of empathy and development for child viewers. However, it is undermined by the fact that Troy and Dillon's solution to the problem (giving him invisibility power so that he can torment his main antagonist) seems rather morally doubtful, as well as making it likely that Willie will get an even worse treatment once he is visible again, particularly if, as here, he runs around waving his new warrior badge and shouting 'guess what I got!'

In addition, the story is full of infodumps. While this is less obvious in the early scenes on the *Galactica*, as it is presented fairly naturally in the context of people being briefed about Earth, the plot on Earth itself periodically grinds to a halt for information sessions on nuclear power, the origins and history of WWII, and so forth. One fairly major problem from the point of view of the value of this exercise is that real information is presented alongside, and frequently in the same speech as, made-up science; a small child might well come away from '*Galactica* Discovers Earth' believing that invisibility is scientifically possible, since they have just heard a technically-accurate lecture from Doctor Zee about optics, followed by the fantasy-science statement that this allows them to make the Vipers invisible to the human eye, which exposes the infodumps as being less for the benefit of children and more an exercise in the network giving the impression of being concerned about education. The story also milks the invisibility concept for comedy potential to the point of boredom, and the flying bikes come across as like a ten-year-old child's fantasy.

THE BLIND LEADING THE BLIND: TROY AND DILLON ON EARTH

Most of the story, as, indeed, the series that follows, revolves around the comedic potential of alien visitors not understanding Earth, which, unfortunately, strains credibility in its search for laughs. While Dillon's remark about how he envies the warrior who was sent to the Union of Soviet Socialist Republics – 'I'm in favour of unions, it's not often you get a whole continent of women to choose from' – raises a legitimate smile (although thereafter the sauciness gets toned right down), Doctor Zee appears to have let the warriors go out criminally unprepared, seemingly not having either outfitted them with currency or suggested to them how to obtain some. His choice of plain clothes for Troy and Dillon also speaks of a really bad fashion sense. The information provided by the languatrons[24] is also worse than useless (defining a phone simply as a means of communication); the presence of these devices, furthermore, draws attention to the fact that, inexplicably, the Colonials are speaking more or less fluent American English. However, Troy and Dillon also lack initiative, evidently failing to make the connection between the phonelike handsets on the *Galactica* and the handset on the pay-phone which they find on Earth, and not bothering to get into their Earth clothes until well after they have left their Vipers, which is partly responsible for their attracting the unwanted attention of an appallingly characterised biker gang. The problem with the line 'I hope these things look like the vehicles we saw in the Earth transmissions' is so obvious it's not even worth mentioning.

While on Earth, they encounter Jamie Hamilton, who will unfortunately become one of the series' regulars. She is a walking cliché, being a plucky and impetuous girl reporter always in pursuit of the story, and, on first meeting, she comes across as amoral, berating Troy for stealing currency, then using the very currency she believes is stolen. She swings from being totally suspicious to totally credulous during her initial meeting with Troy and Dillon, acting as if their implication that they know Doctor Mortinson makes

---

24 The name of the wrist devices has never been officially designated; onscreen material and draft scripts refer to them variously as 'languatrons' (which, in the original series, was the name of a handheld translation device) 'wrist scanners', 'wrist bands', 'wrist analysers' and 'communicators' (and one despairing writer on 'The Day They Kidnapped Cleopatra' calls it a 'wrist contraption'), while some outside sources refer to them as 'wrist computrons'.

them automatically good people. Although she mentions having worked for KNO Reno, presumably a local television or radio station, here she gets the world's most haphazard job interview, first being told that she is one of many candidates, and then being informed that she has a job for life if she can get an interview with the elusive Doctor Mortinson (she herself seems mildly deluded about her prospects, since she refers to this as her 'first day on the job', even before she has had the interview). She is willing to string along Doctor Mortinson on false pretences so that she can covertly film him, and later blackmails Troy and Dillon into taking her back to the *Galactica* with them, threatening to tell everything she knows to the authorities, then, once she's on the ship, she starts shrieking about journalistic immunity as if *they* were the ones who kidnapped *her*. Her reaction to the *Galactica* is a dumb 'so you're not from Earth?' which would seem to be obvious by this point. She is also obsessed with 'getting the story' to an unbelievable degree, with it seemingly not occurring to her that reputable publications might not want to print a news story about flying motorbikes and giant spaceships. By the third episode, she has also completely forgotten her earlier suspicion about the Galacticans, hugging them and promising to keep their secret.

As the story progresses, Jamie comes across like an impulsive child, insisting on dashing off after the American parachutist in 1944 simply because he has dropped from an Allied plane (without considering that he might not want attention drawn to his mission) and insisting on rescuing the Jews without thought for the possible historical ramifications. Her altruistic streak is also fairly limited, as she is a mad homicidal lunatic as far as the opposite side is concerned, urging Troy and Dillon to 'knock those rotten Nazis out of the sky', and later encourages them to shoot down Xaviar rather than bring him to justice. She also isn't bright enough to realise, in part three, that it's best to wait until the Vipers are airborne before dropping her invisibility field and revealing that she has stowed away on one (one might also ask where the extra helmet in the Viper for her to wear came from if the Galacticans weren't planning on taking passengers, but this is the least of the story's credibility problems). At the end of the episode she is delighted with the prospect of going back in time to the eighteenth century, as she has heard that Benjamin Franklin was 'quite a ladies' man' – since rumours persist that he suffered from syphilis, she might want to rethink her eagerness to meet him.

The other major figure the pair encounter is Doctor Mortinson. The plotline through which they get in touch with him is ripped straight off from *The Day the Earth Stood Still* (1951), writing a formula on Doctor Mortinson's computer, only to have Miss Carlyle switch it off, then, when Mortinson reboots it, he finds out that it is the answer he needs. The only reason this sequence occurs is visibly to provide melodrama, so that there is a bit of tension while the viewer thinks the formula is lost and so that Doctor Mortinson doesn't grasp the importance of the visitors straight away; Miss Carlyle's fuss about them 'ruining' the formula seems all the more overblown when one considers that, this being a computer rather than a chalkboard, Doctor Mortinson could easily reload an earlier version of his calculations rather than having to start again from scratch. Mortinson's subsequent change of heart about appearing on television does make sense, however, as, since the pair mentioned having seen him on PBS, he knows they watch television and thus can catch his interview.

The presentation of the situation on contemporary Earth generally strains credibility. The air force pilots fire on the Vipers without requesting identification, and the air force contact the President straight away upon encountering them, rather than, say, trying to identify them or ascertain their nationality, which one would assume would be the first recourse. Miss Carlyle, at the university, calls the protesters a 'street gang', even though street gangs don't normally stand outside labs wielding placards, which would rather suggest student protesters instead. She also assumes that the two men who come to her lab are the two intruders the security guard is after, rather than considering that they might be legitimate visitors of Doctor Mortinson's (in which case she would be in trouble for turning them over to the security guard). Nobody at the police station frisks the warriors or confiscates their equipment; the policeman in the jail opens the cell door when he discovers that the two prisoners are apparently not in there, which seems an odd move (in the drafts, he checks for them under the bunk). Willie's father gives some idea of where his son gets his brains from, in that he appears to be the sort of idiot who goes out in the dead of night (somewhat inexplicably, as it had been daylight shortly before) to look for a spaceship on the word of a boy whose idea of a credible witness to events is his dog Skipper. The police are massively ignorant, finding out that Troy and Dillon are wanted fugitives only from reading the paper (and the authorities assume Jamie to be one of them, for unexplained reasons), and the air force aren't that much better, protesting that secrecy is required for their operations on the Vipers and yet ignoring the fact that the local school bus pulls up right in front of them. It never seems to occur to them to try to shoot, or at least forcibly remove, Xaviar when he gets into the Viper on the base. Finally, Jamie's new boss seems uncharacteristically lenient, continuing to employ Jamie even though he thinks she's mixed up with terrorists or suffering from Stockholm syndrome.

A BRIDGE TOO FAR: THE 1944 SEQUENCE

The WWII-set scenes are, if anything, more credibility-straining than those set on contemporary Earth. Right from the outset, the time-travel scenario would cause a 'time loop', as, if Xaviar goes to the past to encourage the Nazis to form a central world government, then in the present, there would be a centralised government for the *Galactica* to deal with, meaning that there would be no reason for Xaviar to go into the past, and the central government would not form (while solutions to this paradox do exist in fiction, the problem is not even remarked upon in '*Galactica* Discovers Earth'). Jamie argues that she should be allowed to go along on the expedition by saying 'who knows more about Earth's past than a person from Earth?' which, considering the historical inaccuracies in the 1944 sequence (of which one of the most visible is that many the planes which Jamie identifies as Nazi are, in fact, Spitfires), would seem a dubious claim. Jamie's explanation of World War II as being a clash of political ideologies with the USA, Great Britain, China and the USSR on one side and Germany, Italy and Japan on the other suggests that the USA shares a political ideology with China and the USSR, which, even given the spirit of détente in the 1970s, would seem to be stretching credibility.

As for the scenes revolving around the rocket testing facility, leaving aside the cringeworthy cod-Nazi triumphal dialogue, if the Nazis shot their scientists every time a rocket blew up, they would have had no scientists left; rockets blowing up or otherwise failing to perform were a frequent phenomenon at Peenemünde, this is why such places are referred to as 'test facilities'. On the other hand, however, it seems odd that they would trust Xaviar to help them even though they are suspicious of the fact that they have never heard of an English scientist named Xaviar working in rocketry, and one wonders what credentials he presented to convince them that he was a scientist at all (the fact that he passes himself off as 'English', affecting a mid-Atlantic accent, recalls the English traitors of the past season, and rather casts doubts on Doctor Zee's own reliability by implication).

There are other problems with the scenario. The SS officer[25] who shot himself in the foot during the raid is back front and centre next day for the test firing (though he does use a stick and limps a little, for form's sake). Troy is actually wearing a German helmet from the *First* World War in the location footage. Although it's unclear what Xaviar has done to improve the V2, the

---

25 Who is referred to by Stockwell's resistance contact as being a member of the Gestapo, even though his uniform is missing the distinctive SD diamond insignia on the sleeve, and the Gestapo never wore sig-runes on their collar patches, or dressed in black uniforms after 1939. He is, furthermore, incorrectly referred to as a colonel, and not an *SS-Oberführer*.

line that it is 'programmed to land where we want it to land' suggests that he has somehow turned it into a cruise missile (which would be an incredible feat given the primitive nature of computing in the 1940s). No one seems to notice that the American pilot and the two Galacticans have 1980s hair, and Jamie seems able to successfully pass herself off as a man when in Wehrmacht uniform. Before stunning the Nazi guards, it sounds like Dillon indistinctly refers to them as 'bastards'.

This is all the more irritating when one considers that there is an interesting moral dilemma which could have been wrought out of the sequence. By saving the prisoners from the camps, the Galacticans have changed history every bit as much as Xaviar would have by killing people, and yet their act is presented as unmitigatedly good, without even the briefest of nods in the direction of *Star Trek*'s famous 'The City on the Edge of Forever'. The ending might not even be as happy as the heroes seem to think it is. While it is plausible that the refugees could flee from Peenemünde to the Baltic Sea, there is no real idea what they will do once they get there, or why Jamie seems to think that soldiers in northern Germany, near the Polish border, will be too preoccupied with events thousands of miles away in Normandy to stop the refugees.

EVEN A BLIND PIG CAN COME UP WITH AN ACORN: GOOD ASPECTS TO 'GALACTICA DISCOVERS EARTH'

The story is not an unmitigated disaster. It is pacy and does hold the attention, admittedly largely as a form of horrified fascination. Miss Carlyle has very impressive breasts, and the music and visuals in the travelling-through-time sequences are cool in an early-eighties sort of way. Willie's father's line 'sorry I didn't believe you son – now I know how you felt' has the amusing implication that he's been trying to convince the sheriff that there are invisible spaceships in his backyard. There is also a fun reference to the film *The Battle of the Bulge*, specifically the early scene in the movie where General Kohler discusses the fantastic innovations which the Germans are making in terms of rocketry and aviation, in the way the German officers in this story discuss how soon they will have planes without propellers, super-weapons, and so forth.

The villain also comes in for a couple of good moments. Xaviar's hailing a police car instead of a cab (having been told that cabs come in yellow, checkered and black and white) is one of the few genuinely intentionally funny moments in the whole story. The fact that Xaviar puts forward his own plan to interfere with history to Doctor Mortinson as being what Troy and Dillon are up to, culminating in the idea that they want to rule the Earth, suggests not only that he is himself bent on world domination, but that he knows that this plan is amoral and wrong, and the motivations of a character who knows that what he is doing is wrong and does it anyway could do with some exploration. He also gets a great line, saying 'an outlaw can live a good life in any of those periods ... if one had a true vision of what was to come, where and when ... Or rule the world. That's what Troy and Dillon want'. The draft scripts contain a sequence where Doctor Zee/Zero speculates that Xaviar/Baltar could live in the same place at many different times, conjuring up entertaining images of millions of Xaviars populating the past. Jamie's telephone conversation with Doctor Mortinson in part three, where she warns him about Xaviar and he lets her know, implicitly, that Xaviar is in his house, is a mirror of the telephone conversation which Miss Carlyle had with the security guard in part one to warn him about Troy and Dillon's presence in the lab, which is a nice touch.

There are also some entertaining bits of period detail of interest to the modern viewer. Doctor Mortinson's computer appears to be a single unit, such that turning off the screen turns off the entire system. The focus on nuclear power in the Earth sequences references something which was a big issue in the early 1980s, and the series is provided with a gratuitous contemporary pop tune ('My Life' by Billy Joel had been a major top forty hit in 1978 and early 1979). The fact that Jamie doesn't own a credit card seems very odd for a modern viewer, but was more acceptable in the cash-focused economy of the early 1980s. The car chase scene in part two rips off *Diamonds Are Forever* (1972) which features a stunt sequence of a car, pursued by police, driving along on two wheels, and the idea of travelling into the past by flying faster than the speed of light against Earth's rotation echoes *Superman* (1978) and is done to visual effects similar to those used in the warp drive sequences of *Star Trek: The Motion Picture* (1979).

'*Galactica* Discovers Earth' is overlong, poorly characterised, and full of gratuitous children and forced humour. Unfortunately, it is far from the worst story which will come out of the *Galactica 1980* series.

2 • THE SUPER SCOUTS (PARTS ONE AND TWO)

US TRANSMISSION DATES: 16 March 1980 and 23 March 1980
WRITER: Glen A Larson
DIRECTOR: Vincent Edwards
CREDITED CAST: George Deloy (Doctor Spencer); Mike Kellin (John Stockton); Carlene Watkins (Nurse Valerie); Caroline Smith (Bank Teller); Jack Ging (Air Force Officer); Simon Scott (Captain); Helen Page Camp (Saleslady); Ken Scott (Co-Pilot); Michael Swan (Deputy Collins); John Quade (Sheriff Ellsworth)

SYNOPSIS: An unexpected Cylon attack on the Fleet, targeting its schooling ship, results in Troy and Dillon landing on Earth with twelve children, disguising them as a Boy Scout troop to avoid detection. Meanwhile, Colonel Sydell of the US Air Force, who is investigating a reported UFO sighting, becomes suspicious of the Scouts. On Earth, the children manifest advanced physical powers, jumping fifteen feet in the air at a time. Some of the children fall ill and have to be taken to a local clinic. The cause turns out to be pollutants in a local watercourse from which the children drank, stemming from a chemical plant. Troy, Dillon and Jamie find themselves in conflict with the owner of the factory, Stockton. Doctor Zee brings an experimental ship to Earth to rescue and treat the children, and Troy and Dillon enlist Stockton's help to transport them, although not without some resistance, and with pursuit from Sydell (assisted by the local sheriff), who is now convinced they have something to do with the UFO. On board the ship, Doctor Zee shows Stockton a projection of the future consequences of environmental pollution, including his own son's death, and Stockton vows to be a better citizen.

ANALYSIS: The second *Galactica 1980* serial continues the downward spiral, with its main advantage over 'Galactica Discovers Earth' being that it is one episode shorter. We are introduced to a recurring cast of annoying child semi-regulars, and the tediously obsessive Colonel Sydell; the main point of interest, however, is that the need for topical and informative info-dumps has forced a change in political orientation on the *Galactica* franchise.

SO, THIS ISN'T NEW YORK: PRODUCTION AND DEVELOPMENT
The story is written by Glen Larson, and a draft script exists (part one dated 20 February 1980, revised 25 February 1980) which confirms reports that the scripts were written in haste and in a fairly stream-of-consciousness fashion.

The title of the draft of part one is, mysteriously, 'So, This Is New York', which could either be a reference to the 1948 screwball comedy of that title (which has a tenuous connection here in that it involves humour about a rural family coming to the big city), or could be taken to indicate that Larson was originally intending to set the series in New York (certainly he does seem keen on coming back to it, with 'The Night the Cylons Landed' being set in New York – and Dillon's final line in that serial being 'So, this is New York!' – and the ending to the draft of 'The Super Scouts' having Troy and Dillon telling Jamie they are leaving the Scouts with her because they have received information that Xaviar has returned to their timeframe and is in the abovementioned metropolis). Part two (dated 3 March 1980 and revised 5 March 1980) is in fact entitled 'The Super Scouts', and five pages in we have the first use of that phrase, from Jamie, suggesting that the story was retitled when Larson came up with the phrase. The cliffhanger between the parts is a clear indication of the haste in which the story is written: the original draft of part one has Act Four ending with Dillon and Troy being thrown in jail (following a phone call to the sheriff from Stockton informing him of some 'serious troublemakers' in town aiming to close down the plant), with the 'tag' scene featuring a discussion between Dillon, Troy and Jamie (who is visiting them) about the existence of environmental pollutants in the town's water system, followed by the sheriff informing them that one of the children is dead. The teaser for part two then opens with the sheriff learning that the Scout troop is false and urging his men to arrest the phony Scoutmasters (their arrest in the previous cliffhanger being forgotten) and ends with Dillon and Troy taking off on their bikes, which is the end of part one as screened.

The events of the draft script are broadly similar to the screened version (with some scenes brought forward or back, and minor dialogue changes), with the main interesting point of difference being that Andromus and Andronicus, the two humanoid Cylons (who, ultimately, do not appear until 'The Night the Cylons Landed') are briefly introduced, and a 'new Cylon warship' was to have been flying amongst the old-style ones during the space battle sequences, which, as well as setting up an interesting new twist on the classic foe, also explains how Doctor Zee is able to say with such certainty that the Cylons have advanced technologically in the intervening time (as it stands, it makes one wonder if Doctor Zee isn't secretly working for the Cylons), as well as what the 'new technology' that they want to test out might be.

There are a few amusing cut lines, such as the rather unfortunate one from one of the California Highway Patrol officers (CHiPs) confronted with flying motorcycles: '... and those bikes don't even look Japanese!'[26] Dillon tells a child who uses the expression 'flaming Felgercarb' to watch his language. There are a couple of cuts which remove material which actually contributes to the story, where Jamie explains that she once worked as a 'candy striper' (hospital volunteer) as a teenager due to having a crush on TV doctor Ben Casey (explaining where her suddenly-acquired medical knowledge has come from), and another, in which we learn in a flashback that Sydell encountered a UFO ten years previously while flying a plane, explaining his obsessive pursuit of aliens. Doctor Spencer also reveals that he used to box in high school, and Troy and Dillon need the concept of boxing explained (ironically, given the focus on boxing as a pastime in the reimagined series). In a cut line, we learn that the children have a blood pressure of 60/40 and a heart rate of 36, and that Spencer expects the adult Galacticans to have the same vital statistics (since children and adults have different metabolic rates, this seems a bit of a stretch); he puts the differences between these and normal human rates as being down to long-term exposure to a different environment (recalling similar ideas in 'Greetings from Earth'). There is also a sequence where Officer Packer sees some of the children looking curiously at his sidearm and offers to show it to them, but Troy says 'no ... I'd rather not encourage that interest' in an uncharacteristically pacifist gesture, and another in which Troy offers to leave town, and cease agitating against the plant, if Stockton will allow them to treat the children.

Some of the names and details change from the draft to the finished version. The voiceover when the children mess around with the air force staff car was dubbed on later to indicate (somewhat unnecessarily) what is going on, and/or to underline for younger viewers that playing about in cars is wrong. Mr Stockton was originally called Mr Stockwell (probably changed due to the fact that the pilot in the previous story was called Stockwell), with the change happening at the outset of part two, and his son was originally called Jamie (the reasons for his transformation into 'Jimmy' should be obvious). The plant was initially called the Paradise Chemical plant (with the change to Stanford Chemical coming in the 5 March revision), which would have given it a connection with the Paradise Valley Medical Centre. Doctor Spencer originally says that the children's blood contains 'antibodies' he's never seen before, as opposed to saying more vaguely that, if he goes by his textbooks, what's in the blood sample shouldn't even exist. Jamie's career is also briefly recalled at the end of the draft script, when she insists that she

---

26 There is a sly inside joke here, as the turbine props were in fact modified Yamaha MX 175s.

wants to bring a camera team to record the landing of the Galactican ship, and, in an unfortunately-lost point of continuity, Adama is said to wear white when aboard it.

On the production front, this story was apparently rather fraught, with Larson unhappy with what he saw as the slow pace of the direction (according to Allan Cole), and an incident occurred in which a support beam failed to fall during an explosion scene, and, when the director, Vince Edwards, wandered out onto the set, asking what had happened to the beam, the prop man, thinking he had just heard his cue, dropped the beam, nearly onto Edwards. Patrick Stuart, the new Doctor Zee, was also reportedly terrified during his scenes to the point of being unable to turn his head (Cole is quoted as saying 'during dailies, [Larson] kept muttering loudly "what's wrong with his neck? Call his teacher! Call his mother! Call anybody who can fix his neck!"') and also, understandably for a boy in his early teens, had problems controlling the pitch of his voice. The model scenes depicting what is said to be the *Delphi* are in fact stock footage of the *Gemini* freighter from the original series (the name 'Gemini' is clearly visible at one point), and there are a couple of clips from 'Fire in Space' and the film *Operation Crossbow* during the fire sequences. The unconscious child being checked over by Doctor Spencer visibly smiles during the inspection. The pyramid device on the console in Doctor Zee's ship also appears in the first-season *Buck Rogers* episode 'Escape from Wedded Bliss'. Three of Glen Larson's children, Eric, David and Michelle Larson, appear among the Super Scouts (having all previously appeared in 'Greetings from Earth'), with Eric playing 'Moonstone'. Finally, following on from the troubled subsequent career of Little Willie, one of the other child actors playing Super Scouts, Mark Everett, was shot dead by police in 2008, having been wanted by the FBI since 2004 for the murder of his girlfriend.

STRETCHING THE POINT: STORY DEVELOPMENT AND CONTINUITY

The series is developing along a slow narrative, with the *Galactica* now leading the Cylons away from Earth as a decoy. Zee has built a prototype flying-saucer device called an 'anti-gravity ship', but the Fleet lacks the resources to build more (while it may seem coincidental that it resembles a flying saucer, which is the shape most associated on Earth with aliens, it could be that Doctor Zee got the design idea from watching Earth transmissions; the craft is described as 'saucer-like' in the draft script). A line from one of the children indicates explicitly that the Fleet has artificial gravity. Colonial guns now shoot different coloured beams, white for blowing down doors, and cyan for stun. Doctor Zee has now adopted Jamie's neologism, referring to 'the Galactican Fleet', although 'yahrens' and 'microns' still recur. 'Frip' is heard as a childish insult, and 'auric' as a synonym for 'gold' (contradicting the fact that we hear Colonials using the latter word as far back as 'Saga of a Star World'). The Council of Twelve get another namecheck (when the floorwalker asks Troy, thinking he is a Scoutmaster, which council he is with, and he gives the obvious answer). We learn that in the Colonies, 'death is a threshold far beyond this child's condition', indicating advanced technology (as well as recalling the lightship people's line in 'War of the Gods' when they say that Apollo was 'only dead by primitive measures'), and there are a few references to the original series, with Adama calling Troy 'Boxey' (and he calling Adama 'Grandfather'), and with the classroom scene being straight out of 'Greetings from Earth', with Dillon taking Athena's role. Doctor Zee says that Cylons can't imagine, but can 'only copy', building on similar remarks made during the original series. Egyptian and new-age themes are referenced in the presence of a pyramid as part of the saucer's console, and, although Boomer is now a colonel, it seems he still flies missions.

Doctor Zee does another of his sadistic computer simulations for Stockton, and Troy and Dillon imply that he does them a lot, which again casts aspersions on Doctor Zee's character; on the other hand, Doctor Zee, faced with the decision over whether to risk the whole Fleet for one child's life (Adama alludes to a cut scene in 'Saga of a Star World' in telling Doctor Zee that he has contemplated resigning over similar decisions), decides instead to risk himself. Meanwhile, on Earth, we learn that Colonel Sydell is a member of a branch of the US Air Force which 'deals with unexplained phenomena' and the fact that the sheriff implies that Jamie is using the children in order to manufacture a story about environmental damage may seem extreme, but is also in keeping with the slightly insane way she was portrayed in the previous serial.

More interestingly, however, the series' politics appear to have taken a sharp swing to the left, with environmentalists being exalted and even military authority figures being portrayed as stupid and/or corrupt. This is a development which is somewhat off-message given the right-wing leanings of the original series, but perhaps more in keeping with the general tone of children's series of the day.

As before, there are a few pop culture references. CB radios, a popular late-seventies/early-eighties means of in-car communication, feature heavily (while it makes sense for a rural medical clinic to have one, Stockton's is less explicable on practical grounds, suggesting he's a hobbyist). The anti-gravity ship looks much like the alien craft in *Close Encounters of the Third Kind*. The nurse, Val, under the influence of the stun ray, recites a little speech which appears to reference a test pattern: 'my skin is blue and my dress is pink. If you are receiving these colours bright and clear on your television ...' The sequences with the highway patrolmen also explicitly reference the contemporary bike-cop series *CHiPS*, with the script describing one of them as being Hispanic and the other blond as in the latter series, and one of the officers saying 'how come this never happens to the guys on TV?' when confronted with flying motorbikes (the two cops actually come across as much more interesting characters than Troy and Dillon). As the programme was made by another studio for another network, this seems to be simply in for a laugh rather than cross-promotion.

On the child-friendliness front, the whole story is a gratuitous advert for the Scouting movement, with speeches about how much fun Scouting is and how responsible, intelligent and good Scouts are. To be fair, the idea of concealing the children as a Scout troop is a sensible one, providing a plausible explanation for why twelve children of mixed ages are wandering around rural areas in the custody of a couple of men in their twenties, but the execution is fairly heavy-handed, and, also, the girls in the story masquerade, improbably, as boys, rather than having the script use the device of having them belong to a mixed organisation. Adama makes a homiletic speech about responsibility and using one's brain (somewhat undermined by the fact that he's not really providing an example in either regard), and, towards the end of part one, the story segues off into a gratuitous environmental-crusaders-against-plant-bosses plot, complete with unsubtle infodumps about the effects of environmental pollution.

SUPER OR SILLY? GOOD AND BAD ASPECTS TO 'THE SUPER SCOUTS'

There are a few redeeming aspects to the story. Dillon's accidentally holding up a bank is actually rather funny, with a priceless moment when he asks the cashier benignly where she lives so he can repay her the money she has forced on him, and she, panicking, replies '327 Howard Street – but I'm moving just as soon as you finish robbing this bank!' and another later when he attempts to explain the turn of events to Troy: 'it's called "robbing a bank." I couldn't help it, it just happened'. Dillon also gets a good line when he says 'the glory of the universe is intelligence; never be afraid of discovery' (in a paraphrase of a line from the Mormon Doctrine and Covenants, 'the glory of God is intelligence'), and earlier, when one of the children hurls the apple at the sheriff, he admonishes them by saying 'you're behaving like children'. Lorne Greene's facial expressions when confronted with a hysterical Stockton are also fun to watch. It is possible to work out exactly where the story is set, in that the APB that comes over the telex in the sheriff's office is headed 'Clark County', which is the name of a county in Southern Nevada, near the California border (the telex describes Dillon as 'male Caucasian, blond, late twenties, suspect is armed and considered extremely dangerous', and Troy as 'male Caucasian, dark hair, also late twenties'). The experimental ship is very well done, with some lovely scenes of Adama advancing before a wall of lights, and gorgeous red-lit interior shots.

The environmental plotline is interestingly multi-faceted for a programme aimed at children: rather than just pitting good environmentalists against bad factory bosses, it's made clear that the people of the town depend on the plant for a living, so closing it down might cause an equal amount of suffering to leaving it open. Mr Stockton is portrayed as someone who is not inherently bad, just selfish and slightly prejudiced. He is less inclined to look favourably on vigilantism than his workers, and he babbles incoherently about the plant when confronted by the anti-gravity ship, suggesting that the environmental messages are getting through to him. There is also a mild slap at jobsworthiness, in that the nurse says that she can't take action to help the children because it's against regulations and the doctor will have her suspended, and, later, when the doctor returns and sees the work the Galacticans have done in putting in the glucose drips, he praises what he thinks is her initiative, thus indicating that mindless rule-following is not the best way to proceed.

Unfortunately, the problems outweigh the good aspects. The children all have awful names like 'Moonstone' (a boy) and 'Starla'. The fact that the Fleet has produced only a hundred and thirty-seven children after thirty years of not much to do suggests serious fertility problems. It's also rather asking for trouble to put all the children on one ship (as well as it being a massive coincidence that Troy and Dillon just happen to be there when disaster does strike), and, if the *Delphi* is now the 'schooling' ship, one wonders what happened to the classroom on the *Galactica*. The song 'Galactic Scouts', sung around the campfire, is pretty hokey (with the lyrics 'Zay, zee, I know you …' suggesting further idolisation of the irritating Doctor Zee)[27]. The idea that the children find Earth's gravity so light that they can jump fifteen feet in the air at a time begs the question of why Jamie, a physiologically normal Earth woman, isn't weighed down correspondingly by the greater gravity on the *Galactica*. When the children mess around with the staff car, an Air Force sergeant is clearly visible sitting in the vehicle, and yet he takes no action throughout, and

---

27 The song was credited to John Andrew Tartaglia, Sue Collins and Glen A Larson.

appears to be simply reading a pamphlet rather than reacting in any way to the children's activities. At the end of the story, Troy and Dillon dump twelve children on Jamie without even asking if she's physically able to take care of them for a few days.

Other problems come in the details of the adventure. Dillon and Troy have their bikes and 1980s clothes handy on board the shuttle, suggesting that, counterintuitively, such things are now routinely stored on Fleet craft. The gimmicks of invisibility, super-strength/super-jumping and motorbike flight are used to extreme, with it being particularly stupid of Troy and Dillon to launch their turbines into flight in the middle of a crowded town street. Dillon appears to be capable of competently riding a motorbike on American roads without exciting attention for anything other than the design of the bike and its lack of a license plate, which suggests an understanding of traffic laws, and yet he apparently doesn't know enough about the transport system to be able to cross the road safely. The 'high-pitched, coded transmissions' (as the script defines them) that Major Jensen picks up are audibly just speeded-up dialogue, making one wonder why he doesn't notice this, and Zee's solution to environmental problems is more than a little bit lame, amounting to just bottling up the dioxin and trying to think of some way of getting rid of it. The fact that the *Delphi* blows up after the shuttle escapes means that the fire crews and everyone else on board must have perished, a fact which sits ill with the rather jolly, child-friendly tone of the episode. The story ends with an annoying *Scooby-Doo* style forced laugh.

Part two is also the first episode which ends with a card reading: 'The United States Air Force stopped investigating UFOs in 1969. After 22 years, they found no evidence of extra-terrestrial visits and no threat to national security', which will continue to be shown throughout the rest of the series (with the exception of 'The Return of Starbuck'). This seems rather an absurd measure, as *Galactica 1980* is hardly a convincing source on the issue of the veracity of UFO sightings, and begs the question of why other contemporary programmes did not bear similar obvious warnings (*Knight Rider*, for instance, could have done with a title card reading 'cars cannot drive themselves or talk', and *The Dukes of Hazzard* with a title card reading 'not all Southerners are crazed inbreds').

The biggest problem, however, lies with what the story tells us about the series' timeline. We learn here that it has been thirty Earth years since the last Cylon attack, as this is the figure Doctor Zee gives (although why they give the figure in cumbersome terms like 'Earth years' as opposed to their own familiar measurement of time is a mystery). If this is the case, however, the absolute earliest the story can take place is 1999, assuming that a) the Cylon attack seen in 'The Hand of God' was the last one (which it clearly isn't, as another happens in 'The Return of Starbuck'), and b) that 'The Hand of God' takes place contemporaneously with the moon landing (as, unless the transmission went through some kind of extracanonical time warp, it cannot take place any earlier). However, leaving aside the name of the series and other details, Mr Stockton explicitly states that 1990 is 'ten years from now', meaning that, even allowing for rounding up and estimating, there is no canonical way of reconciling the timing of *Galactica 1980* with that of the events of the original series (particularly since the original series implies at a few points, such as 'The Long Patrol' and 'Experiment in Terra', that it takes place in Earth's future).

'The Super Scouts' is, on the whole, tedious, silly, and full of poorly-characterised children and unbelievably thick local people, redeemed by a few moments of humour; furthermore, it appears to drive a cart and horses through the timeline of the series relative to its parent show.

3 ● SPACEBALL

US TRANSMISSION DATES: 30 March 1980
WRITERS: Frank Lupo & Jeff Freilich and Glen A Larson
DIRECTOR: Barry Crane
CREDITED CAST: Paul Koslo (Billy Eheres); Bert Rosario (Hal Fredricks);
KNOWN UNCREDITED CAST: Marla Heasley (Lieutenant Nancy Trent);
Gil Stratton (Steve Baldwin [announcer])

SYNOPSIS: Troy and Dillon meet with Lieutenant Nash, who informs them that they have been assigned a special mission to track down Xaviar, and gives them the coordinates at which, he says, Xaviar may be found, saying that he will guard the children. However, Nash proves to be Xaviar in disguise, and Troy and Dillon are trapped in a non-functioning Viper in deep space. Meanwhile Jamie, who is caring for the Super Scouts in Troy and Dillon's absence, takes them on assignment with her to a baseball camp for disadvantaged children run by disabled former athlete Billy Eheres. There she learns that the camp is in financial difficulty, and can only gain sufficient funding to continue if their team wins the regional playoffs, but half the players are ill with the flu. Jamie suggests that the Super Scouts, with their enhanced abilities, should play instead; however, when she learns that Colonel Sydell has tracked them down and is in the audience for the baseball game, she urges the children to lose. Upon learning that Xaviar plans to use the children to ensure that the *Galactica* allows him to live in freedom upon Earth, and that the winning team is normally mobbed by reporters, Jamie tells the children to play to the utmost of their abilities. They win the game at the last minute, just as Troy and Dillon arrive. Following a brief chase in which Colonel Sydell is shot and injured by Xaviar, Xaviar escapes.

ANALYSIS: Although 'Spaceball' is the episode with the title which best lends itself to rude punning on the poor nature of this series, it is far from the most excruciatingly bad story of *Galactica 1980*, being largely a fairly dull underdog-baseball-team-saving-the-summer-camp story which is heavily indebted to *The Bad News Bears* (1976), and only slightly enlivened by the twist of giving the kids superpowers but forbidding them to use them in case of discovery by the authorities.

THREE STRIKES AND YOU'RE OUT: PRODUCTION, STORY AND DEVELOPMENT
The story follows on narratively from 'The Super Scouts', almost as a kind of

third part, in that it opens with Troy and Dillon heading out on what they think is a mission from Adama, leaving the children with Jamie. The overall level of acting ability has not improved among the children, which is a problem as they are expected to carry much of the action of the story with Troy and Dillon trapped in space. The presence of Jeremy Brett as Xaviar, and the introduction of the idea that he can change his appearance, suggests that Richard Lynch was unwilling to return for the part, and so the team are making a virtue of necessity. More problematically, though, the sequence of the Super Scouts learning about television appears to have been shot backstage at Universal Studios, which simply looks like a budget-saving measure. In a clear inside joke, two of the children at the baseball tournament are named 'Frankie Lupo' and 'Jeffy Freilich', and careful listeners can also hear mention of another named 'Gary Winter', referring to two of the story's writers, and its co-producer.

The story itself is rather predictable (right up to the not-particularly-funny ending in which Starla displays prodigious basketball abilities as well), but also is not well thought through, since the look on Jamie's face when Eheres accuses her of working for the developers who are threatening to buy the land and close the camp, in that she has put him up to fielding a losing team at the championships, suggests that it never occurred to her that telling the Super Scouts to lose the game would mean the closure of the camp, even though that information was explicitly spelled out earlier in the story. For that matter, the scenario begs the question of why she doesn't simply tell the children to play well but within normal human parameters rather than telling them to lose. The pro-sports message of the story, while a worthy one, is just as hackneyed as the pro-Scouting message in the previous adventure. While it might seem a coincidence that a story involving a children's camp should crop up at Jamie's workplace at the same time as she is tasked with caring for the Scouts, it is not totally unreasonable, given that such stories are staple fodder for local news stations; more problematically, Sydell appears to know that the Super Scouts have unusual physical abilities, despite having never witnessed their use in the previous story.

In continuity terms, the action has moved back to California from Nevada (as the banner at the baseball game reads 'California Regional Little League Championships', and the opposing team are from Encino). It is revealed that Xaviar is a member of the Council, something only hinted at previously, and Viper pilots entering 'sleep mode' is mentioned. More ominously, Adama says that their purpose *vis-a-vis* Earth is to find 'a place where we can send our young to prevent their destruction in what we know will be an imminent and final Cylon battle', which differs from their earlier plan to infiltrate the Earth and augment its technology and suggests that they are now growing desperate. Xaviar also seems to have abandoned his idea of going back in time and changing Earth's history. Mr Brooks and Colonel Sydell both appear for the last time here.

We can also compare the final version to three drafts, the first dated 9 March 1980, the second 11 March 1980, and the third, while undated, is closest to the final version (and thus the most recent). As before, barring the order of events and the addition or removal of a few scenes or sequences, the story remains more or less unchanged from the first draft onwards. The most significant change is that the earliest two drafts contain a sequence where an American satellite registers the stranded Viper, causing surprise among the observation team on Earth, which is expanded in the third draft to a running subplot in which the observers are Russian, and they mount an attack on the Viper through the satellite (which is apparently equipped with a laser), adding tension to the scenes with Troy and Dillon. Some minor points of interest include the revelation in the earliest draft that Billy lost his arm in Vietnam, and the two earlier drafts also contain a brief rant by Billy against excessive professional sports salaries and how the money should be ploughed back into programmes to support sports for deprived children (arguably continuing *Galactica 1980*'s political swing to the left). In Sydell's first scene, the earliest two drafts have him talking to his superior, Lancaster, in the office rather than holding a phone conversation, and the first draft also contains a sequence in which Jamie offers to provide soft drinks and cookies for the children as they visit the studio, and they insist they would prefer carrots and celery (which then leads to an exchange where the Scouts discuss Bugs Bunny, with Moonstone remarking 'they have talking rabbits … what a planet').

BOTTOM OF THE NINTH: GOOD AND BAD ELEMENTS

The story does have a few noteworthy aspects. Jeremy Brett is head and shoulders above the rest of the cast (Lorne Greene aside), and is particularly impressive in that, in the one brief scene in which he plays the 'real' Lieutenant Nash, he manages to convey quite clearly that this is a different person. He is also quite sinister as the fake, even with his inexplicable adoption of a cod-Eastern European accent which evokes Bela Lugosi. It can be more fun to watch the episode knowing the 'twist', so that one can appreciate the subtleties in Brett's performance. It is also good to see a disabled person being presented as charismatic, handsome and athletic (although the fact that he is played by an able-bodied actor detracts from the message). Adama shows a slight return to his *Battlestar Galactica* principles, refusing to compromise the safety of the

Fleet to save the Super Scouts. The space suits, previously seen in 'Fire in Space' (although the ones in the original-series episode have different headsets, and oxygen-tanks present) are nice-looking if not very practical (since they should really not be able to breathe without oxygen cylinders) and, if one ignores a few obvious wires, the Viper-fixing sequences are also effective, although the fact that space suits appear to be routinely carried in Vipers makes one wonder why the pilots don't simply fly in space suits rather than flight gear, as the possibility of a Viper canopy being blown open must be a real one.

The Super Scouts, however, are a distinctly weak link. Wellington is particularly annoying, continually spouting know-it-all trivia in a smug voice, and one has to ask why Starla hurls the baseball half a mile when asked to throw it back (she has surely been on Earth long enough to have gained some control over her abilities, and even a six-year-old should know that the phrase 'give us back the ball' does not mean 'throw it into the next county'). All are subject to lots of excruciating 'humour' as they take expressions like 'hit the bench' and 'catching flies' literally. They are still wearing the same clothes as in the previous story, making one wonder if they have managed to wash them in between, and the fact that the children at Billy Eheres' camp are visibly multicultural raises the question of why the Super Scouts are not, given the ethnic diversity on board the Fleet. Neither Mr Brooks (who refers to them as 'Boy Scouts') nor Billy Eheres (who addresses them as 'boys') seems to have noticed that some of the children are girls (although, in the earliest drafts, Billy finally notices at the championship game when one of the girls takes her hat off and her hair falls down), which might be excusable on the part of Mr Brooks as he sees them only briefly, but Billy is supposedly their baseball coach. Jamie commits an act of criminal negligence in leaving a group of under-twelves unsupervised in her workplace while she swans off to a meeting, particularly ones known to be unfamiliar with Earth technology and culture, and elsewhere displays her brilliant strategic mind by informing Xaviar straight away that she has overheard him talking to Adama, when, had she kept her mouth shut, she might have been in a better position to undermine his plans.

The development regarding Xaviar also presents some problems within the story. In the first place, if he can change his form, the *Galactica* don't know his whereabouts, and he is willing to do anything to ensure his freedom, then the obvious idea would be to change his appearance,[28] blend in with the locals, and live as an Earthman, since Adama is unlikely to waste resources tracking him down when he has a Cylon attack to worry about. Furthermore, it's

---

28 As a side note, the fact that the Galacticans have had some success with what Doctor Zee refers to as 'our epidermal transformation' might suggest a reason for Doctor Zee's own change in appearance.

unclear why he seems to assume that Adama will deal with him on his terms, rather than, for instance, acquiescing to Xaviar's wishes, then reneging on the deal the moment Troy, Dillon and the Scouts are safe. Xaviar also criticises Doctor Zee, saying 'I will not be led by an adolescent'; this, however, means that the one anti-Zee voice on the *Galactica* is still that of an evil nutcase. Finally, whereas in 'Galactica Discovers Earth' Xaviar was a ruthless man out to gain power, in this story he has become a generally evil, murderous and child-threatening blackguard, with no real explanation of why he has gone down this route.

'Spaceball' is a tedious comedic runaround focused on Little League baseball and on dragging out the Super Scouts storyline, with the main point of interest being the performance of its special guest star, which lends a touch of class to an otherwise undistinguished character.

4 • THE NIGHT THE CYLONS LANDED (PARTS ONE AND TWO)

US TRANSMISSION DATES: 13 April and 20 April 1980
WRITER: Glen A Larson
DIRECTOR: Sigmund Neufeld, Jr (Part one) Barry Crane (Part two)
CREDITED CAST: William Daniels (Norman); Lara Parker (Shirley); Peter Mark Richman (Colonel Briggs); Roger Davis (Andromus); Wolfman Jack (Himself); Sheila DeWindt (Stewardess); Rene LeVant (1st Officer/Max); Ed Griffith (2nd Officer); Jed Mills (Cabbie); Timothy O'Hagan (Kanon); Robert Lunny (Briton); Marj Dusay (Mildred); Val Bisoglio (Arnie); Bernie Hamilton (Chief Clifford); Heather Young (Star); Ken Lynch (Grover); Arthur Batanides (Cabbie); John Finnegan (Officer in Trauma Room); Herb Vigran (Pop); John Widlock (Chuck); Dan Ferrone (Police Sergeant); Alexander Petala (1st Tough); Cosie Costa (2nd Tough); T Miratti (3rd Tough); Louis Sardo (4th Tough); Paul Tuerpe (Fireman); Chip Lucia (MC)
KNOWN UNCREDITED CAST: Neil Zevnik (Andromidus); Rex Cutter (Centuri); Ed Griffith (Leroy)

SYNOPSIS: On patrol, Recon Probe Delta encounters an unusual Cylon craft. In the ensuing fight, both vessels are damaged, and the Cylon ship, containing three Centurians and two humanoid Cylons, plummets to Earth, landing near New York City. The survivors, one humanoid, Andromus, and one Centurian, Centuri, are picked up by a couple on their way to a Hallowe'en party. Meanwhile, Troy and Dillon fly across the country to stop them, preventing an airplane hijack on the way, but arrive at the crash site too late, and are pursued by the local police on suspicion of being drug runners whose plane has crashed, evading them ultimately by driving their car into the harbour. At the party, Andromus meets radio DJ Wolfman Jack and persuades him to take him to his radio station, so that the Cylons can send a signal to their cohorts and inform them of their location. Dillon and Troy chase Andromus through New York, finally confronting the Cylons on the roof of the International Trade Centre (where the radio station is located), and shoot them. Their bodies land in a disposal bin and are taken away to the dump.

ANALYSIS: 'The Night the Cylons Landed' is less tedious than the earlier ones, with the Super Scouts largely out of the way and the narrative briefly shifting to a New York-based action romp. However, it also features some of the series' all-time lows, including an inexplicable airplane-hijacking subplot and a musical revue number.

HOW B-MOVIES GET MADE: BACKGROUND AND PRODUCTION

'The Night the Cylons Landed' is principally distinguished in production terms by the appearance of Bob 'Wolfman Jack' Smith, a New York DJ and MC. Wolfman Jack shot to fame following an appearance 'as himself' in 1974's *American Graffiti*, and, by the late 1970s, was making a lot of guest appearances as himself in such programmes as *The Odd Couple* and *What's Happening*. The episode also features a return appearance by actress Sheila DeWindt, who played Deitra in the *Battlestar Galactica* story 'Lost Planet of the Gods', as an airline stewardess, and some new modelwork. Robyn Douglass receives a credit for part two, even though she does not appear.

The story is also notorious as the flashpoint for some of the conflict between the crew and the censors. Chris Bunch recalls that the censor, Susan Futterman, demanded to know where they had obtained the astronomical facts cited in the planetarium sequence, and, when she was told that they were from the *Encyclopedia Britannica*, replied 'that's not good enough' (the production team responded by demanding that she put that in writing, at which point she apparently dropped the subject). Later, however, Futterman apparently objected to one of the lines about meatballs (probably Norman's remark in part one about how the Cylons will feel after 'Arnie forces a couple of his meatballs down their throats'), claiming that it was a dirty joke. Larson responded by writing in more references to meatballs (visibly so, since one major difference between the 26 and 28 March drafts of part two are that Norman and Shirley's initial dialogue, which in the 26 March draft revolves around the idea that their hostess, Mildred, is sexually rapacious and will likely make a play for Centuri, is replaced in the 28 March draft by the discussion about Arnie's famous meatballs), and, since the final edit was delivered only minutes before the programme was due to be put on air, the censors were unable to alter the broadcast. A quick count indicates that the word 'meatballs' appears no less than ten times in part two (and four more times in the 28 March draft of this episode; regrettably, one of the cut lines is the delightful exchange: 'What happened?" 'His meatballs exploded …'), including the recap, which, presumably in another nod to the censors, repeats the original meatball joke in full.

Allan Cole also recalls in an interview that the episode was unusually difficult to film, due to the fact that the planetarium sequences had to be shot at night; while night shoots normally incur overtime, and also mean the loss of the next morning's filming (unless shot on a Saturday, in which case the crew have a natural break over Sunday, which, due to the show's fraught schedule, was not possible), the situation was complicated by the fact that they were

filming with children, who were, in his words, 'all either sleepy, or hyper …
driving the planetarium staff out of their gourds' due to the unaccustomed
late night.

This story is unusual for *Galactica 1980* in having a first-draft script which
deviates significantly from later, and screened, versions. In the opening of the
first-draft script (dated 13 March 1980), we have the *Galactica* encountering
the new Cylon craft, which Zee, Boomer and Adama assume to be on a mission
to observe the Earth and report back; we then have scenes in the Cylon craft
which make it clear that in fact, their ship has been damaged in a meteor storm,
and that they do not actually expect to encounter the humans; in a reverse
perspective on 'The Super Scouts,' the Cylons remark that they have not had any
attacks from the humans in 30 years. There is also an extensive scene in which
Boomer, Zee and Adama discuss the new humanoid Cylons, who are said by Zee,
based on close-range scans, to be both machine and organic, and, he speculates,
are capable of living for hundreds of years, and also to be programmable with
the knowledge of past generations. Boomer becomes despondent about their
prospects of winning against such a foe, but Zee points out that if they carry on
progressing along these lines, they will start to develop human passions and will
wind up warring against each other, foreshadowing the plot of 'The Return of
Starbuck', and of the reimagined series.

The first draft's early scenes on Earth are better than the final. Jamie and
the Super Scouts do not appear, and it is Doctor Mortinson who sends Troy
and Dillon to New York; he also explains that the Cylon craft is sparking
international tensions, as it is believed to be an illegally armed Russian satellite,
harking back to the device seen in the later draft of 'Spaceball'. Mortinson
books their tickets for them because the serial numbers of the money they
'stole' have been circulated (possibly explaining Troy and Dillon's concerns
that giving the money to the muggers in New York would implicate them in
the bank robbery). The first draft does not mention Wolfman Jack, and Shirley
at one point blurts out 'I hope they're not gay', referring to Andromus and
Centuri, which must have further endeared the series to the censors.

Drafts of part two, dated 26 and 28 March 1980, are both much closer to
the screened version, but stop abruptly on the final page (59 in the 26 March
draft, 65 in the 28 March draft) at the point at which Troy and Dillon arrive at
the radio station, with the words 'To be Continued,' confirming the idea that
Larson's practice on the series was simply to write about sixty pages and then
go on to the next episode. The two drafts are very close to each other, with the
main differences, apart from the changes to the initial scene mentioned above,
the fact that the meatballs originally were brought to the party by Norman

rather than supplied by Arnie, and finally the addition of the rescue of the child and dog from the fire, the dialogue scenes with Adama and Zee, and a brief scene on a second Cylon ship, to the later draft; Arnie is also 'Danny' in the 13 and 26 March drafts.

In a slightly self-referential twist, this story features B-movies heavily (with the scenario of a bland human male arriving on Earth with a mute, gigantic robot servant being yet another nod to *The Day the Earth Stood Still*) and even includes a few: the Cylons watch a clip from *Abbott and Costello Go to Mars* (1953) and then one from what appears to be the same vampire film Doctor Zee viewed in '*Galactica* Discovers Earth'. Troy, Dillon and the children also watch *This Island Earth* (1955) in the cinema, although, as two of the clips are shown twice, one gets the impression that the projectionist is winding the film backwards and forwards. The first draft also features Troy and Dillon taking in a B-movie named *Creatures from Outer Space*, out of curiosity as to how Earth people portray aliens, and notes that the footage from this film should be represented by a clip from *War of the Worlds* (1953) of the US army attacking alien craft. The draft also mentions *Close Encounters of the Third Kind* as the inflight movie on the plane to New York. Another, non-B-movie, film is briefly referred to by the party-goers to explain Andromus' energy-firing fingers: *Mister Moses* (1965), starring Robert Mitchum.

LINKING SEGMENTS: CONTINUITY AND WORLDBUILDING

As with the original *Battlestar Galactica*, there seems to be a certain amount of episode-to-episode continuity. The references to New York in the draft of 'The Super Scouts' finally pay off when Troy and Dillon do actually visit the city. Doctor Mortinson and Billy Eheres are namechecked (the former is scanning for distress signals on Troy and Dillon's instructions, due to their initial assumption that the crashed ship is a Viper; the latter looks after the Super Scouts in their absence). Although Colonel Sydell is not present, his replacement, Colonel Briggs, mentions that he has a colleague who is out of action due to Troy and Dillon's activities, which, the draft confirms, means Sydell (the character's absence in the filmed story and the 28 March draft, despite being present in the earliest draft of the script, suggests that, as with Xaviar in the previous story, the actor was either unavailable or didn't want to continue: Briggs' screened remark that Sydell is 'suffering from some kind of shock … his brain is someplace else' suggests that the characters are finding the series as difficult to take as most viewers do). Allusions are made to Dillon's accidental bank robbery during one of the mugging sequences (apparently they are still spending the money he 'stole'), and the time since the Fleet's last encounter with the Cylons is stated again to be thirty Earth years. The Cylons also refer to Earth as the last outpost of humanity, confirming the idea that the other human planets have been destroyed. Outside of this, an alien race called the 'Gorkons' are namechecked; the similarity of this word to 'Gorgons', plus the slightly Greek sound to the humanoid Cylons' names, suggests that Larson is still occasionally using the pin-in-the-classical-dictionary method to choose characters' designations.

By far the most interesting developments, however, come with regard to the Cylons. For the first time, we now have humanoid Cylons (who were originally to have been introduced in 'The Super Scouts'; they are called 'androids' in the draft scripts, though not onscreen). The ones we encounter are male in appearance, and named Andromidus and Andromus. They are weaker than the Centurians, but, unlike the similar humanoid Cylons in the reimagined series, they have mechanical insides, and, assuming Andromus is typical, can fire energy beams from their fingers (as well as, possessing the ability to briefly hypnotise New York taxi-drivers). The helmets they wear are similar to Baltar's in 'The Living Legend', complete with third-eye motif. The 3 March draft script states they are to be 'identical', and the 28 March draft of part two has a deleted scene involving two other humanoids (designated 'Android #1' and 'Android #2'), said to look the same as Andromus and Andromidus. Andromus also rapidly outdoes Dillon and Troy in terms of his ability to adapt to Earth, blending in much better after only a few hours than the warriors have managed in a longer stretch of time (although Dillon and Troy have now finally picked up a few words of American slang, such as 'a beaut' and 'take the fall'). Andromus' greeting 'happy Hallowe'en, little people', to the children at the party suggests that he has a similar deadpan wit to his Centurian cousins (then again, given the ignorance Cylons appear to have of human reproduction in 'The Return of Starbuck', he might genuinely think that they are just small adults). The new Cylon ship, said to be larger and faster than previous craft, is visibly different, with a new sound effect; it now features three Centurians and two humanoids as regular crew. The Cylons still have an empire, and the signal beam is being sent to the star Balcon, which presumably possesses a Cylon outpost, or else is where the Cylon fleet is currently stationed.

The humanoid Cylons seem to be the source of a cultural discontinuity. On the one hand, Andromus, viewing the machines running the overnight broadcasting system at the radio station, remarks that humans may soon discover machines more efficient than they are, at which point they will be replaced. Furthermore, the fact that the humanoids assume that they will be able to request assistance from the natives of the planet they encounter, up until they discover that the natives are human, suggests that Cylons in fact share friendly relations with most if not all species in the known universe, except the human race. At the same time, however, Andromus explicitly says that he was 'created in man's image', and both the humanoids' names contain the Greek root *andro-*, or 'man'. The Cylons thus seem split between reviling humans and wishing to emulate them, perhaps providing the intellectual spark for the Cylon-human divisions and connections in the reimagined series.

Andromus also seems to have a fairly friendly relationship with the Centurian which accompanies him, who is largely addressed as 'Centurian' and at one point 'Centurian 9', within the ship, but appears to also have the name 'Centuri', which becomes Andromus' default name for him while they are on Earth. As well as suggesting affection or respect for the machine (as being addressed by name seemed to be a mark of high rank among the Cylons in the original series, as with Vulpa and Lucifer, though it has to be said that 'Centuri' is a bit of a naff name to give a Centurian), this also suggests that the humanoids share the human need to personify and give names to things. On Centuri's part, his programming to keep the humanoids safe overrides his programming to follow their orders.

THE NEW YORK CITY BLUES: GOOD AND BAD ASPECTS

'The Night the Cylons Landed' does contain some good elements, indeed, more than the previous three stories. Much of the Cylon action is great, with some nice modelwork (the crash-landing sequence in particular is worth a second look), an eerie moment when part one ends with the Cylon noise echoing over the freeze-frame for a few seconds, and more examples of the famed Centurian deadpan humour (when the humanoids note that the craft's chance of survival is less than 3%, but the Centurians' chance is 1%, the Centurians all silently turn and regard the humanoids for a minute, and Centuri nods solemnly when Shirley tells her husband, 'you're terrible'). The sequence of Centuri gradually recovering on board ship, with his light becoming brighter and voice forming distinct words, and, later, the one where he punches his way out of the ship, are also good, and the final scene of Centuri's decapitated head, pathetically repeating 'I will protect you', as it is taken off to the dump, is poignant. Elsewhere, the traumatised partygoers attempting to describe Centuri to the police, complete with impressions of his noise and light, are funny, as is the Super Scouts' appalled reaction to the death of the alien in *This Island Earth*.

There are also some entertaining popular culture and media inside references for the astute viewer to watch out for. Billy Joel's 'My Life' makes another appearance, as does Linda Ronstadt's 1976 cover of 'That'll Be the Day'. An air force officer refers both to Skylab's then-recent fall to Earth on 11 July 1979, as well as another incident in which a Russian satellite landed in Canada by accident. Hijackings, a common problem of the late 1970s, are referenced, and the microwave oven used to disable Centuri was at the time a very new and fashionable piece of technology (and reference is made to the fact that they could have a bad effect on old alternating-current pacemakers, which hints at where Larson got the idea from). There is a massive irony in that, had Dillon and Troy witnessed the incident in question, they would have learned a quick way to incapacitate the Cylons which would not harm a normal human, and would also have provided a satisfying narrative payoff for the series' premise, as primitive Earth would have given the Galacticans the means to finally defeat their enemy. The fact that Dillon and Troy go by the pseudonyms Jones and Smith might be an allusion to Larson's earlier series *Alias Smith and Jones*, on which Roger Davis, who plays Andromus, was a regular, replacing Pete Duel as Hannibal Heyes after the latter's suicide, and the chief of the New York City Police is played by Bernie Hamilton, better known for his role on another ABC series, *Starsky and Hutch*, as the eponymous policemen's boss, Captain Dobey (a policeman named Grover also appeared in the 1978 *Starsky and Hutch* episode 'Foxy Lady'). Lara Parker, who played Shirley (who spends both episodes dressed as a vampire) is better known for playing Angelique on the vampire-based series *Dark Shadows*. Somewhat perplexingly, although an institution called the 'International Trade Center' does exist, it is not a building, but the technical cooperation agency of UNCTAD and the WTO; in the *Galactica 1980* universe, however, it appears to be the equivalent of the World Trade Centre (a large and well-known building containing the offices of a variety of companies), but why the WTC has incurred this pseudonym here, particularly as it is namechecked in the draft script, is unknown.

Unfortunately, the story, as is typical for *Galactica 1980*, revolves around a number of unbelievable coincidences. The Cylon craft happens to crash-land in the USA, handy for Troy and Dillon, and does so on Hallowe'en, the one day of the year when two strange-looking humanoids are not likely to be noticed. When Norm and Shirley see Andromus and Centuri, they offer them a lift rather than simply commenting on their costumes, and then turn out to be involved with a local radio station, and thus precisely what the Cylons need to allow them to signal their counterparts. Troy and Dillon, similarly, arrive at the party just in time to rescue the inevitable child (clad in an ill-fitting silver jumpsuit left over from 'Greetings from Earth' and possessing a dog named 'Skippy', presumably no relation to 'Skipper' from 'Galactica Discovers Earth').

The rescue sequence is more extensive in the draft, involving Troy rescuing stranded party-goers as well as the child and dog, but is no less contrived, and contains that section's gratuitous science info-dump as Troy controls the fire through creating a vacuum by causing an explosion with his laser pistol.

The story also abounds with bad fish-out-of-water humour. Evidently Colonials have no concept of fiction as, although Troy and Dillon recognise *This Island Earth* as entertainment, they assume the story to be literal. Centuri and Andromus being mistaken for Hallowe'en revellers is utterly predictable, as are the sequences with the muggers in Central Park. The whole idea of having Troy and Dillon take the plane to New York rather than simply fly their Vipers (which, after all, have the power of invisibility) is simply an excuse for more predictable humour, contributing nothing to the story. Although airline hijackings had reached their peak in the mid-1970s, and thus should have been something very much on the minds of all airline personnel in 1980, the airline desk clerk does not seem at all suspicious of Troy and Dillon, even though they act oddly and use transparent pseudonyms, nor does anyone stop the two hijackers, even though it is obvious from the start that the 'baby' they are carrying is a doll. Even Troy finds it strange that their pictures haven't been circulated to airport personnel, which, as they are wanted by the police, would seem a sensible move to prevent them from leaving town. Troy and Dillon are also bizarrely innocent of the concept of hijackings when one considers that there had been at least two such incidents in the Fleet during *Battlestar Galactica* (in 'Baltar's Escape' and 'Take the *Celestra*') plus at least one attempted hijacking (during Starbuck's prison break in 'Murder on the *Rising Star*'). It is also criminally negligent of Jamie not to explain airport procedure to the warriors before they take their flight, if not particularly inconsistent with Jamie's general irresponsibility.

There are other bad aspects to the story. The press find out about the hijacking remarkably quickly, given that very little happens during it, and all the pilot does is contact the FBI. Troy and Dillon hold hands to get off the plane together while invisible, which seems unusually sensitive even for *Battlestar Galactica* men (in the draft, one holds on to the other's coat). Although the Super Scouts are mercifully absent for the most part, the party scenes feature other gratuitous children (who are interestingly absent from the draft script, barring the one child needing rescuing from the fire, suggesting they were forced in at the network's insistence), and even Wolfman Jack catches the infodump disease, spouting off random trivia about radio broadcasting. The leader of the gang of muggers wears sunglasses after dark. Dillon also displays unusual stupidity when he wonders if the airline crew would let him take the controls (as they have public transport in the Fleet, with the shuttles in 'The Man With Nine Lives' being not dissimilar to Earth commercial aircraft, he can't be unfamiliar with the concept), and neither he nor Troy are acquainted with the idea of 'smoking' (despite the fact that Starbuck smoked his way through the entire original series).

Mention should also be made of the sequence where Troy and Dillon crash a musical variety show featuring actors dressed in Hanna-Barbera character suits (identifiable as Scooby-Doo, Hair Bear, Hong Kong Phooey, and Maw and Paw Rugg from *The Hillbilly Bears*) dancing to 'Zip-a-dee-do-dah', (which, since this sequence is not in the draft script, and since Hanna-Barbera's cartoons were then being screened on ABC, seems like more shameless cross-promotion) and wind up in a chorus line of dancers while an overmature Shirley Temple impersonator belts out 'On The Good Ship Lollipop' (which goes further in the draft script, with the impersonator feeling upstaged by Troy and Dillon's turning invisible, and the latter two end the number by throwing her into a 'sumptuous gigantic birthday cake'). Apparently Dillon found this sufficiently entertaining to want to go back at the end of the story.

More generally, the episodes lack all drama, since, as there's no way the Cylons can destroy the Earth in 1980, we know that Troy and Dillon will succeed in stopping them. In a particularly bad example of cost-cutting, the sequence where Adama and Doctor Zee discuss Cylon technological developments is literally lifted wholesale from 'The Super Scouts', albeit with the lines which refer specifically to the events of 'The Super Scouts' cut out and a few frames of the Delta Probe's scan of the humanoid Cylon inserted to change the context. There is also the question of why Troy and Dillon continually talk like dorks, using language that is far more stilted than Apollo and Starbuck's ever was, and why, if they have compromised themselves in the USA to the extent that every policeman is after them, Adama doesn't consider removing them from the assignment and putting in someone less notorious instead.

'The Night the Cylons Landed' has plenty to amuse fans of late 1970s/ early 1980s popular culture, and has some interesting developments which would influence the later reimagined series. However, it also has the by-now-inevitable discontinuities, plot problems and forced humour which characterise *Galactica 1980*.

5 • SPACE CROPPERS

US TRANSMISSION DATE: 27 April 1980
WRITER: Robert L McCullough
DIRECTOR: Daniel Heller
CREDITED CAST: Dana Elcar (Steadman); Ana Alicia (Gloria Alonzo); Anna Navarro (Louise Alonzo); Bill Cort (Trent); Bill McKinney (Barrett); Ned Romero (Hector Alonzo); Booth Colman (Rogers); Joaquin Garay III (Chris [Alonzo]); Andy Jarrell (Maze); Phil Levien (Dante); Dennis Haysbert (The Creature [Voice of the Imperious Leader]); John Dantona (Foley); Gordon Haight (Deacon); Stefan Haves (Channon); Lance Mugleston (Pilot)

SYNOPSIS: The Cylon Imperious Leader orders the Cylon Fleet to attack the Galactican Fleet's agro-ships, believing that this will force the humans to lead them to Earth. The attack is successful, which prompts Adama to begin the establishment of a secret Galactican agricultural colony on Earth, and Troy and Dillon are sent to acquire suitable land. The warriors enter into partnership with Hector Alonzo, a Hispanic farmer whose livelihood is under threat from his white neighbour Steadman, head of the local Grower's Association and controller of the local water supply. Steadman tries various ploys to force the warriors to abandon Hector, including tricking Dillon into riding a wild horse named Satan (which Dillon succeeds in taming) and cutting off the farm's water (Doctor Zee intervenes by causing a rainstorm). However, the Galacticans prevail, and seed Hector's land with rapidly-growing crops. Secretly observing the Galacticans' fantastic technical and physical abilities, Steadman tries to turn first the Grower's Association, then the local sheriff, against Hector and his partners, with tales of alien activities, but he is not believed, and the colony is established.

ANALYSIS: This is the final *Galactica 1980* episode to follow the storyline set up in '*Galactica* Discovers Earth' and is by far the best of these episodes. Sadly, this suggests that, had it been given proper time, care and enthusiasm, *Galactica 1980* could have been at least a decent successor to its parent, as opposed to the travesty it is widely regarded to be.

BUYING THE FARM: PRODUCTION AND STORY

'Space Croppers' (which, coincidentally, shares its title with a 1966 episode of *Lost in Space*, 'The Space Croppers', revolving around a family of alien hillbillies) is the only story in the series not written, at least in part, by Glen Larson, but by story editor Bob McCullough. Much of the exteriors were filmed at the Disney movie ranch in Los Angeles County, while the first five minutes consist entirely of stock footage from *Battlestar Galactica*, aside from a few Viper-cockpit cutaways. Following on from the previous story's B-movie themes, the sequence where young Chris Alonzo looks out his bedroom window to see Doctor Zee's flying saucer landing is a straight homage to the classic B-picture *Invaders from Mars* (1953). In terms of the casting, Ned Romero is in fact of Spanish, French and Native American origin rather than purely Hispanic, and is otherwise well-known for playing a mysterious Native American shaman in the series *Roswell*, while Ana Alicia is in fact Mexican, and had previously appeared as Aurora in the *Battlestar Galactica* episode 'Take the *Celestra*'.

As with many episodes of the original series, this story makes heavy use of Western-film clichés, in this case that of the poor but worthy farmer being attacked by a bullying local boss, and then saved by the timely intervention of heroic strangers. The setup for the story, with the loss of the agro-ships precipitating a food crisis in the Fleet, is also heavily indebted to 'The Magnificent Warriors'. Again, there is confusion as to how many agro-ships the Fleet has at any point: the stock footage shows three agro-ships flying together, implying that there are three agro-ships in the Fleet (contradicting 'The Magnificent Warriors', in which the original three agro-ships are reduced to one), but Adama refers first to the loss of 'two agro-ships' and then says 'of all the ships in the fleet, the chance of that one being destroyed ...' (the drafts state that the Fleet had only a single agro-ship – which, if that is the case, would support 'The Magnificent Warriors', but contradict 'War of the Gods'), giving the impression of a lack of communication between the different parts of the production team.

In continuity terms, the Fleet's mission has changed back to its original form from the variation stated in 'Spaceball', with the plan now being to establish 'a colony' of Galacticans on Earth, to feed the Fleet, provide a home for the children, and start infiltrating Earth society. The villainous Maze's fondness for cigars may be a sly allusion to Starbuck's own bad habit and the problems it led to with the censors, while we have more references to the earlier series in D Squadron, nicknamed 'the Daggits', whose leader, Lieutenant Dante, has a name recalling the demon/devil references in *Battlestar Galactica*. Adama, deadpan, remarks on his squadron's 'devil may care' attitude. Adama and Boomer do the Colonial forearm-clasp. Steadman, reflecting some of the original series' imagery, wears a white suit on occasion, and Troy also references the fraternal symbolism of both series by saying 'all of you farmers are brothers of a kind'. Dillon mentions that they have seen similar animals to horses before and alludes to there having been beasts like these on Caprica. Zee's flying saucer makes a brief return. In a development which both references the unmade *Battlestar Galactica* story 'Showdown' and looks forward to the reimagined series, we meet a member of the battlestar's ground crew, whose frustration over pilots' cavalier attitude towards their Vipers foreshadows similar tirades made by Chief Tyrol in the reimagined series. The Cylon Imperious Leader makes a welcome return, albeit in a brief and uninteresting scene (again consisting of overdubbed stock footage), and the Cylons also appear to have abandoned the term 'Colonial' for their enemies, referring to the 'Galactican Fleet'.

There appears to have been some development among the Cylons. The fact that the Imperious Leader is no longer voiced by Patrick Macnee (the actor presumably being either unwilling, unavailable, or too expensive) might suggest that there have been some political changes among the Cylons in the past thirty years, including a weakening of the influence of Count Iblis, and it is tempting to wonder if there is any connection between this and the development of the humanoid Cylons.

Perusal of the draft scripts shows that the story has improved a good deal under development. While the basic premise is the same from the earliest to the final drafts, in earlier drafts (where the story title is 'Harvest Home') the family are not Hispanic (with the farmer being named 'Ray Markham' and his daughter 'Kate,' though Louise and Chris' first names are unchanged), and there is also an extensive subplot to the effect that the Cylons have found a means of detecting Galactican ships through a device (inaccurately referred to as 'radar') which can detect ionic radiation in the Fleet's hulls. Doctor Zee develops a process to de-ionise the ships, but obviously cannot treat Troy and Dillon's craft, leading to a deeply predictable space battle in Act Four as the pilots try to bring the crops back to the Fleet (the drafts lack the idea that the Galacticans want to set up an agricultural colony on Earth). In the earlier draft Troy and Dillon plough and seed the field themselves, using the turbines (the Super Scouts only appearing in a brief jokey sequence where they play hide-and-seek using the invisibility process); in the second, Jamie and the Scouts are present (though, perplexingly, the Scouts also appear to be back on the Fleet in an earlier scene, in which Starla complains about the food, raising the question of how they got back down to Earth and into Jamie's custody). Dillon's means of taming the horse in the earlier drafts is, distressingly, to stun it with his laser. In both drafts, Colonel Briggs makes a brief cameo, turning up to investigate reports of flying saucers, but Troy and Dillon are warned in time by Steadman, who, in the drafts, experiences a Stockton-like change of heart and destroys his dam, vowing to behave better in the future. Both drafts end with a slightly hokey 'Galactican Thanksgiving' feast on the Fleet.

The drafts also contain some peculiar inaccuracies: the earlier draft refers to the Cylon craft as 'Cylon Vipers' and misidentifies Boomer as a Captain, and both drafts refer to the Centurions as 'Centuri' (errors which are somewhat perplexing from one of the series' own story editors). The first draft contains yet another *Buck Rogers* inside joke (when young Chris asserts that he knows all about spaceships because he watches this series on TV). The later draft refers to a 'robot tender' being seen caring for plants on the agro-ship, in what looks like another allusion to *Silent Running*. Both drafts also have the conceit that the Galactican plants grow giant vegetables, leading Ray to speculate on the problem of 'hunting up a twenty-foot-long hog for the bacon, lettuce and tomato sandwiches.'

HECTOR'S HOUSE: POSITIVE ASPECTS OF THE STORY

Although 'Space Croppers' gets off to a fairly slow start, it comes together quite nicely towards the end. While the Super Scouts, in their by-now-surely-filthy uniforms, make an unwelcome return, complete with a reprise of the silly Galactican campfire song which featured in 'The Super Scouts', their use is kept to a minimum, their ignorance of agriculture makes sense rather than seeming contrived (their misconceptions about where food comes from are not too dissimilar to those of modern urban children who have never seen a farm), and they manage to get in one or two reasonably funny lines (as in the sequence where Steadman blusters 'Everybody knows who I am!' and two Super Scouts pipe up with 'I don't!' and 'I don't want to!'). Jamie also acts like a proper reporter for once, rather than a criminally irresponsible info-dump machine; the scene where she plays the slightly unscrupulous journalist looking for a good 'kooky hillbillies' story, asking if Steadman regularly sees spaceships and if the sheriff usually goes out to inspect the area for alien activity on his instructions, making both men look even more ridiculous, is well played. Although having Chris Alonzo pray for someone to come help his father immediately before Troy and Dillon show up is another cliché of this type of story, it works in this case because of the running theme, in *Battlestar Galactica*, of divine intervention.

Dana Elcar manages to make John Steadman both charming and bullying, and wrests some great comedy out of the sequences where he reports, quite truthfully, what he saw on the Alonzos' farm (spaceships, miraculous rainstorms, and people leaping great distances), but is assumed to have gone insane by everyone who hears him (it's implied that he changes his story subtly over the course of the episode: when he initially refers to seeing 'alien beings' he is laughed at, but the fact that the sheriff is looking for 'illegal aliens' on his testimony suggests that he became more generic in his use of the term 'aliens', presumably so that people would listen to him). Kent McClure and Barry van Dyke are also good in this story, suggesting that when they have a script which plays to their strengths, they perform well. Unusually (and refreshingly) for the normally chaste *Galactica 1980*, there is a strong indication of romantic interest between Dillon and Gloria (played by an actress who had taken the part of an old girlfriend of Starbuck's in the original series); although her parents try to dismiss this as a teenage crush, Dillon's remarks to Troy in private suggest, Starbuck-like, that he doesn't particularly object to the attention.

The racism theme is also dealt with in a much more nuanced fashion than one would expect from *Galactica 1980*. There are subtle expressions of prejudice as well as obvious ones, for instance the fact that Steadman and his henchmen, who are openly aggressive to Hector, take a more polite tone with Troy and Dillon, and that the Growers' Association members treat Hector with more respect when he has white partners than when he is operating on his own. When Steadman accuses Hector of harbouring aliens, the sheriff and Grower's Association assume he means illegal (and thus Hispanic) aliens, but, when they see that the people on the farm are white, they do not even ask for identification.

The link between racism and power relations is also indicated. Hector himself says that the locals are not bad people, but will not help him because they are afraid of Steadman. Steadman's henchmen openly admit to burning Hector's seed bags, evidently because they feel themselves to be invulnerable, and seem surprised when Steadman says he will punish them for this (which appears in turn to be an attempt to lull Troy and Dillon into thinking he's a reasonable man, so that he can get them under his control). It is also significant that the Grower's Association only turn on Steadman when the rainfall breaks the drought (making his control over the water supply less significant) and when he shows himself in a bad light by going on about aliens. The story also, bravely, does not succumb to the temptation to offer up a pat solution for prejudice, to the effect of announcing at the end that the farmers have all learned a valuable lesson and have given up racism for good; in fact, Troy and Dillon have not actually managed to eliminate the prejudice against Hispanic farmers, and could be argued to have perpetuated it, since their presence simply offers Hector the support of the dominant ethnic group rather than questioning why there should be ethnic divisions, leaving the issue of whether the human race can overcome its negative tendencies open.

HECTORED TO DEATH: PROBLEMS WITH THE STORY

Unfortunately, 'Space Croppers' is far from flawless. Adama has still seemingly checked his brain in at the door, dumbly stating the obvious and providing a sounding-board for Doctor Zee's tedious info-dumps. The Cylons also show a shocking degree of ignorance, since, as the *Galactica* is stated to be 'in orbit', either around the Earth or some nearby planetary or lunar body (as the Viper pilots are able to reach Earth with ease from the *Galactica*), it seems astonishing that the Cylons can find the *Galactica* but can't find Earth, but instead go on about how the *Galactica* will lead them to it.

There is more grating humour when Troy and Dillon fail to recognise a scarecrow for what it is, first mistaking it for an Earthling, then speculating that it might be a grave marker or form of crude art; even if they have never seen a scarecrow before, one would think that they have now been on Earth for long enough to allow them to rule out the other possibilities. Similarly, although Troy and Dillon have difficulty grasping such simple Earth concepts as how to cross the street at an intersection (in 'The Super Scouts') they absorb the concept of prejudice against Hispanic Americans without question (indeed, without the slightest inquiry into the origins and extent of the discrimination they face, let alone the meaning of such potentially confusing terms as 'wetback'), leaving the inevitable info-dump about racism to be conducted for the benefit of Chris Alonzo, who, having experienced this prejudice all his life, would seem to be a less likely subject. The problem is clearly structural, as the writer sensibly does not want to slow the action down with a long discussion on the oppression of Hispanic Americans at the point at which the concept is introduced, and instead reserves the explanations for a slower moment in the narrative, but the end result sits ill with what the audience should expect of the characters.

The story also contains the usual obvious educational info-dumps, this week about plant biology, Hispanic-American culture, and cloud seeding, with a quick plug for both the Scouts and the 4H Clubs (an association for children living in agricultural areas) thrown in as well. There is also a commendable attack on animal cruelty, when the audience learns through Dillon that the cause of the horse Satan's viciousness is simply maltreatment, and that treating the animal kindly encourages a return to normal equine behaviour. There is also a slight continuity problem in that the Super Scouts have difficulty grasping the concept of putting seeds in the ground and letting them grow, saying that in the Fleet, plants are grown through hydroponics, whereas the stock footage of the agro-ships clearly indicates that conventional soil-based gardens also exist.

'Space Croppers' marks a belated upturn in quality for *Galactica 1980*, leading in to the story which many viewers consider to be the high-water-mark of the series, 'The Return of Starbuck', and providing an upbeat conclusion to the adventures of Troy, Dillon, Jamie and the Super Scouts.

6 • THE RETURN OF STARBUCK

US TRANSMISSION DATES: 4 May 1980
WRITER: Glen A Larson
DIRECTOR: Ron Satloff
CREDITED CAST: Dirk Benedict (Starbuck); Judith Chapman (Angela); Rex Cutter (Centurion); Ellen Gerken (Girl)
KNOWN UNCREDITED CAST: Gary Owens (voice of Cy)

SYNOPSIS: Doctor Zee comes to Adama and relates a strange dream. In it, Starbuck crashes on an unknown planet during a Cylon raid; the Fleet are unable to stop and must abandon him. Starbuck rigs up a makeshift shelter and, lacking in companionship, revives a Cylon from a Cylon ship which has also crashed on the planet. He names it 'Cy', and the pair develop an uneasy companionship. Cy brings to the camp a pregnant woman named Angela, and her presence puts a strain on their relationship. She refers to the child as Starbuck's, and asks him to put together a craft for herself and the child. Starbuck, with Cy's help, assembles a life capsule of sorts out of the remains of the two ships. Angela's baby is born, but another Cylon craft arrives, looking for the crashed one. Starbuck gets Angela and the baby into the life capsule, and he and Cy fight off the Cylons, but Cy is destroyed, and Starbuck is again alone on the planet. Angela appears and says that Starbuck has been judged good. Adama reveals to Doctor Zee that his dream was real, and Doctor Zee was the child, having been found by the Fleet drifting alone in the spacecraft.

ANALYSIS: 'The Return of Starbuck' is generally considered the single best story of the *Galactica 1980* run, and is a real return to form, being poignant and dramatic, with a strong message and development of the original series.

MANY HAPPY RETURNS: DEVELOPMENT AND PRODUCTION
'The Return of Starbuck' was developed from a script reportedly intended for the second season of *Battlestar Galactica*, 'The Final Flight', which would have featured an ordinary woman rather than Angela, and Starbuck being rescued at the end by Boomer. According to *Somewhere Beyond the Heavens*, Larson revived this story due to the large amount of fan mail asking about what happened to Apollo and Starbuck. Dirk Benedict has said in interviews that he suggested to Larson that it would make a good premise for a spinoff series along the lines of *The Fugitive*, with Starbuck wandering through space trying to find his way home. The concept of the story draws on both *Robinson Crusoe*

and the film *Hell in the Pacific* (1968), and bears strong similarities to Barry B Longyear's near-contemporary novella *Enemy Mine* (1979), with yet another reference to *Silent Running* when Starbuck teaches Cy to play Pyramid.

The story, the title of which changed to 'Starbuck's Greatest Journey' and 'Starbuck's Last Journey' before finally settling on 'The Return of Starbuck', also exists in the form of a draft entitled 'Starbuck's Greatest Journey' and dated to 15 April 1980, with revisions on 21 and 25 April. The draft is broadly similar to the finished version, but the framing sequences of the story are longer (and the final framing sequence also includes a flashback to Boomer discovering the hybrid spacecraft drifting in space, which presumably was omitted for reasons of time and the fact that it would have required new effects work). The planet has two suns in the script, and three suns (and five moons) in the filmed version. The draft script also describes Cy's Cylon craft filling with CO_2 during the battle sequence to indicate the damage which Starbuck's direct hit has caused it. There is also an omitted sequence where Starbuck considers the various other planets in the system as crash sites, ruling each out in turn, and an extended version of the voice-over where he outlines the normal waking-up procedure for warriors on the *Galactica*, describing his morning ablutions and the terror of facing the enemy day after day.

The longer version of the initial framing sequence has Adama referring, with a slight double meaning, to the events of 'Space Croppers', saying 'we now reap the harvests of our first enclave on Earth … a colony from which we can learn and plan towards the day when we can come forth as a people and join with all of our Earth brothers'. Another noteworthy omission comes when Adama explicitly refers to 'the loss of my own son' (although the precise circumstances of Apollo's fate are not stated), and the sequence which appears in the opening 'teaser' but not in the story, where Starbuck threatens to put the inert Cylons on report, saying ' I'm sick and tired of this silent treatment!' is part of a much longer scripted (and presumably filmed but abandoned) sequence where Starbuck rants about his situation to the Cylons before coming up with the idea of reactivating one of them. The script also contains a continuity error, stating twice that Starbuck has only enough charge in his hand laser to start a single fire, but later depicting him cutting wood, and firing on Cylons, with his laser (presumably this error was noticed, which is why the earlier statements were removed). A couple of points where Starbuck refers to 'years' rather than 'yahrens' make it into the finished version, although one line where Starbuck tells the inert Cylons that they will muster out in a few 'minutes' is changed from the draft to refer to 'centons'.

The filming of the episode took place at the Scenic Cliffs site in Red Rock

Canyon State Park in California. Director Ron Satloff has bad memories of the location shooting, saying that 'there was a hailstorm and [the temperature] was in the 30s. The actress Judith Chapman had a little thing to wear, it was see-through and she was out there with her knees shaking, trying to act. It was unbelievable. We'd wrap blankets around her and [she would] say her lines and try to act before the shakes started. It was just horrible' (this also explains why, although the draft script describes Starbuck as being shirtless in the Pyramid-playing sequences, he is fully clad in the final version). Adama displays a daring choice in Japanese-inspired leisurewear, and he is not bearded in the scenes of *Galactica* in the past. McCord and van Dyke are listed in the opening credits, though neither appears. Some of the footage of Starbuck and Boomer's battle with the Cylon fighters, including a few lines of dialogue, was previously used in 'The Young Lords', although an examination of the available draft script suggests that this was not the intention from the start. Rex Cutter, who played Cy, had previously appeared in 'The Lost Warrior' as Red-Eye, and Centuri in 'The Night the Cylons Landed'. Cy is given an unusual voice for a Cylon, with a gravelly, human-sounding, undertone, making the character more sympathetic and less monotonous to listen to. Alan Cole comments that it was Larson's personal influence which persuaded Benedict to return briefly, and that this is the only story which actually came in on budget, due to its small cast and limited number of locations.

Although this is the last episode of *Galactica 1980*, the producers had started shooting the episode 'The Day They Kidnapped Cleopatra' when the series was cancelled. While 'Wheel of Fire', another unmade script, is often cited as a potential sequel to 'The Return of Starbuck', 'Wheel of Fire' was actually written almost a month before the 'Starbuck's Greatest Journey' draft, suggesting instead that references to Starbuck's fate and the Ship of Lights in this script inspired the changes Larson made to his original 'The Final Flight' Starbuck-marooned scenario, rather than 'The Return of Starbuck' inspiring 'Wheel of Fire'.

The story is one which has received almost universal critical acclaim, with both Glen Larson and Dirk Benedict avowing that they are proud to be associated with it. While some might find the frame story slightly off-putting (with Doctor Zee's awkwardly telling Adama that he's had a significant dream practically crying out for jokes about male puberty), and Starbuck shows a rather unrealistic level of technical ability (constructing a hand-cranked generator and, albeit with help, a spacecraft out of debris from the crash, and rebuilding a Cylon from parts, the latter of which even Doctor Wilker was unable to do in 'Baltar's Escape'), the story is generally well put together and performed, with a number of great lines (such as Starbuck's 'I've been in charge three days and I've already doubled the population', and Cy, on Starbuck's shock upon learning that he has, unbelievably, found a human woman: 'I'm sorry, there wasn't much of a selection'). Even the info-dumps are less intrusive, evolving naturally out of the story; in fact, Starbuck's explanations of human reproduction and infant physiology seem almost like a send-up of earlier, more tediously worthy, info-dumps.

The influence of this episode on the reimagined series is also worth mentioning. As well as providing the immediate basis for the episode 'You Can't Go Home Again', in which Starbuck is stranded on a planet with a crashed Cylon Raider, and the first-season subplot in which Helo and Sharon fall in love while stranded on Caprica, the story also foreshadows the themes of Cylons and humans finding common ground, the birth of miraculous children, and, in the draft script, some of Doctor Zee's remarks to Adama about true visions ('It was in a dream that I clearly saw Earth and knew in my very soul where she was amongst all the stars') recall the continued use of visions as guides to action in the reimagined series.

THE LADY'S NOT FOR RETURNING: CONTINUITY, DEVELOPMENT AND WORLDBUILDING

In continuity terms, the Fleet has had at least one major battle with the Cylons since 'The Hand of God' (and undoubtedly more). Although Cassiopea and Athena are namechecked, Apollo is not, suggesting that he may be dead or disappeared by this point. Starbuck still smokes fumarellos, and apparently keeps some in the cockpit of his Viper. Energisers are again referred to as a source of power. Starbuck alludes to having 'angered the gods' (plural), calls himself a Colonial warrior and mentions the Colonies; the phrase 'Galactican' returns only when the rescue craft is described by Starbuck as 'part Galactican, part Cylon'. The fact that Adama says, in the draft, that the events of Zee's discovery took place 'nearly a decade ago' places Doctor Zee's age at roughly ten years (although the early drafts of 'Galactica Discovers Earth' have Adama stating that Doctor Zee is fourteen).

The story also revisits familiar themes of the series, chiefly the idea of the individual sacrificing themselves for the good of the many, and of superior beings aiding, developing and judging inferior ones, who can eventually hope to reach the superior level themselves. In a cut line, Starbuck says 'all lifeforms are brothers of a sort'. The ending, with a baby being set adrift in a primitive craft to save it from its enemies, and it surviving to become a great leader, references, like the early episodes of *Battlestar Galactica*, the story of Moses (with the power being slightly diminished through our knowledge that the leader it will grow up to become is Doctor Zee).

Angela, also, embodies many of the associations with the 'angels' of the Ship of Lights, although her origins are never explicitly stated apart from saying that she is 'from a dimension beyond'. She asks Starbuck if he wants to progress, and judges him based on his actions towards the baby and herself, declaring him good based on his abandonment of selfishness and embracing of self-sacrifice. Asked about her ship, she says 'it didn't stay', indicating that she did come from a vessel of some sort. She dresses in white, and talks of predestination; one cut sequence has her producing vegetables which she has miraculously grown that very day, apparently without seeds and in hard ground, alluding to the Ship of Lights' influence over plant life seen in 'War of the Gods' (in the same sequence, she refers to Starbuck as 'only human', implying that she is more than human), and another cut line, when Starbuck first meets her, has him saying that 'her clothes were of a fabric as soft as spun angel's hair'. She refers to the baby as Starbuck's 'spiritual child', and he ultimately seems to accept it as his own, implying a deeper connection.

Some new details are also provided, such as the Colonial expression 'they're on me like wet on rain' (as opposed to 'white on rice'). We learn that Viper cockpits can turn into a kind of jettisonable lifepod, with parachutes, in emergencies. Starbuck explains that the Viper cockpit can lower body temperature so as to use less life-support equipment, which might be taken to refer to 'sleep mode' (though the fact that, in 'Spaceball', one person in a two-man cockpit is able to go into sleep mode while the other stays awake, and the early draft scripts of that story describe sleep mode as an 'almost hypnotic trance' suggests a different system). The Colonies also, it seems, have a concept of godparenthood.

One unfortunate continuity error is that Zee appears, at the start of the story, to be unfamiliar with Starbuck, and then, in the extended version of the final framing sequence in the draft script, remarks that he vaguely recalls reading about him in the Fleet's history. This lack of knowledge is surprising, considering that Starbuck is the sort of character whose exploits tend to pass into legend, and, given his friendship with Apollo, it seems odd that Adama didn't mention him more often.

Starbuck is afforded a good deal of personal exploration and development in this story. Here, he comes across as the eternal optimist, fantasising about rescue even as he acknowledges the impossibility of this, suggesting that his difficulty in maintaining permanent relationships comes from a belief that another one will always be coming along. His jokey but self-aggrandising daydream about the planet housing a society of primitives who will worship him rings true with his portrayal in the original series, as does his naming of the planet after himself (prompting Cy to remark, upon learning of his and the planet's names being the same, 'what an interesting coincidence'). In a cut line, he tells Angela 'I was always mechanically inclined' when she appreciates his work on the ship, and he and Cy are said to stand admiring it 'like proud inventors' when they finish it. In the extended version of the scene where he talks to Angela as he cuts wood, he says 'since I never really knew my parents … I kind of built up this defence mechanism … You know … like nothing bothers me … I can get along without anyone … But I'll tell you … when you find yourself the only human being on an entire planet … It makes me wish I had been a whole lot nicer to everyone in my life'.

The sequence where Starbuck crashes is quite touching. Boomer cries when saying goodbye to him (the draft script even states that this should be so), and Adama has an equally poignant moment when he acknowledges that he can't mount a rescue mission without risking the Fleet, but says 'I love you; we all do' when saying goodbye to the absent Starbuck, brilliantly played with a display of conflicting emotions by Lorne Greene.

The idea of Starbuck being judged by his actions comes through continually; even on his first night on the planet, he wonders if he isn't being punished for his selfish ways (and in a cut line, he explicitly refers to the idea of his having died and doing penance in an afterlife). Although, when he is told by Angela 'we all judge ourselves', he replies 'I plan to be very lenient on myself in certain categories', and although he does not volunteer outright to sacrifice himself for Angela and the child, he has clearly developed through his association with her, and accedes to her request to give himself up for them without a murmur, saying 'I love you' as the ship goes (echoing Adama's unheard farewell to him earlier in the story). The episode's ending is poignant and ambiguous, as Starbuck sits on the rocks contemplating his future, and the audience never learns whether he died on the planet or whether he was able to escape (perhaps rigging up the recently-landed Cylon ship); all that is known is that he never made it back to the Fleet.

RETURN TO SENDER: 'CY' AND THE CYLONS

This story, through Starbuck's interactions with Cy, reveals more than ever before about Cylon culture. We learn that 'Cylons work as a team; we are equal' and are strictly democratic (although this apparently does have its drawbacks; Cy's description of the crash indicates that the Cylons' first recourse was to consult the ship's manual, and ends with the line 'we were taking a vote [on what to do next] when the ground came up and hit us'). Cy certainly refuses to let Starbuck take command, pointing out to him that he has no real authority. Cylons are also compelled to answer the automatic distress beacons of their ships (whereas the humans are here forced to abandon their own), suggesting that the one belonging to the Cylon ship in 'The Lost Warrior' must have been damaged somehow. However, the Cylon Empire appears to have a slightly fascist character, in that we learn that it has as its goal the organisation of the universe, but when Starbuck asks 'what are you going to do with it when it's organised?' Cy responds 'I don't recall anyone ever asking that question', indicating a focus on organisation and a lack of questioning of paradigms. They also strive for perfection, as when Cy remarks, in a partially cut line, 'why am I not perfect? Eternal perfection and order is the goal of the Cylon Empire'. The Cylons use pistols here, as in 'The Night the Cylons Landed', as opposed to the rifles seen in *Battlestar Galactica*.

The familiar Cylon sarcasm is evident throughout, with, as the Cylon ship goes out of control, one commenting 'that was an unexpected move; he is a very good warrior', and another replying 'that is a small consolation; we are going to crash'. As in 'The Night the Cylons Landed', Cy 'charges up' when reviving, and the draft script calls for a shot from Cy's point of view of the world coming into focus, with a green tint to the image (as with infrared photography, presumably); the gradual return of the Cylon noise, rendered as 'whommmmm ...' in the draft, is also scripted. In physical terms, Starbuck is apparently able to use parts from the other Cylons to repair Cy.

We learn that Cylons see humans as evil, and Cy and Starbuck argue over this, with Cy asserting that they must be enemies, but Starbuck replying that since there are only two of them, it doesn't matter: 'we're cultural dissidents. That means our cultures don't get along, but that's in their world', and eventually presents Cy with a dilemma, in that he saved Cy's life and they both need each other to survive, meaning that they cannot continue to be enemies. Doctor Zee says that the Cylons were created for one purpose, namely, the extinction of man (which would seem to contradict the scenario presented in the added scenes of the 'Experiment in Terra' telemovie, where we learn that the Cylons were created prior to the war with the humans, and rebelled against their lizard masters). Starbuck comments on Cylon ignorance of humans, despite the fact that they've been fighting for a thousand yahrens (although the same could easily be said of the humans themselves vis-a-vis Cylons). Cy's opinion of human reproduction and infant development is that it is inefficient and 'it is not a wonder you lost the war'; he suggests 'you people really ought to try our method ... fast ... efficient ... and painless ...'; when Starbuck says 'I'll mention it if we make it back to the Fleet', he adds 'don't mention that the idea came from a Cylon … you humans are emotional about our having destroyed you'.

Cy adapts to human culture with a rapidity that rivals Andromus' in 'The Night the Cylons Landed'. In a cut sequence, Starbuck speculates that 'in being exposed to human beings, he was beginning to reveal human traits of envy and possessiveness … Maybe even those emotional characteristics that make men most vulnerable and unpredictable', developing the theme in this earlier story of Cylons becoming more human, and building on the suggestion in the original series that the humans and Cylons might have more in common than either is willing to acknowledge. Starbuck wonders 'how do you hurt a Cylon's feelings?' in surprise at learning that Cy does have emotional vulnerabilities. Cylons understand the concept of physical pain, even though they cannot feel it themselves (which begs the question of why the seats on Cylon craft are visibly padded). We see jealousy of Angela from Cy; he is seen as being slouched, with folded arms, as he watches Starbuck talk with her, and pointedly states that they built the rescue craft 'without her help'.

Cy himself is well characterised. When Starbuck, fairly typically, teaches the Cylon to play Pyramid, Cy notes perceptively that Starbuck is cheating and concludes that this is because he is bored; bringing back 'a woman' for Starbuck, he says 'I feel I've already compromised everything I believe in; what's one more human more or less?' He introduces himself as 'Group Leader Cyrus', and the other Cylons don't challenge this, further indicating that they have personal names; the draft script reinforces this by having him add what appears to be an identification code, '… Ot, ot, zen …' after giving his name (although it's an unforgivable coincidence that Starbuck's nickname for him, based on his species, turns out to also be a contraction of his personal name). He says 'to you I'm nothing more than a machine …' implying that he believes he is greater than that. Cy is also self-sacrificing, dying in Starbuck's arms, but, it seems, being judged by no one except himself.

'The Return of Starbuck' provides a great end to an otherwise largely undistinguished programme, with an uplifting and redemptive finale which evokes all that is best about the original series, and suggests that some common ground may be discovered between warring factions, and that anyone can change for the better.

UNMADE STORIES 1 • WHEEL OF FIRE

LEWIS A KELLY AND ALAN S YOUNG

STORY BY ALAN S YOUNG

SYNOPSIS: Troy and Dillon are in pursuit of Xaviar's Viper, when they are attacked by Cylons. Xaviar goes back in time, inadvertently taking one of the Cylon craft with him. Troy, meanwhile, is sucked into the Ship of Lights. The Fleet presume he is dead. On the Ship, Troy meets Starbuck, who tells him that he will be sent back in time to stop the Cylons. On *Galactica*, Doctor Zee identifies the time which Xaviar has gone back to (the year 592 BC, in Chaldea, near the river Chebar), and Dillon and Jamie also go back in time to stop him. In the past, an aerial battle ensues between the Galacticans and the Cylon, with Xaviar joining forces with his one-time enemies and shooting down the Cylon fighter; however, he escapes under confusion of the battle, to an unknown point in time. The shooting down of the Cylon ship is observed by a man near an oasis. The warriors land and fight a battle with a survivor of the crash, before blowing up the remains of the Cylon ship with charges. Returning to the present, Jamie figures out that the events they have precipitated will form the basis for Ezekiel's vision of the Wheel of Fire in the Old Testament.

ANALYSIS: The draft of 'Wheel of Fire' is dated 19 March, 1980, and marked 'Spec'. No details are available about its authors' previous or subsequent careers. Although it is of a reasonably high standard for *Galactica 1980*, it would have been unlikely to have been made in this form, firstly because of budget issues (the story would require, at minimum, new effects work, the rebuilding of several *Galactica* and Ship of Lights sets, and a desert location shoot), secondly because Dirk Benedict would have been unlikely to return for such a small role (it took Larson quite a bit of persuasion to get him to come back for a much larger part in 'The Return of Starbuck'), and, most crucially, because it is unlikely to have passed the censors. While Larson admits he was partly inspired in developing *Battlestar Galactica* by a book written by a NASA scientist which speculated in great detail that Ezekiel's Wheel of Fire was an alien spacecraft, and while suggesting that Aztecs and Ancient Egyptians were influenced by aliens is one thing, openly giving the Old Testament the von Däniken treatment (implying in the process that Ezekiel's divine vision was false) on mainstream television is likely to offend substantial numbers of believing Christians, Jews and Muslims, while the passage where Jamie describes Jesus Christ simply as a religious leader, rather than the Son of God, is potentially offensive to Christians. While the writers avoid direct controversy by not actually naming Ezekiel, in a country well-known for its vocal religious conservatives, the treatment of the story is a dubious risk for mainstream family television.

The script suggests that the writers were thinking more of *Battlestar Galactica* than *Galactica 1980*. Although Jamie is no brighter than usual, and displays her now-familiar homicidal tendencies by gunning down a Cylon (saying, in a contrived late-70s cod-feminist fashion, 'men aren't the only ones who are good with blasters'), the story is largely free of children (aside from a few mentioned as forming part of the tribe by the river Chebar), info-dumps and Earth-based hijinks with languatrons, while Adama seems more or less returned to his normal intelligence level. Additionally, Troy and Starbuck's conversations make direct references to 'War of the Gods' and 'Experiment in Terra', and the Viper simulators and prison barge are mentioned elsewhere. Adama refers to 'yahrens', and says 'good luck, and may the Lords of Kobol be with you at all times' (in the only reference to the Lords of Kobol in any story related to *Galactica 1980*), while Xaviar swears using the epithets 'frack' and 'for Sagan's sake'. There's a reminiscence about Troy and Dillon smuggling in alcohol for Boomer's promotion celebration, in a nod to the Viper pilots' similar act for Apollo's bachelor party in 'Lost Planet of the Gods' (giving us the first and only mention of ambrosa in *Galactica 1980*). The story also features a Viper exploding, which, considering that there are no onscreen human deaths in *Galactica 1980* (and the only offscreen ones are the implied deaths in the Cylon attack in 'The Super Scouts'), seems more like the sort of thing one might have seen in the earlier series.

In continuity terms, we hear of the use of a tractor beam, described as 'a thin green beam', for the first time in any *Battlestar Galactica* series. The wrist device is now a 'wrist analyzer'. Xaviar refers to 'that asinine Doctor Zee', which, while it may reflect the audience and/or writers' feelings about the character, also recalls his complaints about Doctor Zee's leadership in 'Spaceball'. Troy and Starbuck recognise each other, and Starbuck addresses the younger man as 'Boxey'. The script indicates that Universal's main gate is to stand in for the front of UBC's studios (confirming that Universal's backstage areas are used for some UBC sequences). This is the first time Jamie has heard of Cylons, and she reacts accordingly. Adama apparently keeps a set of family photos, including his wife (whose name, given in the early draft of 'Saga of a Star World' as 'Ila', is here misspelled 'Illa'), Athena, Apollo, Boxey and Serina, in his cabin, and is described as looking at them with a sense of loss in his eyes, implying that he believes or knows all of them to be dead, and he reacts to the news that Troy is missing and presumed dead by 'watching the screen with deep hurt in his eyes'. When he drinks in the officer's lounge, the bartender and Boomer's reaction indicates that this is a rare event (although he has been seen drinking in the original series, for example 'Lost Planet of the Gods', part two, 'Murder on the *Rising Star*' and 'Take the *Celestra*'). The system of time travel, however, appears to have been changed, being now a matter of 'fields' rather than of faster-than-light travel against the Earth's rotation, and there is also a continuity error regarding Boomer, in that, in the sequence in which he and Adama share a drink in the officer's lounge, he says that he regrets his promotion sometimes and misses his Viper, despite the fact that he is seen flying his Viper twice over the course of *Galactica 1980*.

The story also develops the concept of the Ship of Lights and its people, here referred to as the Guardians of the Universe (or simply the Guardians). As before, its appearance includes a painful sound (again raising the question of why supposedly good beings employ such techniques), the costumes on the lightship are white (notes in the script say that they are based on those seen in 'Experiment in Terra', and Starbuck's outfit is said to be similar to John's in that story), as is Troy's uniform both while he is on the lightship and while he is in the past carrying out his mission. In terms of what the beings are, when Troy asks Starbuck, 'are you in another time frame?' he replies 'we're in another dimension, but your present frame of time', and when Troy asks, 'then you didn't die?' Starbuck says 'not exactly. I simply … evolved to another plane of existence'. He adds that he no longer has 'a physical body, as you know it … all you are looking at is a reflection of my spiritual essence'. They are also able to return Troy to his own dimension such that only an instant of time has passed since his leaving it. According to Starbuck, the Guardians sometimes interfere directly with history and sometimes simply advise and guide; however, they have a concern about the potential danger of leaving any trace of the Cylons in the past, and, in a sort of predestination, ensure that Ezekiel's prophecy about the Wheel of Fire is written (their use of Troy as a means to destroy the Cylons does also have parallels with the idea that they might be behind the downing of Iblis' ship in 'War of the Gods'). Although Troy asks what happened to his father (who is continually referred to in the past tense), Starbuck says that he hasn't got time to go into it, suggesting that Apollo's fate is more mysterious and complicated than simple death, in battle or otherwise.

That having been said, 'Wheel of Fire' is no 'The Return of Starbuck'. The opening is something of a retread of earlier Viper-chase sequences, and Jamie is dragged into the plot on a very thin premise, with Dillon going to the trouble of finding her and bringing her to the *Galactica* in the hope that she will provide detailed information about Chaldea in the sixth century BC, and brings her along on the mission even though all she has done is to tell them that conditions were primitive (in fact, she says that there was no technology whatsoever in this era, which seems an exaggeration). Viper chronometers apparently measure time using a BC/AD chronology (as Dillon says that his indicates 'negative five hundred and ninety-two'), which seems surprising (as is Jamie's assertion that 'the people of Earth' measure time from Christ's birth, which ignores the fact that the Jews, Muslims, Chinese, and others use different calendars). While it could be suggested that the Viper chronometers were adjusted to keep up with Earth/American norms, this would then beg the question of why Dillon is surprised to get a 'negative five hundred and ninety-two' reading, and why he doesn't understand about BC/AD dating. In one sequence, a Viper uses braking flaps in space, which ought to be impossible. The Ship of Lights scenes aren't actually necessary to the plot, but seem to be there simply to tie up a loose narrative end regarding the fates of Starbuck and Adama's children, and to draw links between angels, Biblical prophecy, and the *Galactica*. The story is generally rather like part one of a two-parter, with a lot of setup and not much payoff.

The sequence in the 'tag' section of the story, which ties the warriors' recent adventures with the Book of Ezekiel, is slightly contrived, and, as Jamie doesn't actually come out and say what happened in Chaldea in 592 BC of any significance, presupposes a good knowledge of the Bible among the audience (as well as giving Jamie another unlikely field of expertise). Furthermore, the events of this script only actually resemble the Biblical narrative inasmuch as both involve a wheel of fire and beings which appear to be made of metal: the Cylons do not actually resemble the four-faced, multi-winged creatures which Ezekiel describes as accompanying the wheel, and God does not speak to Ezekiel at any point in the story (although, as he is unconscious for some of the battle, the writers may be, again blasphemously, suggesting that he dreamed the prophetic vision).

Although it might, indirectly, foreshadow Ronald D Moore's idea of having Dirk Benedict appear and reveal himself to be God in the draft of the reimagined series story 'Kobol's Last Gleaming', 'Wheel of Fire' unfortunately doesn't live up to its interesting premise, and the Ship of Lights sequences are disappointingly cursory, even if they do suggest a definitive, and positive, development in Starbuck's existence.

UNMADE STORIES 2 • A FLIGHT FOR LIFE

ROBERT W GILMER

SYNOPSIS: The Cylons aim a wave of satellite probes at the *Galactica*. The Viper pilots shoot down most of them, but one probe escapes and crashes on Earth. Adama dispatches Troy and Dillon to locate it, as, if the Earthlings discover it first, they will have irrefutable proof of alien life, which could complicate the Galacticans' mission. However, Colonel Sydell beats them to it, and Troy and Dillon, with Jamie's help, have to infiltrate the air force base to recover it. Meanwhile, Doctor Zee discovers that the probes are infected with a lethal bacterium, and Troy, Dillon and Jamie have thirty-six hours to vaccinate the three men exposed to it (Sydell, Master Sergeant Canon and Colonel Downey) without them discovering this. Canon and Downey are tracked down at a parachute training facility and gym respectively, but they are almost too late in reaching Sydell, who is showing signs of infection. The warriors take Sydell aboard the *Galactica*, where he is treated, and then return him to Earth, with his memory of the events erased.

ANALYSIS: 'A Flight for Life' appears to have been commissioned fairly early on. The writer, Robert W Gilmer, has close associations with other Larson series, having written for *Buck Rogers* and, later, being both writer and co-producer of *Knight Rider*. The first revision of the script is marked 'March 20, 1980', placing it after the writing of 'The Super Scouts'; the author is clearly familiar with the premise if not the events of this story, as Sydell refers to Troy and Dillon as 'the Scoutmasters'. However, it was also evidently written before it was known that Allan Miller would not be returning as Sydell. In terms of its viability as a filmable story, the opening sequence as described would include a lot of new effects work (of the Cylon ship and its probes), and the story would also require a trained bull and some elaborate new car/motorbike stunt sequences, which would presumably also have stretched the budget.

The story is full of the usual silly humour, with an extended 'comedy' scene of Troy and Dillon encountering a bull, not recognising it initially as an animal (they speculate that it may be a tractor) and then questioning whether it has fur or feathers, all of which contradicts established facts (in that we know that the Colonies do have agricultural livestock, and, in 'Space Croppers', Troy and Dillon demonstrate that they are quite familiar with these). Dillon even expresses concern that he doesn't know how to talk to agricultural livestock, suggesting either that they have talking animals on Caprica, or that the pair of them are sufficiently stupid that one worries about their ability to remember to keep breathing. The characters generally state the blatantly obvious to such a degree that they actually seem subnormal, and, when Troy and Dillon discover that one of them has an air force uniform that is too small and the other, one that is too large, it doesn't occur to either of them to swap clothing. As ever, the Galacticans continually refer to 'Earth miles' (had they landed in France, would they be referring to 'Earth kilometres'?) and 'Earth hours' in a very clunky manner.

The sequence where Dillon visits the gym is also doubtful. The gym instructors' comments imply that Dillon is flabby and in need of fitness training, where Barry van Dyke appears quite buff. Dillon somehow manages to get into a gym, use a number of items of equipment, and even have a personal training session, all without paying. Jamie's homicidal tendencies are back, with her implying, after the warriors kidnap Sydell, that they should rid themselves of a thorn in their side by simply killing him, and Adama says that the Galacticans have respect for life (implying that Jamie herself doesn't, and making her rather a poor role model for children).

Elsewhere, the story is utterly predictable, involving yet another space plague, huge coincidences (in that Jamie is visiting the air force base at exactly the same time that Troy and Dillon show up, and the two officers she approaches to ask for directions just happen to be them) and plot holes (in that Jamie somehow knows that Major Pelham was wearing a protective suit and not exposed to the bacterium, but where she acquired this information is unclear). Information imparted to impressionable young minds in this story includes how to find out someone's room number when the hotel clerk won't tell you (for the benefit of any future hotel burglars, this involves simply asking to leave a note and observing the room number on the pigeonhole the clerk puts it in). Doctor Zee, also, has a rather convenient 'memory deletion unit' which keeps Sydell from remembering his visit to space.

The script does have one or two good lines, as when Master Sergeant Canon says 'jump school is three weeks. First week separates the men from the boys. Second week, the men from the idiots. And the third week … the idiots jump!' Elsewhere, when a delirious Sydell starts saying 'yes, General … no, General … Certainly, General …' in his feverish ravings, Jamie remarks that it's not easy being a Colonel sometimes. The bull sequences amusingly call the bull 'Ferdinand', referring to the popular children's book *Ferdinand the Bull*. The sequence in the gym reminds the viewer that fitness clubs were on the verge of becoming very popular at the time. In continuity terms, Jamie is described as driving 'the now familiar yellow Mustang' and Troy calls

Adama 'grandfather' again; Troy and Dillon don't know what a salute is, and we would have seen the interior and exterior of Jamie's apartment for the first time. Mercifully, the script is relatively free of info-dumps, apart from a long discussion of the role of white blood cells in fighting infection. A much better storyline involving a contaminated probe would appear in the reimagined series.

Overall, the story is rather weak, predictable and prosaic; it's actually a poor story even by *Galactica 1980* standards, with all the usual problems (Jamie's psychopathy, predictable aliens-on-Earth jokes) combined with worse-than-average displays of stupidity on the part of both Galacticans and humans.

UNMADE STORIES 3 ● EARTHQUAKE

SYNOPSIS: Troy and Dillon come to the rural town of Lemoncreek, at the request of Jamie, who has been following up reports of unusual earth tremors in the area. A local scientist, Jack Kirkwood, has been predicting more earthquakes (based on his method of detecting earthquakes using natural phenomena, principally animal activity), but is facing opposition from scientists at a nearby government research centre, as well as local people, many of whom work at this facility. Although its true purpose is kept secret, the facility involves drilling into the Earth's crust. Doctor Zee discovers that there is in fact a faultline which runs through the area, which has been dormant for five hundred years, but which would cause massive catastrophes were it to be reawakened. Troy and Dillon make contact with Doctor Kirkwood, providing him with Galactican technology to assist his research. They determine the source of the seismic disturbances which are reawakening the faultline to be the activity at the research centre. Jamie and Kirkwood confront the director of the facility, and discover that there are also plans to detonate a nuclear device in the shaft. Troy and Dillon are given a collapsar by Doctor Zee, which, should it be detonated in the shaft, will render the ground impenetrable. Troy and Dillon sneak into the facility, learn about the nuclear device, and rush to place the collapsar in position to block the drilling and neutralise the bomb.

ANALYSIS: Although the circulating draft of this script has no indication of time of writing, author or number of drafts, an interview with Chris Bunch quoted on BattlestarWiki states that it is the second draft of a script written by himself and fellow story editor Allan Cole, which originally featured Xaviar as the villain, and was rewritten when it was decided that the character would not return. The script is also missing its final six pages, though it is known that Troy and Dillon would succeed in preventing the destruction of the West Coast, and Hargreaves, director of the research centre, would apologise to the pair; presumably, Jamie and Kirkwood, who are being held captive in the facility at the point at which the script cuts off, would be released, Kirkwood's theories would be vindicated in the eyes of the community and the government would have learned a valuable lesson about not dropping nuclear bombs down drilling shafts.

The plot is fairly predictable, being straight out of 1950s hero-scientist movies: a maverick researcher who has uncovered a scientific truth is not believed (the script goes so far as to liken him to Galileo, although in doing so it does make a valuable point that our era is no more 'enlightened' in terms of prejudice than was the seventeenth century), while government scientists interfere with natural processes which they don't understand, although here it is not even explained what the scientists hope to achieve by drilling a hole in the Earth's crust and dropping a nuclear bomb down it. There are strong coincidental similarities with the 1970 *Doctor Who* serial 'Inferno', which also dealt with a secret experiment involving drilling into the Earth's crust, which very nearly causes a catastrophic seismic disaster. There are the inevitable jokes in which Troy and Dillon misunderstand such Earth/US concepts as the Auto Club, and a very stupid scene in which Troy reveals that although he understands what eggs are, he doesn't recognise one and doesn't know what to do with it (although it does prompt the subsequent funny exchange between Samantha and Dillon: 'are you sure you guys are scientists?' 'We have led very sheltered lives ...'). There is also a slight continuity disparity in that Troy and Dillon are now using metric measurements, such as kilogrammes and kilometres. The drilling system, described as looking like an oil pump, but with a 'high-intensity laser drill' instead of the pumping mechanism, would also have necessitated a new model at the very least. The 'collapsar' is yet more vaguely-explained fake science, being somehow capable of making the ground impenetrable (apparently by causing 'all atoms in the vicinity [to] collapse upon themselves') and at the same time neutralising nuclear devices.

That having been said, the script is actually better in some ways than most of the ones produced for *Galactica 1980*. The Super Scouts are again mercifully absent (though the child content is provided through the presence of the garage owner's children and Kirkwood's daughter Samantha, and a subplot involving Samantha's problems with being teased at school about her father's theories). Kirkwood also appears to be a lone parent. There is a nice subversion of the usual *Galactica 1980* formula when Troy and Dillon innocently go to a service station when Troy's bike develops a fault, which seems like the usual setup for comedy, but, in fact, they simply borrow some tools and get on with the repairs themselves (and the fact that they ask for a 'bi-pendular lever' and 'quadra-planed shaft', which turns out to be a pair of pliers and a Phillips screwdriver, is also a nice variation on the usual aliens-on-Earth jokes).

There are some good lines, such as Kirkwood's 'there's nothing an American believes more quickly than a machine', and when he likens himself to the messenger who brings bad news and is killed for it, but knows that if he does not bring his message, no one will learn of the danger. There are some inside jokes, as when we learn that Jack's dog is named Pliny (after a Roman writer famous for documenting the eruption of Vesuvius in 79 AD) or when

Doctor Zee says that one consequence of the earthquake will be the loss of 'all the Pacific islands including Hawaii', the latter being of course Glen Larson's place of residence.

In continuity terms, Doctor Zee again makes one of his rather sadistic projections, involving the impact of a major earthquake on the Western seaboard of North America and the nations of East Asia. Referencing trends of the late 1970s, Kirkwood has a home-built computer, and Ben says that the flying bike looks like 'one of them new Yamabuchis' (mixing up Yamaha and Mitsubishi to suggest Japanese dominance of the automotive sector). When Dillon unpacks a computer which has a woman's voice, Samantha, overhearing, asks who spoke, and Dillon covers by saying that it was him, Samantha assumes that he 'does impressions' and asks him to 'do Dolly Parton'. The information moments in this script are for the most part, unsurprisingly, on a geological theme, including the nature of earthquakes and continental drift, historical beliefs about seismology, and the idea that animal behaviour can predict oncoming earthquakes.

'Earthquake' is, as it stands, a fairly typical and predictable story along the usual *Galactica 1980* formula, which is nonetheless redeemed by good dialogue and clever subversions of some of the series' clichés.

UNMADE STORIES 4 • THE DAY THEY KIDNAPPED CLEOPATRA

Participating writers: Mark Jones, Anne Collins, Chris Bunch and Allan Cole.

SYNOPSIS: Xaviar has travelled back in time to 48 BC in his Viper, where he woos Cleopatra, telling her he is a god. To test his divinity, she poisons him, and he flees to present-day Earth, Cleopatra in tow, where he contacts Troy and Dillon through Jamie and says he will give himself up if they save his life. Troy and Dillon agree to help him, with Xaviar going with Jamie and Troy to the hospital while Dillon takes Cleopatra back to Ancient Egypt. On Xaviar's secret instructions, however, Cleopatra gives Dillon the slip and goes to the Museum of History, where an exhibit on Egyptian queens is being shown. Dillon tracks her down, but she escapes by charming an archaeologist, Williams, who is holding a party that evening to raise funds for an expedition, led by his colleague Professor Johnson, to discover Cleopatra's tomb. At the hospital, Xaviar's life is saved by a doctor friend of Jamie's, with a little advice from Troy on what antitoxins might work, and he escapes from hospital to find Cleopatra, tracking her down to Williams' party after discovering a placard at the museum giving details of the event. At the party, Troy and Dillon are recognised by Mr Brooks, who is reporting on the party, and he accuses them of being terrorists. A chase ensues, with Troy, Dillon and Jamie pursuing Xaviar and Cleopatra, ultimately going back to Cleopatra's time, where Cleopatra rejects Xaviar as a false god, and he escapes. Returning to the present, Troy and Dillon leave a gift for Williams – a photograph of an ancient map which vindicates Johnson's theories about the location of Cleopatra's tomb.

ANALYSIS: 'The Day They Kidnapped Cleopatra' very nearly got made, with filming having started when news came through of the series' cancellation. Certainly it does seem to be more budget-friendly than many of the unused draft scripts, calling only for some location filming, a Cleopatra costume and some vaguely Egyptian sets (although the stage direction 'Ext: Alexandria – Ancient Egypt – Night – Stock' does amusingly suggest that the team expect Universal to own actual stock footage of Classical Egypt; this was apparently to have been accompanied by captions informing the audience that this represents 'Alexandria, Egypt – 48 BC'). The circulating draft script identifies the first draft as 15 April 1980, with one revision on 21 April and two on 22 April, placing it very close in development to 'The Return of Starbuck'. Anne Collins had written extensively for Larson's *Nancy Drew* series, and acted as story consultant on *Buck Rogers* and *Matlock*. Mark Jones had written for a number of cartoons (including, significantly for reasons to be shortly explained, *Fangface*), and went on to write for *The A-Team* and the comedy-horror film series *Leprechaun*.

The story overall bears more than a slight resemblance to 'The Night the Cylons Landed', featuring amusing chases around a major American city, gratuitous product placement (Xaviar and Cleopatra are stated in the script as going to the Sheraton-Universal Hotel, and *Fangface*, a 1978 cartoon made by Ruby-Spears for ABC and now largely found on websites devoted to identifying the worst cartoons of all time, appears on television), parties and run-ins with authority figures. The script displays the usual confusion over terminology, referring to the vehicles as both 'turbo bikes' and 'turbocycles', and the wrist devices as 'communicators', 'wrist bands', and 'wrist contraptions'. The infodumps are mercifully brief and scattered, but focus on providing a somewhat sanitised version of Egyptian history (in that it is asserted that Cleopatra 'married' Julius Caesar and Mark Antony, when in fact her relationships with them were rather more informal) and, at one point, on how plumbing works (as Cleopatra attempts to understand modern technology).

In continuity terms, Jamie now has an office at UBC, and seems brighter than usual, coping admirably with Xaviar's unexpected phone call, and covering for Cleopatra's high-handed behaviour with a shopkeeper by claiming that the Queen is an actress. However, she does display an unlikely expertise in Egyptian history, as well as a convenient ex-boyfriend who happens to be a doctor (and, considering the difficulty that the Paradise Medical Centre had in treating the sick children in 'The Super Scouts', one wonders why they bother trying Earth medicine on Xaviar at all), and he and his colleague identify the poison as coming from an asp (which is quite a cliché given the themes of the story) despite the fact that most doctors would simply identify it initially as an unknown snake venom and work their way through the local reptiles before considering more exotic possibilities. Doctor Mortinson is briefly namechecked, and Mr Brooks makes an appearance, somewhat inexplicably reporting on the charity event (surely he would be too high up in the studio hierarchy to have to do the roving reporting himself).

The usual problems with the series continue, albeit with comedy scenes about Cleopatra's inability to understand twentieth-century life as well as the Galacticans' (typical example: when asked for a date by a cab driver, she replies 'I prefer kumquats'). There are also internal contradictions, as when Troy says that they are landing in 'what Earth calls a forest', suggesting, despite the evidence to the contrary in 'The Man With Nine Lives', that there are no forests of that name in the Colonies. Troy and Dillon are yet again accused of being terrorists, and end the story by helping yet another worthy scientist to carry out his work (though, considering that Johnson and Williams come across as materialistic idiots obsessed with petty jealousies, it hardly seems worth assisting them).

There are other problems with this story particularly. Although Cleopatra's ability to quickly figure out modern customs and devices (tricking Dillon by leaping out of the elevator before the doors close) makes sense, her ability to speak modern English is less excusable. Jamie's ex-boyfriend, David Rubin, is a bit of a Jewish stereotype, going on about his mother and bragging about the size of his medical practice. As is too often the case on television, archaeology is portrayed as glorified tomb-robbing and archaeologists as greedy treasure-hunters, and there is an example of irritating late-seventies anti-feminist humour when a group of women in the museum defend Cleopatra against what they perceive as an attack by a 'chauvinist'. Silliest of all, however, is Doctor Zee's assertion that if Cleopatra does not continue as Queen of Egypt, her country will prematurely fall to the [here a blank is left in the script, indicating that the writer wasn't sure who the enemy were either], and then goes on to extrapolate from this that the USA will not be discovered for another hundred years, and that, in the twentieth century, the US will be in a period equivalent to 'what Earth once called the Dark Ages', which seems a tall extrapolation, and appears to be only put into the story to make Cleopatra seem relevant to the modern middle-American.

On the plus side, however, we do get scenes of Xaviar flirting with Cleopatra ('Oh! You shouldn't tease the Queen of Egypt!' she admonishes him), and a couple of jokes (as when Dillon accidentally runs in front of a cab, the cab driver shouts 'what do you think you're doing?' Dillon replies 'going to the Museum of History', and is promptly told to hop in). Contemporary pop culture also features in that the Cleopatra exhibition is likened to the King Tut exhibit, which, as mentioned earlier, had just finished touring North America the previous year.

The story is another basic comedy runaround, with time travel, product placements and jokes of varying degrees of silliness. Although it isn't as terrible as some, following 'The Return of Starbuck' with an episode like this one would have been rather like following a screening of *The Mission* (1986) with an hour of Hanna-Barbera cartoons.

OTHER UNMADE GALACTICA 1980 SCRIPTS

While four unmade episodes of *Galactica 1980* exist in draft script form, several more are known to have been developed to some stage, but only fragmentary information about their content is available. As Allan Cole and Chris Bunch have reported, the script-commissioning process on *Galactica 1980* was confused, with Larson writing his own scripts at the same time as others were being commissioned, meaning that a number were abandoned at an early stage. Stories which are reported to have been considered, apart from the ones known to exist in draft form, include:

The Money Machine by Alan S Godfrey: This was to have been a comedy in which Troy and Dillon are hiding out in an orphanage with a Galactican machine which can print currency. The children at the orphanage find the machine and start printing their own money, but, when it subsequently falls into the hands of some inept criminals, the warriors must stop them, apparently not so much because counterfeiting is wrong than because the secret of the *Galactica's* existence is compromised. Sydell, and also some more serious criminals who are after the machine, would have joined the pursuit as well. Bunch and Cole have claimed they thought it was a funny script, but that Frank Lupo hated it, and thus they don't believe the story got as far as Glen Larson.

The Battle of Troy by an unknown writer: Even less is known about this story, as 'The Battle of Troy' apparently is not its actual title, but a description of what it would have been about. Rather than this involving the former Boxey getting into a fight, however, it would have featured Troy and Dillon going back in time to the Trojan War to stop Xaviar altering the course of history. Helen would have fallen for one of our heroes, and eventually they would have not only ensured that the battle, complete with horse, pans out as in the myth, but would have been seen by a young Homer. This sounds like a similar idea to 'The Day they Kidnapped Cleopatra' crossed with 'Wheel of Fire', albeit more silly and predictable, and is another indication of the team's strange obsession with sword-and-sandals movies (even more odd when one considers that these were not particularly fashionable in the 1970s).

Bullfighting Script by Chris Trumbo: Little is known about this story beyond the somewhat intriguing designation. Trumbo is the son of Dalton Trumbo, the screenwriter for, among others, *Spartacus* (1960), who was blacklisted by the House Un-American Affairs Committee.

Gun Script by E Nick Alexander: Again, little is known about this, bar that the story would have revolved around a juvenile delinquent getting hold of one of the *Galactica*'s guns, and Troy and Dillon having to find it, again more to hide their existence from the authorities than as part of any anti-violence message. The story was reportedly hamstrung from the start in that the censors would not allow any onscreen shootings during the 7pm timeslot.

Biker Script by Richard Christian Matheson and Tom Szollosi: This story would have pitted Troy and Dillon against a group of bikers, picking up on the biker-gang sequence of '*Galactica* Discovers Earth'. Richard Christian Matheson is the son of Richard Matheson, author of the 1954 horror novel *I Am Legend*.

BATTLESTAR GALACTICA: 'THE WILDERNESS YEARS'

Following the cancellation of the original *Battlestar Galactica* programme, the series lived on in the form of merchandise, comic books and original novels. What follows is a brief, idiosyncratic, look over the spinoffs from the original series and *Galactica 1980*.

MERCHANDISE

The late 1970s were a boom time for TV-related merchandise, with toy companies capitalising on the popularity of early-evening drama series among children as well as adults to sell toys relating to almost every series of the era, from *The Bionic Woman* to *Space: 1999* to *Welcome Back Kotter*. Predictably, *Battlestar Galactica* had its own range of tie-in items, including lunch boxes and Hallowe'en costumes. The most well-known are Mattel's range of 3½ inch action figures, including Adama, Cylons in bronze and silver, the Imperious Leader, Starbuck, an Ovion, a rather generic-looking 'Colonial Warrior', Baltar, a Boray and Muffit. Also produced were Colonial spacecraft toys, guns, handheld video games, and, perhaps the strangest (but now one of the rarest) item of merchandise, cuddly Muffit dolls. Monogram released a range of model kits, which were re-released in the late 1990s to cash in on the revival of interest in *Battlestar Galactica* in the wake of the release of the remastered *Star Wars* films. In March 1997, Treadmasters also released a new set of action figures and models. These unfortunately bear little resemblance to the original series characters (a curiously muscular Starbuck, for instance, and an Imperious Leader apparently sporting wings). Today, the 1970s and, to a lesser extent, 1990s revival merchandise from the series is popular with collectors, with toys in various conditions turning up frequently on Internet auction sites.

Following the surge in interest in the original series after the success of the reimagined series, a number of action figures for the adult collector market were released. In 2005-6 Majestic Studios produced a range of 12-inch action figures, featuring Starbuck, Apollo, Adama and a Cylon Centurian, and including, in partnership with Time and Space Toys, an 'Experiment in Terra' limited edition box set, featuring Starbuck and Apollo in their white uniforms. After the collapse of Majestic Studios, the range was taken over by the company Amok Time, which subsequently released a number of figures, including Athena (dressed in a Colonial Warrior uniform), Boomer, Cain, Lucifer and Tigh. In 2005 a company named Joyride Studios also acquired the license to produce 5-inch original series action figures for the adult collector market, but thus far they have only produced figures of Apollo, Starbuck, silver and bronze Cylons, and some Colonial and Cylon ship models (the latter inaccurately designated as 'Raiders'). Hasbro, as part of its diecast *Battlestar Galactica* vehicle range, included a 1978 Viper and a 1978 Cylon fighter (also inaccurately referred to as a 'Raider'). Replica props, insignia and costume items are also available via websites and Internet auctions.

COMIC BOOK SERIES

The original series also continued in comic form. Several of these were contemporary or near-contemporary with the series: British comic magazine *Look-in* and the similar French publication *Tele-Junior* featured comics based on *Battlestar Galactica* in 1979-80 and 1980-81 respectively. Two British annuals are also known to exist. The best-known near-contemporary series was the one published by Marvel Comics, which finished in 1981 after 23 issues. Initially, a comic adapting the events of 'Saga of a Star World' was released as Marvel Super Special #8, and, when this proved successful, Marvel gave the series its own line, adapting 'Saga of a Star World' as its first three issues, 'Lost Planet of the Gods' in issues 4 and 5, and then, as they had run out of serials which they had the rights to adapt, continued from issue 6 onwards to develop original stories about the Fleet. These were mostly set in the magnetic void encountered in 'Lost Planet of the Gods', although also featuring flashback stories, and end with an adventure in which Jolly discovers the coordinates to Earth. As such, they are generally considered to have a separate continuity from the original series.

Between 1995 and 1997, Maxim Press issued a new *Battlestar Galactica* comic book mini-series called 'The War of Eden'. This ignored the events of *Galactica 1980,* and began with the Fleet's arrival at a prehistoric Earth. Albeit non-canonical, this series proved popular enough that four sequel series followed, 'The Enemy Within', 'Starbuck', 'Apollo's Journey', and 'Journey's End', before the company published an omnibus edition, *The Batttlestar Galactica Compendium* and quietly ceased producing *Battlestar Galactica* stories. In 1998, Realm Press also published a one-shot comic based on the original series called *Battlestar Galactica The Search for Sanctuary*, and this proved successful enough for them to do two mini-series set after 'The Hand of God', as well as a few one-shot comics. In 2006, Dynamite Entertainment, publishers of comics based on the reimagined series, began an original-series range, which incurred negative comments from fans due to continuity errors. After doing five issues of *Classic Battlestar Galactica* in 2006, plus four of a classic-series-set story called *Cylon Apocalypse* (dealing with the discovery of a virus which could wipe out the Cylons) in 2007, they returned to concentrating on the reimagined series. In 2009 they returned with a 'reimagining' of *Galactica 1980* in four-part comic book form, loosely based on the television series (featuring such developments as an evil Doctor Zee, the return of Baltar and explicit references to contemporary politics, such as the Presidency of Jimmy Carter) and as such having the distinction of being the only known piece of official *Galactica 1980* merchandise.

ORIGINAL NOVELS

Although ten official novelisations by various authors and four original *Battlestar Galactica* novels (all written by Robert Thurston, although some give Glen Larson a co-writer's credit) were published by Berkeley in the 1980s, the best known series is the one written between 1997 and 2005 by Richard Hatch and, severally, Christopher Golden, Stan Timmons, Alan Rodgers and Brad Linaweaver. These were probably at least partly sparked by the success of the *Star Wars* tie-in novels (beginning in 1992 with the Thrawn Trilogy, which continued the series after *Return of the Jedi*), although also being affected by a general revival of interest in *Battlestar Galactica* in the mid-90s, with the series being repeated on the Sci-Fi Channel in 1993-4 and 1996-7 and Maxim Press' comic series proving a success. While generally not regarded as canon, the stories pick up the Fleet about twenty years after 'The Hand of God', starting with the death of Adama and ending with half the Fleet marooned on the doomed planet Paradis, in a thus-far-unresolved cliffhanger (Hatch has reportedly written another book in the series, but legal disputes which arose over the publishing rights mean that it remains unreleased at the time of writing). The series features many of the original characters, albeit older and more advanced in rank, as well as Lucifer, Baltar, Iblis, Cain and the *Pegasus*, and a grown-up Boxey going by the name of Troy (although this is the only reference to *Galactica 1980*). Aspects of the novels are a clear influence on the reimagined series (for instance, Cylons capable of 'downloading' their personalities into new bodies, a race of creatures who fly through space in armoured shells like reimagined-series Cylon Raiders, Starbuck and Cassiopea having a blonde daughter who seems to have inherited many of her father's bad character traits). The novels also give some indication as to what Hatch's abortive revival effort might have involved.

FOR SAGAN'S SAKE: THE LEGACY OF *BATTLESTAR GALACTICA*

While *Battlestar Galactica* has undoubtedly made a contribution to later American telefantasy, it is unfortunately difficult to say precisely what its wider legacy has been, due to the fact that it is overshadowed by *Star Wars* and grounded in SF concepts with a more general application: while the 1980s and 1990s threw up religious- and/or politically-themed space-operas such as *Babylon 5* and *Space: Above and Beyond*, and von Däniken-inspired fantasies such as *The X-Files* and *Roswell*, it is debatable how much of this is down to *Battlestar Galactica* specifically.

The series' more obvious legacy is, of course, the development of the reimagined series, beginning in 2003 and with the main series concluding in 2009. While some critics have derided this programme as '*Galactica* In Name Only', and argued that the designations of the ship and some of the central characters are the only link it has with the 1978 series, in fact, there are deep thematic connections between the two.

On the political level, for instance, both are grounded in neoconservatism, although the original series treats it as a new and idealistic philosophy, where the reimagined one comes after the movement has been through a range of real-world political trials. Both also focus around debates about the legitimacy of leadership and the problems of authoritarianism: while the original series does have the subtext that an authoritarian regime is justified if the leader is the right person, the stories 'The Living Legend' and 'War of the Gods' both address the fact that it is very easy to mistake the wrong leader for the right one – and *Galactica 1980*'s portrayal of Adama contains the implication that even the 'right' leader can lose their ability to command over time.

Both series also have a similar treatment of religious themes. The lightship people, who, by implication, must themselves have been helped to enlightenment by a being or beings which are as far advanced relative to them as they are to the Colonials and Cylons, have a parallel in the reimagined series with the actions of God and God's messengers (the 'Head People'). Both series explore the idea of battles in the divine sphere being played out through the activities of mortals, with Brother Cavil, in the reimagined series, becoming a kind of Iblis-figure. The hybrid child, Hera, of the reimagined series, arguably has antecedents in Doctor Zee, a miraculous child engineered through divine intervention, who has preternatural insights into the Fleet's situation, and who holds the future of his species in his hands (albeit Hera is considerably less annoying). Both series take the position that conflict is necessary for growth and evolution, and peace only leads to stagnation and decadence.

Morally, both series revolve in part around the issue of whether humanity is worth saving, and what it is to be a hero. The idea that the humans and Cylons, although they are at war and convinced they are polar opposites, in fact have a lot in common, runs through the original series and *Galactica 1980* as well as the reimagined one. The premise that the Cylons emulated (and, in *Galactica 1980*, continue to emulate) the humans also first appeared in the original series. Both series also are suspicious of the benefits of technology, with the survival of the *Galactica* in the reimagined series being down to its antiquated computer systems, and with the original stating that the Lords of Kobol abandoned their technology because of its destructive effects.

In character terms, both feature a dynamic Fleet with a variety of individuals, including, as well as the military, a range of politicians, technicians, reporters, prostitutes and entrepreneurs. Both cultures are multiethnic, and obsessed with the number twelve. Although the original series is more explicitly a family show, through the focus on the multigenerational, blended, Adama family and Starbuck's search for relationships, themes of family life are also explored in the reimagined series, with the loving family of the Agathons contrasted with the dysfunctionality of the Adamas, and the quadrangle of Tigh, Ellen, Caprica-Six and Baltar, and the complexities of Chief Tyrol's personal life, illustrating how complicated relationships can become. Many characters in the reimagined series are close to their original-series equivalents: both Starbucks, for instance, are feckless gamblers with troubled childhoods and difficulty making a commitment, while, although Cain may be a more visibly disturbing character in the reimagined series, both iterations are built on the idea that a charismatic leader faced with a crisis can take their followers into self-destructive actions. Some characters also reappear under different names in the reimagined series: while the reimagined-series Apollo is not much like his original-series counterpart, a closer parallel can be found in Helo, a deeply moral, self-sacrificing family man.

The reimagined series also is able to both explain, and make an intriguing plot point of, the time discontinuities and recurrent coincidences of the original series and *Galactica 1980*. By introducing the element, first of all, that the events which we see recur cyclically (the 'all this has happened before; all this will happen again' mantra which runs through the narrative), and second, that a being with divine or near-divine powers is orchestrating events, then even seeming problems like the fact that the Fleet receives the 1969 moon landing broadcast but, when they arrive on Earth over 30 years later, it is only 1980, can be explained (clearly, the Earth which sent the broadcast is not the same Earth that the Fleet later encounters). Furthermore, what might seem like unbelievable coincidences (for instance, the recurrence of Earth names and measurements on Terra, to say nothing of the Galacticans strange fluency in English) can be rationalised when one has the premise that all the people of the series are literally being guided by the 'hand of God'.

In sum, then, the original series, despite its tragically short run, has seen its themes and characters developed in the 2000s, the specifics of which will be explored in more detail in Volume Two.

ABOUT THE AUTHORS

ALAN STEVENS has written, edited and developed numerous works on telefantasy series, including *Doctor Who, Blake's 7* and *The Prisoner* (notably *Liberation: The Unofficial and Unauthorised Guide to* Blake's 7 and *Fall Out: The Unofficial and Unauthorised Guide to* The Prisoner, both for Telos). Since the early 1990s, he has produced a number of documentaries, serials and dramas for radio and independent audio release, including the *Blake's 7/Doctor Who* spin-off series *Kaldor City* and the Gothic horror time-travelling adventure *Faction Paradox*. He is currently based in the South East of England, where he runs his own audio production company, Magic Bullet Productions (www. kaldorcity.com).

FIONA MOORE was born and raised in Toronto, but has lived in the UK since 1997. She has a doctorate in Social Anthropology from the University of Oxford, and is currently Senior Lecturer in International Human Resource Management at Royal Holloway, University of London. She has written non-fiction on a wide variety of subjects, from the identities of Taiwanese businesspeople to the culture of drag queens, and is co-author of *Liberation: The Unofficial and Unauthorised Guide to* Blake's 7 and *Fall Out: The Unofficial and Unauthorised guide to* The Prisoner. Her fiction and poetry have been published in, among others, *Asimov, Interzone* and *Dark Horizons*. She will admit to owning a 3½-inch action figure of Muffit.

INDEX BY TITLE

Titles in italics are working titles or unmade episodes.

Other Doctor Who Telos Titles Available

THE HANDBOOK: THE UNOFFICIAL AND UNAUTHORISED GUIDE TO THE PRODUCTION OF DOCTOR WHO by DAVID J HOWE, STEPHEN JAMES WALKER and MARK STAMMERS
Complete guide to the making of *Doctor Who*
(1963 – 1996).
£14.99 (+ £5.00 UK p&p) Standard p/b ISBN: 1-903889-59-6
£30.00 (+ £5.00 UK p&p) Deluxe signed and numbered h/b
ISBN: 1-903889-96-0

BACK TO THE VORTEX: THE UNOFFICIAL AND UNAUTHORISED GUIDE TO DOCTOR WHO 2005 by J SHAUN LYON
Complete guide to the 2005 series of *Doctor Who* starring Christopher Eccleston as the Doctor
£12.99 (+ £3.00 UK p&p) Standard p/b ISBN: 1-903889-78-2
£30.00 (+ £3.00 UK p&p) Deluxe signed and numbered h/b
ISBN: 1-903889-79-0

SECOND FLIGHT: THE UNOFFICIAL AND UNAUTHORISED GUIDE TO DOCTOR WHO 2006 by J SHAUN LYON
Complete guide to the 2006 series of *Doctor Who*, starring David Tennant as the Doctor
£12.99 (+ £3.00 UK p&p) Standard p/b ISBN: 1-84583-008-3
£30.00 (+ £3.00 UK p&p) Deluxe signed and numbered h/b
ISBN: 1-84583-009-1

THIRD DIMENSION: THE UNOFFICIAL AND UNAUTHORISED GUIDE TO DOCTOR WHO 2007 by STEPHEN JAMES WALKER
Complete guide to the 2007 series of *Doctor Who*, starring David Tennant as the Doctor
£12.99 (+ £3.00 UK p&p) Standard p/b ISBN: 978-1-84583-016-8
£30.00 (+ £3.00 UK p&p) Deluxe signed and numbered h/b
ISBN: 978-1-84583-017-5

MONSTERS INSIDE: THE UNOFFICIAL AND UNAUTHORISED GUIDE
TO DOCTOR WHO 2008 by STEPHEN JAMES WALKER
Complete guide to the 2008 series of *Doctor Who*, starring David Tennant as
the Doctor.
£12.99 (+ £3.00 UK p&p) Standard p/b ISBN: 978-1-84583-027-4

END OF TEN: THE UNOFFICIAL AND UNAUTHORISED GUIDE TO
DOCTOR WHO 2009 by STEPHEN JAMES WALKER
Complete guide to the 2009 specials of *Doctor Who*, starring David Tennant
as the Doctor.
£14.99 (+ £3.00 UK p&p) Standard p/b ISBN: 978-1-84583-035-9
£30.00 (+ £3.00 UK p&p) Signed h/b ISBN: 978-1-84583-036-6

WHOGRAPHS: THEMED AUTOGRAPH BOOK
80 page autograph book with an SF theme
£4.50 (+ £2.50 UK p&p) Standard p/b ISBN: 1-84583-110-1

TALKBACK: THE UNOFFICIAL AND UNAUTHORISED DOCTOR
WHO INTERVIEW BOOK: VOLUME 1: THE SIXTIES edited by
STEPHEN JAMES WALKER
Interviews with cast and behind the scenes crew who worked on *Doctor Who*
in the sixties
£12.99 (+ £3.00 UK p&p) Standard p/b ISBN: 1-84583-006-7
£30.00 (+ £3.00 UK p&p) Deluxe signed and numbered h/b
ISBN: 1-84583-007-5

TALKBACK: THE UNOFFICIAL AND UNAUTHORISED DOCTOR
WHO INTERVIEW BOOK: VOLUME 2: THE SEVENTIES edited by
STEPHEN JAMES WALKER
Interviews with cast and behind the scenes crew who worked on *Doctor Who*
in the seventies
£12.99 (+ £3.00 UK p&p) Standard p/b ISBN: 1-84583-010-5
£30.00 (+ £3.00 UK p&p) Deluxe signed and numbered h/b
ISBN: 1-84583-011-3

TALKBACK: THE UNOFFICIAL AND UNAUTHORISED DOCTOR WHO INTERVIEW BOOK: VOLUME 3: THE EIGHTIES edited by STEPHEN JAMES WALKER
Interviews with cast and behind the scenes crew who worked on *Doctor Who* in the eighties
£12.99 (+ £3.00 UK p&p) Standard p/b ISBN: 978-1-84583-014-4

HOWE'S TRANSCENDENTAL TOYBOX: SECOND EDITION by DAVID J HOWE & ARNOLD T BLUMBERG
Complete guide to *Doctor Who* Merchandise 1963–2002.
£25.00 (+ £5.00 UK p&p) Standard p/b ISBN: 1-903889-56-1

HOWE'S TRANSCENDENTAL TOYBOX: UPDATE No 2: 2004-2005 by DAVID J HOWE & ARNOLD T BLUMBERG
Complete guide to *Doctor Who* Merchandise released in 2004 and 2005. Now in full colour.
£12.99 (+ £2.50 UK p&p) Standard p/b ISBN: 1-84583-012-1

HOWE'S TRANSCENDENTAL TOYBOX: UPDATE No 3: 2006-2009 by DAVID J HOWE & ARNOLD T BLUMBERG
Complete guide to *Doctor Who* Merchandise released from 2006 to 2009. Now in full colour.
£25.99 (+ £3.00 UK p&p) Standard p/b ISBN: 978-1-84583-033-5

THE TARGET BOOK by DAVID J HOWE with TIM NEAL
A fully illustrated, large format, full colour history of the Target *Doctor Who* books.
£19.99 (+ £5.00 UK p&p) Large Format p/b ISBN: 978-1-84583-021-2

WIPED! DOCTOR WHO'S MISSING EPISODES by RICHARD MOLESWORTH
The story behind the BBC's missing episodes of *Doctor Who*.
£15.99 (+ £3.00 UK p&p) Standard p/b ISBN: 978-1-84583-037-3

TIMELINK: THE UNOFFICIAL AND UNAUTHORISED GUIDE TO THE CONTINUITY OF DOCTOR WHO VOLUME 1 by JON PREDDLE
Discussion and articles about the continuity of *Doctor Who*.
£15.99 (+ £3.00 UK p&p) Standard p/b ISBN: 978-1-84583-004-5

TIMELINK: THE UNOFFICIAL AND UNAUTHORISED GUIDE TO THE CONTINUITY OF DOCTOR WHO VOLUME 2 by JON PREDDLE
Timeline of the continuity of *Doctor Who*.
£15.99 (+ £3.00 UK p&p) Standard p/b ISBN: 978-1-84583-005-2

TORCHWOOD

INSIDE THE HUB: THE UNOFFICIAL AND UNAUTHORISED GUIDE TO TORCHWOOD SERIES ONE by STEPHEN JAMES WALKER
Complete guide to the 2006 series of *Torchwood*, starring John Barrowman as Captain Jack Harkness
£12.99 (+ £3.00 UK p&p) Standard p/b ISBN: 978-1-84583-013-7

SOMETHING IN THE DARKNESS: THE UNOFFICIAL AND UNAUTHORISED GUIDE TO TORCHWOOD SERIES TWO by STEPHEN JAMES WALKER
Complete guide to the 2008 series of *Torchwood*, starring John Barrowman as Captain Jack Harkness
£25.00 (+ £3.00 UK p&p) Deluxe signed and numbered h/b
ISBN: 978-1-84583-025-0

The prices shown are correct at time of going to press. However, the publishers reserve the right to increase prices from those previously advertised without prior notice.

TELOS PUBLISHING
c/o Beech House, Chapel Lane, Moulton, Cheshire, CW9 8PQ, England
Email: orders@telos.co.uk
Web: www.telos.co.uk

To order copies of any Telos books, please visit our website where there are full details of all titles and facilities for worldwide credit card online ordering, as well as occasional special offers, or send a cheque or postal order (UK only) for the appropriate amount (including postage and packing – note that four or more titles are post free in the UK), together with details of the book(s) you require, plus your name and address to the above address. Overseas readers please send two international reply coupons for details of prices and postage rates.

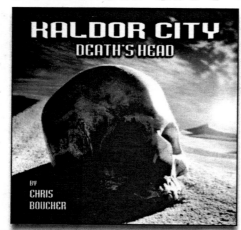